French Studies in and for the Twenty-first Century

Edited by

Philippe Lane and Michael Worton

LIVERPOOL UNIVERSITY PRESS

First published 2011 by
Liverpool University Press
4 Cambridge Street
Liverpool L69 7ZU

Copyright © 2011 Liverpool University Press

The right of Philippe Lane and Michael Worton to be identified as the editors
of this work has been asserted by them in accordance with the Copyright, Designs
and Patents Act, 1988.

British Library Cataloguing-in-Publication data
A British Library CIP record is available

ISBN 978-1-84631-6-555 (cased)
ISBN 978-1-84631-656-2 (limp)

Liberté • Egalité • Fraternité
RÉPUBLIQUE FRANÇAISE

AMBASSADE DE FRANCE
AU ROYAUME-UNI

Typeset in Plantin by R. J. Footring Ltd, Derby
Printed and bound in the United States of America

French Studies in and for
the Twenty-first Century

Contents

Notes on Contributors   viii

Foreword by Baroness Jean Coussins   xix
*Chair of the All-party Parliamentary Group on
Modern Languages*

Foreword by His Excellency Bernard Emié   xxi
French Ambassador to the UK

Part I: Contextualisations

1   Introduction   3
Philippe Lane and Michael Worton

2   A Short History of French Studies in the UK   12
Diana Holmes

Part II: Research and Public Engagement Strategies

3   The *exception anglo-saxonne*? Diversity and Viability of
French Studies in the UK   27
Adrian Armstrong

4   Why French Studies Matters: Disciplinary Identity and
Public Understanding   37
Charles Forsdick

5   Learning from France: The Public Impact of French
Scholars in the UK since the Second World War   58
Michael Kelly

Part III: The Place of Women and Gender in French Studies

6   Gender and the French Language: The *longue durée* of
French Studies in the UK   75
Michèle Cohen, Hilary Footitt and Amy Wygant

7   Contemporary Women's Writing in French: Future
    Perspectives in Formal and Informal Research Networks   86
    Gill Rye

8   French Studies and Discourses of Sexuality   95
    Emma Wilson

Part IV: The Place of Literature

 9 Integrated Learning: Teaching Literature in French   107
    Simon Gaunt and Nicholas Harrison

10 Oxford, Theatre and Quarrels   118
    Alain Viala

11 Defining (or Redefining) Priorities in the Curriculum
    when the Good Times have Flown   129
    William Burgwinkle

Part V: The Place of Linguistics in French Studies Today

12 French Linguistics Research and Teaching in UK and
    Irish HE Institutions   141
    *Wendy Ayres-Bennett, Kate Beeching, Pierre Larrivée
    and Florence Myles*

13 The Rise of Translation   155
    Jo Drugan and Andrew Rothwell

Part VI: Theatre, Cinema and Popular Culture

14 Teaching and Research in French Cinema   171
    Phil Powrie and Keith Reader

15 Popular Culture, the Final Frontier: How Far Should
    We Boldly Go?   184
    David Looseley

**Part VII: Area Studies, Postcolonial Studies and War and
Culture Studies**

16 An Area Studies Approach in European and Global
    Contexts: French Studies in Portsmouth   197
    Emmanuel Godin and Tony Chafer

17 French Studies and the Postcolonial: The Demise or
    the Rebirth of the French Department?   207
    David Murphy

18 The Development of War and Culture Studies in the UK:
    From French Studies, Beyond, and Back Again   220
    Nicola Cooper, Martin Hurcombe and Debra Kelly

Part VIII: Adventures in Language Teaching

19 French Studies at the Open University: Pointers
    to the Future   235
    Jim Coleman and Elodie Vialleton

20 Opportunities and Challenges of Technologically
    Enhanced Programmes: Online and Blended Learning at
    King's College London   247
    Dominique Borel

21 French Studies and Employability at Home and Abroad:
    General Reflections on a Case Study   262
    Maryse Bray, Hélène Gill, Laurence Randall

22 Sartre in Middlesex, De Beauvoir in Oxford:
    The Contribution of the ASMCF to the Study of France   272
    Máire Fedelma Cross

23 Culturetheque: A New Tool for French Culture   288
    Laurence Auer

Appendices. Addresses to the *Future of French Studies* Conference

    Appendix 1. Opening Speech. A Vast and Dynamic
    Field of Research and Teaching   293
    Maurice Gourdault-Montagne

    Appendix 2. A View from France   296
    Jean-Paul Rebaud

Index   300

Notes on Contributors

Adrian Armstrong is Professor of Early French Culture at the University of Manchester. His major research interests comprise late medieval French poetry, textual materiality and illustration, and text editing. He is the author of *Technique and Technology: Script, Print, and Poetics in France, 1470–1550* (Oxford, 2000); *The Virtuoso Circle: Competition, Collaboration and Complexity in Late Medieval French Poetry* (forthcoming); and, with Sarah Kay, *Knowing Poetry: Verse in Medieval France from the 'Rose' to the 'Rhétoriqueurs'* (Cornell, 2011).

Laurence Auer, diplomat, has been the Secretary General of the Institut Français, Paris, since January 2011. From 2006 to 2010, she was Cultural Counsellor at the French Embassy in London and Director of the Institut Français there. She has a first degree in English literature, and her graduate studies were in Arabic literature, and political science, Institute d'Etudes Politiques. She was granted a Fulbright Scholarship, Berkeley and UCLA, 1987.

Wendy Ayres-Bennett is Professor of French Philology and Linguistics at the University of Cambridge and Fellow at Murray Edwards College. She works on the history of the French language and the history of linguistic thought, particularly in seventeenth-century France. Her major publications include *Vaugelas and the Development of the French Language* (MHRA, 1987), *A History of the French Language through Texts* (Routledge, 1996), *Les Remarques de l'Académie Française sur le Quinte-Curce de Vaugelas* (PENS, 1996), *Problems and Perspectives: Studies in the Modern French Language* (Longman, 2001) and *Sociolinguistic Variation in Seventeenth-Century France* (Cambridge University Press, 2004).

Kate Beeching is Reader in Linguistics and French at the University of the West of England, Bristol. She is on the executive committee of the Association of University Heads and Professors of French and was President of the Association for French Language Studies until

September 2009. Her research interests are in sociolinguistics, pragmatics and spoken corpora, specifically in the analysis of spoken French. Publications include *Gender, Politeness and Pragmatic Particles in French* (2002), and a volume co-edited with Nigel Armstrong and Françoise Gadet: *Sociolinguistic Variation in Contemporary French* (2009) (both published by Benjamins).

Dominique Borel is Director of the Modern Language Centre at King's College, London. She is responsible for delivery of academic and specialist language programmes. She oversees the centre's external provision of programmes in language and intercultural studies for client organisations, which include London Business School and The Foreign Office. Additionally, she supervises an extensive e-learning programme which includes the design of a cross-college platform for language and cultural training to undergraduates, graduates and staff. She holds an MA in Romance Languages and Literature from Birkbeck College and a PGCE from the Institute of London.

Maryse Bray is Principal Lecturer in French in the Department of Modern and Applied Languages at the University of Westminster. Her research interest is focused on representations of France's colonial past in contemporary popular culture. She has published in French and in English on various productions such as French colonial songs and post-colonial cinema. Recent publications include joint articles with Hélène Gill on the film output of Mahamat-Saleh Haroun for *Nouvelle Revue Francophone* (2009) and *L'Eloge de la Francophonie* (Michael Abecassis, ed., Cambridge Scholars Publishing, forthcoming in 2011). She is the academic leader for language learning at undergraduate level. Under her impulsion, an innovative applied Bilingual Skills strand has been introduced in all languages on the University's Modern Languages degrees which, in addition to language skills, is designed to develop undergraduates' employability skills.

William Burgwinkle is a specialist in Medieval French and Occitan literature, gender and sexuality, and critical theory. He is the author of *Sodomy, Masculinity and Law in Medieval Literature, 1050–1230* (Cambridge University Press, 2004), *Love for Sale: Materialist Readings of the Troubadour Razo Corpus* (Garland, 1997), and *Razos and Troubadour Songs* (Garland, 1990), co-author of *Sanctity and Pornography: On the Verge* (Manchester University Press, 2010) and co-editor of *The Cambridge History of French Literature* (Cambridge University Press, 2011) and *Significant Others: Gender and Culture in Film and Literature, East and West* (Hawaii, 1992). He is currently head of the department of French at Cambridge.

Tony Chafer is Professor of Contemporary French Area Studies at the University of Portsmouth and Director of its Centre for European and

International Studies Research. His specialist research area is French-speaking Africa and he has published widely on Franco-African relations in the late colonial and postcolonial era. He is the author of *The End of Empire in French West Africa: France's Successful Decolonization?* (Berg, 2002) and of a number of articles on French African policy in the contemporary period. He is course leader for the University of Portsmouth's new MA Francophone Africa.

Michèle Cohen teaches history at Richmond American International University in London. She has long been interested in the culture wars between England and France in the eighteenth century, especially those concerning language and 'conversation', and their relation to the construction of masculinity and national character in each nation. She has also been exploring the notion of 'conversation' in relation to informal education in eighteenth-century domestic spaces. Her publications include *Fashioning Masculinity: National Identity and Language in the Eighteenth Century*. She is currently working on a cultural history of education in eighteenth-century England.

Jim Coleman is Professor of Language Learning and Teaching at The Open University, current Chair of the University Council of Modern Languages, and Editor of *System: An International Journal of Educational Technology and Applied Linguistics*. Previously at Glasgow and Portsmouth Universities, he co-authored French courses *Le français en faculté* and *Lyon à la Une*, and has published on French literature and area studies, but especially on aspects of university language education, focusing on policy and practice, institutional contexts, pedagogy, applications of technology, e-learning, skills and employability, language testing, intercultural competence, and especially study/residence abroad.

Nicola Cooper is the Director of the Callaghan Centre for the Study of Conflict, Power and Empire in the College of Arts and Humanities at Swansea University. She is one of the co-editors of the *Journal of War and Culture Studies*, and associate editor of *French Cultural Studies*.

Jean Coussins (Baroness Coussins), is an adviser on corporate responsibility and a member of the Better Regulation Commission. Lady Coussins is a member of the Advertising Standards Authority and was until recently the Chief Executive of the Portman Group, a not-for-profit organisation that promotes sensible drinking by the consumer and responsible marketing by the industry. Since 2008 she has been Chair of the All-Party Parliamentary Modern Languages Group.

Máire Fedelma Cross, Professor of French in the School of Modern Languages at Newcastle University, is Head of French and teaches the history of feminism and politics in France. President of the Association for the Study of Modern and Contemporary France since 2005, she is a member of the executive of the Association of Professors and Heads of French and was decorated by the French government in 2008 as *Chevalier dans l'Ordre des Palmes Académiques*. Her works on French feminism and politics in history include *The Letter in Flora Tristan's Politics, 1835–1844* (Palgrave, 2004), an English edition of *Flora Tristan's Diary: The Tour of France, 1843–1844* (Peter Lang, 2002), an edited volume *Gender and Fraternal Orders in Europe, 1300–2000* (Palgrave, 2010), and co-edited books with Caroline Bland, *Gender and Politics in the Age of Letter Writing, 1750–2000* (Ashgate, 2004), and with David Williams, *The French Experience from Republic to Monarchy, 1792–1824: New Dawns in Politics, Knowledge and Culture* (Palgrave, 2000).

Joanna Drugan is Senior Lecturer in Translation Studies at Leeds University, where she has run one of the UK's largest masters programmes in applied translation for over a decade. Her research focuses on translation ethics, quality, translation tools and training. Continuum will publish her book *Quality in Professional Translation* in 2011. She also performs French-English translations for NGOs and campaigning groups.

Hilary Footit is Senior Research Fellow in the Department of Modern Languages and European Studies in the University of Reading. She has written on women in politics (*Women, Europe and the New Languages of Politics* [Continuum, 2002]), and on Franco–British relations at the Liberation (*War and Liberation in France: Living with the Liberators* [Palgrave Macmillan, 2004]). She is currently Principal Investigator for the AHRC project *Languages at War*, led by the University of Reading, with the University of Southampton and the Imperial War Museum, London.

Charles Forsdick is James Barrow Professor of French and Head of the School of Cultures, Languages and Area Studies at the University of Liverpool. He is the author of *Victor Segalen and the Aesthetics of Diversity* (Oxford University Press, 2000), *Travel in Twentieth-Century French and Francophone Cultures* (Oxford University Press, 2005) and *Ella Maillart, 'Oasis interdites'* (Zoé, 2008); and co-author of *New Approaches to Twentieth-Century Travel Literature in French* (Peter Lang, 2006). He is also editor and co-editor of a number of collections, including *Francophone Postcolonial Studies* (Arnold, 2003), *Human Zoos: Science and Spectacle in the Age of Colonial Empire* (Liverpool University Press, 2008), *Postcolonial Thought in the French-Speaking World* (Liverpool University Press, 2009) and *Transnational French Studies: Postcolonialism and Littérature-monde* (Liverpool University Press, 2010).

Simon Gaunt is Professor of French Language and Literature at King's College London. His most recent publications include *Love and Death in*

Medieval French and Occitan Courtly Literature (Oxford University Press, 2006) and (with Sarah Kay) *The Cambridge Companion to Medieval French Literature* (Cambridge University Press, 2008).

Hélène Gill is Principal Lecturer at the University of Westminster where she teaches French Language and Area Studies. Her research and pedagogic interests include French and Francophone Studies with particular reference to Francophone African cinema. She is the Editor of the *Bulletin of Francophone Africa* and organises events on Francophone Studies and other related areas. Publications include *The Language of French Orientalist Painting* (monograph, Mellen Press, 2003), articles in scholarly journals including *Modern and Contemporary France* and the *International Journal of Francophone Studies*, as well as recent articles jointly with Maryse Bray on the film output of Mahamat-Saleh Haroun for *Nouvelle Revue Francophone* (2009) and *L'Eloge de la Francophonie* (Michael Abecassis, ed., Cambridge Scholars Publishing, forthcoming in 2011). She is the Year Abroad Tutor in the Department of Modern and Applied Languages.

Emmanuel Godin is Principal Lecturer in French Studies, University of Portsmouth, UK. His research interests are in French and European politics. He has edited several volumes in this field, most recently, with Tony Chafer – *The End of the French Exception?* Basingstoke: Palgrave: 2010). He is presently working on a research monograph on France since the 1970s to be published by Reaktion book.

Maurice Gourdault-Montagne was the French Ambassador in the United Kingdom from December 2007 to March 2011 (since when he has been Ambassador in Germany). He is a graduate of the Paris *Institut d'Etudes Politiques*; DEUG (two-year undergraduate degree) in German, University of Paris IV Sorbonne (1976); with a master's degree in law, University Paris-Assas (1977); and a graduate of INALCO (French school of oriental studies) (Hindi and Urdu).

Nicholas Harrison is Professor of French Studies and Postcolonial Literature at King's College London. His publications include two books, *Circles of Censorship* (Oxford University Press, 1995) and *Postcolonial Criticism: History, Theory and the Work of Fiction* (Polity Press, 2003), and two edited collections, *The Idea of the Literary*, a special issue of *Paragraph* (July 2005) and *Pontecorvo's Battle of Algiers, 40 Years On*, a special issue of *Interventions: International Journal of Postcolonial Studies* (November 2007). He is on the editorial boards of *Paragraph*, *Comparative Literature*, and *Research Monographs in French Studies*. His current research centres on colonial-era schooling in the Maghreb, with particular emphasis on secularism and literary education.

Diana Holmes is Professor of French at the University of Leeds, where she teaches twentieth and twenty-first century French literature and film. Her publications include monographs on *Colette* (1991), *French Women Writers 1848–1994* (1996), *Rachilde – Decadence Gender and the Woman Writer* (2001) and *Romance and Readership in Twentieth-Century France: Love Stories* (2006). She co-edited (with Carrie Tarr) *A 'Belle Epoque'? Women in French Society and Culture 1890–1914* (2005) and (with John Gaffney) *Stardom in Postwar France* (2007). Her second research field is cinema: she co-edits the Manchester University Press series *French Film Directors*, in which she co-authored the volume on François Truffaut. Her current research is on popular fiction and the pleasures of reading.

Martin Hurcombe is Senior Lecturer in the Department of French at the University of Bristol, with an interest in political commitment and the memory of the First World War in twentieth-century French culture, with related interests in French crime fiction, particularly the novels of Sébastien Japrisot. He is author of *Novelists in Conflict: Ideology and the Absurd in the French Combat Novel of the Great War* (Rodopi, 2004) and *France and the Spanish Civil War: Cultural Representations of the War Next Door, 1936–1945* (Ashgate, 2011). He is a member of the executive committee of the Group for War and Culture Studies (GWACS) and one of the editors of the *Journal of War and Culture Studies*.

Debra Kelly is Professor of French and Francophone Studies at the University of Westminster. Her research interests cover text and image studies, French and francophone literary and cultural studies, and war and culture studies. She is the Director of the Group for War and Culture Studies (GWACS). She is co-editor with Valerie Holman of *France at War in the Twentieth Century. Propaganda, Myth and Metaphor* (Berg, 2000) and editor of *Remembering and Representing the Experience of War in Twentieth Century France* (Mellen, 2000). Other publications include *Pierre Albert-Birot* (Associated University Presses, 1997) and *Autobiography and Independence. Selfhood and Creativity in North African Postcolonial Writing in French* (Liverpool University Press, 2005).

Michael Kelly is Professor of French at the University of Southampton and a specialist in modern French culture and society, especially the history of ideas and intellectuals. His most recent book was published by Palgrave Macmillan on the cultural and intellectual reconstruction of France after the Second World War. Previous books have dealt with the work of Emmanuel Mounier, with Modern French Marxism, and with the reception of Hegel in France. He is a member of the steering group of a Franco-British research network on cultural relations and associate editor of the journal *French Cultural Studies*. He is Editor of *Synergies Royaume Uni et Irlande* and the *European Journal of Language Policy*.

Philippe Lane, Attaché de Coopération Universitaire at the French Embassy in London, has been a Visiting Fellow at the University of Cambridge since 2009. He gives seminars on French cultural and scientific diplomacy. His recent publications include *Présence française dans le monde: l'action culturelle et scientifique* (La Documentation française, 2011) and, co-edited with Maurice Fraser, *Franco-British Academic Partnerships: The Next Chapter* (Liverpool University Press, 2011).

Pierre Larrivée is a Reader in French Linguistics at Aston University (Birmingham, UK). The author of five monographs and nearly 70 articles, his research interest lies in meaning through language. He is currently working on the impact of pragmatics for language change, and was the principal investigator of the Leverhulme International Network 'Cycles of Grammaticalization'.

David Looseley is Professor of Contemporary French Culture in the School of Languages and Culture at the University of Leeds. His research concerns the contemporary history of cultural practices, policies and institutions, in particular popular culture. He has written on such topics as the Nancy Theatre Festival, the Bibliothèque nationale de France, postcolonial approaches to cultural policy, youth culture, and the social and cultural theorist Antoine Hennion. He is the founder of the Popular Cultures Research Network.

David Murphy is Professor of French and Postcolonial Studies at the University of Stirling. He has published widely on African – particularly Senegalese – culture, and on the relationship between francophone and postcolonial studies. He is the author of two monographs, *Sembene: Imagining Alternatives in Film and Fiction* (James Currey, 2000), and (with Patrick Williams), *Postcolonial African Cinema: Ten Directors* (Manchester University Press, 2007). He is also co-editor of several collections of essays, including: *Francophone Postcolonial Studies: A Critical Introduction* (Arnold, 2003); *Postcolonial Thought in the French-Speaking World* (Liverpool University Press, 2009); *Transnational French Studies: Postcolonialism and Littérature-Monde* (Liverpool University Press, 2010).

Florence Myles is Professor of French Linguistics and Director of the Centre for Research in Linguistics and Language Sciences (CRiLLS) at Newcastle University, but will be moving to the University of Essex in September 2011. She was President of the Association for French Language Studies 2004–7 and is currently Vice-President of the European Second Language Association (EUROSLA) and Editor of the *Journal of French Language Studies* (CUP). Her research interests are in the area of second language acquisition, especially of French, and she is particularly interested in morphosyntactic development, and in theory building in the field. She has directed research projects with the dual aim of investigating learner development in French and of constructing an electronic database of French learner language oral corpora.

Phil Powrie is Dean of the Faculty of Arts and Human Sciences and Professor of Cinema Studies at the University of Surrey. He has published a number of books on French cinema, including *French Cinema in the 1980s: Nostalgia and the Crisis of Masculinity* (1997), *Jean-Jacques Beineix* (2001), *French Cinema: An Introduction* (2002), *The Cinema of France* (ed., 2006), *Changing Tunes: The Use of Pre-existing Music in Film* (ed., 2006), *Carmen on Film: A Cultural History* (2007), and *Pierre Batcheff and Stardom in 1920s French Cinema* (2009). He leads the Association for Studies in French Cinema and is the chief general editor of its journal, *Studies in French Cinema*.

Laurence Randall is Senior Lecturer in French in the Department of Modern and Applied Languages at the University of Westminster. Her research interest is focused on discourses elaborated by European and non-European critics around colonial and postcolonial cultural production. She has published a travel journal entitled *Dix jours au pays des crevettes* (Bod, 2008). As the employability coordinator in the Department of Modern and Applied Languages, she has set up an integrated programme designed to enhance students' employability at all levels on the undergraduate languages programme.

Keith Reader is Professor of Modern French Studies, University of Glasgow, having previously held chairs at the universities of Newcastle and Kingston. He has published extensively in the fields of French cinema, theory, intellectual history, literature and cultural topography, and his most recent book is *The Place de la Bastille* – in press with Liverpool University Press. He is a member of the editorial board, *French Studies* and is on the editorial advisory boards of *Paragraph* and *Modern and Contemporary France*.

Andrew Rothwell is Professor of French and Translation Studies at Swansea University. His main research interests are in modern and contemporary French poetry and the visual arts, literary and technical translation, and computer-based translation technologies. He has written on the early French avant-garde, Bernard Noël, Yves Bonnefoy as translator, and machine translation of Dada, as well as publishing his own translations into English (Zola, Dupin, Maulpoix, Noël). He coordinates Swansea's PhD Translation programme, Translation Research group, and membership of the European's Master's in Translation network.

Jean-Paul Rebaud is Sous-Directeur du Français, Ministère des Affaires Etrangères et Européennes.

Gill Rye is Professor of French at the Institute of Germanic & Romance Studies, University of London, where she is Director of the Centre for the Study of Contemporary Women's Writing and convenor of the Contemporary Women's Writing in French Seminar and network. Her publications include *Reading for Change* (2001), *Women's Writing in Contemporary France* (2002, co-edited with Michael Worton), *Narratives of Mothering* (2009), and edited special issues of *Dalhousie French Studies* (2004), *L'Esprit Créateur* (2005), *Nottingham French Studies* (2006, with Carrie Tarr) and the *Journal of Romance Studies* (2009, with Debra Kelly). She is currently researching the representation and politics of new reproductive technologies in recent French literature.

Alain Viala is Professor at the University of Oxford and Fellow of Lady Margaret Hall, as well as Professeur émérite at la Sorbonne Nouvelle and Directeur de rechecher associé au CRH-EHESS. His main publications are: *Naissance de l'écrivain* (Editions de Minuit,1985), *Racine, la stratégie du Caméléon* (Seghers,1990), *Histoire du théâtre* (Puf, 1996 and 2008), *Lettre à Rousseau sur l'intérêt littéraire* (Puf, 2005), *La France galante, histoire d'une catégorie culturelle des origines à la Révolution* (Puf, 2008) ; he is also a co-author of *Le Dictionnaire du littéraire* (Puf, 2002, 2005, 2008).

Elodie Vialleton is Head of French at the Open University. A graduate of the École Normale Supérieure de Fontenay St Cloud, she has taught at the Sorbonne Nouvelle in France, at Dartmouth College in the USA and at the University of Oxford. She is a published translator and has co-authored languages course books in France and in the UK. Her main research interest is the linguistic analysis and teaching of spoken French and English, in particular the use of authentic speech in language teaching. She is also conducting research in the use of technology and computer-mediated communication for language teaching and learning.

Emma Wilson is Professor of French Literature and the Visual Arts at the University of Cambridge and a Fellow of Corpus Christi College. Her publications include: *Sexuality and the Reading Encounter: Identity and Desire in Proust, Duras, Tournier and Cixous* (Oxford University Press, 1996); *French Cinema since 1950: Personal Histories* (Duckworth, 1999); *Memory and Survival: The French Cinema of Krzysztof Kieslowski* (Legenda, 2000); *Cinema's Missing Children* (Wallflower, 2003); *Alain Resnais* (Manchester University Press, 2006); and *Atom Egoyan* (University of Illinois Press, 2009). Her latest book, *Love, Mortality and the Moving Image*, is forthcoming.

Michael Worton is Vice-Provost of UCL (University College London) and Fielden Professor of French Language and Literature. He is also Higher Education Advisor to the British Council. He was a founding member of the Arts and Humanities Research Board, later the Arts and Humanities Research Council, on which he served from 1998 to 2006, chairing several of its major committees. He is also a member of the Comité International de Consultation en Sciences Humaines et Sociales de l'ANR and of the Advisory Board for the Programme of Artistic Research of the Austrian Research Council (FWF). His research focuses on twentieth- and twenty-first-century European litera-ture and on aspects of critical theory, feminism, gender politics, and painting and photography. He has published 10 books and more than 70 articles and chapters in books. Recent books include *Women's Writing in Contemporary France: New Writers, New Literatures in the 1990s* (with Gill Rye) and *Liberating Learning: Widening Participation* (with Patrick Derham). His forthcoming publications include an essay on gender for the first book on gender theory to be published in North Africa, and several articles on why the study of foreign languages and culture is important in today's world. He is an Officier of the Ordre des Palmes Académiques and in 2009 was awarded the Medal of Honoured Worker in Higher Education of the Republic of Kazakhstan.

Amy Wygant is Senior Lecturer in French at the University of Glasgow. She is the editor (2006–11) of *Seventeenth-Century French Studies*, and a co-founder of Women in French in Scotland (WIFIS). Her expertise is in early modern studies, psychoanalysis, historical witchcraft, opera and tragedy. She is particularly interested in the history of sugar, and melons. As a component of a long-standing research project on the historiography of French Studies in the UK, she is a member, with Hilary Footitt and Michèle Cohen, of the Groupe de recherche sur l'histoire du français en Angleterre (GRHIFA).

Foreword

Baroness Jean Coussins
Chair of the All-party Parliamentary Group on
Modern Languages

At the time of writing, a review of the national curriculum in England and Wales is imminent. As far as languages are concerned, this will be a crucial opportunity to reverse some of the disastrous consequences of previous policies and to introduce new ones, which positively promote both the importance and the pleasure of learning modern foreign languages.

It is self-evident that the place of languages in schools will have a critical impact on their presence in higher education (HE), but the opposite is also true. University modern language departments should be much more closely attuned to the ways in which they can influence what goes on in schools. For example, if more universities had a language requirement for matriculation, schools would have to take account of this when advising pupils on their GCSE option choices and ensure that the timetable allowed sufficient time for languages. Currently, according to an OECD survey published in September 2010, secondary school pupils in the UK spend less time studying languages than anywhere else in the developed world. Only 7 per cent of the lesson time of 12 to 14-year-olds is allocated to languages, which is half the amount of time spent on sciences. This puts England joint bottom of a table of 39 countries, alongside Ireland and Estonia and behind Indonesia and Mexico. Unless schools produce sufficient numbers of prospective HE students who are qualified and motivated to take modern language degrees, cutbacks will inevitably follow in universities.

Sixty per cent of UK employers say they are dissatisfied with the foreign language skills of school leavers, and research by Cardiff University's Business School suggests that the UK economy could be losing up to £21 billion a year in lost contracts because of a lack of language skills in the workforce. In addition to the business case, knowledge of other people's languages opens doors to understanding other people's cultures. Competence in languages also provides us with the wherewithal to function in international institutions and to participate in research. Graduates from the USA, China, India, and other EU countries are more likely to have a language, or two, in addition to their main subject, whether that be law, chemistry, geography or economics. The British Academy is rightly concerned that this may damage the internationally recognised distinction of UK scholarship within the humanities and social sciences and the ability of UK-educated researchers to contribute to international projects.

This situation will not be improved until all children once again have the right and the opportunity to learn languages up to the age of at least 16. To deprive them of this is to narrow their whole educational experience and to place them at a competitive disadvantage later in a global labour market.

Enlightened self-interest on the part of universities should extend to helping schools with the practical delivery of their language teaching. Some universities have programmes to send native speaker students into local schools to provide extra conversation practice. Detailed careers advice is another area which should provide a pragmatic link between the sectors, particularly for those who hope to work as linguists, for example by highlighting the benefits of studying not just one but two languages.

Lord Browne concluded in his review of university funding that languages should be a priority subject for public investment. The Higher Education Funding Council for England (HEFCE) describes languages, along with the science, technology, engineering and mathematics (STEM) subjects, as 'strategically vulnerable and important'. It is extremely disappointing, therefore, that some universities are considering significant cuts in modern language provision and apparently jumping too quickly to the conclusion that languages are 'unsustainable'. I hope that instead of being tempted down this path, they will take a closer look at the Worton Report and resist short-sighted and damaging cuts. Professor Worton suggests that the principal language issues needing attention by universities are not necessarily financial but strategic, organisational and policy based. To be seen as international centres of excellence in teaching, learning and research, they must (like schools) ensure that their institutional policies, or mission statements, acknowledge the importance of preparing young people to be global citizens and the place and value of language competence and intercultural understanding within that framework. No one should graduate, whatever their degree subject, without some form of assessed language competence.

If you really want to get under the skin of another culture, or have influence, then you need their language, not just a louder voice in your own. This book of essays on French Studies takes a timely and valuable lead in assessing our achievements and our shortfalls as a nation and in pointing us in the right direction for future improvement. Experts, advocates and practitioners in other languages should do likewise, so that we can build our momentum as language champions.

Foreword

His Excellency Bernard Emié
French Ambassador to the UK

The publication of this book comes at a time when humanities in general, and the teaching of modern foreign languages in particular, feel threatened because of uncertainty in relation to financial and economic circumstances. French Studies departments already faced difficulties when, in 2004, the education department for England decided that a foreign-language GCSE was no longer required to access higher education, a decision that resulted in the dropping of language teaching in many secondary schools. Learning a foreign language is perceived in the UK as being difficult and, the subject having in essence become optional, few pupils enrol in language classes, even where these are still offered. This has led to a drop in the number of students with the language skills required to enrol in French Studies at university. Organisations involved in the defence of language learning, and French Studies departments throughout the UK, have pointed out that British professionals in both public and private sectors often lack the language skills they need to pursue international careers. Already, for instance, there is a shortfall of graduates applying for posts within EU bodies or entering international organisations which require the command of a European language.

French Studies departments have argued that with the teaching of French language comes the teaching of French literature, French history, French politics, French cinema and theatre, French linguistics, and so on. Also prominent in French Studies are subjects such as postcolonial studies, war and culture, and women's studies. As the present book shows, French Studies in the UK covers a wide range of subjects which have for many decades made a huge contribution to the dissemination of French language and ideas.

The very high standards in research achieved by French Studies departments were given official recognition by the high ratings they obtained in the last Research Assessment Exercise in 2008. The RAE will now be replaced by the REF (the Research Excellence Framework) which gives a greater place to the impact of research across a range of audiences, including the general public. This will place an extra burden on French Studies departments: in addition to their focus on rigour and quality, they will also need to develop visibility within the country as a whole.

I share the view that the ability to speak a foreign language has never been so important in a world where countries interact on a daily basis through the internet and other information networks, even if the language most often used to communicate is English. Learning a foreign language, and becoming acquainted with a foreign culture, prepares students to operate in a social and cultural context different from their own, and so will help them interact with people from different backgrounds, wherever they happen to be later in their careers.

In addition, the command of a foreign language has been shown to be a valuable asset which boosts the employability of students and their access to international careers. In the particular case of French, recent events in Africa, both north and south of the Sahara, have reminded the world that French is spoken by millions of people there. It is clear that in Africa, as well as in Europe, familiarity with French language and culture will be a great asset in the years to come. In addition to their role in the dissemination of French ideas, British academics have produced rigorous and unbiased research on many aspects of French culture, ensuring that accurate and objective representations of French culture are transmitted to future generations of students. I feel greatly indebted to them for this invaluable work.

The French Embassy in the UK will offer its full support to projects proposed by French Studies societies and associations in higher education through the programmes run by its cultural and scientific department, managed by M. Laurent Burin des Roziers, Cultural Counsellor and Director of the Institut Français du Royaume-Uni.

Part I: Contextualisations

1

Introduction

Philippe Lane and Michael Worton

The central purpose of this book is to offer a picture of French Studies today, an analysis – from the inside – of what the discipline has become and where it might and, indeed, must go in the future. We hope that this anatomisation of French Studies and the way in which it is taught, researched and managed in the UK will help to energise debates around the place of modern languages in the modern university.

The world of higher education has been changing radically since the beginning of the twenty-first century, and the next ten years will witness the most significant changes experienced over the past half century, as many countries prioritise higher education and invest considerably in it. On the other hand, in the UK, especially after the October 2010 Comprehensive Spending Review, which was the most severe austerity budget for 60 years, universities and other higher education institutions (HEIs) are facing considerable challenges in terms of their funding, of recruitment of students at all levels, of international competitiveness and, crucially, of their own missions and identities. Furthermore, the government's decision on student funding means that there will be considerably more competition to attract the best students from the UK and from overseas, and in a context of severe financial constraints.

It is now axiomatic that much is changing in the new world of international education – and changing very fast. Students are travelling more and more to different countries for their higher education, and they have high expectations both of their student learning experience and of their employment prospects. For their part, employers expect broad skill sets and evidence of some work experience as well as disciplinary knowledge, and national and regional governments increasingly expect higher education to deliver on national priorities.

In this world of challenges but also of opportunities, universities and subject communities are having to think much more strategically. Key strategic directions are: (a) towards a broadening of the curriculum; (b) towards ever more interdisciplinarity; (c) towards internationalisation of universities, both at home and overseas. There is also an important shift in the ways in which universities perceive, redefine and reconstruct themselves, with a return of social and moral values to the curriculum, at the same time as there is ever more engagement with business and industry.

In this new world, modern languages have a vital role to play. However, one of the key findings of the *Review of Modern Foreign Languages Provision in Higher Education in England*, which HEFCE commissioned from Michael Worton,[1] was that the modern language community felt itself vulnerable and beleaguered up to the point of being in a crisis of confidence. Since that review was published in September 2009, the situation has, if anything, got worse, with more departments closing down or significantly reducing the number of language degrees offered. The decline in secondary pupils studying GCSE and A Levels in modern languages continues and, worryingly, it seems that a class divide is opening up, with significantly fewer comprehensive school pupils studying languages, compared with those in selective schools or independent schools (in 2009, only 41 per cent of comprehensive school pupils were entered for a modern language GCSE, compared with 91 per cent of selective school pupils and 81 per cent of independent school pupils).[2]

It must be said that the precarious position of languages today is due in part to the fact that the different stakeholders have failed to articulate a powerful, shared message about the value of languages, with government giving a different message from that of the employers, while both of these are themselves often different from those of educators and researchers. It is therefore not simply timely, but urgent for the modern languages community to take a lead in advocacy, explaining and demonstrating why and how languages are vital to every higher education experience, be it in the UK or elsewhere in the world. And the modern languages community needs at the same time to transform itself not only academically but also conceptually in order better to face the challenges ahead.

In this work, French Studies has a particularly important leadership role to play, since French remains the most widely studied and researched language in the UK. While it is the future that must concern us most, the reasons that led French to its place at the core of the modern curriculum in UK higher education are illuminating. For this reason, several essays in this volume trace pathways in the development of French Studies, highlighting, for instance, the ways in which the discipline has adopted what can be seen as a feminine bias, while paradoxically remaining a male-dominated profession, and the progressive shift away from

1 Michael Worton, *Review of Modern Foreign Languages Provision in Higher Education in England* (London: Higher Education Funding Council for England [HEFCE], 2009), online resource, consulted 25 November 2010.
2 For full details, see the national statistics on KS4 results in England, 2008–09 given at Table 11 in Department for Children Schools and Families, *GCSE And Equivalent Results In England 2008/09 (Revised)*, SFR 01/2010 (London: Department for Children Schools and Families, 2010), online resource, consulted on 25 November 2010.

pre-modern literature and culture to an ever increasing focus on the contemporary period. The history of French Studies reveals a discipline, which, while remaining largely committed to a 'language and literature' approach, has steadily embraced other disciplines in the humanities and the social sciences, to the extent that it often now defines itself essentially through its interdisciplinarity rather than through any linguistic or geographic specificity. Yet throughout most of its history, it has been the dominant language, despite the many and significant geopolitical and cultural changes that have occurred since the early nineteenth century. It is therefore interesting to note that when modern languages were first introduced into the modern university curriculum by UCL (then the University of London), when it opened in 1828, Chairs were established from the very beginning in German, Italian and Spanish, as well as in Latin, Greek, Hebrew and Hindustani. French was also taught from the very beginning, but P. F. Merlet, the original teacher of French, was not given the title of Professor until 1834! French did not therefore have a visible position of seniority in the new modern languages community, but over the decades it grew in the UK to be the most studied of languages, both in schools and in universities.

Today, although there are falling registrations for GCSE, AS and A Levels, year on year for the past decade, French remains what could be described as the flagship language, and its fortunes are central not only to the understanding of the place of modern languages today, but also of its future. This book arose out of a seminar convened by us, which brought together colleagues from across the country to discuss the present state of French Studies in the UK and also to look forward to what the future holds for the discipline. The workshop took place in the context of some concern about both funding for teaching and for research, and about the standing of French Studies in the UK. During the workshop, all participants sought to give a greater sense of the breadth and depth of French Studies as well as beginning to shape a common sense of how we could help to shape the future. These ideas were taken forward as these essays were drafted and we invited further specialists from the field to contribute to the volume.

Since that workshop, the landscape has changed yet further, with the HEFCE set to withdraw all teaching funding for humanities and social sciences and fees for undergraduates rising to at least £6,000 per annum, with some universities charging up to £9,000 per annum as a result of the government's response to the Browne report.[3] There will also be a gradual decline in research funding, which will be maintained in cash terms over the next four years, but will be reduced by inflation. However, the Browne report itself made mention of the need to continue

---

3 John Browne, *Securing a Sustainable Future for Higher Education In England: an independent review of higher education funding and student finance* (London: Department for Business, Innovation and Skills, 2010), online resource, consulted 25 November 2010.

funding for 'strategically important languages'. While this gave some hope, no one is yet quite clear exactly what is meant by 'strategically important' in this context and, at the time of writing, we are still lobbying for this to include all languages and not simply languages which are important to business (e.g. Mandarin and Arabic) or to national security and counter-terrorism measures (e.g. Pashtu and Persian). The increase in tuition fees will also have a very significant impact on student recruitment, and the reduction in research funding, although not as severe as feared, will adversely affect modern languages and other humanities, since the sciences, technology, engineering, mathematics and medicine are to be prioritised.

The rapid expansion of international and transnational education may well offer a major opportunity for all those teaching and researching in the modern languages, but it represents also a significant challenge. In this context of challenge and opportunity, it is vital that we are able to define, articulate and communicate not only what is excellent about French Studies but what is distinctive, and we trust that this volume will contribute to that vital process.

As students travel more and more to different countries for their higher education, and as they have different expectations in terms of their student experience and of their employment prospects, all disciplines need radically to rethink their curricula with regard to the changing needs of students and of employers (including universities). A thorough overhaul of the curricula of French Studies and other languages is clearly called for, as is much closer cooperation with, and creative challenge to, primary schools and secondary schools in their own development of French Studies curricula. As far as research is concerned, collaboration must be the way forward, both with other departments within individual universities, between modern foreign language departments and language centres, between UK and overseas universities – and collaboration with business, industry and government must be stepped up at all levels. While we must never adopt a purely utilitarian approach, we need to work strategically with organisations like the Confederation of Business and Industry (CBI) who stressed the importance of language skills two seminar reports,[4] and we also need to lobby government more effectively, stressing the fact that interlinguistic competencies and intercultural skills have key roles in 'soft power' as well as in business and the fostering of global citizenship. French Studies can give a lead in the various redefinings that are necessary, stressing how the study of French, as a flagship discipline for modern foreign languages in the UK, helps our students fully to become active and creative global citizens.

---

4 Confederation of British Industry (CBI), *Emerging Stronger: the Value of Education and Skills in Turbulent Times* (London: CBI, 2009); CBI, *Stronger Together. Businesses and Universities in Turbulent Times: a report from the CBI Higher Education Task Force* (London: CBI, 2009).

The decade ahead will be a time of some painful reconstruction, but as a community, we do well to remember that globalisation and transnational education have changed for ever the circumstances within which we operate as educators and researchers and are necessitating radical changes in the ways in which learning, teaching and research can take place. Since the development of the 'infinite library' of the internet, we are having to question our traditional conceptions of how much we can actually know and also our conceptions of how we should actually learn when knowledge is constantly expanding and changing, and when it is managed by no single authority. Both reality and knowledge in the virtual world are constructed consensually by communities of readers and texts, and hierarchies between learners and teachers are dissolved. We also need to teach scepticism much more actively than in the past, since the authority of the reference book is no longer what it was. In this new world, our programmes and the learning materials that we use need to be ever more self-consciously aware and we need constantly to explore how language and culture are bound up with issues of owner-ship and with the question of how any given language and culture is managed, both by its 'originating' or its host country and globally.

In the case of French Studies, questions of cultural ownership and of national, cultural or linguistic identity have become vital research questions and are slowly becoming important elements of some taught courses. With this interrogation of ownership and identity come other questionings, which aim both to determine the specificity of the Frenchness of French culture and, indeed, of French Studies and con-versely to explore the ways in which French culture has been 'exploded' conceptually and geographically and how French Studies is increasingly defined in terms of its cross-cultural interactions. Several of the essays in this volume precisely argue that French Studies is now best defined in terms of its multidisciplinarity. This has great benefits in research and in teaching and learning, yet it poses problems in terms of developing and articulating a coherent identity. Taking another perspective, some essays also argue for the 'feminine' nature of French culture and of French Studies in the UK, while yet others highlight the diversity of provision in French Studies in the UK. And while we would want to celebrate such multiplicity of approach, it does pose problems in terms of developing and communicating a coherent, if complex message about the purpose and identity of French Studies.

The discussions and debates that led to this volume have been wide-ranging and energetic, with attention being paid both to important sub-disciplines, such as literature, linguistics, translation, cinema, popular studies, postcolonial studies, and so on and to the new con-texts in which French Studies operates, such as a greater focus in universities on interdisciplinarity, the challenging funding situation, the importance of establishing new partnerships with business and in-dustry, including a much greater focus on employability, the potential for UK French Studies to engage in 'soft power' and diplomatic engagements, and so on.

The mood of debates around languages in the UK remains dark and gloomy, yet it is vital that we find ways not only to face the challenging future but also to find ways of helping to shape that future. In this, we clearly need to work together, establishing new partnerships and a culture of creatively challenging collaboration. We give details in Annexe 1 of the ways in which the French government, through a variety of agencies and approaches, is collaborating with universities in the UK, and many of the essays in this volume set out how the UK French Studies community is redefining both itself and its agenda through ever-increasing interdisciplinary work and interdepartmental and inter-institutional working.

The future for the discipline and for those working in it is fraught with challenges, but if we learn to create innovative partnerships both within the national and international academic community and with the world of business, we shall create a discipline that will be creatively and effectively responsive to the needs and demands of our complex, globalised twenty-first century.

Bibliography

Browne, John, *Securing a Sustainable Future for Higher Education In England: An Independent Review of Higher Education Funding and Student Finance* (London: Department for Business, Innovation and Skills, 2010), available at www.info4local.gov.uk/documents/publications/1737515 (consulted 25 November 2010).

Confederation of British Industry, *Emerging Stronger: The Value of Education and Skills in Turbulent Times* (London: Confederation of British Industry, 2009).

Confederation of British Industry, *Stronger Together. Businesses and Universities in Turbulent Times: A Report from the CBI Higher Education Task Force* (London: Confederation of British Industry, 2009).

Department for Children Schools and Families, *GCSE and Equivalent Results in England 2008/09 (Revised)*, SFR 01/2010 (London: Department for Children Schools and Families, 2010), available at: www.education.gov.uk/rsgateway/DB/SFR/s000909/sfr01–2010.pdf (consulted on 25 November 2010).

Worton, Michael, *Review of Modern Foreign Languages Provision in Higher Education in England* (London: HEFCE, October 2009), available at www.hefce.ac.uk/pubs/hefce/2009/09_41/ (consulted on 25 November 2010).

Annexe 1
French Government Support for UK French Studies

There has always been a close relationship in higher education between France and the UK. However, over the past two decades there have been significant changes and reforms in both the French and the UK systems, with yet more being implemented or planned. The face of higher education throughout Europe and, indeed, globally is changing, and therefore it is even more urgent that France and the UK cooperate as closely and effectively as possible. The French government is taking forward this cooperation in a variety of ways, which are set out below.

The Value of Vigilance: Keeping a Watching Brief

The global market for higher education needs to be closely watched. Our ongoing analysis of UK higher education allows us to assess the advantages and drawbacks of UK policy choices, the hopes and worries that they raise, and the lessons to be drawn for France.

Actions
- production of reports on academic developments in both countries
- creation of a forum of 'best practices' and 'benchmarking'
- development of exchanges and intense executive education programmes between university vice-chancellors and their administrative teams in both countries.

The Promotion of French Higher Education

The international league tables do not include most French universities and this fact has been harmful to their image. One of the main objectives of the Attaché for Higher Education is to promote French universities and *grandes écoles*, and to encourage student mobility between the two countries.

Actions to raise the profile of French HE
- participation in carefully selected student fairs
- support of partnership projects between British and French universities (visits by representatives of French universities and *grandes écoles* to gather information about the governance of UK universities to be used in the implementation of the French reform on university autonomy)
- strengthening of the *entente cordiale* scholarship scheme, as this scheme allows an orientation of students towards the best institutions and laboratories, where they will be given a warm welcome; as years

go by, the alumni network grows in size and influence in Franco-British circles
- development of fundraising to support international student mobility.

The Development of Scientific and Academic Networks (Student and Researcher Mobility; Dual Diplomas; Agence Nationale de la Recherche; CNRS; Invitations and Visiting Professorships)

The Bologna Process for the creation of the European Higher Education Area has given a new impetus to cooperation in higher education between the member countries of the EU, including France and the UK. The forthcoming completion of the 2000–2010 phase of the Bologna Process will allow us to make a first positive assessment (since a majority of partner institutions now regard the development of a European Higher Education Area as vital) and to open new perspectives for the next phase – after 2010. These objectives will be achieved through a close collaboration between the Maison Française d'Oxford and the Science and Technology Department of the French Embassy.

Actions
- as in past years, creation of dual diplomas and joint PhDs, including new areas of research
- arrangement of visiting professorships for French academics and researchers
- development of research networks with the help of the Science and Technology Department of the French Embassy (ANR projects, Research Councils, etc.)
- exploration of cooperation opportunities in professional training (in collaboration with the Department of Business, Innovation and Skills), especially in the field of ecology and renewable energies.

Conferences and Seminars, French Studies, Debates

In recent decades, many French Studies departments have become part of other departments such as European studies, international studies, media studies, cinema studies, and so on, thereby widening the impact of our cooperation. Furthermore, learned societies specialising in French Studies are privileged partners with whom to hold debates on important current issues. Many of the officers of these societies hold positions of responsibility in the most prestigious universities.

Actions
- as in past years, invitations to the UK of academics from French institutions

- support of conferences and seminars by the French Studies network
- participation of French universities and *grandes écoles* in important international conferences organised by British institutions.

This represents a significant programme of support and cooperation across the full range of HE provision in the UK. As our two countries take forward their national strategies, it is clear that there is divergence in many of the aspects of the reforms, but there is also a shared vision of placing HE at the heart of the social and economic developments of our two countries. The number of collaborations in both teaching and research grows steadily from year to year. We need to ensure that this growth continues – and also that our collaborations are increasingly strategic.

2

A Short History of French Studies in the UK

Diana Holmes

Preamble

In October 1999 the journal *French Cultural Studies* brought out an original and engaging special issue entitled 'Personal Voices, Personal Experiences'. It was composed of eight essays by academics of different backgrounds and generations, each working in some aspect of French Studies, all but one within the UK, and it put the emphasis on autobiographical trajectories, on how each had come to choose French as their discipline and its teaching and study as their career. Brian Rigby, the volume's editor, commented in the introduction on how little has been written on the development of French as an academic discipline, and on the paucity in such accounts as do exist of any 'traces of the personal and autobiographical'.[1] 'It is as if studying a foreign language and culture – as opposed to one's native language and culture – demands the repression of the scholar and critic's own personal, social, linguistic and cultural identity.'[2]

This is not an autobiographical account of my own engagement with French Studies, but rather an attempt to frame the chapters that follow within a history that has seen massive change, and a fair amount of continuity, linear development, and cyclical patterns of decline and renewal. However, Brian Rigby's statement chimes with my own recognition as I prepared this paper that any history was going to be shaped by personal experience: my sense of what French means to British people, of how it is classed and gendered, as well as my examples of particular universities that seem to illustrate a broader tendency – these are inevitably determined in part by an individual story, which should therefore be briefly acknowledged.

---

1 Brian Rigby (ed.), 'Personal Voices, Personal Experiences', *French Cultural Studies* 10: 3, no. 30 (October 1999), p. 241.
2 Rigby, 'Personal Voices', pp. 241–2.

In the 1960s I was at school in a Lancashire town with a large Catholic population, where Catholic and what we called 'non-Catholic' educational systems ran in parallel: passing the 11-plus, as a Catholic girl, meant going to Notre Dame Convent Grammar. The nuns' real ambition for us – at least that was our impression – was that we should become good pious wives and mothers, but languages were encouraged and relatively well taught. They were considered feminine subjects. Few girls aimed at university (rather more for Catholic training colleges), and those of us who did were almost all the first generation in our families to do so. Once every few years a Notre Dame girl would get in to Oxford, and the school would be given a half-holiday. I chose French, Spanish, English and General Studies at A level. The school put me in for Oxford, but Sussex by the sea, with its then reputation for drugs, rebellion and general wickedness, as well as a thrillingly unfamiliar curriculum, 'The Modern European Mind', looked so much more exciting. I studied French at Sussex in its heyday, when French literature was contextualised within a broader European history of political change, thought and culture, and it was the intellectual excitement of that education (as well as falling in love in, and with, France during my year abroad) that led me to continue studying post graduation, with a *maîtrise* in Paris and then a return to Sussex to undertake a PhD.

Somewhere between Brighton and Paris, I met second-wave feminism, and lots of things fell into place: the doctorate was on 'images of woman' (we were still using the singular) in the inter-war novel. Looking for a job in the mid to late 1970s, I aimed for what seemed then to be the egalitarian comprehensives of the higher education (HE) sector, and got my first post in a quite new, but large and thriving, department at Wolverhampton Polytechnic. Since then I have taught in a variety of institutions: North London Polytechnic and Ealing College of Higher Education (now Thames Valley University) during a half-decade in London, Keele University, then (and still) the University of Leeds. Like most senior academics, I have also been an external examiner in a further range of universities (and polytechnics), and been part of the national associations in which we meet to exchange ideas and scholarship, and to campaign. This particular experience – in some respects typical – will have its effect on the account below.

French in the UK – From the late Nineteenth to the Twenty-first Century

The study of French in British universities began in the mid-nineteenth century, mainly taking the form of (presumably extra-mural) conversation classes for young ladies, and the teaching of the French language to those destined for a career in secondary education. Those doing the teaching were mainly French nationals, and their competence therefore assumed to be natural or at least contingent on birth and biography rather than scholarly. If French was to gain the status of a university subject or discipline, it had to distinguish itself from the mere acquisition of linguistic fluency, taking as a model the study of dead languages (classics). This meant defining French as French philology, used in its broader sense to mean the study of the historical development of a nation's language and literature. The philological turn seems to have begun by the *fin de siècle*: the first chair in French (and German) at Southampton University, for example, was awarded in 1899 to a Dr E. du Bois; Leeds University, which received its charter in 1904, immediately appointed Professor Paul Barbier (*fils*) to a chair of French language and romance philology. Oxford University, after much passionate debate over the relative academic status of Greek and modern languages, introduced the latter as a full subject in 1905.

The First World War strengthened the ties between France and Britain and also revealed a national need for better language skills: both the failure to pick up forewarnings of war and the difficulty of communication with allies were blamed on an outmoded educational system that neglected modern languages. The government commissioned reports on various aspects of education: the Leathes Committee reported on modern studies – mainly, in fact, modern languages – in 1918. Its *état des lieux* showed that French was far and away the dominant language taught in British schools and universities: in Britain's 22 universities there were 70 people involved in teaching French, as opposed to 42 German, 11 Italian, 11 Russian and 7 Spanish. Native fluency remained a primary criterion for appointments, so that out of 15 professors of French, 10 were French nationals.[3] The Leathes Report, published in 1918, argued strongly for a radical upgrading of modern languages in secondary and higher education, both on the pragmatic grounds that language competence was 'directly and abundantly remunerative' in foreign trade,[4] and on the less instrumental grounds that studying languages within their cultural context represented an 'ideal of human learning', developing 'the higher faculties, the imagination, the sense of beauty and the intellectual comprehension, clear vision, mental harmony, a just sense of proportion, higher illumination'.[5] The study of modern languages was thus being promoted as the intellectual and moral equivalent of studying the classics, but with the added benefit of serving a very practical purpose. A 1920 report concurred on the vocational dimension:

---

3 Susan Bayley, 'Modern Languages: An "Ideal of Humane Learning": The Leathes Report of 1918', *Journal of Educational Administration and History* 23: 2 (1991), 11–24, p. 14.
4 Bayley, 'Modern Languages', p. 15.
5 Bayley, 'Modern Languages', p. 13.

The Universities should train up for the service of the nation an abundant supply of men and women capable of acquiring, digesting, arranging and imparting the vast amount of knowledge concerning foreign countries which can be obtained by study, and travel, and personal intercourse.[6]

The Leathes Report made a number of recommendations, some of which were too expensive, or conflicted with the recommendations of committees on other disciplines, but some of which were implemented. By 1919, seven UK universities had a separate honours school of French Studies; by 1920 modern languages were established as part of the curriculum in all British universities, in the majority of cases with an established chair. As the report recommended, all new appointments to chairs were of British nationality, so that qualifications and publications were seen to be as important in this as in any other discipline. Numbers of students graduating in modern languages, the majority of these in French, rose from 60 in 1904 to 300 in 1923.

The French department of the University of Leeds exemplifies the national trend. In 1919–20, the department had three academic members of staff including (less commonly) one woman, a Miss Doris Gunnell who was a doctor of the University of Paris. By 1925–26 there were five colleagues in French, by the mid-1930s, six.

To pursue the narrative in very broad terms: the growth of French departments (and of modern languages departments generally) continued steadily throughout the inter-war period and beyond. By 1951–52, Leeds had two professors, one senior lecturer, three Lecturers and four assistant lecturers (eleven in all) plus three lecteurs/lectrices; by 1967–68 this was up to nineteen, more or less the size of the department in 2010. Staff–student ratios were rather more favourable than half a century later: the university's Annual Report records totals of 240 'single subject' undergraduates in French, 82 'two subject' (nowadays joint honours), and 254 'general/service', or (presumably) students in other disciplines taking elements of French.

By the late 1960s, a major expansion of higher education (HE) had taken place, thanks in large part to the 1963 Robbins Report. Robbins's recommendations, including to observe a demand-led policy and thus create more additional places in the arts than the sciences, had been fully accepted and funded by the government. New universities were created with new visions of how knowledge should be organised and imparted, including in modern languages. White Papers in 1965 and 1972 also led to the establishment of a new HE sector, the polytechnics, intended to enjoy parity of esteem with the universities while pursuing a rather different mission of direct responsiveness to social needs.

---

6 *Report of the Committee on Modern Languages* (1920), p. 55; cited in Christophe Campos, 'Le Français dans les universités britanniques', *Franco-British Studies* 8 (1989), 69–108, p. 84.

Polytechnic languages departments would also play an important role in the development of modern language studies, particularly before the polytechnics were absorbed into the university sector in 1992. HE expansion continued throughout the 1970s.

The 1980s brought a new, and now all too familiar, discourse of cuts and contraction: the expenditure plans of the new (1979) Thatcher government, announced in March 1981, meant a cut of more than 8 per cent in spending on further and higher education. For Salford University –one of the worst hit – this led, for example, to a 44 per cent cut in income from the University Grants Committee and to the loss of 8 out of 40 jobs in the modern languages department. Nonetheless, by the 'where are we now?' conference held at Birmingham in July 1991 (*French in the 90s*),[7] the scene had changed again. Anxious as many of the deliberations at that conference were, they took place within a confident sense of expansion: Mike Kelly traced advertisements for 35 new lecturer posts in French in 'old' universities alone in 1988–89, as well as a sharp increase in undergraduate recruitment: 7 per cent in universities and 20 per cent in polytechnics in the year preceding the conference. If this also meant increasing casualisation of academic labour and a distinct rise in staff–student ratios, French did at least appear to be a fully established discipline and a necessary component of any self-respecting institution of higher education, supported by healthy student demand.

Little did we know what the following two decades would bring. Under the influence of the perceived global dominance of English, the failure of many state schools to promote language learning, particularly after the 2004 withdrawal of ML from the compulsory post-14 curriculum, and a number of other factors, A level entries in most languages including French declined sharply – French dropped by 47 per cent between 1996 and 2007. Applications for degrees in French, as in ML generally, declined accordingly. University language departments contracted and in many cases closed, particularly, but by no means only, in the once vibrant ex-polytechnic sector. It is poignant to look down the list of institutions represented at *French in the 90s* and to see just how many of the departments of French and/or modern languages no longer exist, or exist only in the most minimal and threatened form. A quick and incomplete run through the list produces the following roll call of the fallen (three of which are part of my own French Studies history): Bradford, Bristol Polytechnic (later University of the West of England), Coventry, Keele, Kingston, South Bank, Sussex, Wolverhampton. One decade into the twenty-first century, French Studies in the UK is vibrant but embattled.

---

7 Jennifer Birkett and Michael Kelly (eds), *French in the 90s: A Transbinary Conference July 1991* (Birmingham: Birmingham Modern Languages Publications, 1992).

Defining French

From its earliest days as a university discipline, the degree syllabus in French meant literary translation and a historically contextualised study of language and literature. Thus the distinction was clearly marked between being a French scholar, and merely mastering the language; the curriculum was informed by the Leathes concept of a language discipline as 'an ideal of humane learning'. Already in 1904–5 the honours syllabus at Leeds covered translation in both directions with questions on grammar, an oral exam, Old French, 'historical grammar', and a prescribed period of French literature (Victor Hugo's *Préface de Cromwell* and *Hernani* were set books in the final year). With minor changes, this type of syllabus remained the norm up to – and in many institutions well beyond – the 1970s: a 1965 guide to courses of study in European languages at universities tells potential applicants that:

> university language courses vary ... but the majority can be described as academic courses of study in language and literature, generally based on the conviction – and with good reason – that a study of the language should be coupled with the study of its literary masterpieces.[8]

In the same guide, King's College London articulated very clearly the ideal at which such degree programmes aimed: apart from a high degree of language competence:

> Every student should achieve (1) a general knowledge of who wrote what, when; (2) knowledge of the contents and historical significance of most of the main works, even if some must be at second hand (3) first-hand acquaintance with a comparatively limited number of writers.

There was always an alternative view: the quotation from the 1920 report above is quite clear on the need to 'train up' specialists in language 'for the nation's service', and the call for a more practical, vocationally oriented approach to language degrees seems always to have formed a sort of descant accompaniment to the serene continuity of the lang-lit model. In the 1960s and 1970s, with expansion and the incentives this provided for new thinking, alternatives began not just to be proposed but to be put into practice.

The University of Sussex (charter 1961), for one, challenged the emphasis on canonical coverage and emphasised instead the study of how knowledge was constructed. The study of French – like all other arts subjects – took a different form, depending on the school in which it was studied. For the majority, this was the school of European studies, which meant a broad introduction to philosophy, history and critical

---

8   H. H. Stern (ed.), *Modern Languages in the Universities. A Guide to the Courses of Study in 5 European Languages at Universities in the UK* (London: MLA, 1961), p. 7.

approaches in year 1, then an emphasis on the contextualisation of national cultures through school courses that included the foundations of European thought, and the celebrated, wonderfully diverse *Modern European Mind*, running alongside an option-based curriculum in French that dispensed with all pretention to inclusivity. The syllabus, however, remained largely literary, and language fluency remained a subsidiary aim.

Meanwhile, universities like Bradford (1966) and Salford (1967) – both previously colleges of advanced technology – placed language at the centre of their degree programmes, and innovated in language learning methods with language labs, higher class contact hours, and work placements. They thus appealed to those many language enthusiasts who (as applicants used to say at interviews for the BA modern languages at Wolverhampton) 'didn't really like literature'. The 30 polytechnics almost all established departments of languages and interpreted their mission of relevance and vocationality in more than one way. Wolverhampton provides a good example, since it had one of the largest and the most diverse of polytechnic ML departments. The School of Languages and European Studies, of which French was a division, integrated four main languages (French, Spanish, German, Russian) and a number of minor ones, plus European politics and economics, into a unitary school, and offered:

- a flagship BA Modern Languages: two languages with Europe-wide core courses and national-specific options in politics, history, economics and (to a lesser extent) culture
- a BA European Studies with one language plus a social-science based study of contemporary Europe
- a Diploma in Languages for Business (essentially to train bi- or trilingual secretaries – the gender of 99 per cent of the students will cause no surprises)
- in collaboration with the rest of the Arts faculty, a BA Humanities, where the many lecturers in language disciplines whose interests remained literary had a free hand to invent interesting courses. 'Hums' also provided the framework for the development of French film studies.

The dearth of jobs towards the end of the 1970s, and still more in the 1980s, meant that many literary/cultural postgraduates who might otherwise have headed for universities like their own went instead to the expanding polytechnics. Whether recruited to 'old' university or polytechnic departments, we joined the same professional associations, went to the same conferences, faced the same questions about curriculum, pedagogy and research. Partly through the influential work of the Council for National Academic Awards (CNAA), the body charged with awarding degrees and monitoring quality in the polytechnics, contacts were also made and maintained higher up the managerial scale, so that more traditional university departments became aware of what was going on in the polytechnics and of its popularity with students. The general expansion of HE, combined with a sharper sense of the social relevance of language study and the employability of its graduates, widened the class base from which undergraduates were drawn: the newer universities and the polytechnics provided small but useful correctives to the traditional identification of French as a thoroughly middle-class subject.

There was conflict: those who saw the study of literature as the heart of the discipline were often outraged by the new breed of French scholars for whom the socio-political was of primary relevance, and the relative importance of language fluency (and how to produce it in students) was a permanent subject of controversy. But for pragmatic reasons of student demand and, in many cases, the movements of academics between different types of institution, the overall pattern was one of convergence. Leeds, a 'traditional' university department, already offered a course on 'contemporary French history and institutions' in 1961, but this socio-political element certainly expanded in the 1970s. Even the longest established departments became more self-conscious about their language teaching. The increasingly porous nature of the binary line also meant that French in the polytechnics moved in a 'cultural' direction. By the time the binary line went in 1992, the difference between polytechnic and university languages departments was far from obvious.

By the 1990s, French Studies, both as a degree subject and as a research field, included linguistics, translation studies, literature, film, history, politics, economics, popular music, thought and philosophy, and stretched from the medieval period to the present and across the entirety of the francophone world rather than just metropolitan France. Though the inclinations of academic staff plus, perhaps, the inertia of tradition meant that literary options remained in the majority, by the late 1980s, as one correspondent wrote to Colin Evans as the latter researched his 1988 book *Language People: the Experience of Teaching and Learning in Modern Languages in British Universities*:

> You can put anything in a French course as long as it has some link with France, is intellectually respectable and makes the students work.[9]

As Evans commented:

> The surprising thing (was) that this multiplicity, while confusing to the university, actually enabled the discipline to adapt with great rapidity to the changing environment.[10]

9 Colin Evans, *Language People: The Experience of Teaching and Learning Modern Languages in British Universities* (Milton Keynes: The Society for Research into Higher Education and Open University, 1988), p. 173.

10 Evans, *Language People*, p. 177.

So there has always been a problem of definition, and one of representing the subject (or discipline?) to the world outside, starting with our own colleagues in the university. University subjects are clearly not labels for divisions that naturally occur in the world, but 'institutionalised, operational territories inhabited by communities of people who defend their boundaries and compete with other communities',[11] and, as Colin Evans also points out, Britain (at least) has always liked its subjects strongly differentiated and framed, corresponding to a clear body of knowledge and set of intellectual methodologies (the prolonged and still fruitless struggle to replace A levels with a broader qualification confirms this). The story of French Studies is one of repeated and diverse struggles – sometimes successful ones – to define the nature and purpose of our multiple, complex, sometimes internally divided subject area in ways that convince those on whom our existence depends.

The internal battles over what French Studies is have raged around the syllabus – those committed to the lang-lit model did not go down without a fight against what they perceived as a philistine utilitarianism – and been reflected in research. The journal *French Studies* was founded after the Second World War (1946) to bring a briefly eclipsed French culture back to a general and academic readership, but became (not surprisingly) the preserve of the traditional lang-lit departments, as did the annual conference that began in 1959 when the *Society for French Studies* was formed. The *Association for the Study of Modern and Contemporary France* was founded in 1979 as – in a sense – a riposte to the assumptions that still underlay *French Studies*: bringing together French specialists from ML departments – mainly in polytechnics and newer universities – as well as from history and politics, it foregrounded 'new combinations of French Studies such as history, politics, geography and cinema, alongside innovative methods of teaching the language'. The *Association for French Language Studies*, founded in 1981 to 'encourage and promote language teaching activities and research in French Language and Linguistics as areas worthy of consideration in their own right', did something similar for language. *Paragraph* founded in 1983, also interpellated the discipline by foregrounding the critical theory now central to French intellectual life but curiously absent from most UK French (as opposed to English) departments. *Women in French* conferences, from 1990 on, pointed up the curious gender bias of the subject (to which I turn below). As with departments, the outcome of these challenges was not the drawing up of battle lines but rather the gradual expansion and increase in scope of the *French Studies* association and journal, both now distinctly more multi- or interdisciplinary and inclusive, if maintaining an accent on literature.

11 Evans, *Language People*, p. 162.

To summarise, the competing justifications for our existence, often unarticulated but nonetheless informing practice, have been these:

- We practice and teach one of the world's major languages. The UK needs competent graduates – as the 1920 report put it: 'an abundant supply of men and women capable of acquiring, digesting, arranging and imparting the vast amount of knowledge concerning France' – who are both highly fluent and culturally literate in French. What has changed, in line with broader definitions of culture, is the definition of 'culturally literate'. The argument for the national relevance of the subject assumes that France and the francophone world *matter*, economically and politically, and that the British and French can be valued interlocutors for each other.
- Modern languages graduates, regardless of specific language, are likely to emerge not only able to deploy the core skills of the humanities scholar (analysis, critical judgement, communication), but also with the additional qualities of 'flexib(ility), empath(y) and free(dom) from insular thinking'[12] – hence as highly employable and generally useful citizens. The emphasis on the nature of language that is inseparable from the ML degree is intrinsically valuable for it 'frees the mind from the tyranny of words. It is extremely difficult for a monoglot to dissociate thought from words but he who can express his ideas in two languages is emancipated'.[13]
- As a field of research and teaching, French (like other modern languages) embodies a particularly valuable form of intellectual enquiry because the focus on a national culture licenses us to connect disciplines, to foreground the interplay of disciplinary knowledge and (always) the role of language in the construction and framing of knowledge and of social relations.

Gender

The paradox in the relationship between French Studies and gender is this: French (even more than other modern languages) has long been associated in Britain with the feminine, and yet within French Studies women, for a very long time, remained quite invisible.

Why should studying French be seen as feminine? Michèle Cohen provides an excellent analysis of the ways in which the British national character was forged,[14] in the eighteenth century, in part by opposition to Britain's closest 'other', France, on a series of binaries that contrasted

---

12 Evans, *Language People*, p. 186.
13 S. J. Evans, quoted in Evans, *Language People*, p. 190.
14 Michèle Cohen, *Fashioning Masculinity: Masculinity, National Identity and Languages in The Eighteenth Century* (London: Routledge, 1996).

French refinement, sophistication and submission to absolute monarchy to a sort of rough-hewn British authenticity and freedom. Frenchness was effeminate, and a threat to taciturn British manliness. Interest and fluency in French became 'girly' – a form of feminine refinement – in the nineteenth century, and remained so.

One might speculate too about the relation between self and other in the advanced study of a language: the need to shift identity, to see the world through another's eyes and tongue, and relate this to the fact that girls, throughout the nineteenth and twentieth centuries, have been directed more towards empathy, towards the construction of a self whose ego boundaries are more porous, more fluid than those of men.

Whatever the reasons, far more women than men have opted to pursue the study of modern languages at university level. In 1983, typically for the whole period, female students of ML outnumbered men in a proportion of 3:1. However, the proportions were reversed when it came to academic staff, with only 29 per cent women in French Studies departments, and these mostly at the base of the pyramid of seniority. Female undergraduates may have felt an affinity with French language and culture, but as a university discipline, French was male. The syllabus told the same story: at Sussex, for all its progressiveness, the *Princesse de Clèves* was the only indication that 'woman writer' was not an oxymoron. During my undergraduate career I was taught by only one woman – Margaret McGowan. My experience was typical of the times – and appeared simply normal.

When Elizabeth Fallaize and I were appointed simultaneously in 1975 to lectureships in French at Wolverhampton Polytechnic, young women lecturers were so few and far between that two at once defied credibility, and we were widely assumed to be the same person for quite some time. We were also generally assumed to be students, and berated for daring to park in the staff car park. The fact that Elizabeth would go on to become the first female fellow of St John's College Oxford, with a research specialism in Simone de Beauvoir studies, is both a significant part of the story of women in French, and a measure of progress made.

The point here is this: it took a long time to extricate ourselves from a gender imbalance so familiar as to be invisible, but part of the history of French Studies has been the identification of the gender deficit as a real problem, and the resulting changes to the discipline and the way it is staffed. At the inaugural meeting of the loose support and research network we now call Women in French, in December 1987 – a meeting I recall as a heady mix of anger and optimism – we found that while women made up two-thirds of French undergraduates, there were just six women professors of French in the UK, and one head of department in a polytechnic. The absence and silence of women in the major scholarly associations – especially *French Studies* – was agreed to be disgraceful. Rather than simply analysing the intricate workings of patriarchal culture (though we did that too), we organised, and to a considerable extent it has worked. By 2002/3 25 per cent of professors in French in the UK were women, 37 per cent of senior lecturers, 58 per cent of lecturers. As French women themselves know only too well, the achievement of parity is a slow and painstaking business, and women still make up the vast majority of lower-paid and less secure 'other' staff' on part-time or temporary contracts (76 per cent in 2003/3). Nonetheless, in the twenty-first century, French Studies is much less likely to mean the study of the language, history and worldview of one half of the French.

Conclusion

This narrative overview has shown French establishing itself in the first two decades of the twentieth century as an intellectually respectable humanities discipline within which language is central not only as a skill but as an object of study. Thereafter, French is present in just about all universities (and, between the late 1960s and 1992, polytechnics), until very recently. The definition of what constitutes 'French Studies', and of the balance between language and 'culture' on undergraduate programmes, becomes increasingly diverse, but the value of the field and of degree programmes in French is rarely questioned – again, until recently. The intellectual project of French Studies has diversified and been enriched by new disciplinary perspectives and by challenges to certain hegemonic assumptions and exclusions that inform (or have informed) French culture itself, postcolonial and feminist perspectives being the most obvious examples. What has remained constant is the fundamental project of studying and teaching a language and culture that are of intrinsic importance, and at the same time using French as a prism for intellectual enquiry. Currently this project is challenged by a paradoxical strengthening of the complacent monolingualism of the British, just as the country becomes officially more 'European', and by the growing concentration of advanced language study in private schools rather than in those attended by the majority. The subject's history shows a capacity for growth, adaptation, intellectual vibrancy and (a very French) spirit of *contestation* that promises well for the fight back.

Bibliography

Bayley, Susan, 'Modern Languages: An "Ideal of Humane Learning": The Leathes Report of 1918', *Journal of Educational Administration and History* 23: 2 (1961), 11–24.

Birkett, Jennifer and Michael Kelly (eds), *French in the 90s: A Transbinary Conference July 1991* (Birmingham: Birmingham Modern Languages Publications, 1992).

Campos, Christophe, 'Le Français dans les universités britanniques', *Franco-British Studies* 8 (1989), 69–108.

Cohen, Michèle, *Fashioning Masculinity: Masculinity, National Identity and Languages in the Eighteenth Century* (London: Routledge, 1996).

Evans, Colin, *Language People: the Experience of Teaching and Learning Modern Languages in British Universities* (Milton Keynes: The Society for Research into Higher Education and Open University, 1988).

Rigby, Brian (ed.), 'Personal Voices, Personal Experiences', *French Cultural Studies* 10: 3, no. 30 (October 1999).

Stern, H. H. (ed.), *Modern Languages in the Universities. A Guide to the Courses of Study in 5 European Languages at Universities in the UK* (London: MLA, 1961).

Thanks to Margaret Atack for the loan of her file on the history of French at Leeds, and to the Leeds archivists.

Part II: Research and Public Engagement Strategies

3

The *exception anglo-saxonne?* Diversity and Viability of French Studies in the UK

Adrian Armstrong

In March 2009, the Ministère des affaires étrangères et européennes held an international seminar in Sèvres, in collaboration with the Centre International d'Études Pédagogiques.[1] It emerged clearly from discussions at the seminar that French provision in UK universities contrasts with that in most other EU countries in three important respects.[2] First, UK French departments are relatively unusual in delivering a curriculum that includes a high volume and a wide variety of 'content courses', as practitioners often term them, alongside core language provision. Second, innovation in the delivery of that curriculum appears to be more widespread in UK universities. Increasing use is made of virtual learning environments; assessment often includes presentations and project work, as well as traditional examinations and coursework exercises; there is a high level of explicit engagement with the 'transferable skills agenda', which has come to occupy a central position in reflection on undergraduate teaching since the 1990s.[3] Finally, career prospects tend to be much wider for UK graduates in French than for most of their European counterparts, for reasons that have become familiar to many language teachers in higher education. In the context of a relatively flexible graduate-level job market, where many opportunities do not require

---

1   CIEP, *Situation et perspectives d'évolution des départements d'études françaises des universités européennes* (2010), online resource, consulted on 26 July 2010.

2   Diana Homes and Susan Harrow, Report on CIEP seminar, 'Situation et perspectives d'évolution des départements d'études françaises des universités européennes' (2009), online resource, consulted 26 July 2010.

3   Anny King (ed.), *Languages and the Transfer of Skills: The Relevance of Language Learning for 21st Century Graduates in the World of Work* (London: The Centre for Information on Language Teaching and Research (CILT), 2000); Mike Fay, 'Knowing What You're Doing: The Skills Agenda and the Language Degree', in Subject Centre for Languages, Linguistics and Area Studies (2003), online resource, consulted 26 July 2010; Julie Lawton and Catherine Franc, 'Employability and Enquiry-Based Learning in Languages', Subject Centre for Languages, Linguistics and Area Studies (2009), online resource, consulted on 26 July 2010.

a degree in a specific subject, modern language graduates are attractive to employers: they have not only highly developed communication skills, but an autonomy and an understanding of cultural diversity that have been particularly fostered through a period of residence abroad.[4] In other words, from a continental European standpoint, the teaching of French at UK universities appears polyvalent and innovative. To have our discipline 'defamiliarised' in this way, to use a venerable term from Russian Formalist aesthetics, is salutary.[5] In what follows I explore how this defamiliarised perspective may illuminate the capacity of French Studies to evolve in the near future. As French loses its traditional preponderance within modern foreign languages in British education, what are the challenges for recruiting students – and indeed staff – and for devising curricula? Is the discipline's diversity threatened by larger processes of change, or does it enable UK departments to deal with those processes more effectively, even to take an international lead in the teaching of foreign language and culture?

Any reflections in this area must begin by considering the gradual shifts in the position of French in relation to other languages. Most obviously, as Table 1 indicates, long-term trends are visible in the secondary sector. Although French remains the single most widely studied foreign language by a large margin, it no longer has absolute predominance, especially not at A level.[6] This tendency needs to be viewed alongside

---

4   Keith Marshall, 'General introduction to modern languages in today's UK universities', in Subject Centre for Languages, Linguistics and Area Studies (2001); John Canning, *Enhancing Employability: A Guide for Teaching Staff in Languages, Linguistics and Area Studies* (2004), online resource, consulted on 26 July 2010; Michael Worton, *Review of Modern Foreign Languages Provision in Higher Education in England* (London: HEFCE, 2009), pp. 21–3.

5   Viktor Shklovsky, 'Art as Technique', in Lee T. Lemon and Marion J. Reis (eds), *Russian Formalist Criticism: Four Essays* (Lincoln, NE and London: University of Nebraska Press, 1965), pp. 3–24, p. 12.

6   Trends in Scotland offer a fascinating contrast. At Standard Grade, the share of French in modern language examination entries rose from 65.4 per cent in 2000 to 71 per cent in 2009. During the same period, the share of German fell from 27 per cent to 18.3 per cent, and that of Spanish rose from 5 per cent to 8.4 per cent. At Higher Grade during this period, the share of French rose from 57.1 per cent to 59.5 per cent, while that of German fell from 28.2 per cent to 16.4 per cent and that of Spanish rose from 10.4 per cent to 17.7 per cent. Of the Advanced Higher Grade examination entries for modern languages in 2009, 64.3 per cent were for French, 13.7 per cent for German, and 17.7 per cent for Spanish. (Percentages have been calculated from the numbers of examination entries indicated in the 2010 Scottish CILT reports, *Standard Grade Exams in Languages*; *Higher Grade Exams in Languages*; and *Advanced Higher Exams in Languages*). The rising share of French appears to reflect larger patterns of provision, with a decline in German but – in contrast with the rest of the UK – no significant corresponding rise in Spanish. The number of specialist German teachers in Scottish secondary education dropped by almost a third between 2004 and 2009; that of specialist Spanish teachers dropped by some 15 per cent in the same period (2010 Scottish CILT report *Secondary Language Specialists*; compare estimated figures in 2010 CILT report *How Many Language Teachers are there in Secondary Schools?*).

Table 1 *GCSE and A-level entries in modern languages: percentage shares of individual languages, 1995–2009*

	GCSE 1995	GCSE 2009	A level 1995	A level 2009
French	62.6	49.7	56.5	39.1
German	23.1	19.3	21.8	15.7
Spanish	7.3	17.7	9.9	20.0
Chinese	0.4	0.9	2.0	8.5

Percentages have been calculated from the numbers of examination entries (in England, Wales, and Northern Ireland) indicated in the two CILT *National Trends* reports. Data for 2009, deriving from the Joint Council for Qualifications, are provisional.

others: the increasing provision for community languages within education at all levels;[7] the general diversification of qualifications across the UK secondary sector; the changing language needs of employers in a multicultural and globalised environment; within higher education, the introduction of beginners' streams more widely across modern language departments and the increasing provision of non-specialist language learning streams.[8] These all point in substantially the same direction: although university entry to French degrees currently appears broadly stable,[9] departments that require entrants to have an A level or equivalent qualification are fishing in a pool that looks rather limited by comparison with other languages, and that in some cases may become too limited to be optimally sustainable. This does not necessarily imply, of course, that all French departments will find themselves obliged to introduce beginners' provision – although in the longer term some departments may consider it worth exploring that option, with everything that it means for their staffing policy. Nor does it imply that French departments should be fighting their own corner for student recruitment at the expense of their counterparts in Spanish, or Chinese, or Arabic: fragmentation of the modern languages sector is a danger that must be avoided.[10] What these trends *do* imply is that in the foreseeable future, long-established and sizeable French departments will no longer be able to assume that a substantial cohort of students with advanced qualifications in the language will choose to continue with it as a major named degree subject. Some departments will doubtless have to acknowledge the changing demographics earlier than others, but all will eventually have to consider what those demographics mean for them.

7 CILT, *Community Language Learning in England, Wales and Scotland* (2005), online resource, consulted on 27 July 2010.
8 Marshall, 'General introduction', appendix 2; Worton, *Review*, p. 26.
9 Worton, *Review*, pp. 16–18.
10 Worton, *Review*, pp. 35–6.

Even when advanced learners do embark on a degree in the subject, their learning experience may well become 'less French' in some respects than that of their predecessors. Current and future trends in higher education funding are likely to accelerate the rationalisation of university curricula. Language departments are usually of small size in comparison with many other humanities disciplines, and may therefore seek to maintain viability through maximising economies of scale in teaching. This can be achieved, for instance, by developing more synthetic curricula, with different language departments sharing the delivery of individual courses. Already in place in various institutions,[11] such cross-language provision is likely to generate courses on topics such as 'The European Enlightenment' or 'Literary Adaptation in European Cinema', with a common core of materials taught in translation and complementary pathways devoted to work in specific languages. If this practice develops to any significant extent, it will have very significant pedagogical implications. On a formal level, institutions may find themselves obliged to review any policies they may have concerning teaching in the target language, or teaching materials in translation.[12] More generally, if students are exposed to significantly less material in the target language, this may need to be compensated elsewhere in their degree programme in order to safeguard overall learning outcomes and benchmarking standards. Raising the proportion of core language provision within the degree, or introducing practical language elements into 'content courses', would be obvious solutions. French Studies may need to learn strategies from other language disciplines that have historically relied more upon an intake of beginners, and that consequently have always had to think very carefully about how to balance students' ongoing language acquisition with their exposure to authentic materials.

All these developments are likely to change the balance between language and 'content', and in this respect UK French departments may find themselves looking rather more like their European counterparts in the future. In particular, there may be much less opportunity for research-active academics to teach in their specialist area. Yet the findings of the Sèvres seminar demonstrate that these academics are much better placed to face this challenge than they might think. French specialists in the UK are accustomed to delivering diverse content – very often outside their immediate area of expertise – through generic first-year curricula, team taught thematic courses, and suchlike. Moreover, they are accustomed to delivery methods that promote integration between teaching and research – not by relying on their own research to produce curriculum content, but by developing research as a mode of student enquiry.[13]

11 Worton, *Review*, p. 26.
12 Worton, *Review*, p. 25.
13 Worton, *Review*, p. 25.

If curricula are uncoupled from specific areas of staff expertise, if only in a partial and relative way, the long-term implications for staffing and the future of research in the field are manifold. At present, departments' perceptions of need in *teaching* provision tend to orientate staffing developments around particular areas of *research*. Hence in recent years, to simplify the picture considerably,[14] the discipline has seen an increasing emphasis on both courses and staffing in modern cultural studies. Conversely, provision in literary studies has remained strong in most pre-1992 universities, at least with regard to the nineteenth century and after. While these general trends are common to all modern foreign languages, they have particular implications for French Studies because of the discipline's historical position. Because French departments have traditionally been larger than other modern language departments, they have often regarded 'coverage' of their field as a realistic aspiration, if not a sine qua non. The very notion of 'coverage' is, of course, chimerical. It is apt to conceal, even to perpetuate, expectations about what constitutes an appropriate field of study for a university department: in many quarters 'coverage' is exclusively understood to mean provision in all periods of French literary history (rather than, say, in all cultural forms produced in the French-speaking world, regardless of chronology). It can also mask inequalities of provision: is there genuine 'coverage' in a department where most or all fields of French Studies are represented, but where most expertise is concentrated in one or two of those fields?

Leaving these issues aside, the fact remains that many French departments have been wedded to a concept of coverage that their counterparts in German or Spanish would never have entertained. Herein lies a potential structural problem for the discipline. Coverage is increasingly proving unsustainable in practice: departments are unable to maintain their staffing complement in traditional areas while also developing provision in new fields. However, if departments cannot imagine themselves as *not* offering some form of coverage, they may simply redefine the notion in line with unexamined assumptions about canonicity or relevance. In such circumstances, academics and managers may find themselves adopting positions that they would not hesitate to challenge in student essays: presuming, for instance, that a subject's relevance or interest decreases as its chronological distance from the present increases; that a department cannot do without a research specialist in a given field; or that particular research specialisms cannot be accommodated if staffing falls below a certain level. There is some evidence to suggest that, as undergraduate curricula and hence staffing evolve, the breadth of current and future research across the discipline is at risk.[15]

14 Worton, *Review*, pp. 25–7.
15 Worton, *Review*, p. 6.

Yet the imperative to appoint research-active staff in a specific field could appear much less important if curricula take on a different shape, with fewer and more general 'content courses' and a higher profile for core language teaching. When most undergraduate teaching is relatively generic, the research expertise of the teacher is a relatively insignificant criterion for appointment. Much more important is her ability to devise high quality broad-based teaching, grounded in a sufficient understanding of fields outside her immediate specialism. That ability may come to occupy an important position in the training of future research students, but even today it is strongly represented in French departments, thanks to the experience that staff have developed – as individuals, across departments, and across the whole discipline – in contributing to the varied curricula that are so typical of French Studies in the UK.

If the employment prospects of potential academics will depend increasingly on flexibility and adaptability, the same has long been true of UK language graduates. The Worton report points out that for graduate employers, linguistic fluency is less important than inter-cultural competence, the ability to engage constructively and sympathetically with alterity – a skill that language students do not always seem to value sufficiently highly in themselves.[16] For French Studies, the issue of inter-cultural competence has far-reaching implications for teaching and learning. Many students of French seem more familiar with their subject than students of other modern languages, to the extent that university courses hold relatively few surprises for them. There are good reasons for this familiarity: the sheer length of students' previous exposure to the language, typically seven years before university entry; the geographical proximity of France, and the relatively rare opportunities to develop experience of different French-speaking regions (far fewer students of French than of Spanish seem to spend their period of residence abroad outside Europe).[17] But familiarity may breed, if not contempt, then at least a certain lack of excitement and engagement in comparison with other languages. That possibility is exemplified in a recent prize-winning student essay, on the theme of inspiration through university study in modern languages, published in the biannual magazine of the Subject Centre for Languages, Linguistics and Area Studies. The essay is a highly impressive advert for inter-cultural competence, but what is particularly significant from the perspective of French Studies is what it does *not* say:

16 Worton, *Review*, p. 22; Robert Crawshaw, 'Intercultural Awareness as a Component of HE Modern Language Courses in the UK', in *Subject Centre for Languages, Linguistics and Area Studies Good Practice Guide* (2005), online resource, consulted 27 July 2010.

17 There is a need for a systematic survey of student destinations during periods of residence abroad, which could inform university policies and practices across the modern language disciplines.

When I first made my decision to study French and Spanish, I envisaged hours of dull lessons stuck in a drab lecture theatre listening to a boring old professor drone on about the subjunctive and other complicated tenses [*sic*].[18] I certainly didn't imagine learning about indigenous South American tribes in the deepest darkest depths of the Amazon, or how to say 'I like cake' in a Native American language.[19]

The extract above contains the only reference to French-related culture in the whole essay. For this student, inspiration has come from exposure to Latin American culture, through academic study and through spending a year in Peru; she mentions llamas more frequently than French.[20]

This is a single case, but very much in keeping with the larger picture. Tables 2 and 3 approximately indicate the relationship between undergraduate modern language cohorts, postgraduate enrolment, and the availability of funded postgraduate studentships under the Arts & Humanities Research Council's (AHRC) Block Grant Partnership (BGP) scheme. While not wholly reliable, these tables indicate the relative sizes of undergraduate and postgraduate cohorts, as well as the historical patterns of high quality activity at master's and doctoral levels on which the BGP allocations were primarily based. It emerges very clearly that both the postgraduate population and the availability of studentships are proportionally less for French than for *all* other major European languages taught at UK universities. An undergraduate studying Italian is, in very broad terms, more than twice as likely to proceed to postgraduate study – and to receive AHRC funding – than a student of French. Notwithstanding the possibilities for statistical nuancing, the message is stark. French is the language of which post-A level candidates make up the highest proportion of university students; it is therefore a language of which one might expect to encounter a strong cohort of highly motivated experts at postgraduate level; yet it is the language that exhibits the weakest history of postgraduate achievement.[21]

18 It is striking that such expectations did not discourage the author – although her experience suggests that schools and universities may need to adopt new approaches when seeking to raise awareness of modern language degrees.
19 Laura Gent, 'From the River Tyne to Lake Titicaca', *Liaison* 3 (2009), 38–9, p. 38.
20 Laura Gent subsequently makes frequent reference to using her French language skills in various non-European contexts in her 'From Finals to Fiji … via Ghana', *Liaison* 5 (2010), 34–5.
21 A further avenue for research suggests itself here. How far might previous A level study actually hinder language students' performance at university level, for instance by encouraging the acquisition of habits or routines that are appropriate to 16–19 study but that prove restrictive thereafter? For some of the curricular discontinuities facing language students between 16 and 19 and higher education see Jocelyn Wyburd, Elinor Chicken and John Doherty, *LATCOF: Lessons from a Secondary/sixth-form – HE Consultative Forum for Language Teachers* (2005), online resource, consulted on 27 July 2010.

Table 2 *UK first degree and postgraduate enrolments 2007–8: FPEs (full person equivalents)*

	First degrees	Postgraduates (taught and research)	Postgraduates as % of first degrees
French	8005	340	4.2
Spanish	5100	305	6.0
German	3105	200	6.4
Italian	1320	120	9.1
Russian & E. European	890	295	33.1

FPE figures from CILT, *HE language student enrolments*, which expresses concerns over the reliability of the data (submitted by institutions to Higher Education Statistics Agency). Variable reporting practices mean that individual totals for each language are likely to under-represent the true figures.

Table 3 *UK first degree enrolments 2007–8 and AHRC Block Grant Partnership awards (all types) 2009–13*

	First degrees	AHRC BGP awards	Awards as % of first degrees
French	8005	132	1.6
Spanish & Portuguese	5405	98	1.8
German	3105	90	2.9
Italian	1320	51	3.9
Russian & E. European	890	41	4.6

First degree enrolments from CILT, *HE language student enrolments*, as for Table 2. AHRC awards from AHRC 2009, based on the following subject areas: French Language and Culture; German Language and Culture; Iberian and Latin American Language and Culture; Italian Language and Culture; Russian, Slavonic and Eastern European Language and Culture.

Is this, then, to be the position of French Studies within British higher education – a springboard for studying other languages, which in most cases ultimately claim students' greater loyalty? A gateway drug, so to speak? From the viewpoint of the modern languages sector as a whole, there is nothing necessarily wrong with that position. But it is a position that may prove untenable in the not too distant future. The 'gateway' status of French in the UK is rooted in two historical tendencies that have simultaneously guaranteed its widespread sustainability. In the first place, French has traditionally been the first foreign language studied in school, hence ensuring that a large cohort passes into higher education. In the second place, French has been the most widely studied foreign language in higher education, producing a sizeable postgraduate body through sheer weight of numbers. Current trends suggest that both these tendencies may end in the foreseeable future; French Studies cannot afford to conceive and present itself as if they will continue in perpetuity.

It is up to university departments, therefore, to take the French-speaking world and defamiliarise it, designing and delivering curricula that can inspire through the unexpected. That process does not at all mean a wholesale turn towards modern cultural studies, or indeed towards any particular area within the discipline. It involves Racine and the Strasbourg Oaths just as much as it involves cinema and *bande dessinée*. Different institutions will inevitably rethink their provision in different ways, but there is no shortage of possible strategies. French Studies could learn a great deal from Classics, which has an excellent track record in knowledge transfer and public engagement:[22] how to blow the dust off apparently 'dead' materials, how to redefine notions of relevance, how to celebrate the ways in which encounters with the unfamiliar can produce more fulfilled members of more tolerant societies. The Sèvres seminar reminds us not only that UK French departments are equipped to meet this challenge, thanks to a disciplinary history of diversity and innovation, but that they are almost uniquely well equipped to meet it. University teachers of French, like their students, can afford to have more respect for the skills they already have.

Bibliography

AHRC, *Summary of BGP studentships* (2009), available at www.ahrc.ac.uk/Funding Opportunities/Pages/BGP.aspx (consulted 27 July 2010).

Beard, Mary and John Henderson, *Classics: A Very Short Introduction* (Oxford: Oxford University Press, 1995).

Canning, John, *Enhancing Employability: A Guide for Teaching Staff in Languages, Linguistics and Area Studies* (2004), available at www.llas.ac.uk/resources/paper/2124 (consulted 26 July 2010).

CIEP, *Situation et perspectives d'évolution des départements d'études françaises des universités européennes* (2010), available at www.ciep.fr/conferences/evolution-des-departements-etudes-francaises-des-universites-europeennes/docs/situation-et-perspectives-d-evolution-des-departements-d-etudes-francaises-des-universites-europeennes/index.html (consulted 26 July 2010).

CILT, *Community Language Learning in England, Wales and Scotland* (2005), available at www.cilt.org.uk/home/research_and_statistics/language_trends/community_languages.aspx (consulted 27 July 2010).

CILT, *HE language student enrolments in the UK, 2002–3 to 2007–8, by language and qualification type* (2009), available at www.cilt.org.uk/home/research_and_statistics/statistics/higher_education/he_learning_trends_in_uk.aspx (consulted 27 July 2010).

CILT, *National trends in GCSE entries 1995 to 2009* (2010), available at www.cilt.org.uk/home/research_and_statistics/statistics/secondary_statistics/gcse_exam_entries.aspx (consulted 27 July 2010).

CILT, *National trends in AS and A level entries 1995 to 2009* (2010), available at www.

22 See, for example, Mary Beard and John Henderson, *Classics: A Very Short Introduction* (Oxford: Oxford University Press, 1995).

cilt.org.uk/home/research_and_statistics/statistics/secondary_education/as__a_level_exam_entries.aspx (consulted 26 July 2010).

CILT, *How Many Language Teachers are there in Secondary Schools?* (2010), available at www.cilt.org.uk/home/research_and_statistics/statistics/secondary_statistics/language_teachers_at_secondary.aspx (consulted 27 July 2010).

Crawshaw, Robert, 'Intercultural Awareness as a Component of HE Modern Language Courses in the UK', in *Subject Centre for Languages, Linguistics and Area Studies Good Practice Guide* (2005), available at www.llas.ac.uk/resources/gpg/2303 (consulted 27 July 2010).

Fay, Mike, 'Knowing What You're Doing: The Skills Agenda and the Language Degree', in *Subject Centre for Languages, Linguistics and Area Studies Good Practice Guide*, 2003, available at www.llas.ac.uk/resources/gpg/1435 (consulted 26 July 2010).

Gent, Laura, 'From the River Tyne to Lake Titicaca', *Liaison* 3 (2009), 38–9.

Gent, Laura, 'From Finals to Fiji … via Ghana', *Liaison* 5 (2009), 34–5.

Holmes, Diana and Susan Harrow, Report on CIEP seminar, 'Situation et perspectives d'évolution des départements d'études françaises des universités européennes' (2009), available at www.auphf.ac.uk/docs/CIEP.doc (consulted 26 July 2010).

King, Anny (ed.), *Languages and the Transfer of Skills: The Relevance of Language Learning for 21st Century Graduates in the World of Work* (London: The Centre for Information on Language Teaching and Research (CILT), 2000).

Lawton, Julie and Catherine Franc, 'Employability and Enquiry-Based Learning in Languages' (2009), available at www.llas.ac.uk/resources/paper/3250 (consulted 26 July 2010).

Marshall, Keith, 'General introduction to modern languages in today's UK universities'. Subject Centre for Languages, Linguistics and Area Studies Good Practice Guide (2001), available at www.llas.ac.uk/resources/gpg/1392 (consulted 26 July 2010).

Scottish CILT, *Standard Grade Exams in Languages* (2010), available at www.strath.ac.uk/scilt/researchandstatistics/statisticsonlanguagesinscotland/standardgradeexamsinlanguages/ (consulted 27 July 2010).

Scottish CILT, *Higher Grade Exams in Languages* (2010), available at www.strath.ac.uk/scilt/researchandstatistics/statisticsonlanguagesinscotland/highergradeexamsinlanguages/ (consulted 27 July 2010).

Scottish CILT, *Advanced Higher Exams in Languages* (2010), available at www.strath.ac.uk/scilt/researchandstatistics/statisticsonlanguagesinscotland/advancedhigherexamsinlanguages/ (consulted 27 July 2010).

Scottish CILT, *Secondary Language Specialists* (2010), available at www.strath.ac.uk/scilt/researchandstatistics/statisticsonlanguagesinscotland/secondarylanguagespecialists/ (consulted 27 July 2010).

Shklovsky, Viktor, 'Art as Technique', in Lee T. Lemon and Marion J. Reis (eds), *Russian Formalist Criticism: Four Essays* (Lincoln, NE and London: University of Nebraska Press, 1965), pp. 3–24.

Worton, Michael, *Review of Modern Foreign Languages Provision in Higher Education in England* (London: HEFCE, 2009).

Wyburd, Jocelyn, Elinor Chicken and John Doherty, *LATCOF: Lessons from a Secondary/Sixth-form – HE Consultative Forum for Language Teachers* (2005), available at www.llas.ac.uk/resources/paper/2266 (consulted 27 July 2010).

4

Why French Studies Matters: Disciplinary Identity and Public Understanding

Charles Forsdick

> A neglected aspect of learning for world citizenship is foreign language instruction. All students should learn at least one foreign language well. Seeing how another group of intelligent human beings has cut up the world differently, how all translation is imperfect interpretation, gives a young person an essential lesson in cultural humility. [...] Even if the language learned is that of a relatively familiar culture, the understanding of difference that a foreign language conveys is irreplaceable.[1]

Two dominant assumptions underpinning Michael Worton's 2009 report for the Higher Education Foundation Council for England (HEFCE) on 'Modern Foreign Languages provision in higher education in England' are: (i) that the field is characterised by a set of persistent uncertainties regarding its present and future; and (ii) that the anxiogenic effects of this unstable context risk becoming detrimental to the sustainability of this essential area of academic activity and enquiry. Modern languages is often seen as divided between, on the one hand, the nurturing of linguistic proficiency among a broad range of students, and, on the other, the development of specialist, research-led disciplinary fields that form an important part of national and international scholarship in the humanities and social sciences. Mary Louise Pratt has identified the evident problems to emerge from a continued inability to negotiate in any clear and cogent way this relationship between differing understandings of purpose:

> There are many kinds and degree of language competence, and all have benefits. Knowing a language well enough to get by in the day to day is very different from knowing a language well enough to read sophisticated texts, write, develop adult relationships, exercise one's profession, move effectively in a range of contexts, and adapt quickly to new situations.

---

1   Martha C. Nussbaum, *Not for Profit: Why Democracy Needs the Humanities* (Princeton and Oxford: Princeton University Press, 2010), pp. 90–1.

Though everyone knows these differences exist, the current public idea about language has no way of talking about them, just as it has no way of talking about the many kinds of language learning.[2]

Michael Worton's report associates this threat of bifurcation, and of consequent uncertainty of mission, with the more widely perceived crisis in the languages community – and with what its author sees as the 'gradual but apparently inexorable reduction in provision nationally'.[3] It may be argued that the situation that Worton describes – regarding these possible tensions between the functional delivery of languages (in association with, and often as a subsidiary to, other subjects), and the commitment to a focus on language study that prioritises close analysis, rigorous socio-cultural and historical contextualisation as well as the development of a wider intercultural competence – has been accentuated in the current climate of higher education in the UK and Ireland. The decline of specialist language study has, however, been accompanied, and in part also counteracted, by a more general internationalisation of the curriculum across a range of subjects (and by the integration of languages that this logically implies).

What is evident is that this tension is not at all new, and may even be considered as one of the foundational aspects of modern languages as a modern disciplinary field in its own right. The early twentieth-century inauguration of the James Barrow Chair of French at the University of Liverpool provides a clear example of the way in which such indeterminacy of mission – or, perhaps more accurately, the failure to ensure that the principal strands outlined above are articulated and understood in such a way as to become genuinely complementary – may be seen as historically constitutive of the subject area. 'Let it be understood at once', wrote a correspondent to the *Liverpool Daily Post and Mercury* in 1905:

> that the Chair endowed with Mrs Barrow's £10,000 *will not be used for the manufacture of correspondence clerks for merchants' offices*. A University does not and ought not to exist to do work of this kind; our own University has suffered some damage from the indiscreet suggestions of some of its good friends that is specially designed to manufacture experts for commercial and technical businesses.[4]

These comments appeared during local controversy on Merseyside over the endowment of the Barrow Chair of French, and clearly reflect those disciplinary ambiguities of French Studies that have persisted since the

2 Mary Louise Pratt, 'Building a new public idea about language', *Profession* (2003), 110–19, p. 116.
3 Michael Worton, *Review of Modern Foreign Languages Provision in Higher Education in England* (London: HEFCE, 2009), p.6.
4 As cited in E. Allison Peers, *Spanish – Now* (London: Methuen, 1944), p. 2, emphasis in original.

emergence of the field in a recognisably modern form in late Victorian and Edwardian Britain. At the same time, the letter writer in the *Daily Post and Mercury* signalled the specific crisis of identity and purpose that is seemingly inherent in our field: the crisis that opposes – as has been outlined above – the cultivation of linguistic proficiency with firmly research-based activity, and accordingly begs the question as to where French Studies belongs, how it functions, and to which intellectual practices and priorities it relates in the modern academy.

As Michael Worton suggests, the dichotomy is not inevitable, although it has often been perpetuated by institutional structures, by funding regimes, and by other issues rooted in contractual, pedagogical and operational considerations. The recent HEFCE report makes it clear, however, that modern languages is still perceived as being, and – according to many of the measures by which it is judged – operates as, 'more of an undergraduate subject than many other humanities disciplines'.[5] I would like to consider in the chapter that follows the reasons for such a perception and focus on the associated risks faced by modern languages, and more specifically by French Studies, as a result of various practicalities of our particular business mix: as with other humanities subjects, the potential for grant capture among modern linguists can never compete with STEM areas; *unlike* many other humanities disciplines, we are faced with decline of our subjects at GCSE and A Level; and practitioners in the field are challenged, moreover, to be particularly innovative when it comes to attracting overseas students who are more inclined, except in a few highly specialised areas and in a handful of institutions with sufficient expertise and reputational capital, to study in countries where our target languages are spoken and where fees are often a fraction of those charged in the English-speaking world.

Faced, in a rapidly changing environment, with vice-chancellors telling language departments that their future is in their own hands (i.e., that they should diversify activity, generate income, or perish), practitioners of French Studies risk being drawn into responding to an internationalisation agenda in practical, functional ways that will shift the balance of our activity towards language provision, while failing to communicate and develop our key intellectual contribution to such developments. In his excellent study of translation and globalisation, Michael Cronin states that: 'the general decline in foreign-language learning in the English-speaking world in recent years can be attributed … to the desire to maintain the benefits of connectedness without the pain of connection'.[6] French Studies – and modern languages more generally – are a reminder that the cultivation of any genuine intercultural experience and consciousness, of any translingual or transcultural

---

5 Worton, *Review*, p. 4.
6 Michael Cronin, *Translation and Globalization* (London: Routledge, 2003), p. 49.

competence, is neither effortless nor painless, yet at the same time remains essential not only to negotiating the hypercomplexity of the contemporary world, but also to allowing the (re)discovery of what Pratt dubs 'the pleasures and pains of living multilingually'.[7]

This is an observation that one might apply equally and specifically to the internationalisation of research practices, an area in which it is modern languages – with French Studies, owing to its continued predominance and influence, acting arguably as *primus inter pares* of modern languages fields – that has a key role to play. It was after all a modern linguist, E. Allison Peers, who – writing under the pseudonym of Bruce Truscott – sought in *The Red Brick University* (first published in 1943) to define the post-war higher education sector. 'What is a University?' he asked. 'A corporation or society which devotes itself to a search after knowledge for the sake of its intrinsic value.'[8] How is this to be achieved, he asks? Through the promotion of research as the chief aim of every university, impacting on teaching and also on what Allison Peers – providing an early formulation of humanities research impact – saw as the essential connection between the university and its region. Yet as higher education institutions seek single solutions to current crises, the possibilities on offer – for example, recruitment of increasing numbers of overseas students; development of a mix of activities in which undergraduates are progressively replaced with postgraduates – are not necessarily suited to what those in French Studies can currently, or can even ever, deliver. The risk is that, in the light of a simple cost–benefit model and standardised staff–student ratios, researchers in French Studies will be faced with ever-increasing teaching loads, and/ or that involvement in institution-wide language programmes, a crucial element of internationalisation strategies, will increase. It seems that we have reached another juncture, seen by some even as a definitive crisis, at which the achievements evident in the development over the past century, of a strong national research culture in French Studies, seem genuinely to be at risk.

Central to any reaction to these current challenges is a reflection on the disciplinariness of modern languages:

> If foreign language departments want to rightsize rather than downsize in the twenty-first century, they are going to have to lay claim to status as a discipline with principles common to all its subfields (language, literature, linguistics, culture) and distinct from other humanities (especially history) and social sciences. Yet most of today's discourses try to define foreign languages as studies about language, literature, linguistics, or culture or as

7 Pratt, 'Building an new Public Idea', p. 111.
8 E. Allison Peers [writing as Bruce Truscott], *Red Brick University* (Harmondsworth: Penguin, 1951 [1943]), p. 65.

interdisciplinary courses, thus suggesting that foreign language study has no common core of investigatory precepts across its subfields.[9]

The wider context for such discussion is shared by many other fields. It is undeniable that the late nineteenth-century emergence of French Studies coincides with the consolidation of the concept of the academic discipline as an institutionalised phenomenon. As Julie Thompson Klein observes:

> The modern connotation of *disciplinarity* is a product of the nineteenth-century ... As the modern university took shape, disciplinarity was reinforced in two major ways: industries demanded and received special-ists, and disciplines recruited students to their ranks.[10]

In one of the first sustained statements regarding the identity of the larger field to which French Studies belonged, the 1918 government report on *Modern Studies*, it is clear that disciplinary fluidity was a foundational aspect of the area. The report underlines the transdisciplinary reach of higher-level language learning, and foregrounds the clear complemen-tarity that has long existed between modern languages and a number of other humanities and social sciences disciplinary fields alongside which it developed. For the first half of the twentieth century, the paradigm of *Lettres Modernes* nevertheless provided focus and stability, but the drift away from a canonical and literary object of study, as well as the cracking of coherence this implied as the century progressed,[11] may be linked to a growing eclecticism of identity and method as disciplinary development depended on interdisciplinary borrowing. Recognition of such shifts is central to an understanding of the growth patterns of French Studies, and also of the tensions between 'definitional closure' and 'definitional competition' that characterise the field with varying degrees of intensity.[12]

In terms of the sliding scales of disciplinary identity that Thompson Klein describes, it might be argued that French Studies is 'configura-tional' rather than 'restricted', 'less codified' rather than 'highly codified', 'nonconsensual' rather than 'consensual'.[13] The openness that such characteristics imply permits an enabling flexibility and eclecticism, but has led at the same time to a perception of disciplinary centrifugation

9 Janet Swaffar, 'The Case for Foreign Languages as a Discipline', *ADFL Bulletin* 30: 3 (1999), 6–12, p. 6.
10 Julie Thompson Klein, *Interdisciplinarity: History, Theory and Practice* (Detroit: Wayne State University Press, 1990), p. 21. (Emphasis in the original).
11 Christophe Campos, 'The Scope and Methodology of French', in Jennifer Birkett and Michael Kelly (eds), *French in the 90s: A Transbinary Conference July 1991* (Birmingham: Birmingham Modern Languages Publications, 1992), pp. 33–8.
12 Thompson Klein, *Interdisciplinarity*, p. 105.
13 Thompson Klein, *Interdisciplinarity*, p. 104.

in the light of which an excessive emphasis on interdisciplinarity may be seen as a threat. In such a context, and in order to prevent the interdisciplinary from becoming the undisciplined, the reassertion of disciplinarity of French Studies – and of modern languages more generally – is an urgent project, not to be reduced to struggles over departmental identity and the allocation of resources, but linked more importantly to 'a stable epistemic community and agreement on what constitutes excellence in the field'[14] – or, in rather more stark terms, 'a field of study with significant intellectual boundaries rather than a set of high-culture affectations'.[15]

In the midst of current change and uncertainty – seen by some as linked to an ongoing proliferation of French Studies (in the plural), situated somewhere between the enriching diversity and fatal fragmentation outlined above – there has been a striking series of statements, from very different sources, that offer welcome coherence or focus. These interventions challenge the disciplinary conservatism inherent in the position represented by Sandy Petrey, according to whom: 'To try to cover everything is to condemn ourselves to watered-down, dumbed-down versions of history, political science, art, economics, sociology, and the many other areas pertinent to things French.'[16] Amy Wygant, quoting from the 1918 *Modern Studies* report, has made it clear, for instance, that nostalgia for lost coherence is in many ways illusory.[17] Although French Studies emerged as a rival to the declining field of classics (hence John Orr's designation of it as the 'third classic'),[18] it has from the outset operated – despite clear literary emphases – as a hybrid field whose distinctiveness, or disciplinariness, is linked not so much to Francophilia or to a desire for cultural insiderism as to a commitment to the close analysis of a range of subjects and phenomena related to Frenchness, which is only possible for a scholar who is both linguistically proficient and culturally (or, more accurately, interculturally) literate. These are the two qualities, supplemented by the clear ethnographic distance, or cross-Channel perspective, that have long characterised much of the best research in French Studies in the UK and Ireland. In Michael Holquist's terms: 'We teach distance, abstraction, reflection, and above all, the mysteries of relation, together with the interpretative skills such matters require.'[19]

14 Thompson Klein, *Interdisciplinarity*, p. 107.
15 Swaffar, 'The Case for Foreign Language', p. 7.
16 Sandy Petrey, 'When Did Literature Stop Being Cultural?', *Diacritics* 28: 3 (1998), 12–22, p. 12.
17 Amy Wygant, 'Modern studies: historiography and directions', *French Studies Bulletin* 30 (2009), 75–8.
18 John Orr, *French the Third Classic: An Inaugural Lecture given at the University of Edinburgh on 10th October 1933* (Edinburgh: Oliver and Boyd, 1933).
19 Michael Holquist, 'Language and Literature in the Globalized College/University', *ADFL Bulletin* 37: 2–3 (2006), 5–9, p. 9.

Christophe Campos, in a contribution to a volume on *French in the 90s*, reflects usefully on the 'French' of 'French Studies', exploring the 'unusual, but not quite unique' designation of a subject area 'by an adjective instead of a noun', or, perhaps more accurately, by an adjective used as a denotative noun, that is, a part of speech whose field of reference is notoriously arbitrary or unpredictable.[20] Whether the term relates to language, geography, literature, history, politics, sociology or other legitimate areas of enquiry, this 'French' has traditionally been understood Hexagonally, and mapped accordingly on to metropolitan France. The steady transformation of France throughout the twentieth century – subject to two world wars, decolonisation, urbanisation, the emergence of the European Community, an often uneasy adjustment to the implications of postcolonial multi-ethnicity – means that this centre could not hold.

The rise to prominence of francophone postcolonial studies is a clear indication of this prizing open of a geographically and culturally restricted object of study. It is undeniable that this shift, away from the *certaine idée de la France* that dominated French Studies for much of the twentieth century, entails 'a possible threat to the genuine intellectual convictions as well as the hard-earned, existing "cultural capital" of many members of French departments'.[21] Aware of the implications of this threat, Lawrence Kritzman asks two questions that may be seen to underpin the contributions to the present volume: 'Can French Studies survive the death of the traditional idea of the nation, and the teleology of its progress? Does France's own identity crisis – the loss of its exceptional status, its role as an imperial messianic nation, its integration into the European community – endanger our own discipline of French Studies?'[22] By way of an answer, in a controversial *Times Higher* article from September 2003, the Latin Americanist Jon Beasley-Murray explained along these lines why he thought the more general languages crisis to which these questions relate could be helpful:

> Globalisation induces the definitive crisis of modern languages. As national borders fade, so does the notion of national languages. […] The crisis, its causes and contexts should become the very substance of modern languages. We should amplify and propagate the crisis, exposing the complacency of disciplines (English and history, again) that carry on as usual. Modern languages, more affected than most by globalisation and the practical and political challenges it raises, are also best placed to study these processes.[23]

20 Campos, 'The Scope and Methodology', pp. 33–4.
21 Dominick LaCapra, 'Reconfiguring French Studies', in *History and Reading: Tocqueville, Foucault, French Studies* (Toronto: University of Toronto Press, 2000), pp. 169–226, p. 170.
22 Lawrence D. Kritzman, 'Identity Crises: France, Culture and the Idea of the Nation', *SubStance* 76–7 (1995), 5–20, p. 19.
23 Jon Beasley-Murray, 'Why I think the Languages Crisis is Helpful', *The Times Higher* (26 September 2003), 18.

The call to resituate languages at the heart of debates in the humanities – drawing on our inherited practices while responding to the processes of 'becoming-transnational'[24] – is a challenging one and this chapter concludes with a focus on this issue.

It is undeniable, as the opening section of these comments made clear, that French Studies currently faces a series of major challenges, relating, in no particular order, to disciplinary sustainability, research environment, public perception and understanding of the field, and undergraduate curriculum design. The progressive erosion of pre-1789 subjects has been regularly remarked, and if there is indeed a creeping 'presentism' in French Studies, there is a need to acknowledge at the same time that any restricted historical focus on the modern and contemporary is potentially as disabling to the field as the assumptions relating to limited geography discussed above that tended to characterise the field for much of the twentieth century. To take the example of francophone postcolonial studies, increasingly innovative work in this field is currently conducted by those working in the medieval and early modern fields, and the sense that postcolonial approaches are only appropriate for a corpus of 'francophone' material that has emerged in the post-war period has long been redundant. The steady contraction of the historical reach of French Studies is linked, however, to a number of other factors that continue to challenge the field. The increasing emphasis on the 'impact' of research and its communication to non-academic audiences is seen by some, for instance, to privilege contemporary areas in which there is existing public interest, or of which the public policy implications are more readily apparent.

There are some marked examples that belie such a critique,[25] and it is likely that the implications of the 'impact agenda', and more specifically of a spoken or unspoken emphasis on 'national' impact relating to 'national' heritage (or impact that inevitably occurs in our national languages), will have a more generally detrimental effect on the subject area. Practicalities relating to publishing in modern languages, as outlined in the report of an MLA ad hoc committee on the future of scholarly publishing, create further impediments to current disciplinary development.[26] Discussing the discontinuation by Cambridge University Press, now almost a decade ago, of its distinguished collection in French Studies, the report claims that 'the symbolic value of closing the series should not be underestimated'.[27] It is encouraging that publishers such as Liverpool University Press have challenged this

24 Françoise Lionnet, 'Introduction', *Modern Language Notes* 118: 4 (2003), 783–6, p. 784.
25 See, for example, *The Online Froissart Project*, online resource, consulted 22 August 2010.
26 MLA, Ad Hoc Committee on the Future of Scholarly Publishing, 'The Future of Scholarly Publishing', *Profession* (2002), 172–86.
27 MLA, 'The Future of Scholarly Publishing', p. 175.

trend, and a proliferation of journals devoted to French Studies, or of which French Studies forms a substantial part, has allowed the emergence of important new outlets in quality edited collections. The reality remains, however, that fewer publishers are interested in monographs in the field, especially relating to work in earlier periods, and that those who are often require subsidies. This means that commercial rather than scholarly decisions have an impact on commissioning, which is disproportionate to that in other humanities fields, a situation exacerbated by the increasing pressure under which university libraries find themselves in budgetary terms and the fact that electronic publishing and open access initiatives in modern languages still seem slow to develop.

The coherence and stature of French Studies as a disciplinary field are further challenged by the sense that the subject area may be downgraded to the status of an 'arena'. Such a shift is in part linked to changes in the external landscape, in particular that relating to the assessment of research. The distinctive French Unit of Assessment employed for all previous RAEs (research assessment exercises) will be replaced in the new REF (research excellence framework) with a general modern languages panel. Although such a move will address perceived discrepancies in standardisation of judgements across languages sub-panels in previous exercises, such a general assessment of languages again challenges the particular and distinctive role of French. The critical mass of a unified modern languages community may provide a stability and degree of protection that, in most institutions in the current climate, can no longer be guaranteed, but there is nevertheless a need to reflect on the place of French Studies in such structures and shifts. Michael Worton cogently identifies this dilemma:

> A further complexity is raised by the fact that the individual language disciplines seek to define themselves individually, rather than as a single collective discipline. One element that links all of them is their interdisciplinary nature, yet this very point of commonality raises questions to 'outsiders' about the specificity of each language discipline beyond that of the individual language in question. We therefore face the challenge of formulating broad, inclusive and yet also clearly delineated messages about 'languages', with, alongside these, supporting and complementing defining statements about each of the individual language disciplines.[28]

In 'Modern studies: historiography and directions', Amy Wygant insightfully explores the privileged role of French Studies within such 'broad, inclusive' definitions, and sees the distinctive contribution of the field, in British intellectual life, as being intimately linked to the cultivation and exploration of 'developing attitudes towards neighbourliness, foreignness, gender, conflict and space'.[29]

---

28 Worton, *Review*, p. 7.
29 Wygant, 'Modern studies', p. 75.

Wygant's positive validation of the distinctiveness of French Studies, presented as an ethnographic and cross-disciplinary project actively central to – as opposed to drawing passively and parasitically on – some of the major strands in current research in the humanities and social sciences, reveals the need to acknowledge current opportunities without, of course, trivialising the challenges that accompany them. Essential to such an approach is a communications strategy – as well as an accompanying set of practices in teaching, scholarship and research – that recognises the need to develop and nurture the 'public understanding' of French Studies as a field in its own right, that is, in the terms of the HEFCE report, to position French within the urgent articulation of 'clear messages about the strategic importance of modern foreign languages and what they represent and do within the UK'.[30] From the platform of the presidency of the MLA, Mary Louise Pratt similarly underlined the need to engage in 'building a new public idea about language', and suggested that modern linguists should deploy their research activities to communicate the 'importance of knowing languages and of knowing the world through languages'.[31]

In such a context, the positionality of French Studies – and in particular its relative links to other fields – is of paramount importance. While maintaining the coherence articulated by Pratt, French Studies has at the same time developed through dialogue and exchange with a range of other disciplinary areas – most notably visual cultures (including primarily film studies), gender studies, postcolonialism, linguistics and comparative/world literature – a clear visibility and a renewed credibility. In such developments, one key aspect emerges: the judicious choice and identification of interlocutors (institutionally, and then nationally and internationally), and the resulting engagement in dialogues that use French Studies as a firm point of departure. French Studies thus becomes one of a number of disciplinary fields that are genuinely and strategically pivotal. Located now on interconnected axes of intellectual exchange (most particularly transatlantic and *trans-Manche*, anglophone and francophone), the field finds itself at a juncture, a situation to which two responses would seem possible: a resignation to any bifurcation, and acceptance of one affiliation or the other; or a recognition that this double articulation may be celebrated as an enabling opportunity, the most successful outcomes of which may allow scholars in French Studies to act increasingly as *passeurs* between other academic fields and traditions.

At the same time, as this chapter has already demonstrated, our interlocutors are also increasingly interdisciplinary, suggesting that there is no longer the traditional time lag as French Studies, *en retard d'une guerre*, is seen to catch up with other areas. This is striking in –

30 Worton, *Review*, p. 38.
31 Pratt, 'Building a new Public Idea', pp. 110–19, p. 12.

but certainly not restricted to – the set of scholarly practices known as francophone postcolonial studies, which has challenged the mono-lingualism of the traditionally anglophone field of postcolonialism, and prised this open to permit the multilingual comparatism that has in many ways given the area a new lease of life.[32] Interdisciplinary dialogue is supplemented, moreover, by the international dimensions alluded to above. Traditional cross-Channel dialogues continue to be valuable, with French Studies scholars in the UK and Ireland maintaining their debates with colleagues in France, Belgium, Switzerland and elsewhere in the Francosphere.[33] But cross-Channel exchanges are increasingly supplemented by transatlantic communication as research in our field is reinvigorated by connections with scholarship in the Americas, notably in Canada and the Caribbean, but more particularly in the USA where major French Studies conferences and key journals regularly welcome a British and Irish contribution. French Studies, at the intersections of the cross-Channel and the transatlantic, enjoys a pivotal location, and this is an aspect of activity that allows us, more than most other disciplinary fields, to internationalise our research practices and increasingly to offer the lead in twenty-first-century arts and humanities research.

How then might French Studies proceed? One of the principal recom-mendations of the HEFCE Review was that the diverse fields on which the report focuses should seek greater unity in striving to identify and articulate a common agenda and purpose:

> One of the most significant outcomes of the consultation was the evidence of a tension between the idea of languages as a collective discipline, and the diversity of experiences across the sector. There are, of course, major differences between languages, and also between their associated cultures, histories and traditions – as well as significant differences in the ways that they are perceived by students. Nevertheless, what links them all together as MFL is the fact that, in each case, culture and history are examined through developing an understanding of and a familiarity with language.[34]

This chapter has made a case that such a process of self-questioning and of self-definition requires at the same time, at a more specific level of granularity, that the constituent areas of 'modern languages' should themselves engage in similar explorations of disciplinary identity. It is likely that there will be considerable overlap in such self-reflexivity, particularly – as the benchmarking statement for languages and related

32 Charles Forsdick, 'Challenging the Monolingual, Subverting the Monocultural: The Strategic Purposes of Francophone Postcolonial Studies', *Francophone Postcolonial Studies* 1: 1 (2003), 33–41.

33 On the spatiality of French Studies and the notion of the 'Francosphere', see Charles Forsdick, 'Mobilizing French Studies', *Australian Journal of French Studies* 48: 1 (2011), 88–103.

34 Worton, *Review*, p. 35.

studies makes clear – in relation to the key skills and scholarly practices that have shaped these fields and continue to reflect their centrality to the arts and humanities. At the same time, however, since there are such clear differences between the various objects of study of the distinctive modern languages fields, and since these areas of enquiry have emerged organically according to such varying factors as international and historical relations or the more local conditions of academic culture, distinctiveness remains. It is evident – as the citation from Amy Wygant makes clear – that a field such as French Studies could usefully seek to identify and retain a certain sense of its disciplinary DNA. Such a process must occur as part of – as opposed to emerging in tension with – a more general advocacy for, and identification of the strategic and intellectual value of, modern languages. It remains essential, however, that such general advocacy should not eclipse the clear distinctions between the different strands of the field that have often been lost institutionally in the creation of larger, post-departmental or extra-departmental structures such as 'schools' or 'colleges'.

In the light of such local shifts, the consolidation of networks – actual or virtual – of regional, national and international communities in French Studies becomes increasingly urgent. This is a project in which traditional and more recently adopted means (i.e., communication through learned societies, and the development of web-based or electronic networking such as Francofil), are becoming increasingly important. This is not to encourage a siege mentality or a sense of disciplinary salvage, with each area retreating into a monolingual and even mono-cultural bunker to the detriment of comparative and interdisciplinary connections and dialogues. Such networks – and the sense of disciplinary identity they will nourish and develop – are indeed only viable and sustainable if they maintain an openness to activity in other language areas and other academic fields, if they display a willingness to engage in the exploratory dialogues on which the development of innovative research practices depends. Having risked, in the final decade of the twentieth century, a potentially harmful fragmentation of purpose and identity, the challenge for French Studies in the early twenty-first century is to manage the field's diversity in a more coherent way, federating current activities across a range of areas in a way that acknowledges the foundational role of French in the study of modern languages in Britain and Ireland (and elsewhere), refuses any risk of complacency associated with being the primary modern language that has historically been studied in Great Britain and Ireland, and foregrounds the persistent distinctiveness of its place in current and future provision.

Such specificity is both intellectual and circumstantial. Writers, thinkers and creators in France and in the wider French-speaking world have created a body of work whose epistemological implications for intellectual life have been, and continue to be, profound. To take but one example already alluded to, the postcolonial turn in the humanities and social sciences is, despite its emergence in the 1980s in the anglophone North American academy, in large part a fundamentally francophone phenomenon, the result of a process of what Edward Said dubbed 'travelling theory',[35] that is, the transatlantic passage and almost alchemical transformation of two bodies of thought of French and francophone origin, on the one hand poststructuralism (in particular in Derrida, Foucault and Lacan) and on the other anti-colonialism (in a wide range of thinkers including Fanon, Memmi and Sartre). In addition to such intellectual and theoretical legacies, our complex proximity to the largest francophone country in the world has implications for French Studies in Britain and Ireland in terms of history, geography, culture and language, implications that become evident periodically in key events such as the seventieth anniversary of de Gaulle's *appel de Londres*, but which are present every day in the provocative, yet not wholly groundless, observation that the English language is in many ways a Creole of French.[36]

French Studies has, in recent years, been concerned with a number of manifestos emerging from France and the wider French-speaking world, most notably that advocating a *littérature-monde en français*, but also a series of other documents and position statements regarding literature, history and identity more generally.[37] I would suggest in addition that the field should take seriously the implications of Stephen Greenblatt's *Cultural Mobility: A Manifesto* (2010), and underline the centrality to activity across French Studies of literal mobility, of the tensions between mobility and rootedness, and of the privileged status of the 'contact zone' – all of which are to be seen as constitutive not only of our objects of study, but also of the scholarly practices with which and the locations from which we approach these diverse fields. I do not intend to contribute further to such debates, many of which gesture towards the desirability or viability of a post-national French Studies, 'libéré', in the terms of the

35 Edward W. Said, 'Traveling Theory', in *The World, the Text, and the Critic* (Cambridge, MA: Harvard University Press, 1983), pp. 226–47.
36 Similar arguments, regarding the occluded francophone substrata of North America, have been made not only by Bill Marshall in his edited *France and the Americas: Culture, Politics, and History*, 3 vols (Santa Barbara, CA: ABC-Cliom, 2005) and his *The French Atlantic: Travels in Culture and History* (Liverpool: Liverpool University Press, 2009), but also by Ronald de St Onge *et al.* in their *Héritages francophones: enquêtes interculturelles* (New Haven, CT: Yale University Press, 2009).
37 See, for example, 'Appel des indigènes de la République', 'Appel pour une République multiculturelle et postraciale', and 'Pour un véritable débat sur l'identité nationale'. On these manifestos, see the following two works: Charles Forsdick, '"On the Abolition of the French Department"?: Exploring the Disciplinary Contexts of *Littérature-monde*', in Alec Hargreaves, Charles Forsdick and David Murphy (eds), *Transnational French Studies: Postcolonialism and Littérature-Monde* (Liverpool: Liverpool University Press, 2010), pp. 89–108; and David Murphy, 'The Postcolonial Manifesto: Partisanship, Criticism and the Performance of Change', in Hargreaves, Forsdick and Murphy (eds), *Transnational French Studies*, pp. 67–86.

littérature-monde en français manifesto, 'de son pacte avec la nation'.[38] Instead, highlighting the two terms of the chapter's subtitle – disciplinary identity and public understanding – I shall sketch out more actively, in conclusion, the beginnings of a manifesto for a dynamic and sustainable French Studies for the twenty-first century, reflecting the priorities of a coherent, research-led project that is capable of: (1) identifying itself as a distinctive disciplinary field in the humanities that privileges intellectual rigour and innovation; (2) ensuring communication of the findings of such research and scholarship to the widest possible audience, both academic and non-academic; (3) contributing to the development in each generation of a cohort of modern linguists for whom proficiency in a chosen language is systematically complemented by the varied tools of intercultural competence; and (4) articulating the centrality of language study to any meaningful process of internationalisation of research and curricula in higher education.

What might such a manifesto look like?

(i) Central to French Studies is a persistent commitment to linguistic proficiency in French and to the varieties of French spoken throughout the francophone world. Such an emphasis on proficiency is in no way, however, to be seen as reductively monolingual, and is to be linked to an awareness that the Francosphere is an inherently multilingual space in which French exists in relation to a range of other languages, regional, heritage, community, or of wider communication. At the same time, the foregrounding of linguistic proficiency is not a means of privileging the functionality of language, but is instead a recognition of the importance for the modern linguist – to repeat Mary Louise Pratt's terms – of 'knowing languages and of knowing the world through languages'.

(ii) Such an approach depends on emphasis of another persistent strength of French Studies, which is its foregrounding of a mode of reading that might be seen as at once close, deep and slow.[39] Implicit in such a commitment is an understanding of the importance of the text, with that term understood in its most open senses as not simply literary or cinematic, but encompassing all sets of symbols, linguistic and non-linguistic, coherent and incoherent, that may be seen to act as the vehicle for understanding of the societies and cultures under scrutiny.

(iii) The development of such tools and approaches is complemented by a keen and clear sense of positionality, and French Studies – the study of France, of the wider Francosphere, and of a more general notion of 'Frenchness' – depends consequently on an outsider perspective that often manifests itself through the implicit engagement with the practices of ethnography and the elaboration of research methods that are *sui*

38 Michel le Bris *et al.*, 'Pour une "littérature-monde" en français', *Le Monde* (16 March (2007).
39 On 'slow reading', see John Miedema, *Slow Reading* (Duluth, MN: Litwin Books, 2009).

generis, that resist replication of those evident in the cultures under scrutiny, and that foreground the importance of intercultural translation, both literal and figurative. The corollary of such an understanding is, at the same time, an enhanced self-reflexivity, permitting what Martha Nussbaum sees as an essential 'ability to see one's own nation, in turn, as part of a complicated world order in which issues of many kinds require intelligent transnational deliberation for their resolution'.[40]

(iv) The result is that those active as French Studies scholars have the potential – and, I would add, the responsibility – to act as *passeurs*, creating dialogues that are at the same time transnational and transdisciplinary. Such an approach permits the development of connections that are both cross-Channel and transatlantic, actively driving rather than passively following debates in other fields (ranging from medieval studies to postcolonialism, from linguistics to film studies), and exploiting the paradoxical element of French Studies, evident since some of its earliest rationalisations as a key component of 'modern studies' (1918), that its disciplinariness depends in part on its potential as an 'interdiscipline'. The possibility that French Studies might assert a leavening effect in other fields, performing an interdisciplinarity that does not destabilise but rather strengthens our distinctiveness, depends in part on a thorough reconceptualisation of what constitutes the 'French' of the field's name. For instance, one of the flaws of the concept of *littérature-monde en français* is that it attempts to articulate a radically post-national position without acknowledging its reliance on the structures (literary prizes, Parisian publishers) of a centripetal, conservative (French) nationalism that is still characteristic of cultural production in, and wider identity politics of, the French-speaking world.

(v) The challenge for such a post-national, transnational, globalised French Studies is to avoid the same trap, meaning that it should present the Francosphere as a space in which national boundaries have been eroded without being eclipsed, have been reconfigured without the accompanying eradication of the asymmetries of power whereby the space has often been constructed and continues to be regulated. Such paradigm shifts necessitate a move away from the foundational assumptions that mapped the boundaries of the field onto those of metropolitan France itself, and permit instead a centrifugal diversion of attention away from any obsession with Paris in order to permit engagement with other key sites such as Montréal, Port-au-Prince and Nouméa.

(vi) Geographical diversification is not – as these three examples of places make abundantly clear – to the detriment of history, and any presentist tendencies are to be challenged by the reassertion of French Studies as a fundamentally transhistorical field, in which teaching, scholarship and research depend on rigorous contextualisation, and the

40 Nussbaum, *Not for Profit*, p. 26.

creation of genealogies and connections that this implies. Such recon-
figuration invites the student or practitioner of French Studies to engage
with the Francosphere in its depth, breadth and complexity, avoiding
the privileging of a certain key, originary zone – or, at best, of certain
key zones – in order to create connections that link texts, artefacts,
sites and historical circumstances in ways that Edward Said dubbed
'contrapuntal'.[41] The method has wide-reaching implications that scholars are only cautiously beginning to explore. As Aamir R. Mufti has
suggested, such an approach highlights 'the *Eurocentrism* of the knowledge structures we inhabit',[42] and may be seen as an epistemological
reflection of what Dipesh Chakrabarty has dubbed the 'provincializa-
tion of Europe'.[43] For reasons that are immediately evident in the
Francosphere (France is arguably the only former colonial power that
has not been eclipsed demographically and linguistically by its former
colonies), a very distinctive form of provincialisation and of its resistance
is of particular interest to French Studies.[44] Counterpoint might provide
a solution to those who seek to know whether it is not only France but
also the wider French-speaking world that is – again to borrow from
Chakrabarty – '*theoretically* … knowable'.[45] The development of a
contrapuntal literacy is one response to the 'becoming-transnational' of
the French Studies field, and it permits sustained engagement with the
hierarchical structures of global culture and with the ways in which the
interactions of different parts of the Francosphere are illustrative of this.
As such, the rhetoric of cultural autonomy and accompanying notions
of exceptionalism appear increasingly mythical as, in Mufti's terms: 'We
come to understand that societies on either side of the imperial divide
now live deeply imbricated lives that cannot be understood without
reference to each other.'[46]

(vii) Emerging from such shifts is a heightened awareness of the constitutive role of mobility in French Studies, both in literal terms in that
the subjects we study are often in movement or the result of border
crossing and other forms of movement, and in figurative terms in that
the accomplished modern linguist is – in Abdelkebir Khatibi's terms – a

---

41 Edward W. Said, *Culture and Imperialism* (London, Vintage: 1993). See also Aamir R.
   Mufti, 'Global Comparativism', *Critical Inquiry* 31: 2 (2005), 472–89.
42 Mufti, 'Global Comparativism', p. 472.
43 Dipesh Chakrabarty, *Provincializing Europe: Postcolonial Thought and Historical Difference*
   (Princeton, NJ: Princeton University Press, 2000).
44 Frederick Cooper, 'Provincializing France', in Ann Laura Stoler, Carole McGranahan
   and Peter C. Perdue (eds), *Imperial Formations* (Santa Fe: School for Advanced
   Research Press; Oxford: James Currey, 2007), pp. 341–77.
45 Chakrabarty, *Provincializing Europe*, p. 29.
46 Mufti, 'Global Comparativism', p. 478.

voyageur professionnel.[47] Michael Cronin adopts the terminology of James Clifford to describe the ways in which such an emphasis on mobility and displacement may be seen as both positive and negative in terms of the history of the field:

> These departments of French, German, Italian or Oriental languages 'dwelt' in a particular country but they were perpetually 'travelling' through scholarship, academic contacts and student visits elsewhere. This may indeed have been their principal handicap in terms of active participation in the intellectual life of the country in which these departments dwelled. Historians, economists, philosophers, sociologists, psychoanalysts and theologians have variously marked the public intellectual life of many countries in the West, but what of scholars in modern language departments? [H]ow many modern language scholars ever appear in the public eye unless there is a very specific issue directly relating to their specialist area?[48]

Anticipating Stephen Greenblatt's recent call for the privileging of 'cultural mobility' across a range of fields,[49] and also reflecting on questions of modern languages and the 'impact' of research, Cronin sees this 'problem of category definition' as an opportunity:

> How are modern language departments [...] to be defined, given that they imply a travelling-in-dwelling? This relative weakness of public identity could be seen in the light of a more recent reflection on travel as a source of disciplinary strength. The long experience of these departments in movement across cultures and borders and languages would appear to equip them ideally for the task of the comparative cultural studies that Clifford envisages – particularly because one of the principal advantages of foreign language acquisition is that it allows for that other element of Clifford's intellectual project, dwelling-in-travelling, the vertical sojourn in the country of the language being learned. If the focus in the past has been very firmly on an integrative, assimilationist approach to the foreign language and culture, with little or no cognisance taken of the native culture or language of the student, it is arguably by a greater attention to the in-between, to the translation dynamic of foreign-language acquisition, that modern language departments [...] can have an impact not just on the countries to

47 Abdelkébir Khatibi, *Un été à Stockholm* (Paris: Flammarion, 1990), pp. 9–10. For a discussion of the 'voyageur professionnel', see Jean-Frédéric Hennuy, '"Examen d'identité": voyageur professionnel et identification diasporique chez Jean-Philippe Toussaint et Abdelkébir Khatibi', *French Studies* 60: 3 (2006), 347–63, and Réda Bensmaïa, 'Political Geography of Literature: on Khatibi's "Professional Traveller"', in Marie-Claude Le Hir and Dana Strand (eds), *French Cultural Studies: Criticism at the Crossroads* (New York: SUNY Press, 2000), pp. 295–308.

48 Michael Cronin, *Across the Lines: Travel, Language, Translation* (Cork: Cork University Press, 2000), p. 125.

49 Stephen Greenblatt, *Cultural Mobility: A Manifesto* (Cambridge: Cambridge University Press, 2010).

which their students or graduates are sent but also on the intellectual life of the countries in which they dwell.[50]

In situating 'movement across cultures and borders and languages' at the centre of the field, Cronin identifies a defining aspect of pedagogical and intellectual practices in modern languages, and highlights an aspect of French Studies with thematic, conceptual and epistemological resonances that may prove central to the elaboration of greater public understanding of the disciplinary field.

(viii) Such an emphasis on travel and mobility foregrounds not only the notion of border crossing, but also the existence of contact zones with which this is related. The result is awareness of the fuzzy boundaries and limits of the field, not in terms of method and approach, but in terms of the legitimate objects of enquiry with which it may engage. For the contrapuntal approach to different elements and sites in the Francosphere is to be complemented by a comparative engagement with similar phenomena, either coexisting, or originating in other linguistic zones. Evident connections may be made with Arabic, Creole or Vietnamese cultures, and it seems increasingly urgent that more and more practitioners of French Studies should be familiar with the languages that permit access to these. At the same time, the bi-cultural and multicultural contexts in which many researchers and students operate, in subfields ranging from the medieval to the postcolonial, reveal the importance of comparatist practices that permit contact with those working across a wide range of linguistic fields.

A French Studies that responds to these issues, retaining key aspects of the disciplinary heritage it has inherited while engaging actively with the new priorities of twenty-first century intellectual and academic agendas, will prove itself to be increasingly attuned to analysis and negotiation of the hypercomplexity of the contemporary world. As such, the field will play a major role in addressing one of the principal challenges faced by the contemporary humanities: 'to think well about a wide range of cultures, groups, and nations in the context of a grasp of the global economy and of the history of many national and group interactions [...] as members of an interdependent world'.[51] The resultant task is at least three-fold. First, there is a need to explore the feasibility of a shared disciplinary identity in French Studies that, avoiding a return to homogeneity, can at least be seen as coherent and un-fragmented. Second, such a sense of identity should play a definitional role in shaping national decisions about the field and its future direction, informing institutional debates at a time when the distinctiveness of French Studies is often eclipsed by a more general commitment to internationalisation

50 Cronin, *Across the Lines*, pp. 125–6.
51 Nussbaum, *Not for Profit*, p. 10.

and linguistic proficiency. And finally, in asserting the status of French Studies as a research-led disciplinary field and in challenging recurrent misconceptions about the activities it encompasses, a priority remains the enhancement of public understanding of the subject. Thomas Spear, critiquing the reductive nation-state model of French Studies presented above, describes the common association of the field with Paris: 'So you're a professor of French?'; 'Yes'; 'Really? I've been to France! I *love* Paris...',[52] – and proceeds to outline a model of French Studies whose guiding principle is that '"la" culture française – même hexagonale – est une culture multiple, métissée, transformée et imbriquée avec d'autres'.[53]

The diverse activity currently federated under the banner of French Studies, and represented not least by contributions to the present volume, reveals how outmoded reductively national misconceptions have become. Michael Cronin concludes his comments on modern languages and on the centrality of the practices and figures of travel by stating: 'If it is now accepted that cultures do travel, that all roots lead to routes, then the foreign-language nomads may find that they have finally come home.'[54] The challenge is to ensure that French Studies is mobilised in such a way that all its practitioners play a role in the consolidation of disciplinary identity, in the foregrounding of academic expertise, in the challenging of public and institutional misconceptions, in the forging of alliances with advocates outside the academy, and in the articulation of public understanding – that is, in those key activities on which such the homecoming to which Cronin refers inevitably depends.

Bibliography

Allison Peers, E., *Spanish – Now* (London: Methuen, 1944).

Allison Peers, E. [writing as Bruce Truscott], *Red Brick University* (Harmondsworth: Penguin, 1951 [1943]).

Beasley-Murray, Jon, 'Why I ... think the languages crisis is helpful', *The Times Higher*, 26 September 2003, p. 18.

Bensmaïa, Réda, 'Political Geography of Literature: on Khatibi's "Professional Traveller"', in Marie-Claude Le Hir and Dana Strand (eds), *French Cultural Studies: Criticism at the Crossroads* (New York: SUNY Press, 2000), pp. 295–308.

Campos, Christophe, 'The Scope and Methodology of French', in Jennifer Birkett and Michael Kelly (eds), *French in the 90s: A Transbinary Conference July 1991* (Birmingham: Birmingham Modern Languages Publications, 1992), pp. 33–8.

Chakrabarty, Dipesh, *Provincializing Europe: Postcolonial Thought and Historical Difference* (Princeton, NJ: Princeton University Press, 2000).

Committee on the Position of Modern Languages in the Educational System of Great Britain (1916), *Modern Studies: Being the Report of the Committee appointed by the Prime Minister to enquire into the Position of Modern Languages* (London: HMSO, 1918).

---

52 Thomas Spear, *La Culture française vue d'ici et d'ailleurs* (Paris: Karthala, 2002), p. 9.
53 Spear, *La Culture française*, p. 29.
54 Cronin, *Across the Lines*, p. 126.

Cooper, Frederick, 'Provincializing France', in Ann Laura Stoler, Carole McGranahan and Peter C. Perdue (eds), *Imperial Formations* (Santa Fe: School for Advanced Research Press; Oxford: James Currey, 2007), pp. 341–77.

Cronin, Michael, *Across the Lines: Travel, Language, Translation* (Cork: Cork University Press, 2000).

Cronin, Michael, *Translation and Globalization* (London: Routledge, 2003).

Forsdick, Charles, 'Challenging the Monolingual, Subverting the Monocultural: The Strategic Purposes of Francophone Postcolonial Studies', *Francophone Postcolonial Studies* 1: 1 (2003), 33–41.

Forsdick, Charles, '"On the Abolition of the French Department"?: Exploring the Disciplinary Contexts of *Littérature-monde*', in Alec Hargreaves, Charles Forsdick and David Murphy (eds), *Transnational French Studies: Postcolonialism and Littérature-Monde* (Liverpool: Liverpool University Press, 2010), pp. 89–108.

Forsdick, Charles, 'Mobilizing French Studies', *Australian Journal of French Studies* 48: 1 (2011), 88–103.

Greenblatt, Stephen, *Cultural Mobility: A Manifesto* (Cambridge: Cambridge University Press, 2010).

Hennuy, Jean-Frédéric, '"Examen d'identité": voyageur professionnel et indentification diasporique chez Jean-Philippe Toussaint et Abdelkébir Khatibi', *French Studies* 60: 3 (2006), 347–63.

Holquist, Michael, 'Language and Literature in the Globalized College/University', *ADFL Bulletin* 37: 2–3 (2006), 5–9.

Kritzman, Lawrence D., 'Identity Crises: France, Culture and the Idea of the Nation', *SubStance* 76–7 (1995), 5–20.

Khatibi, Abdelkébir, *Un été à Stockholm* (Paris: Flammarion, 1990).

LaCapra, Dominick, 'Reconfiguring French Studies', in *History and Reading: Tocqueville, Foucault, French Studies* (Toronto: University of Toronto Press, 2000), pp. 169–226.

Le Bris, Michel, *et al.*, 'Pour une 'littérature-monde' en français', *Le Monde*, 16 March 2007.

Lionnet, Françoise, 'Introduction', *Modern Language Notes* 118: 4 (2003), 783–6.

Marshall, Bill (ed.), *France and the Americas: Culture, Politics, and History*, 3 vols (Santa Barbara, CA: ABC-Clio, 2005).

Marshall, Bill, *The French Atlantic: Travels in Culture and History* (Liverpool: Liverpool University Press, 2009).

Miedema, John, *Slow Reading* (Duluth, MN: Litwin Books, 2009).

MLA Ad Hoc Committee on the Future of Scholarly Publishing, 'The Future of Scholarly Publishing', *Profession* (2002), 172–86.

Mufti, Aamir R., 'Global Comparativism', *Critical Inquiry* 31: 2 (2005), 472–89.

Murphy, David, 'The Postcolonial Manifesto: Partisanship, Criticism and the Performance of Change', in Alec Hargreaves, Charles Forsdick and David Murphy (eds), *Transnational French Studies: Postcolonialism and Littérature-Monde* (Liverpool: Liverpool University Press, 2010), pp. 67–86.

Nussbaum, Martha C., *Not for Profit: Why Democracy Needs the Humanities* (Princeton and Oxford: Princeton University Press, 2010).

Orr, John, *French the Third Classic: An Inaugural Lecture given at the University of Edinburgh on 10th October 1933* (Edinburgh: Oliver and Boyd, 1933).

Petrey, Sandy, 'When Did Literature Stop Being Cultural?', *Diacritics* 28: 3 (1998), 12–22.

Pratt, Mary Louise, 'Building a new public idea about language', *Profession* (2003), 110–19.

Said, Edward W., 'Traveling Theory', in *The World, the Text, and the Critic* (Cambridge, MA: Harvard University Press, 1983), pp. 226–47.

Said, Edward W., *Culture and Imperialism* (London, Vintage, 1993).

St Onge, Ronald de, *et al.*, *Héritages francophones: enquêtes interculturelles* (New Haven, CT, Yale University Press, 2009).

Spear, Thomas, *La Culture française vue d'ici et d'ailleurs* (Paris: Karthala. 2002).

Swaffar, Janet, 'The Case for Foreign Languages as a Discipline', *ADFL Bulletin* 30: 3 (1999), 6–12.

Thompson Klein, Julie, *Interdisciplinarity: History, Theory and Practice* (Detroit: Wayne State University Press, 1990).

Worton, Michael, *Review of Modern Foreign Languages Provision in Higher Education in England* (London: HEFCE, 2009), available at: www.hefce.ac.uk/pubs/hefce/2009/09_41/ (consulted on 8 August 2010).

Wygant, Amy, 'Modern studies: historiography and directions', *French Studies Bulletin* 30 (2009), 75–8.

Websites

The Online Froissart Project (n.d.), available at: www.hrionline.ac.uk/onlinefroissart/ (consulted 22 August 2010).

5

Learning from France: The Public Impact of French Scholars in the UK since the Second World War

Michael Kelly

'L'intellectuel est quelqu'un qui se mêle de ce qui ne le regarde pas.'[1] Sartre's canonical definition of the intellectual suggests a basic question about the public impact of French scholars. To what extent have they intervened in British society, and how far have they stepped outside their areas of expertise to do so? In attempting to answer this question, the following discussion examines how scholars of French have engaged in activities that have shaped different aspects of life in the UK beyond the world of French Studies. Examining the current debate around the question of public impact, it will look at the work of scholars in bringing French intellectual life to a wider public; at their educational role in influencing public policy especially in respect of languages, and at their involvement in broader social and political movements.

The Impact Debate

French has been a focus of degree level study and scholarly research at British universities for more than a century. Throughout this time, there have been recurrent debates about whether the study of French should be expected to serve social objectives.[2] To some extent, they have reflected wider public concerns that universities should produce useful knowledge, encapsulated in the radical utilitarianism of Jeremy Bentham.[3] The social objectives suggested for French have included economic, political and cultural aims, mainly according to the state of Franco-British relations at any one time, and to a lesser extent, the relations

---

1 Jean-Paul Sartre, *Situations VIII* (Paris: Gallimard, 1972).
2 An early example of this is discussed in D. G. Charlton, 'French Studies: A Report to the Prime Minister (in 1918)', *French Studies Bulletin* 25 (1987/8), 10–16.
3 There is a useful discussion of this in Robert J. C. Young, 'The Idea of a Chrestomathic University', in *Logomachia: The Conflict of the Faculties*, ed. R. A. Rand (Lincoln, Nebraska University Press, 1992), pp. 97–126.

between Britain and the wider French-speaking world. Since the Second World War, France has been an important commercial partner and the two economies have become increasingly interdependent. It is clear that the study of French can make a significant contribution to the economic prosperity of the UK. Relations with France have loomed large in British politics. Whether politicians in the two countries have worked together or taken opposing sides on current issues, it has always been important to understand each other's language. Similarly, the creativity and diversity of French culture has been a source of enrichment for Britain in many domains of high and popular culture. Access to this is greatly facilitated by the study of the French language and by knowledge of France's cultural traditions.

This debate is currently being articulated around the proposal that research assessment in UK universities should include significant additional recognition 'where high quality research has contributed to the economy, society, public policy, culture, the environment, international development or quality of life'.[4] Much of the passion invested in these debates derives from political rather than intellectual factors. The attachment of governments to measuring 'impact', or in previous iterations 'relevance' or 'usefulness', is characteristically motivated by a desire to hold universities accountable for the productive use of the large amounts of public funding invested in them. Conversely, the underlying concern among the academic community is that the demand for impact embodies an attempt by the state or by educational authorities to take control of research and scholarship, reducing the ability of scholars to pursue new knowledge and reducing their freedom to choose the direction of their investigations. Often, this concern is associated with resistance to a narrowly defined political or economic agenda that increased state control will enforce.

Resistance to the 'impact agenda' is particularly strong in the humanities area, where the link between research and wealth creation or political relations is mainly indirect. Much of the public benefit of research lies in its contribution to educating future generations of graduates. But while graduates in French often go on to occupy important positions in business or in politics and public administration, it is unusual for their teachers to do so. It is in the cultural area that scholars make the most direct contribution to society.

Spreading French Culture

Much of the work of scholars in French is centred on the domain of culture, and they have often contributed to spreading their knowledge and their enthusiasm to wider audiences. Traditionally, their main focus

---

4   See HEFCE, 'Impact Pilot Exercise' (2010), online resource, consulted 23 August 2010.

was on literary and intellectual life, though in the last twenty years there has been an upsurge of interest in other cultural forms, such as cinema, music and popular culture such as sport and *bande dessinée*.

One of the recurrent concerns of French scholars has been to take French culture out of the lecture hall and make it accessible to a broad educated public. In the immediate post-war period, the journal *French Studies* began with this aim, though in practice it did not prove feasible for a rigorously academic literary journal to gain a wider audience. Instead, French scholars have usually found other routes to share their knowledge and raise the profile of French culture. Articles in literary reviews and in the more serious newspapers have always been a favoured channel. The *Times Literary Supplement*, for example, has carried innumerable pieces by French scholars, though until 1974, their identity was a closely guarded secret. They have made distinguished contributions to the *London Review of Books* and to similar publications at the high-brow end of the periodic press. Conversely, few British scholars have contributed translations of French works. The conspicuous exception is Richard Nice who, after an academic career, became the main translator of Bourdieu's works.[5] Other contributions include Martin Turnell's translation of Sartre's *Baudelaire*, and Peter Collier's translation of Bourdieu's *Homo academicus*.[6]

It is a matter of intermittent soul-searching that French specialists have rarely been the first to bring major French cultural figures to prominence in Britain. Frequently, the early adopters have been the more alert publishing houses, as was the case with the existentialists in the post-war period. Most of Camus's works were published in translation by Hamish Hamilton. Along with Secker & Warburg, they also published a number of translations of Beauvoir and Sartre. Academic 'passeurs' have more often been scholars in English, sociology or philosophy, as with Michel Foucault, Louis Althusser or Jean Baudrillard more recently. In other cases, the advocates of French writers have been non-specialists with a particular interest, especially in the case of religious thought. For example, Catholic writers like Jacques Maritain, Simone Weil and Georges Bernanos were first sponsored by British Catholic writers and intellectuals.

Scholars of French have more often played a supporting role, lending their expertise to extend public understanding of writers that have already come to public attention through other routes, or to correct misconceptions that so readily arise in the often haphazard process of importing

5 Richard Nice's translations of Bourdieu include *Outline of a Theory of Practice* (Cambridge: Cambridge University Press, 1977), *Distinction: A Social Critique of the Judgement of Taste* (London: Routledge & Kegan Paul, 1984), *Reproduction in Education, Society and Culture* (London: Sage, 1990) and numerous other key works.
6 Jean-Paul Sartre, *Baudelaire* (London: Horizon, 1949); Pierre Bourdieu, *Homo academicus* (Cambridge: Polity, 1988).

ideas from abroad. They have frequently contributed to celebrating the intellectual achievement of particular French writers, whose reputation is already well established. The centenary of the birth of Simone de Beauvoir, for example, was the occasion for a flurry of contributions. No doubt, the special significance of Beauvoir for the feminist movement was the key factor that sparked invitations to contribute. By contrast, Sartre's centenary three years earlier passed almost unnoticed outside academic circles.

Frequently, French scholars have played a practical role in introducing French writers and artists to a wider academic audience, through invited visits and lecture tours, often with the support of French cultural institutions. These events occasionally break out of a purely academic setting to draw public attention. For example, in 1947, Enid Starkie succeeded in securing an honorary doctorate at Oxford for André Gide, in the teeth of influential opposition. Similarly, in 1992, Marian Hobson Jeanneret spearheaded a successful campaign to award Jacques Derrida an honorary doctorate at Cambridge, against concerted resistance from the philosophy department. Both of these events were taken up in the wider press, which always responds with interest to a hint of controversy.

Some French scholars have participated in radio and television broadcasts. Malcolm Bowie, for example, was a regular contributor to the BBC Radio 4 programme '*In our time*' from 1999 to 2003, speaking on topics about literature, Proust and Freud. Half a dozen other French scholars have contributed to the same programme since it was first broadcast in 1998.[7] On the other hand, it is very rare to see a scholar presenting French cultural material on a television programme, or in non-academic areas of the internet. They have certainly participated in local and regional radio broadcasts, generally on the occasion of a particular event in France or a significant anniversary. And there are many examples of departments organising public lectures and seminars, especially when a particular topic in the news concerns France or the French-speaking world. Most recently, several departments have arranged briefing events on the culture and society of Haiti in the wake of the earthquake.[8]

For a long time, French departments had a tradition of mounting plays in French, drawing from the classical and contemporary repertoires. On the one hand, these were a valuable experience for students who took part, and on the other hand they provided an opportunity for people in the local community to attend a cultural event in French. This opportunity was most often taken up by sixth-form students, especially when

7   Details can be found on the BBC website *In Our Time*, online resource, consulted 19 August, and a convenient listing is presented in the Wikipedia entry *In Our Time* (BBC Radio 4) online resource, consulted 19 August 2010.

8   See for example, the University of Birmingham events during the spring of 2010 entitled *Haiti: Beyond the Earthquake*, online resource, consulted 19 August 2010.

the play figured on their school syllabus, as an A-level text, for example. Many departments offered a play annually, usually in the spring, and departments such as the University of Bristol would often draw attendance from a wide hinterland. In recent years, this practice has declined, as academic and administrative staff have been increasingly unable to sustain the large commitment of time involved.

It is equally rare to see a French scholar play a prominent role in high profile exhibitions, since these are the province of professional curators, who tend to work with historians and art historians rather than French specialists. This was the case, for example, with the 1993 exhibition *Paris Post War Art and Existentialism 1945–55* at the Tate Gallery in London.[9] However, a number of French scholars contributed to a colloquium at the Gallery that was held to mark the opening of the exhibition, and participated in a number of cultural events organised while it was open. Scholars have frequently organised smaller exhibitions, generally to coincide with conferences and visiting lectures. For example, an exhibition of publications and memorabilia of the Franco-British Exhibition of 1908 was mounted at the *Institut français* in June 2008 to accompany a two-day conference marking the centenary of the event.

In summary, scholars have mainly worked to promote knowledge and understanding of French culture among their students and their academic communities. That has always been their mission and, as it were, their job description. They are quite often called upon to offer their expertise to a wider audience, but tend to act in a supporting role rather than as initiators. They have not generally seen themselves as cultural animators, but have been happy to assist those whose job it is to carry out cultural activities aimed at a broader public.

Associations and Networks

One of the most active engagements of scholars and educators is their involvement in associations and networks concerned with different aspects of France and French Studies. The Society for French Studies is the oldest of the associations, dating back to the immediate post-war period, and focuses on promoting 'teaching and research in French Studies in higher education'.[10] It set the basic pattern for later associations in organising its activities around a learned journal and an annual conference. During the 1980s, as the university population expanded, other associations were formed to take forward particular areas of study. They included the Association for the Study of Modern

---

9 The catalogue was published with a lengthy background essay by the art historian Sarah Wilson, 'Paris Post War: In Search of the Absolute', in Frances Morris (ed.), *Paris Post War: Art and Existentialism 1945–55* (London: Tate Gallery, 1993), p. 238.

10 *Society for French Studies*, online resource, consulted 19 August 2010.

and Contemporary France, established in 1979 'to advance and develop research and education concerning modern and contemporary France in the United Kingdom';[11] the Association for French Language Studies, founded in 1981 'to encourage and promote language teaching activities and research in French Language and Linguistics in higher education';[12] and the Society for the Study of French History, established in 1986 'to encourage research and interest in all aspects of the history of France and its possessions from its beginnings to the present day'.[13] More recent groups include the Association for Studies in French Cinema,[14] and the Society for Francophone Postcolonial Studies.[15]

These associations are mainly focused on academic aims, often encouraging interdisciplinary collaboration between scholars of French and their counterparts in other subject areas. But they do offer various kinds of bridge to society more broadly. Some of them have undertaken outreach to schools, for example by offering opportunities for visiting speakers who might go into schools, or by arranging study days for sixth-form students. Some of the associations have attempted to involve secondary school teachers in their activities, though in practice this has had little success. More commonly, associations may involve external non-academic speakers in their conferences. These are most commonly French intellectuals, politicians or members of social movements, but on occasion associations have invited representatives of comparable UK stakeholder groups such as employers or policy makers.

French scholars also participate in less academic networks that have an interest in France and things French. Most prominent of these is the Alliance française, which had branches in many major UK cities. For a long time, the Alliance was a loose network in which local groups maintained an energetic cultural programme with some assistance from the headquarters in London. These groups typically comprised native French speakers living in the area, language teachers and a spectrum of Francophiles, meeting approximately monthly through the school year. They were often attached to universities and involved academic staff. In Southampton, for example, the Alliance branch had been in existence since 1911 and met regularly in premises made available by the University French department. In the 1970s and 1980s a member of the department was deputed to be the link person, and successive professors of French took a turn as President of the branch. In most years, one or more members of the department were invited to present a talk on some aspect of French history or culture. However, more recently,

---

11 *Association for the Study of Modern and Contemporary France*, online resource, consulted 19 August 2010.
12 *Association for French Language Studies*, online resource, consulted 19 August 2010.
13 *Society for the Study of French History*, online resource, consulted 19 August 2010.
14 *Association for Studies in French Cinema*, online resource, consulted 19 August 2010.
15 *Society for Francophone Postcolonial Studies*, online resource, consulted 19 August 2010.

the Alliance federation has focused its energies mainly on providing French language teaching and has consolidated its activities into a smaller number of larger centres, which operate as separate organisations within a loose federal structure.[16] Branches like Southampton, which were cultural affinity groups rather than language teaching centres, have been vulnerable to financial pressures and competing attractions, and many have now closed.

The role of developing cultural relations is a central focus of the Franco-British Society, an independent charitable organisation, founded in 1924. It seeks to act as 'a focus for those individuals, groups and companies who wish to keep in touch with France, her culture, history and current affairs'. Based in London, it draws in some highly influential figures in British life and has Her Majesty the Queen as its patron.[17] The names of senior French scholars appear intermittently in its programme of events.

Education Policy

Perhaps the most consistent engagement of scholars in French has been their involvement in influencing the British education system. This is close to home for any educator, and it is a logical step to move from their own practice of teaching to seek to shape the way teaching and research are carried out more broadly. A first route is the management career, which many French scholars have followed, proceeding from head of department or school to dean of a larger faculty and on into senior management. Innumerable colleagues have served a stint in middle management positions, and many have gone on to make distinguished contributions at a more senior level, a few even reaching the pinnacle of vice-chancellor (Sir Martin Harris may be the sole example) or master of college (recent examples are Malcolm Bowie and Robert Lethbridge).

A second route of engagement is through national institutions. Perhaps the most distinguished of the institutions is the British Academy, which has counted many French scholars among its fellows, though not often among its officers. In recent years, for example, Nicholas Mann served as its vice-president and foreign secretary (1999–2006). French scholars have occupied positions of responsibility in research councils and similar bodies. Naomi Segal, for example, has served on a number of panels and committees for the Arts and Humanities Research Council, and its predecessor Board. They have also acted in advisory roles for funding bodies, where, for example, James Laidlaw wrote influential reports for the University Grants Committee in the 1980s. Michael

16 See, for example, the Alliance française operations in London (*Alliance française de Londres*), online resource, consulted 19 August 2010, and in *Alliance française de Manchester*, online resource, consulted 19 August 2010.

17 *Franco-British Society*, online resource, consulted 19 August 2010.

Worton currently acts in a similar capacity for the Higher Education Funding Council for England (HEFCE).

A third route of educational engagement is participation in support organisations. There have been various initiatives in this area. For example, from 1989 to 1999 the Computers in Teaching Initiative (CTI) included the CTI Centre for Modern Languages, based at the University of Hull. The centre pioneered innovative approaches to computer assisted language learning (CALL) across all modern languages, and was led by Graham Chesters, Professor of French.[18] A successor initiative, which began in 2000, established a learning and teaching support network including the Subject Centre for Languages, Linguistics and Area Studies (LLAS), based at the University of Southampton. Now under the auspices of the Higher Education Academy, the subject centre has provided staff development, support and advice across a wide range of subject areas, and is directed by Michael Kelly, also Professor of French.[19]

The subject centre has led two large government-funded programmes based on collaborative networks across the nine English regions. The *Routes into Languages* programme enables universities to work with secondary schools to increase the take-up of languages.[20] *Links into Languages* has provided professional development and support for school teachers to improve the teaching of languages.[21] Together, these programmes have played an important role in raising the profile of languages in the UK. They have also supported the efforts of other organisations whose main focus is on the school sector, including CILT, the National Centre for Languages, and the Specialist Schools and Academies Trust.

Finally, there is the associative route to educational engagement, where scholars volunteer their services to contribute to pro bono organisations. Many have been active members of their trade union, though mainly in their home institution. Few have aspired to national office in their union, though Steve Wharton served as President of the University and College Union, formerly the Association of University Teachers, from 2005 to 2007.[22] For the most part, when colleagues have had the time and energy to donate, they have invested it in one or more of the learned and professional associations that provide such a valuable infrastructure of collaboration and exchange. The role of learned associations has been discussed above. Many of them are routinely invited to comment on

---

18 Some of the archive material for this programme can be found on the website of Fred Riley (who was Website Developer and Technical Coordinator), *Call@Hull*, online resource, consulted 20 August 2010. Other material was transferred the LLAS website: *Subject Centre for Languages, Linguistics and Area Studies*, online resource, consulted 20 August 2010.

19 *Subject Centre for Languages, Linguistics and Area Studies*, online resource, consulted 20 August 2010.

20 *Routes Into Languages*, online resource, consulted 23 August 2010.

21 *Links into Languages*, online resource, consulted 23 August 2010.

22 *Dr Steve Wharton*, online resource, consulted 20 August 2010.

some aspect of education policy, such as research assessment or teaching quality, and sometimes they do respond. But more frequently, this role is carried out by professional associations which have been established to speak to policy makers on behalf of the academic community.

Soon after the Second World War, senior scholars led by Alan Carey Taylor established the Association of University Professors of French (AUPF), to deal with the more administrative aspects of French Studies, such as organising year abroad schemes or responding to government policy documents. For many years, it ran parallel to the Society for French Studies (SFS), usually occupying a half day to coincide with the society's annual conference. During the 1980s it extended its remit to include non-professorial heads of French and changed its name to reflect this.[23] It also began meeting for a full day separately from SFS and adopted a more activist approach towards government policy in the light of the funding reductions introduced by the Thatcher administration in 1981. Since that time, it has acted as the representative organisation speaking on behalf of French to policy makers.

In 1992, a major reform gave university status to the then polytechnics, ending the 'binary line' that had previously divided them into two distinct sectors. A special meeting arranged by AUPHF in 1991 explored the implications of the planned changes.[24] It brought in senior scholars from both sectors, and was addressed by senior figures from outside French Studies. They included Professor Martin Harris, then Vice-chancellor of Essex, Dr Anthony Kenny, President of the British Academy, and the Labour Party spokesman on Higher Education, Andrew Smith MP. As a result of two days of reflection, AUPHF led a move to coordinate the response of associations in other languages to the new situation. Negotiations were initiated with the representative body for the polytechnic sector, the Standing Conference of Heads of Modern Languages (SCHML) and with the Directors of University Language Centres (now AULC). As a result, a new association was formed, entitled the University Council of Modern Languages (UCML), which now acts on behalf of languages in higher education to lobby government and to support language departments.[25] Five of the chairs of the association have been senior scholars in French.[26]

In the mid-1990s, UCML joined with associations representing schools, including the Association for Language Learning and the National Association of Language Advisers. They successfully put

23 Naomi Segal, *AUPHF: Partial History* (2000), on line resource, consulted 20 August 2010.
24 The proceedings were published in Jennifer Birkett and Michael Kelly (eds), *French in the 90s* (Birmingham: Birmingham Modern Languages Publications, 1992).
25 *UCML University Council of Modern Languages*, online resource, consulted 20 August 2010.
26 Michael Kelly, Hilary Footitt, Richard Towell, Pam Moores and Jim Coleman.

a proposal to the Nuffield Foundation to establish a major inquiry into the state of modern foreign languages in the UK. The Nuffield Language Inquiry, chaired by Sir Trevor McDonald and Sir John Boyd, drew up a major report which was published in 2000, and set the agenda for government strategy throughout the 2000s.[27] Senior academics in languages, many in French, participated in a variety of resulting initiatives, through the following decade, including the design of new qualifications, increased cooperation between universities and schools, a government-chaired Higher Education Languages Group, and a major report for HEFCE by Michael Worton in the summer of 2009. The number of government consultations and initiatives has continued to increase, and has been given greater momentum by the change of government in the spring of 2010, and the prospect of significant policy changes resulting from it.

Political and Social Movements

Political developments in France have been endlessly fascinating to French scholars. Increasingly, there are many whose research and teaching directly focuses on contemporary French and francophone politics and society. A long list of British academics have written books and articles on the subject for an academic audience, and in many cases have contributed feature articles to the daily and periodic press. However, the fascination of France is not confined to an academic interest, and many teachers and researchers have been inspired in their own life by what they have encountered in France.

In many cases, the first-hand experience of France has been a catalyst for individuals to change their life at home. The first post-war generation of French scholars was deeply marked by the experience of war. Some who began their academic careers before the Second World War had been called on to use their expertise in the war effort. C.A. (Sam) Hackett, for example, served in the Field Security and Psychological Warfare Branch of the Intelligence Corps, where among other things, in conjunction with the writer and publisher Max-Pol Fouchet, he arranged to have miniature editions of Resistance poems and other 'Free French' texts scattered by RAF planes over occupied France.[28] The experience confirmed his lifelong commitment to the human value of poetry, and inspired him to produce his much reprinted *Anthology of Modern French Poetry*.[29]

27 Nuffield Languages Inquiry, *Languages: The Next Generation* (London: Nuffield Foundation, 2000), p. 104. Michael Kelly was a member of the inquiry. A number of individuals and associations in French made submissions to it.
28 R. L., 'Obituary. C. A. Hackett (1908–2000)', *French Studies* LIV (2000), 560–2.
29 C. A. Hackett, *An Anthology of Modern French Poetry: From Baudelaire to the Present Day* (Oxford: Blackwell, 1952).

The experience of the late 1960s propelled many French scholars into more direct political activity. There were relatively few who espoused the more radical agendas of 1968, but many were inspired to take part in protests and join political parties of the Left. Among them were a fair proportion of activists in their local Labour party, and even a small number who served as elected local councillors. Although these personal commitments may have been inspired by French events, for practical purposes, they took place outside the ambit of French Studies. The content was inevitably British, albeit with a flavour of Gauloises. To borrow a distinction developed by Jacques Maritain, they were activists 'en enseignants' rather than 'en tant qu'enseignants'. They carried their French expertise with them, but it was not the defining focus of their commitment.

Certainly, some scholars did engage politically with France, but it was almost never in the form of joining a French-based movement. It is unlikely there were many card-carrying members of the French Communist Party, though there were certainly a number of sympathisers and fellow travellers, such as Max Adereth, a poetry specialist who, at the end of his career, published a history of the Parti communiste français (PCF).[30] More typically, a number of scholars took on the role of honorary foreign correspondent for reviews and newspapers, as in the case of Brian Darling, who was the English contact for the review *Esprit*. Similarly, David Hanley wrote a regular chronicle for *La Croix*. No doubt also a number of French lecturers offered their services to translate documents for political and social movements, though this 'grey literature' is rarely recorded.

Subsequent generations have found their lives marked in less party political ways by the French connection. From the 1970s, it was social movements that caught the imagination. Ecological movements, women's movements, gay and lesbian movements all exercised their attraction. To some extent, this attraction was part of the upsurge of 'rainbow politics' across Europe in the aftermath of the upheavals of 1968. In western European countries, people were investing more time and energy on campaigning over issues about which they felt passionate, rather than giving their commitment to a particular political party. The result was a more fluid experience of the political sphere, in which allies and opponents could emerge from different quarters, and be configured differently from one issue to another.

The new social movements drew French scholars for a number of reasons. First, it was easier to engage with the movements, since their patterns of organisation were generally less formally structured. It was sufficient to attend events to feel part of the movement, and the sense of belonging arose more readily with the feeling that 'you are in it, if you

---

30 Max Adereth, *The French Communist Party: A Critical History (1920–1984)* (Manchester: Manchester University Press, 1984).

think you are in it'. The gay and lesbian movements were particularly effective in achieving this, organising flamboyant events such as parades in which anyone could participate.

Second, the new fluidity attenuated the barriers between nationalities. The issues were similar, though not identical, from one country to the other, and in many cases, the aim was to influence decision makers that were not national governments. Perhaps the UK's entry into the European Community also helped to reduce the segregation of the political sphere along national lines. It was a key perception of the ecological movement, for example, that environmental issues do not respect national borders, but do require concerted cross-border cooperation to address major challenges. Some scholars engaged in green activism in both countries, and at the same time brought their ideas into their teaching and research. The regular inclusion of a question on the environment in essay papers was a faint echo of this.

A third attraction of social movements was that it became easier to transfer aims and forms of action from one country to the other. French scholars found models of political involvement in France that could be adapted to campaigns in Britain. And at the same time, they became representatives and carriers of a British movement which could hold lessons and examples for their French colleagues. The women's movement was particularly adept at sharing experiences in this way, and in developing interventions across issues from rape and domestic violence to birth control and abortion.

In all three movements, a decisive advantage of engaging with France was the access it gave to a body of theory, which could inspire with a sense of the wider significance of the issues. The country's philosophical tradition gives French activists an important resource in developing theoretical analyses of great clarity and force. Their analyses are characteristically pitched at a universal level, which enables them to be seen as relevant to many different contexts.

The theorists of social movements crucially provide the essential bridge between social activism and academic work. For French scholars in Britain, the academic study of French theorists is a central part of their professional responsibilities. And at the same time, it enables scholars to be the vectors of key ideas which can be of value to the social movements in Britain. Perhaps the most conspicuous example is the extent to which the study of French feminist intellectuals has informed the British women's movements. A good deal of impetus has come from participants in the Women in French group, which was established in 1988 as an informal support network to counter the minority status of women both in university departments and on the university syllabus.[31]

31 The network does not have a website, and this information is gleaned from the obituary of Elizabeth Fallaize, one of its founders; see 'Professor Elizabeth Fallaize: scholar in French studies', online resource, consulted 19 August 2010.

The group's participants have been among the most energetic scholars in studying key thinkers such as Simone de Beauvoir, Hélène Cixous, Luce Irigaray and Julia Kristeva. In addition to women's social and political issues, these writers have contributed to reflection on female sexual identities. Similarly, French theorists of male homosexuality have formed a significant focus of academic study. The pioneering works of Michel Foucault on sexuality and Roland Barthes on desire have been highly influential in this respect, but younger gay writers such as Hervé Guibert and Guy Hocquenghem have also had an impact.

Conclusion

The picture that has been painted here suggests some responses to Sartre's challenge about the public impact of scholars as intellectuals. It is clear that French scholars have intervened in British society in a variety of ways. They have helped to bring French intellectual life to a wider public. They have played a role in influencing public policy in education, especially in respect of languages. And they have been involved in a range of social and political movements. On the other hand, their most conspicuous contributions have been located well within their areas of expertise, understood to include not just French Studies but also the broader realms of education and research. Beyond these areas, they have contributed their expertise in French theories and practices to a range of social and political movements. The more difficult question is whether in so doing they have stepped outside their areas of expertise. In a pragmatic sense, they step outside their area when they take to the streets, and at the same time they also step outside their scholarly persona. It is impossible to say, for example, how many French lecturers demonstrated against the South African rugby tour of Britain in 1969, or how many joined the vast demonstrations on 15 February 2003 against the impending invasion of Iraq. Undoubtedly, many were involved, but in their capacity as citizens rather than specifically as French scholars.

The line between socio-political commitment and academic work is often debated. For the most part, scholars are well aware of the interface between academic freedom and professional deontology, and the difference between citizenship and professional practice. They recognise that there is a point at which they step outside their professional role into their role as citizens. In managing different roles and identities, there is no area of social life which 'does not concern them' as human beings and as citizens, though there are clearly areas in which their professional identity as scholars does not explicitly inform their involvement.

British academics are therefore not intellectuals in Sartre's sense, since their identity is not exhausted by their professional expertise. But they may well be intellectuals in the broader sense of 'spécialistes du savoir pratique' who involve themselves in public debates and activities, which concern them as citizens rather than as specialists. In the case of French scholars taken collectively, their zone of expertise is very wide-ranging. It covers almost all aspects of culture, politics and society in France, and includes a considerable ability to transfer this expertise at least to some extent to a British context. As a result, scholars of French in Britain have mostly managed to enjoy the best of both worlds, pursuing studies that are academically important in advancing knowledge and personally important in providing tools for social engagement. In the process, they have undoubtedly had a pervasive impact on the texture of public life in Britain.

Bibliography

The Times, 'Professor Elizabeth Fallaize: scholar in French studies', *The Times* (6 January 2010), available at http://times.cluster.newsint.co.uk/tol/comment/obituaries/article6976887.ece (consulted 19 August 2010).

Max Adereth, *The French Communist Party: A Critical History* (1920–1984) (Manchester: Manchester University Press, 1984).

Birkett, Jennifer and Michael Kelly (eds), *French in the 90s* (Birmingham: Birmingham Modern Languages Publications, 1992).

Bourdieu, Pierre, *Homo academicus* (Cambridge: Polity, 1988).

Charlton, D. G., 'French studies: a report to the Prime Minister (in 1918)', *French Studies Bulletin* 25 (1987/8), 10–16.

Hackett, C. A., *An Anthology of Modern French Poetry: From Baudelaire to the Present Day* (Oxford: Blackwell, 1952).

HEFCE, 'Impact pilot exercise' (2010), avalable at www.hefce.ac.uk/research/ref/impact/ (consulted 23 August 2010).

Morris, Frances (ed.), *Paris Post War: Art and existentialism 1945–55* (London: Tate Gallery, 1993).

Nuffield Languages Inquiry, *Languages: The Next Generation* (London: Nuffield Foundation, 2000),

R. L., 'Obituary. C. A. Hackett (1908–2000)', *French Studies* LIV (2000), 560–2.

Sartre, Jean-Paul, *Baudelaire* (London: Horizon, 1949).

Sartre, Jean-Paul, *Situations VIII* (Paris: Gallimard, 1972).

Segal, Naomi, *AUPHF: Partial history* (2000), available at www.auphf.ac.uk/history.html (consulted 20 August 2010).

Wilson, Sarah, 'Paris Post War: In Search of the Absolute', in Frances Morris (ed.), *Paris Post War: Art and existentialism 1945–55* (London: Tate Gallery, 1993).

Young, Robert J. C., 'The Idea of a Chrestomathic University', in *Logomachia: The Conflict of the Faculties*, edited by R. A. Rand (Lincoln: Nebraska University Press, 1992), pp. 97–126.

Websites

Alliance française de Londres, available at www.alliancefrancaise.org.uk/index.htm (consulted 19 August 2010).

Alliance française de Manchester, available at www.alliancefrancaisemanchester.org/ (consulted 19 August 2010).

Association for French Language Studies, available at www.afls.net/ (consulted 19 August 2010).

Association for Studies in French Cinema, available at http://research.ncl.ac.uk/crif/sfc/home.htm (consulted 20 August 2010)

Association for the Study of Modern and Contemporary France, available at www.asmcf.org/ (consulted 19 August 2010).

Call@Hull, available at www.fredriley.org.uk/call/index.htm (consulted 20 August 2010).

Dr Steve Wharton, available at www.bath.ac.uk/pip/directory/profile/1230 (consulted 20 August 2010).

Franco-British Society, available at www.francobritishsociety.org.uk/index.html (consulted 19 August 2010).

Haiti: Beyond the Earthquake, available at www.french.bham.ac.uk/news/haiti.shtml (consulted 19 August 2010).

In Our Time, available at www.bbc.co.uk/radio4/features/in-our-time/archive/ (consulted19 August 2010).

In Our Time (BBC Radio 4), available at http://en.wikipedia.org/wiki/In_Our_Time_%28BBC_Radio_4%29 (consulted 19 August 2010).

Links into Languages, available at www.linksintolanguages.ac.uk/ (consulted 23 August 2010).

Routes Into Languages, available at www.routesintolanguages.ac.uk/ (consulted 23 August 2010).

Society for Francophone Postcolonial Studies, available at www.sfps.ac.uk/ (consulted 22 August 2010).

Society for French Studies, available at www.sfs.ac.uk/about.htm (consulted 19 August 2010).

Society for the Study of French History, available at www.frenchhistorysociety.ac.uk/index.htm (consulted 19 August 2010).

Subject Centre for Languages, Linguistics and Area Studies, available at www.llas.ac.uk/index.html (consulted 20 August 2010).

UCML University Council of Modern Languages, available at www.ucml.ac.uk/index.html (consulted 20 August 2010).

Part III: The Place of Women and Gender in French Studies

6

Gender and the French Language:
The *longue durée* of French Studies in the UK

Michèle Cohen, Hilary Footitt and Amy Wygant

This chapter seeks to explore the notion that the study of French in the UK today is framed by a series of historical assumptions about the nature of the French language, and about the implications of speaking French for those of us who are British-based. In this perspective, much of what we observe today in our university French departments may have deep-set historical roots. In the *longue durée* of French in the UK, the language has been represented, this chapter argues, as essentially feminine, and as alien to an English national identity constructed as masculine. A specifically English view about the value and implications of actually speaking the language has developed over time, from the eighteenth century through to the nineteenth century and, in some measure, it is this representation that continues to influence the status we accord today to the discipline of learning French.

Studying French in UK universities remains a traditionally female activity. The overall student cohort, undergraduate/postgraduate taught/postgraduate research combined, has continued to be overwhelmingly feminine over the past decade: in 1996–97, 69 per cent of all those enrolled were women, and ten years later, in 2007–8, the percentage was the same.[1] Admittedly, this is not such a large gender imbalance as in subjects like engineering for example, where the percentage of male students is consistently around 88 per cent in this same decade, but it is still notable. In French however, unlike engineering, it is the minority sex which comes to direct and lead university departments of study. The pattern of engineering as a male discipline continues from undergraduate level, through to research, and then on into the staffing of higher education institutions. French departments, on the other hand,

---

1 Higher Education Statistics Agency, *Students: Subject of Study Tables, 1996/1997 – 2007/8*, 'French', online resource, consulted 5 February 2010. The way in which the Higher Education Statistics Agency (HESA) records numbers, and the categories it uses, has changed over this period, hence the notes specify the nomenclature of data quoted.

start off female at degree level, then become more gender balanced in research, and finally become strongly male at senior levels, and only feminised at junior, and very junior grades.

The gender split in languages for doctoral research hovers around the 50/50 mark, depending on the year.[2] While this propensity for more men to opt to do doctorates may well be a general phenomenon which extends across other subjects (humanities for example, in one sample year had 52 per cent women undergraduates, but only 36 per cent researchers), the drop in such a strongly feminised subject at undergraduate level is surely still surprising. The same trend is apparent in staffing levels. Amy Wygant's web-based study of staff in university French departments in Scotland from 2002 to 2010 suggested that the percentage of women employed in promoted posts in 2010 was 44 per cent, a slight decrease over previous years, while the percentage of women at professorial grade, which had increased from 20 per cent in 2002, still stood at only 35 per cent in 2010.[3] The percentage of men in promoted positions showed a slight increase from the 2009 figure, the average over the period from 2002 to 2010 being 80 per cent. From the Scottish survey, it would seem that women cluster in the ranks of lecturer and senior lecturer, while the largest group of men is at the rank of professor. In addition, further UK statistics indicate that the percentage of women staff has increased most sharply in language departments in what is termed the 'others' category, where they represented approximately 70 per cent of staff.[4] This category is related to teaching-only contracts, and in the specific case of French probably refers to members of staff employed to teach the language itself, very often in the context of university language centres.

The pattern that emerges of French in British higher education is thus one of a feminised discipline at undergraduate level, situated in departments dominated by male academics, with women apparently employed on junior (and increasingly language-only teaching) grades. While there are doubtless wider issues which are not specific to French – mentoring, work–life balance, gendered styles of behaviour within institutions – this landscape of French Studies in the UK is both long-standing, and seemingly unchangeable. In the context of much of what has been done in higher education to pursue equality agendas over the past ten to fifteen years, the persistence of this situation, and its apparent intractability over time, merits some investigation. The next section explains how

2   Higher Education Statistics Agency, *'Languages': Students and Qualifiers Data Tables, 1994/5–2002/3*, online resource, consulted 5 February 2010.

3   Amy Wygant, 'History and Hiring: The Case in Scotland' (n.d.), online resource, consulted 30 June 2010.

4   Higher Education Statistics Agency, *Staff Data Tables: Full-Time Academic Staff by Cost Centre, Principal Source of Finance, Grade and Gender: 1995/6–2002/3 'language-based' 1994–1999; 'French', 'German', 'Spanish', 1999–2003)*, online resource, consulted 5 February 2010.

languages and conversation came to be critical sites for the representation, articulation and production of national and gender identities in the eighteenth century.

The Eighteenth Century

Conversation as a practice of sociability for leisured classes has a long history, but it was in seventeenth-century France that it became, as art historian Mary Vidal has argued, 'une marque de noblesse'.[5] One essential condition for conversation upon which all historians agree is the importance of the role of women. The Marquise de Rambouillet is usually represented as the originator of the salon and of practices around conversation.[6] Her early seventeenth-century salon spawned many others, some 'philosophical', others 'scientific', and women became central to cultural, intellectual and social life in seventeenth-century Paris. Women not only reigned over the space of the salon, but, according to theoreticians of *politesse* such as Méré, were essential to the development of the *honnête homme*, the gentleman, because, 'C'est dans la conversation [...] que le caractère d'un honnête homme se fait voir dans son véritable jour.'[7]

By the mid-eighteenth century, the art of conversation had reached its apogee, and was more central than ever to social and intellectual life, and by then, arguably to political life as well. It also continued to be the touchstone and the standard by which the male self was fashioned.[8] Conversation, however, constructed not just the virtues of the gentleman, but a way of being social and of being French around *esprit*. According to the *Encyclopédie* entry, 'Esprit',

> Ce mot, en tant qu'il signifie une qualité de l'âme est un de ces termes vague auquel tous ceux qui les prononcent attachent presque toujours des sens différents. Il exprime autre chose que jugement, génie, goût, talent, pénétration, grâce, finesse, et il doit tenir de tous ces mérites.[9]

5   Mary Vidal, *Watteau's Painted Conversations: Art, Literature and Talk in Seventeenth- and Eighteenth-Century France* (London: Yale University Press, 1992), p. 78.
6   See Marc Fumaroli, 'La conversation', in Pierre Nora (ed.), *Les lieux de mémoire, tome III* (Paris: Gallimard, 1992), pp. 679–743, p. 699.
7   Antoine Gombauld, Chevalier de Méré, *Oeuvres complètes (1668–77)*, 3 vols, ed. Charles H. Boudhors (Paris: Fernand Roches, 1930); François de Fenne, 'Entretiens familiers pour les amateurs de la langue françoise' (1696), p. 81, in Christoph Strosetzki, *Rhétorique de la conversation: sa dimension littéraire et linguistique dans la société française*, Biblio 17 (Paris, Seattle, Tübingen: Papers on French Seventeenth-Century Literature, 1984), p. 20.
8   Jean-Paul Sermain, 'La Conversation au dix-huitième siècle: un théâtre pour les Lumières?', in Alain Montandon (ed.), *Convivialité et politesse: du gigot, des mots et autres savoir-vivre* (Clermont-Ferrand: Faculté des Lettres et Sciences Humaines de l'Université Blaise-Pascal, 1993), pp. 106–30, p. 106.
9   M. Diderot and M. D'Alembert (eds),. *Encyclopédie, ou dictionnaire raisonné des sciences, des arts et des métiers* (Paris: Une Société de Gens de Lettres 1751–72), s. v. 'Esprit'.

Esprit was the distillation of all the qualities of an individual, and conversation enhanced it and the natural talents of speaker and listeners – energising the memory, awakening and focusing the attention, exercising the mind and making it deeper, more vigorous, more precise, and more penetrating. Conversation was *la grande école de l'esprit*.[10] But, argued the Abbé Morellet, conversation was not the product of French *esprit* alone. What made it possible was the free commerce between the sexes, a form of sociability most developed in France:

> Si les femmes communiquent aux hommes une partie de la douceur que la nature a mise dans leur caractère, c'est par la conversation que cette communication se fait, c'est par la conversation que leur délicatesse, leur bonté, cette exquise sensibilité, si doucement et heureusement contagieuse, se déploient et font leur impression; et si c'est par le désir de plaire aux femmes, qui tempère par degrés la dureté naturelle aux hommes; c'est par la conversation que ce désir est manifeste et c'est l'habitude de l'exprimer qui forme l'habitude de le sentir.[11]

For Morellet, conversation and the sociability it entailed were the emblems of civilised society, and conversation the most 'powerful source for the perfecting of the sociability of nations'. It was the habit of conversing that distinguished 'civilised from savage man', and among the nations of Europe, it was in France that this type of sociability was most developed.[12]

Eighteenth-century salons were the sites for the most brilliant conversation and were, Fumaroli explains, 'une école du grand monde'.[13] The composition of the salon was, even more than in the seventeenth century, a mix of social classes, emphasising intellectual aristocracy above lineage. But even though salons were frequented by philosophers, encyclopédistes, scientists, artists and writers, conversation had to be pleasing and charming; Voltaire's conversation was particularly praised because it was seductive, never pedantic, and above all, measured: the discipline of the tongue was crucial. In France, this discipline was attributed not to self-control, but to taste. Thus it was Madame du Boccage's 'delicate taste' which ensured that she did not talk more than others or more than one would have wished.[14] More openly and deliberately than in the seventeenth century, the women who ruled eighteenth-century salons chose their regular guests, organised dinners and disciplined as well as regulated the conversations that took place. Morellet maintains

10 André Morellet, 'De la conversation', in *Eloges de Mme Geoffrin* (Paris: H. Nicolle, 1812), pp. 155–226, p. 158.
11 Morellet, 'De la conversation', p. 163.
12 Morellet, 'De la conversation', pp. 159–65.
13 Fumaroli, 'La conversation', p. 699.
14 Grace Gill-Mark, *Anne-Marie du Boccage: une femme de lettres au XVIIIe siècle* (1927) (Geneva: Slatkine, 1976), p. 44.

that conversation was best when the hostess was either the only woman, or the only woman at the heart of the society. She was 'la muse qui accordait les voix', tuning and harmonising the diverse voices and opinions around her, setting the tone and orchestrating the whole.[15] As one of Mme Geoffrin's guests replied, when she complimented him one evening on his brilliance, 'Je ne suis qu'un instrument dont vous avez bien joué.'[16] 'La conversation française', writes Fumaroli, 'était un espace de jeu qui rend possible les repons entre voix féminines et voix masculines, et qui fait de l'esprit leur point d'accord parfait.'[17]

What made French conversation charming was its lightness, its delicacy and the *esprit* of its participants, male and female alike. But these terms, 'lightness' and 'charm', and even the notions of naturalness and spontaneity conceal the fact that conversation was the supreme expression of a number of qualities which cannot but have been the product of self-discipline, awareness of the self and others, and above all, of a mind trained by study and a thorough control of language. In particular, women in the salons had to know what they were talking about and understand what their guests discussed. They read the contemporary philosophical and political texts, and understood them.[18] At the same time, part of the grace of conversation was the ability to talk lightly about the most serious subjects and make no show of one's knowledge. To take Marmontel's portrait of Mme de Marchais, the future Comtesse d'Angiviller:

> Imagine all the charms of character, wit, language and even of figure blended to the highest degree of perfection, clarity of thought, finesse, accuracy, and a surprising quickness, [...] expressions always well chosen and spontaneous, and as swift as thought. [...] No one spoke with greater ease, accuracy or method. [...] But the most marvellous aspect of her conversation was its variety: the most appropriate word for the thing, for the moment, for the person; the finest distinctions and nuances, and for all and everyone, the best there was to say.[19]

There were attempts to import into eighteenth-century England the idea of the salon as a space for mixed conversation but, apart from a few, such as Elizabeth Montagu's Bluestocking salon, these were never as numerous as in France. The success of mixed assemblies in Paris must have had something to do with 'the national character of the French', Nathaniel Wraxall noted in his *Memoirs*.[20] Travellers noted that in England, when

15 Fumaroli, 'La conversation', p. 698.

16 Morellet, 'De la conversation', p. 12.

17 Fumaroli, 'La conversation', p. 698.

18 See Dena Goodman, *The Republic of Letters: A Cultural History of the French Enlightenment* (Ithaca, NY: Cornell University Press, 1994).

19 Jean-François Marmontel, *Mémoires d'un père pour servir à l'instruction de ses enfants*, 4 vols, trans. Michele Cohen (Paris, An XIII, 1805) II, Livre V, pp. 21–22.

20 Nathaniel William Wraxall, *Historical Memoirs of My Own Time*, 2 vols (London: T. Cadell and W. Davis, 1815), I, 160.

men and women met to converse they remained separate:'The women generally speaking place themselves near the door, and leave the upper hand and the conversation to the men',[21] and conversation itself took on quite distinct characteristics. These were associated with the forging of a national identity which was masculine, and which would eventually position the French language and those who spoke it as effeminate.

While Richard Steele defined the gentleman as a 'man of conversation',[22] English representations of conversation were framed by issues relating to the segregation of the sexes in English society, the English national trait of taciturnity, and concerns about mixed conversation and effeminacy. Musing on the relationship between language and national character in *The Spectator*, its editor Joseph Addison observed that because the English language was 'abounding in Monosyllables', it was perfectly suited to a people wishing to utter their thoughts quickly and frugally. 'Loquacity', he declared, was the 'enemy' of the English.[23] Despite the pressure on men throughout the century to develop the fluency of the tongue necessary for polite conversation and gentlemanliness, a satirical pamphlet, *The Art of Speaking and Holding One's Tongue* still presented taciturnity as a peculiarly English trait. People on the continent, it remarked, regard the Briton as a pensive animal, 'so deeply immersed in thought and spleen that nothing but repeated Draughts of strong liquor can raise his spirits and induce him to express ideas for any length of time'.[24] The English delight in silence, Addison had remarked early in the century,[25] and they still did when Rousseau was writing *La Nouvelle Héloïse*, in which he describes how 'nous avons passé une matinée à l'anglaise, réunis dans le silence'.[26]

Addison, like Morellet, was convinced that the mixed company of the sexes was the ideal social state, because:

> It is the Male that gives Charms to Womankind, that produces an Air in their Faces, a Grace in their Motions, a Softness in their Voices, and a Delicacy in their Complections. On the other hand without Women, Men would be quite different from what they are at present, rude unfinished Creatures; their Endeavours to please the opposite Sex, polishes and refines them out of those Manners most natural to them.[27]

21 Chauncey Brewster Tinker, *The Salon and English Letters* (New York: Macmillan, 1915), p. 134.
22 *The Tatler*, no. 21 (Saturday 28 May 1709).
23 *The Spectator*, no. 135 (Saturday 4 August 1711).
24 *The Art of Speaking and Holding One's Tongue In and Out of Doors* (London: printed for C. G. Seyffert, 1761), p. 1.
25 *The Spectator*, no. 135.
26 Jean Jacques Rousseau, 'Julie ou la Nouvelle Héloïse' (1761), in *Oeuvres complètes*, Bibliothèque de la Pléiade, 5ème partie, Lettre III (Paris: Gallimard, 1956), pp. 557–8.
27 *The Spectator*, no. 433 (Thursday 17 July 1712).

As the quotation suggests, while men made women more feminine and women made men more refined, they did not explicitly make them more manly. Unlike the French, the English worried that mixed company would make men effeminate.

In England, when taciturnity had been attributed to the English character, the reference was to English men, not to women. Throughout most of the eighteenth century, men were said to lack both ease and elegance of expression while women's 'flexible tongue'[28] and verbal talents were celebrated. However, by the end of the century, attitudes to fluency and conversation changed dramatically. Men's inarticulateness became the testimony to the power, penetration and depth of their minds. Women's sprightly conversation and fluent tongue, on the other hand, was now evidence of the superficiality of theirs. It was the strength of men's minds – not their 'taste' as in France – that provided the discipline of the tongue that women lacked constitutionally. The taciturnity of English men distinguished them not just from the shallow sprightliness of English females, but also from that of the French. From an English perspective, there was no difference between French men and French women's tongue. French men had 'many pretty ways of insinuating what they meant', unlike the 'forcible and manly ways' of the English.[29] French men's conversational skills, their 'wit and vivacity' even suggested that they 'must perhaps be proportionately deficient in judgement'.[30] Mary Wollstonecraft weighed into the debate, arguing that the famous conversational skills which the French themselves linked to *esprit*, were merely at 'their tongue's end', and that they lacked the depth of thought acquired only by silent contemplation.[31] 'The English', noted a French commentator in 1771, 'delight not only in seeing themselves but in being regarded as the rivals of France and its superiors in everything regarding strength of mind, vigour of the spirit and energy of the language'.[32]

In France, after the Revolution had destroyed the way of life which produced conversation and which it bonded and secured, the nineteenth century exalted conversation and it became a nostalgic *lieu de mémoire*, celebrated as 'un titre de gloire nationale'.[33] In England, it was the

28 Henry Home, *Loose Hints upon Education; Chiefly Concerning the Culture of the Heart* (Edinburgh, J. Bell and J. Murray, 1781), p. 135.
29 Alexander Jardine, *Letters from Barbary, France, Spain, Portugal, &c.* I, 2 vols (London: printed for T. Cadell, 1788), p. 266.
30 Jardine, *Letters*, I, p. 266.
31 Mary Wollstonecraft, *A Historical and Moral View of the Origin and Progress of the French Revolution and the Effect it has Produced in Europe*, Book V, Ch IV (London: J. Johnson, 1794), p. 505.
32 Simon-Nicolas-Henri Linguet, 'Annales politiques, civiles et littéraires', cited in 'Introduction', in Louis-Sébastien Mercier, *Parallèle de Paris et de Londres*, Claude Bruneteau et Bernard Cottret (eds) (Paris: Didier-Erudition, 1982), pp. 9–50, p. 31.
33 Fumaroli, 'La conversation', p. 718.

'talent of Silence' that Carlyle celebrated, a silence which characterised his strong and manly heroes.[34]

The Nineteenth Century

In the nineteenth century, these attitudes to speaking French largely persisted. In Scotland for example, in the opening lecture of the arts course at Queen Margaret College, Glasgow, on 3 November 1891, the Professor of Humanity, George Gilbert Ramsay, sought to address the question, 'Should Women Study the Classics?'[35] Ramsay was a terrifyingly energetic, or perhaps terrifyingly well-supported, figure: professor for 43 years, author of a three-volume Latin grammar, editor of three volumes of Tacitus, dean of the faculty in his eighties, and the first president both of the Classical Association of Scotland and of the Scottish Mountaineering Club.[36]

Ramsay offered comments on three different aspects of languages. First, the answer to the question posed by his title was that, yes, women should study the classics, but not for the reasons that men do, in order, that is, to enter into the highest ranks of the civil service, to become lawyers and medical doctors. To put the matter uncharitably, Ramsay thought that women should study the classics in order to confirm them in their established roles as commodities on the marriage market and arbiters of polite society. But to read his comments more sympathetically, Ramsay was overwhelmingly concerned with that quality that the Victorians thought was transmitted by the study of the classics, culture:

> The culture we aim at [...] is to be used for ends suitable for women, not necessarily suitable for men. Our aim is women's culture, pursued with a full sense of all the differences of character, of physique, and of future life, which will ever make women as essentially, in their nature, different from men, as they are actually, in their lives, indispensable to them.[37]

Second, with respect to spoken language, Ramsay's educated woman 'will probably speak simpler, homelier, more picturesque English than her companion'.[38] Thus her English was 'picturesque' at a time when the University of Glasgow was at pains to avoid any hint of it. In establishing the chair of Scottish history in 1911, the university 'would remove any

34 Thomas Carlyle, *On Heroes, Hero Worship and the Heroic in History*, 6 lectures (London: James Fraser, 1841), online resource, consulted 18 June 2010.
35 George Gilbert Ramsay, *Should Women Study the Classics? Opening Lecture of the Arts Course at Queen Margaret College, Glasgow, November 3, 1891* (Glasgow: Maclehose, 1891).
36 'Biography of George Gilbert Ramsay', in *The University of Glasgow Story* (n.d.), online resource, consulted 21 June 2010.
37 Ramsay, *Should Women Study the Classics?*, pp. 7–8.
38 Ramsay, *Should Women Study the Classics?*, p. 11.

tendencies to parochialism, picturesqueness, and defective perspective' by requiring that the teaching associated with it be accompanied by a course in history in order to graduate in the subject.[39] 'If she have occasion to use French or German', Ramsay continued,

> she will pronounce them in such a way that she might possibly be understood by a Frenchman or a German. Latin or Greek she will *never* quote, however well she knows them, but if you make sly allusions to the great personages, the great book, the great myths of antiquity, you will find that they are appreciated.[40] (original emphasis).

The anxiety about gender identification in language betrayed by Ramsay's 'never' in italics was most fully deployed when Ramsay came to discuss the role of French. 'Good French', in his opinion, 'is an absolute sine qua non of every lady's education'.[41] It is in connection with French, then, that two remarkable things happened in Ramsay's address. First, this was the only moment in his text when the cultivated woman was referred to as a 'lady'. The study of French was thus overwritten with connotations of social class. Second, Ramsay here did exactly what he had declared to be the defining gesture of the masculine: he spoke Latin. French was the 'sine qua non' of the lady's education, and with this quotation, he both separated himself from any threat of feminisation and positioned the woman student as the one who would never have access to his language. His 'sine qua non', that is, was secured as being not hers. This led on to Ramsay's final formulation, which claimed that his fashioning of the cultivated woman was distinctly Scottish:

> A cultivated woman is like a good old-fashioned Scotch garden. Inside, somewhat screened from view, are all the products of what our English friends call the kitchen-garden; the homely vegetables which feed the family kail-pot; the native fruits of which the winter preserves are made; but there is thyme and lavender in it, as well as carrots, turnips, and potatoes; roses are not wanting; and it is set all round with bright sweet-scented perennial flowers, which grow sweeter and richer as they grow older.

The women to whom Ramsay was speaking in 1891 would go on to become the first female arts graduates of the university. Our evidence of the last decade of French Studies in UK higher education, however, suggests that the ghost of the eighteenth century and of Ramsay – the effeminacy of actually speaking French among taciturn male Britons – continues to cast a surprisingly long shadow over our departments of French to this very day.

---

39 George Edwin Maclean, *Studies in Higher Education in England and Scotland. With Suggestions for Universities and Colleges in the United States* (Washington: Government Printing Office, 1917), p. 60.
40 Ramsay, *Should Women Study the Classics?* (original emphasis), p.11.
41 Ramsay, *Should Women Study the Classics?*, p. 16.

Bibliography

The Art of Speaking and Holding One's Tongue In and Out of Doors (London: printed for C. G. Seyffert, 1761).

'Biography of George Gilbert Ramsay', in *The University of Glasgow Story* (n.d.) available at www.universitystory.gla.ac.uk/biography/?id=WH1418&type=P (consulted 2 June 2010).

Carlyle, Thomas *On Heroes, Hero Worship and the Heroic in History*, 6 lectures (London: James Fraser, 1841), available at www.gutenberg.org/files/1091/1091–h/1091–h.htm (consulted 18 June 2010).

de Fenne, François, 'Entretiens familiers pour les amateurs de la langue françoise' (1696), in Christoph Strosetzki, *Rhétorique de la conversation: sa dimension littéraire et linguistique dans la société française*, Biblio 17, 20 (Paris, Seattle, Tübingen: Papers on French Seventeenth-Century Literature, 1984),

Diderot, M, and M. D'Alembert (eds), *Encyclopédie, ou dictionnaire raisonné des sciences, des arts et des métiers* (Paris: Une Société de Gens de Lettres, 1751–72).

Fumaroli, Marc, 'La conversation', in Pierre Nora (ed.), *Les lieux de mémoire, Tome III* (Paris: Gallimard, 1992), pp. 679–734.

Gill-Mark, Grace, *Anne-Marie du Boccage: une femme de lettres au XVIIIe siècle* (1927) (Geneva: Slatkine, 1976),

Gombauld, Antoine, Chevalier de Méré, *Oeuvres complètes* (1668–77), 3 vols, ed. Charles H. Boudhors (Paris: Fernand Roches, 1930).

Goodman, Dena, *The Republic of Letters: A Cultural History of the French Enlightenment* (Ithaca, NY: Cornell University Press, 1994).

Higher Education Statistics Agency, *'Languages': students and qualifiers data tables, 1994/5 – 2002/3*, available at www.hesa.ac (consulted 5 February 2010).

Higher Education Statistics Agency, *Staff Data Tables: full-time academic staff by cost centre, principal source of finance, grade and gender: 1995/6 – 2002/3 'language-based' 1994–1999; 'French', 'German', 'Spanish', 1999–2003*, available at www.hesa.ac.uk (consulted 5 February 2010).

Higher Education Statistics Agency, *Students: subject of study tables, 1996/1997 – 2007/8*, 'French', available at www.hesa.ac.uk (consulted 5 February 2010).

Home, Henry, *Loose Hints upon Education; Chiefly Concerning the Culture of the Heart* (Edinburgh: J. Bell and J. Murray, 1781).

Jardine, Alexander, *Letters from Barbary, France, Spain, Portugal, &c.*, 2 vols (London: printed for T. Cadell, 1788).

Linguet, Simon-Nicolas-Henri, 'Annales politiques, civiles et littéraires', cited in 'Introduction', in Louis-Sébastien Mercier, *Parallèle de Paris et de Londres*, Claude Bruneteau et Bernard Cottret (eds) (Paris: Didier-Erudition, 1982), pp. 9–50.

Maclean, George Edwin, *Studies in Higher Education in England and Scotland. With Suggestions for Universities and Colleges in the United States* (Washington: Government Printing Office, 1917),

Marmontel, Jean-François, *Mémoires d'un père pour servir à l'instruction de ses enfants*, 4 vols (Paris, An XIII, 1805) [Paris: Chez Xhrouet, 1805].

Morellet, André, 'De la conversation', in *Eloges de Mme Geoffrin* (Paris: H. Nicolle, 1812), pp. 155–226.

Ramsay, George Gilbert, *Should Women Study the Classics? Opening Lecture of the Arts Course at Queen Margaret College, Glasgow, November 3, 1891* (Glasgow: Maclehose, 1891).

Rousseau, Jean Jacques, 'Julie ou la Nouvelle Héloïse' (1761), in *Oeuvres complètes*, 5ème partie, Lettre III, Bibliothèque de la Pléiade (Paris: Gallimard, 1956).

Sermain, Jean-Paul, 'La Conversation au dix-huitième siècle: un théâtre pour les Lumières?' in Alain Montandon (ed.), *Convivialité et politesse: du gigot, des mots et autres savoir-vivre* (Clermont-Ferrand: Faculté des Lettres et Sciences Humaines de l'Université Blaise-Pascal, 1993), pp. 106–30.

Tinker, Chauncey Brewster, *The Salon and English Letters* (New York: Macmillan, 1915).

Vidal, Mary, *Watteau's Painted Conversations: Art, Literature and Talk in Seventeenth- and Eighteenth-Century France* (London: Yale University Press, 1992).

Wollstonecraft, Mary, *A Historical and Moral View of the Origin and Progress of the French Revolution and the Effect it has Produced in Europe* (London: J. Johnson, 1794).

Wraxall, Nathaniel William, *Historical Memoirs of My Own Time*, 2 vols (London, T. Cadell and W. Davis, 1815).

Wygant, Amy, 'History and Hiring: The Case in Scotland' (n.d.), available at http://wifis.edublogs.org (consulted 30 June 2010).

7

Contemporary Women's Writing in French: Future Perspectives in Formal and Informal Research Networks

Gill Rye

In the UK and elsewhere in the anglophone world, contemporary literature in French continues to be a strong field of study in both research and teaching. Traditionally lone scholars, researchers of literature are now increasingly being pressured by their institutions to network, to collaborate and, above all, to generate large sums of external research funding. Contemporary women-authored literature is not the threatened subject that some other contributions to this publication document – it is widely researched and taught on a range of undergraduate and post-graduate courses – except perhaps in the sense that if women's writing is not made visible, there is a risk that it will become invisible again (for instance, many published surveys of contemporary literature are still dominated by male-authored texts). However, working on the very contemporary does have its own issues and challenges.

It is in the above context that I chart here the case of the Contemporary Women's Writing in French (CWWF) seminar and research network, together with its related activities. My aim is to offer CWWF as a relatively low-cost, groundswell example of the possibilities for developing a research field and informal research network. While this in itself does not necessarily address the challenges of generating large collaborative research grants, it does represent a way for individual scholars with shared interests to come together for a common purpose, to explore and develop a field of study, to refine methodologies, to forge collaborations with colleagues they know they can work with, and thus to build a position of strength from which the much desired large research funding can be applied for. It is thus a bottom-up model of collaboration that is formed out of genuine common interest, rather than a top-down version where as yet unknown research partners are required to identify and seek out each other.

Through its activities, events and publication outputs, CWWF has made a strong contribution to French Studies in the UK, and over the past ten years has helped raise the profile of contemporary women's writing in French in the anglophone world. Now, with its recent expansion into a more formalised cross-cultural centre – the Centre for the Study of Contemporary Women's Writing (CCWW) – it aims both to continue to respond to the needs and interests of its growing constituencies and to help meet some of the internal and external challenges that face researchers in modern language studies in the future, in what is a new climate for the humanities. What I describe here is thus continuing work in progress.

CWWF – and CCWW – are based at the Institute of Germanic & Romance Studies (IGRS),[1] School of Advanced Study, University of London, as part of its national and international remit to promote and to facilitate research in its various constituency areas. The CWWF seminar originally grew out of the needs and wishes of its membership – scholars in French Studies and beyond who teach and research contemporary literature by women in French – and it continues to respond to its members' ideas by involving them in the organisation of events and other activities. With minimal funding, over the decade, CWWF has organised a programme of events – seminar meetings, international conferences, study days – developed an open access website of research resources, and produced a monthly email newsletter of publications and events listings. Five of the six major conferences organised under the auspices of CWWF have already resulted in a number of book and journal special issues, and publications for the remaining conferences and study day are in process.

A conference entitled 'Women's Writing in France: New Writers, New Literatures?', held at the then Institute of Romance Studies in January 2000, first brought together scholars who were working on literary texts published during the 1990s. It was originally planned as a small, one-day event, but the call for papers resulted in about fifty proposals, and it ultimately became a major three-day international conference, with external funding support from the British Academy, the Association for the Study of Modern and Contemporary France, and Women in French with which CWWF has very close links. There was a great deal of interest in the field, prompted by what was termed 'a new generation' of women authors who had come to the fore in the 1990s.[2] Following that event, participants expressed such enthusiasm for continuing the exchange,

1 The IGRS was established in 2004 with the merger of the Institute of Germanic Studies and the Institute of Romance Studies, founded in 1950 and 1989, respectively. It is one of ten institutes of the School of Advanced Study in the University of London. The mission of the IGRS is to promote and facilitate the study of the cultures of German-speaking and Romance language countries across a range of disciplines in the humanities. CWWF was launched in 2000, under the auspices of the Institute of Romance Studies.

2 See, for example, Gill Rye and Michael Worton (eds), *Women's Writing in Contemporary France: New Writers, New Literatures in the 1990s* (Manchester: Manchester University Press, 2002), and Nathalie Morello and Catherine Rodgers (eds), *Nouvelles écrivaines: nouvelles voix?* (Amsterdam: Rodopi, 2002).

which the conference had initiated, that a study group, the CWWF seminar, was established. It continued in the tradition of, and aimed to emulate, the inspiring work that the late Professor Elizabeth Fallaize had begun with her Women Reading Women group, which in the late 1980s and early 1990s was part of the activities of Women in French.[3]

As a group emanating from the grass roots, CWWF is an informal network with no formal constitution or membership fees. The seminar normally meets two or three times a year. A peripatetic seminar, its meetings alternate as far as possible between London, at the IGRS, and other universities in the UK. So far, in addition to London, meetings have been held at the universities of Leeds, Nottingham, Oxford (twice), Edinburgh, Birmingham, Cambridge, Newcastle, Cardiff, Reading and Durham. Meetings take a range of different formats, but whatever the format, there is always plenty of time for both formal and informal discussion and networking. In addition to the normal meetings of the seminar, two full-day meetings have been held: a study day on the work of Marie Darrieussecq in June 2009, organised by Helena Chadderton, and a special meeting in March 2009, in Oxford, organised by Ruth Cruickshank, to honour Elizabeth Fallaize, who sadly died in December that year from motor neurone disease. The latter event was generously funded by St John's College, Oxford, and Royal Holloway, University of London.

Given the general reduction in research time that has resulted from increased teaching and administrative workloads and cuts in finance and staffing within institutions, with the best will in the world, informal research groups such as CWWF can fall apart for lack of time for organisation. As convenor of the seminar, my role has been to ensure its continuity via regular meetings and other activities. While it is crucial for at least one person to take on this role, this seminar has surely lasted so long because individual members are involved, especially but not exclusively for the out of London meetings. They host the meeting in their department, choose the theme or topic and organise the speakers. This means that the seminar is effectively owned by its members.

Over the last ten years, CWWF has not received any regular funding, apart from a small internal budget to help postgraduate students travel to attend meetings. Departments have been happy to host the meetings, and speakers and participants generally pay their own travel costs or their institutions support their attendance. Of course, as an IGRS seminar, CWWF benefits from the general publicity and basic administrative services of the Institute, as well as the rooms and equipment available there

3 Fallaize's seminal text, Elisabeth Fallaize, *French Women's Writing: Recent Fiction* (Basingstoke: Macmillan, 1993), was influential in introducing 1970s and 1980s French women's writing to anglophone readers.

for its London meetings.[4] However, more specific administration, events organisation and costs, newsletter and website development, and work on publications have relied on a series of internal and external funding bids or on voluntary input from members.

Since 2000, five more major CWWF international conferences have been held at the IGRS, supported variously by the British Academy, the French Embassy, Women in French, the Modern Humanities Research Association and the Cassal Trust Fund. All conferences so far have resulted in edited publications – both books and journal special issues[5] – and there have been some other collaborative spin-off publications. Many of the studies focus on gendered themes – the way writers express women's lives and experiences, sometimes in controversial ways – the body, sexuality, motherhood, of course, but also violence, trauma, war, memory, migration, love and death. Women's writing is predominantly approached from a cultural studies type of perspective and methodology that does not neglect close readings and literary analysis, and it is also looked at as a socio-cultural phenomenon in itself, via work on literary prizes, translation, bestsellers, and so on. The epithet 'contemporary' is widely applied in French Studies, where even the study of Proust can be included in taught courses on 'contemporary literature'! However, the main focus of CWWF interests and activities relates to recently published texts by living writers from either metropolitan France or elsewhere (i.e. what is being produced *now*) or what is

---

4   The IGRS hosts a number of seminars convened either by staff members or other members of its academic constituency. See http://igrs.sas.ac.uk for further details or to propose a new seminar.

5   Rye and Worton's *Women's Writing in Contemporary France* was drawn from the first conference in 2000; the 2002 conference generated two journal special issues, Gill Rye (ed.), *Hybrid Voices, Hybrid Texts: Women's Writing at the Turn of the Millennium*, special issue of *Dalhousie French Studies* 68 (Fall 2004) and Gill Rye (ed.), *A New Generation: Sex, Gender and Creativity in Contemporary Women's Writing in French*, special issue of *L'Esprit Créateur* 45: 1 (Spring 2005). Gill Rye and Carrie Tarr (eds), *Focalizing the Body in Contemporary Women's Writing and Filmmaking in France*, special issue of *Nottingham French Studies* 45: 3 (Autumn 2006) drew on the conference held in 2003; and Margaret-Anne Hutton (ed.), *Redefining the Real: The Fantastic in Contemporary French and Francophone Women's Writing*, Modern French Identities vol. 81 (Oxford: Peter Lang, 2009) on the 2007 conference. Publications drawn from the October 2006 conference are forthcoming: Marie-Claire Barnet and Shirley Jordan (eds), *Space, Place and Landscape in Contemporary Francophone Women's Writing*, special issue of *Dalhousie French Studies* 93 (Spring 2011) and Marie-Claire Barnet and Shirley Jordan (eds), *Watch this Space: Women's Conceptualisations of Space in Contemporary French Film and Visual Art*, special issue of *L'Esprit Créateur* 15: 1 (Spring 2011); likewise a publication from the 2009 study day on Darrieussecq: Helena Chadderton and Gill Rye (eds), *Marie Darrieussecq*, special issue of *Dalhousie French Studies* (forthcoming). In relation to the latter, Darrieussecq is both a popular and much-studied author in the UK and the USA, but although numerous articles and books chapters have been published on her work, as yet, no complete publication is devoted to it. This special issue will be the first.

sometimes termed 'the extreme contemporary' (*l'extrême contemporain*).[6] Yet it also caters for a wider interest in any post-war women's writing in French by, for example, including details of relevant calls for papers or conferences in its newsletter and on its website. The October 2010 conference and subsequent publications aimed at formulating an *état présent* of themes and issues, texts and authors, forms and aesthetics, of works published in the first decade of the twenty-first century.

Communication with CWWF members takes place via a free monthly email newsletter, which I compile, distributed through JISC.[7] There are now almost 200 subscribers, grown steadily from about 75 when the newsletter was launched in 2001. Most members (about 120) are UK based, and there are 33 in the USA, 15 in France, and smaller numbers in Canada, Eire, Australia, New Zealand, Italy and Algeria. Events are also publicised outside the membership, so that CWWF as a group is always renewing and expanding. At the beginning of the academic year, I regularly receive requests to subscribe from new postgraduate students whose supervisors have recommended CWWF to them, and colleagues tell me they regularly pass on the newsletter to research students, or even their whole department.

Working on literature as it is being produced is exciting for scholars, students and teachers alike. However, it does have its own specific challenges. In addition to an ever-growing corpus of works, there may not always be much scholarship in existence with which to engage, or for students to access, or it is too recent to be searchable via bibliographic databases. The CWWF newsletter endeavours to provide a service to respond to this need. It contains information on new books by female authors and on articles on contemporary writing by women; it also includes calls for papers and events announcements, plus other information of interest to members; and it has a searchable archive. Members regularly comment on its usefulness, despite the fact that coverage is unfortunately rather patchy. We have no dedicated research help, and so content has to rely on contributions from members and information received via other email lists.

Another CWWF activity is its website. This is an open access resource, hosted by the IGRS, containing biographical and bibliographical information on individual authors and on general pages. Like the newsletter, it also includes calls for papers and events announcements, and it has

---

6 Various international research groups exist for the study of 'the extreme contemporary' in French literature (not just in women's writing): for example, the Groupe de Recherche sur l'Extrême Contemporain (GREC) (Bari, Italy) and the Groupe de Recherche et d'Étude sur la Littérature Française d'Aujourd'hui (GRELFA) (Toronto, Canada).

7 JISC is the Joint Information Systems Committee, a support body for the use of information and communications technology in Further and Higher Education, see www.jisc.ac.uk/.

links to a wide range of relevant organisations. Until recently, coverage and updating the website had been something of a problem, since, apart from a small internal grant for help to set it up, no funding has been available to develop it. However, a recent initiative at the IGRS means that the site is now being developed again: current content is being updated, new author pages are envisaged, and coverage will be expanded to include interviews with authors, and so on.

This new development is the Centre for the Study of Contemporary Women's Writing (CCWW), which spans the language areas of the Institute – French, German, Italian, Portuguese and Hispanic. The new Centre, which benefited from some basic start-up funding from an internal School of Advanced Study fund,[8] employs CWWF activities and resources as a model for the development of the other individual language strands, in which there are rich bodies of work and a constituency of established and emerging scholars researching and teaching it. It also aims to promote and facilitate cross-cultural and comparative events and projects. CWWF itself now comes under the umbrella of the centre.

Its launch event in October 2009 brought three writers to the UK, from Austria, Italy and Portugal, with funding from the Coffin Trust Fund and the Austrian Cultural Forum.[9] In addition, a Spanish reading group has been established, a number of one-day conferences and readings have been held on French, German, Hispanic and Italian authors, with more to follow, and a well attended cross-cultural seminar is in progress. A CCWW website has been launched and content is building on the individual language pages, including audio-visual recordings.[10] The centre has a steering committee, an advisory board, a mission statement, and associate members who help with activities and electronic resource content. It is hoped that this new structure will facilitate cross-cultural projects and collaborative funding applications.

What does this development mean for its French constituency in the greater context of modern language studies? With the threat to the survival of modern languages in its current form in higher education and the reduction of single honours modern language degrees, more language departments are being organised in cross-cultural arrangements (schools of modern languages, for example). While this trend offers opportunities for comparative, cross-cultural and interdisciplinary collaboration in teaching – via school-wide degrees and courses, for example – it raises

---

8 CCWW is one of two new Centres at the IGRS to benefit from this start-up support; the other is the Centre for the Study of Cultural Memory, see http://igrs.sas.ac.uk/research/CCM.html.

9 The Coffin Trust Fund is a bequest administered by the School of Advanced Study, University of London.

10 For the CCWW website, see http://igrs.sas.ac.uk/research/CCWW.htm. The CWWF pages are now part of the CCWW site at http://igrs.sas.ac.uk/research/CCWW%20 French.htm.

the question of whether such a broadening out enhances single language teaching or betrays it, especially where it necessitates teaching in translation. As far as CCWW's remit in research facilitation is concerned, the aim is certainly not to abandon single language studies or research facilitation support for them, but rather to enrich them. The centre will support the research of its discrete constituencies by providing resources, events and activities in the individual language areas, but it is also well placed to encourage cross-cultural and interdisciplinary dialogue.

For example, the first meeting of the cross-cultural seminar, which took place in May 2010, took the form of a study day on 'Writing childhood'. Six papers were presented in two sessions – one paper on each of French, German, Italian, Spanish and Portuguese authors and texts, and one theoretical paper. Questions and discussion followed each paper, and the day concluded with a round-table discussion, which ranged across both sessions. As befits a comparative forum, discussion during the round-table started by drawing out the similarities and connections between the different papers and contexts, and then retrenched to the specific national and individual author contexts, exploring how differences were being played out as well as how interconnections could be productive. All speakers found it useful and enriching to present their work in a cross-cultural forum – the insights produced in a comparative format supplement and enhance, and perhaps problematise, those achieved outside that framework.

The speakers and participants at this event were all keen to hold a second event on the same theme, to build on the dialogue of the first session, but to explore the topic more deeply, rather than yet more widely. Again, all languages were represented, but the focus of the next session in January 2011 was narrower, concentrating on narrative and exactly *how* it expresses the perspective of a child. It is expected that a cross-cultural publication will result on the topic, largely drawn from these two study days. This amount of detail is only offered here as it serves to illustrate how cross-cultural, comparative dialogue can enrich the study of literature, despite the putative disadvantage of having to discuss texts – or at least passages – in translation, though normally both original language and translation are made available.

Ultimately, the centre aims to respond – and to help its membership respond – to the challenges that modern languages currently face. In view of the difficult financial climate in the UK public sector, these are likely to intensify rather than lighten over the next few years. There are fewer and fewer internal pots of money with which to underwrite conferences or seminars, and academics have less and less time to devote to research. This means more reliance on external funding, and on what represents a turn to collaborative projects in the humanities, and perhaps especially in modern languages, given their potential in large European funding grants. This turn has, of course, been directed by the Arts & Humanities Research Council, which also favours interdisciplinary collaborations.

Thus, CCWW hopes to facilitate the networking that collaborative applications rely on, and also to provide a home for several cross-cultural projects. While supporting individual scholars and research, its activities, events and resources also respond to the new buzzwords that have become important in higher education, especially 'knowledge transfer' and 'social impact'.

We intend to take a lead in collaborative, cross-cultural and interdisciplinary activities in contemporary women's writing, and to bring together academics, not only from the UK, France, Germany, Italy, Spain and Portugal, but also from a wider range of European countries, in order to discuss specific themes in a pan-European context. Many policies relating to themes covered in contemporary women's writing – not least families, motherhood, violence, work – are dealt with at European level, but little attention is given to the contribution literature can make to understandings and knowledge of these issues. At the centre, we plan to explore the social impact of research in contemporary literary studies, thus enabling our members to respond to the increasing impact agenda. It is in all our interests now to seek to identify and to document the various relationships between literature (or other forms of cultural production) and the social.

The CWWF activities described here have, I believe, made a significant contribution to French Studies in the UK over the last ten years, by developing a research field and network, especially via its publications. Despite its publishing successes, it is still quite difficult to publish contemporary French literary studies, especially in the UK, and particularly in the field of recent metropolitan women's writing – work on francophone authors is arguably more easily placed. Member feedback confirms that CWWF is a valuable resource in terms of information but also as a support network. We have achieved quite a lot with minimal internal funding and some occasional small amounts of financial support from a variety of external funding pots. It represents a model of a bottom-up research network, from which to respond to twenty-first century challenges.

It may have taken CWWF almost ten years to expand into a more formalised centre, and new networks may not wish to spend so much time at what might be considered such a basic level – that is, without major funding – but both national and institutional agendas have changed somewhat over the last ten years. CWWF was conceived as part of the outreach and facilitation mandate of the IGRS, providing facilities and opportunities for researchers nationally and internationally. It has, however, always brought together research and teaching – in that many of its members teach research-led courses on women's writing – and CCWW is particularly well placed to add knowledge transfer to the mix. The IGRS already reaches a broad public (its groups, Friends of Italian, and Friends of Germanic Studies, for example, include both academic and non-academic members, and it organises a number of visual arts events which include non-academic participation). Indeed, CCWW events have also already attracted members of the public, including groups of school children who come to hear international authors read from and discuss their work. The centre's potential for generating cross-cultural and interdisciplinary projects, especially via external funding applications, offers the opportunity to develop this interaction in exciting ways, bringing French literature and culture into dialogue with other national literatures and cultures, and with other disciplines. This will help us engage with the impact agenda and, through this, we aim to raise the profile of literature as an object of study in a wider context.

Bibliography

Barnet, Marie-Claire and Shirley Jordan (eds), *Space, Place and Landscape in Contemporary Francophone Women's Writing*, special issue of *Dalhousie French Studies* 93 (Spring 2011).

Barnet, Marie-Claire and Shirley Jordan (eds), *Watch this Space: Women's Conceptualisations of Space in Contemporary French Film and Visual Art*, special issue of *L'Esprit Créateur* 15: 1 (Spring 2011).

Chadderton, Helena and Gill Rye (eds), *Marie Darrieussecq*, special issue of *Dalhousie French Studies* (forthcoming).

Fallaize, Elisabeth, *French Women's Writing: Recent Fiction* (Basingstoke: Macmillan, 1993).

Hutton, Margaret-Anne (ed.), *Redefining the Real: The Fantastic in Contemporary French and Francophone Women's Writing*, Modern French Identities, vol. 81 (Oxford: Peter Lang, 2009).

Morello, Nathalie and Catherine Rodgers (eds), *Nouvelles écrivaines: nouvelles voix?* (Amsterdam: Rodopi, 2002).

Rye, Gill (ed.), *Hybrid Voices, Hybrid Texts: Women's Writing at the Turn of the Millennium*, special issue of *Dalhousie French Studies* 68 (Fall 2004).

Rye, Gill (ed.), *A New Generation: Sex, Gender and Creativity in Contemporary Women's Writing in French*, special issue of *L'Esprit Créateur* 45: 1 (Spring 2005).

Rye, Gill and Carrie Tarr (eds), *Focalizing the Body in Contemporary Women's Writing and Filmmaking in France*, special issue of *Nottingham French Studies* 45: 3 (Autumn 2006).

Rye, Gill and Michael Worton (eds), *Women's Writing in Contemporary France: New Writers, New Literatures in the 1990s* (Manchester: Manchester University Press, 2002).

8

French Studies and Discourses of Sexuality

Emma Wilson

In his scintillating volume, *Freud, Proust and Lacan: Theory as Fiction*, Malcolm Bowie writes of the 'profoundly unsettling view of human sexuality enshrined' in the later volumes of *A la recherche du temps perdu.*[1] Bowie writes wonderfully about the narrator's attachment to Albertine:

> The asking of questions about Albertine – has she had lesbian relationships in the past? is she having, or contriving to have, such relationships now? how can truth be distinguished from falsehood in Albertine's reports on her actions and feelings? – is presented as one of the narrator's inescapable emotional needs. His mind comes to specialise ever more devotedly in the production and transformation of anxiety, and in the telling of tactical lies designed to surprise Albertine into self-disclosure.[2]

Bowie traces the relation between interpretation and desire in this long novel, responding to the two as interminable, and infinitely involved with one another. Looking beyond previous critical attempts to locate Albertine and define her sexuality, Bowie reminds us that 'Albertine's sexuality remains an enigma'.[3] He continues: 'Albertine cannot be known, unless this interminable passage from structure to structure is itself knowledge and our other notions of what it is to know are the products of a lingering infantile wish for comfort or mastery.'[4]

It has now long been recognised that literary and cultural studies in France have felt the impact of queer studies and of theoretical investigations of gender, pursued in the USA and UK, only latterly. Judith Butler's paradigm-shifting *Gender Trouble: Feminism and the Subversion of*

1   Malcolm Bowie, *Freud, Proust and Lacan: Theory as Fiction* (Cambridge: Cambridge University Press, 1987), p. 46.
2   Bowie, *Freud, Proust and Lacan*, p. 50.
3   Bowie, *Freud, Proust and Lacan*, p. 59.
4   Bowie, *Freud, Proust and Lacan*, p. 59.

Identity (1990) was only published in France in 2005.[5] Subsequently, translations of her works have appeared much more rapidly and Butler has been invited to give prestigious lectures in France (for example at the Ecole des Hautes Etudes en Sciences Sociales and the Ecole Normale Supérieure in 2009).[6] For *la rentrée* 2010, *Le Monde* carried an article on the new compulsory teaching of queer studies at Sciences Po, suggesting at once how far such discourses are now recognised within the academy in France and also how far this is still so novel as to be remarked on in the media. An irony of the belated receptivity to queer studies comes in the fact that Butler's work in its origins develops from critique of the works of theorists and philosophers writing in French, *Gender Trouble*, for example, engaging closely with works by Simone de Beauvoir, Michel Foucault, Luce Irigaray, Julia Kristeva and Monique Wittig.

French Studies in the UK has responded far more quickly to queer theory and its questioning of sexuality than related disciplines in France, in part through increased dialogue with French Studies in the USA, and in part through the productive interaction between academia and political activism in the wake of the AIDS crisis in the 1980s. While drawing attention to such responses and their importance for French Studies as a discipline within the UK, my aim here is also to look outwards to a broader understanding of reflection on discourses of sexuality in UK French Studies. To begin with Malcolm Bowie is instructive in this regard.

Bowie has been widely recognised as the most gifted and influential scholar of his generation in UK French Studies. His work in extending and enriching the discipline is entirely remarkable and is felt both in the extraordinarily generative moves in his own research between the fields of literary criticism, psychoanalysis, the history of art, philosophy, and music, and in the institutional changes he afforded through his work in a number of UK universities, at the Institute of Romance Studies, and at the European Humanities Research Centre. In his exploration of sexuality in the work of Proust, as in his exploration of so many other complex issues in art and literature – morality, difficulty, death – Bowie ensures the most generous, labile attention to his subject. In coruscating analyses, he demonstrates the highly complicated ways in which French literary writings, and Proust's in particular, have shown how sexuality is bound up with what it is to be a self and what it is to know another. Sexuality and interpretation are entirely enmeshed in this perspective.

---

5 Judith Butler, *Gender Trouble: Feminism and the Subversion of Identity* (New York and London: Routledge, 1990). The French edition is *Trouble dans le genre. Pour un féminisme de la subversion*, trans. Cynthia Kraus, with a preface by Eric Fassin (Paris: La Découverte, 2005).

6 Her first book to be translated into French was *The Psychic Life of Power: Theories in Subjection* (Stanford, CA: Stanford University Press, 1997). This appeared in French as *La Vie psychique du pouvoir. L'Assujetissement en théories*, trans. Brice Matthieussent, with a preface by Catherine Malabou (Paris: Léo Scheer, 2002).

Following Bowie, sometimes in dialogue with psychoanalysis, but also in sophisticated readings engaging with Foucault, with French feminism, with queer theory, with recent work in ethics, UK scholars of French Studies have cast light on a very wide territory of desire in literary texts, images and moving image works. I want to draw attention on the one hand to the ways in which this work looks spectacularly beyond binaries of straight and queer, while respecting diversity and political positioning, and on the other to the ways in which such work in its mass and in its complexity makes a concerted case for the seriousness and impact of engagement with discourses of sexuality in our understanding of narrative and interpretation, of ethics and the relation to the other, of identity politics and of what it means to be human. I want to say here that the treatment of these questions in literary and cultural production in French has been significantly critiqued and illuminated in UK French Studies. This has been one of the key developments in the discipline in the UK in the last quarter of a century and it is testimony to the embrace of equality and diversity in UK universities and to the embrace of interdisciplinarity (as represented in the most stellar terms by Bowie's work) and political engagement in the work of UK scholars.

Questions of sexuality, as they relate to interpretation and representation, have been addressed in examination of literary and cultural production in French of all periods. In an *état present* for the UK journal *French Studies* on 'Queer Theory and the Middle Ages', William Burgwinkle writes:

> Though it might surprise many, the Middle Ages are emerging as a kind of queer utopia, a historical period in which institutional state regulation as we know it hardly existed, in which marriage practices were not yet controlled entirely either by state or church and varied widely by class and region, in which same-sex segregation was a norm, particularly in intellectual communities, and in which love stories between men were common, if covert.[7]

Adding to the literature on the queer Middle Ages, Burgwinkle's *Sodomy, Masculinity and Law in Medieval Literature, 1050–1230* rethinks relations between male homosexuality and the legal system. His more recent *Sanctity and Pornography in Medieval Culture: On the Verge*, co-authored with Cary Howie, moves outwards from focus on queer sexualities to examine a specific nexus of relations between sanctity and pornography. The volume explores the persistence of fascination with pain and pleasure, bodily exposure and enclosure, showing how in the imaging and narrating of medieval saints' lives we find representations of desires and practices that continue, in the twenty-first century, to sustain and enable our bodies' transformation.

---

7 William Burgwinkle, 'Queer Theory and the Middle Ages', *French Studies* 60: 1 (2006), 79–88.

Where medieval texts and images here anticipate urgent concerns in thinking sexuality in the modern period, contemporary theory has been used very productively to illuminate desire and sexuality in France and Occitania of the Middle Ages. In his volume, *Love and Death in Medieval French and Occitan Courtly Literature: Martyrs to Love*, Simon Gaunt offers innovative treatment of the concept of martyrdom for love. His work explores the core issues of courtly ethics, rarefied in particular through engagement with the seminars of Jacques Lacan.

In the early modern period, very rich work has been generated by the research group 'Obscenity in Renaissance France', an AHRC-funded network headed by Hugh Roberts at Exeter University. The network is made up of 30 researchers from the UK, France, USA, Switzerland and the Netherlands. In 2007 a symposium on the topic was organised at Clare College, Cambridge. Also of note in the area of the French Renaissance is Gary Ferguson's *Queer (Re)Readings in the French Renaissance: Homosexuality, Gender, Culture*, which addresses authors such as Ronsard and Montaigne. On the seventeenth century, the work of Joseph Harris in his volume *Cross-Dressing in 17th-century France* uses queer theory and particularly the work of Judith Butler to illuminate the ambivalent position of cross-dressing within the literature, culture and history of seventeenth-century France. Nicholas Hammond's *Gossip, Sexuality and Scandal in France (1610–1715)* looks at a range of literary writings and also at areas of popular culture and social history, revising views of the currency and meanings of sexuality in the period.

In the modern period, we may note with less surprise the surge of interest in questions of sexuality, desire, and also adultery, divorce, inheritance, decadence and perversion. Here I would signal in particular the extraordinary contribution to work on discourses of sexuality in French Studies of Lisa Downing, who is Professor of French Discourses of Sexuality at the University of Exeter, and Director of the Centre for the Interdisciplinary Study of Sexuality and Gender in Europe. Downing's first book, emerging from a thesis supervised by Malcolm Bowie, *Desiring the Dead: Necrophilia and Nineteenth-Century French Literature*, ranges across the works of Sade, Baudelaire and Rachilde, whilst also investigating death and psychoanalysis. The volume, like so many others cited, not only explores an aspect of human sexuality, but also reaches outwards to an overarching view of the power of sexuality and its analysis to illuminate social and cultural patterns. As Downing contends, 'there is a different and quite contrary face of the nineteenth-century imagination in France, one which is overlooked if we concentrate only on the larger picture of social expansion'.[8] She demonstrates the ways in which a number of artistic innovations of the period are characterised by

8 Lisa Downing, *Desiring the Dead: Necrophilia and Nineteenth-Century French Literature* (Oxford: Legenda, 2003), p. 10.

'an insidious morbidity which may be seen to reveal the underside of the century's visible optimism'.[9] Downing has gone on to publish a volume on Foucault, with whose work on sexuality she enters into productive dialogue,[10] and also, among other projects, to co-edit special numbers of the *Journal of the History of Sexuality* and of *Psychology and Sexuality*.

If Downing's work has led the way in thinking about sexuality and the nineteenth-century imagination, Hannah Thompson's work in *Naturalism Redressed: Identity and Clothing in the Novels of Emile Zola*, and latterly on the relation between modern critical theories of the body, gender theory and monster theory, illuminates readings of realist and naturalist texts, illustrates strongly the ways in which studies of sexuality open out into questions about body morphology and the normative construction and regulation of identity.

Normative heterosexuality itself, its relation to the French legal system, and to social and cultural regulation, has also come under close scrutiny in the work of scholars of the nineteenth century. Diana Knight is pursuing a major study of realism and compulsory heterosexuality in the *Comédie humaine*. Of particular note, as well, is the critical work of Nicholas White who has variously explored the fictional representation of marriage, the family and divorce in nineteenth-century France in volumes such as *The Family in Crisis in Late Nineteenth-Century French Fiction*. He is currently pursuing work on adultery in late nineteenth- and early twentieth-century French writing. Andrew Counter has also produced groundbreaking work on the interrelation of sexuality and the family in the nineteenth century in his volume on literature, law and cultural politics, *Inheritance in Nineteenth-Century French Culture: Wealth, Knowledge and the Family*. He is currently working on representations of sexuality in nineteenth-century fiction, from Astolphe de Custine in the 1820s to Emile Zola at the *fin de siècle*.

Moving from the nineteenth into the twentieth century and the modern period, and also across language areas, Naomi Segal has, in an extensive body of work, brought together questions of psychoanalysis, the body, gender and sexuality. She brings the works of André Gide, and the questions they raise about sexuality, under close scrutiny in her important monograph *André Gide: Pederasty and Pedagogy*. Her most recent volume, *Consensuality: Didier Anzieu, Gender and the Sense of Touch*, looks at the ways in which Anzieu's work on the skin offers different psychoanalytic modes of thinking sensuality and contact.

In the twentieth century, questions of sexuality have often intersected with issues about life-writing and the construction of the self. These issues arise in the modern chapters of Michael Sheringham's influential *French Autobiography: Devices and Desires*. It is evidenced further in

---

9 Lisa Downing, *Desiring the Dead*, p. 11.
10 Lisa Downing, *The Cambridge Introduction to Michel Foucault* (Cambridge: Cambridge University Press, 2008).

Alex Hughes's prize-winning *Heterographies: Sexual Difference in French Autobiography*[11] that examines writings by Violette Leduc, Jean-Paul Sartre, Hervé Guibert, Marguerite Duras, André Gide, Marie Cardinal and Simone de Beauvoir. The imbrication of sexuality and the construction or performance of the self is explored by Claire Boyle in her volume *Consuming Autobiographies: Reading and Writing the Self in Post-War France* and in her current work on sexuality and the first person in film. Questions of sexuality, variously construed, also illuminate individual critical works on some of the major writers of the twentieth century, such as Ursula Tidd's *Simone de Beauvoir: Gender and Testimony* and James Williams's *The Erotics of Passage: Pleasure, Politics and Form in the Later Work of Marguerite Duras*.

Michael Worton and Judith Still edited an important anthology about interpretation and sexuality, *Textuality and Sexuality: Reading Theories and Practices*. My own *Sexuality and the Reading Encounter: Identity and Desire in Proust, Duras, Tournier and Cixous* attempted, around the same time, to draw together questions about reading and sexual identification across a range of major writers. More recently, further work integrating concerns with sexual tropes and the ways in which sexuality is bound up with larger issues of representation, exposure and crisis, has been done by Keith Reader in his volume *The Abject Object: Avatars of the Phallus in Contemporary French Theory, Literature and Film*, which uses theoretical writing by Julia Kristeva and Jacques Lacan to examine works by writers and filmmakers such as Georges Bataille, Christine Angot, Jean-Luc Godard and Gaspar Noé. In their co-written volume, *The New Pornographies: Explicit Sex in Recent French Fiction and Film*, Victoria Best and Martin Crowley extend critical examination to writers and filmmakers such as Michel Houellebecq, Catherine Millet and Catherine Breillat, whose use of pornographic material is seen to be indicative of important contemporary concerns.

While work on the modern and contemporary period has been typified by its attention to an extraordinarily diverse range of investments in sexuality, beyond straightforward categories of homosexual and heterosexual, it is important to recognise as well the work done in UK French departments to establish a queer canon of writing and filmmaking. The work of Lucille Cairns has been particularly influential in this respect in her edited volume, *Gay and Lesbian Cultures in France* and in the compendious critical investigations *Lesbian Desire in Post-1968 French Literature* and *Sapphism on Screen: Lesbian Desire in French and Francophone Cinema*. Important too, with relation to lesbian sexuality, has been the work of Renate Günther and Wendy Michallat in their co-edited volume, *Lesbian Inscriptions in Francophone Society and Culture*.

---

11 Alex Hughes, *Heterographies: Sexual Difference in French Autobiography* (Oxford: Berg, 1999). This volume was the winner of the first R. H. Gapper prize awarded by the Society for French Studies.

Drawing together lesbian and gay representations, Günther was also co-editor, with Owen Heathcote, of a special issue of the journal *Modern and Contemporary France*, 'Gays and Lesbians in Contemporary France: Politics, Media, Sexualities'. Heathcote himself was also previously co-editor, with Alex Hughes and James Williams, of *Gay Signatures: Gay and Lesbian Theory, Fiction and Film in France, 1945–1995*. Where Cairns has written thoughtfully on representations of lesbianism in French film, Nick Rees-Roberts has produced a strong critical overview of representations of male homosexuality on film in *French Queer Cinema*.

As exemplified in the critical engagement of many of the works cited, scholars in the UK have worked closely and directly on French discourses of sexuality, literary, cultural, political and theoretical. Where a critic like Downing has engaged with the work of Foucault, Bill Marshall in his monograph *Guy Hocquenghem* looked at one of the founders of the contemporary gay movement. Sarah Cooper inter-related questions arising from queer theory in the USA with concerns for identity and identification in French feminism in her *Relating to Queer Theory: Rereading Sexual Self-Definition with Irigaray, Kristeva, Wittig and Cixous*.

This chapter can only offer a sketch of this verdant research area in UK French Studies. A further indicative snapshot of the field can be found in looking at the programme of the 2007 conference of the Society of French Studies held in Birmingham. Here, in a panel on 'Queer Theory' chaired by James Williams, papers were given by Lisa Downing ('Michel Foucault and the Queer Self/Other'), Hector Kollias ('Making the Gay Self: Constructionism and the Resistance to Theory in Didier Eribon's work') and James Hartford ('Interaction and Transfer: On Queer Theory Finding Itself'). A keynote talk was given by Didier Eribon who has proved one of the most prominent researchers on queer issues in France. Engagement with discourses of sexuality has allowed researchers in French Studies in the UK to transform analysis of literary and cultural works in the French language. Such work is vital and ongoing in our diverse society as we continue through the twenty-first century.

Bibliography

Best, Victoria and Martin Crowley, *The New Pornographies: Explicit Sex in Recent French Fiction and Film* (Manchester: Manchester University Press, 2008).

Bowie, Malcolm, *Freud, Proust and Lacan: Theory as Fiction* (Cambridge: Cambridge University Press, 1987).

Boyle, Claire, *Consuming Autobiographies: Reading and Writing the Self in Post-War France* (Oxford: Legenda, 2007).

Burgwinkle, William, *Sodomy, Masculinity and Law in Medieval Literature, 1050–1230* (Cambridge: Cambridge University Press, 2004).

Burgwinkle, William, 'Queer Theory and the Middle Ages', *French Studies* 60: 1 (2006), 79–88.

Burgwinkle, William and Cary Howie, *Sanctity and Pornography in Medieval Culture: On the Verge* (Manchester: Manchester University Press, 2010).

Butler, Judith, *Gender Trouble: Feminism and the Subversion of Identity* (New York and London: Routledge, 1990) .

Butler, Judith, *The Psychic Life of Power: Theories in Subjection* (Stanford, CA: Stanford University Press, 1997) .

Butler, Judith, *Trouble dans le genre. Pour un féminisme de la subversion*, trans. Cynthia Kraus, with a preface by Eric Fassin (Paris: La Découverte, 2005).

Butler, Judith, *La Vie psychique du pouvoir. L'Assujetissement en théories*, trans. Brice Matthieussent, with a preface by Catherine Malabou (Paris: Léo Scheer, 2002).

Cairns, Lucille (ed.), *Gay and Lesbian Cultures in France* (Bern: Peter Lang, 2002).

Cairns, Lucille, *Lesbian Desire in Post-1968 French Literature* (Lampeter: Edwin Mellen Press, 2002).

Cairns, Lucille, *Sapphism on Screen: Lesbian Desire in French and Francophone Cinema* (Edinburgh: Edinburgh University Press, 2006).

Cooper, Sarah, *Relating to Queer Theory: Rereading Sexual Self-Definition with Irigaray, Kristeva, Wittig and Cixous* (Bern: Peter Lang, 2000).

Downing, Lisa, *Desiring the Dead: Necrophilia and Nineteenth-Century French Literature* (Oxford: Legenda, 2003).

Downing, Lisa, *The Cambridge Introduction to Michel Foucault* (Cambridge: Cambridge University Press, 2008).

Downing, Lisa, special issue of *Journal of the History of Sexuality*, ed. with Peter Cryle, on 'Feminine Sexual Pathologies in Nineteenth- and Early-Twentieth-Century Europe', vol. 18, no. 1 (January 2009).

Downing, Lisa, special issue of *Psychology and Sexuality* ed. with Peter Cryle, on 'The Natural and The Normal in the History of Sexuality', vol. 1, no. 3 (September 2010).

Ferguson, Gary, *Queer (Re)Readings in the French Renaissance: Homosexuality, Gender, Culture* (Aldershot and Burlington: Ashgate, 2008).

Gaunt, Simon, *Love and Death in Medieval French and Occitan Courtly Literature: Martyrs to Love* (Oxford: Oxford University Press, 2006).

Günther, Renate and Wendy Michallat (eds), *Lesbian Inscriptions in Francophone Society and Culture* (Durham: Durham Modern Languages Series, 2007).

Günther, Renate and Owen Heathcote (eds), 'Gays and Lesbians in Contemporary France: Politics, Media, Sexualities', special issue of *Modern and Contemporary France* (2006).

Hammond, Nicholas, *Gossip, Sexuality and Scandal in France (1610–1715)* (Oxford: Peter Lang, 2011).

Harris, Joseph, *Cross-Dressing in 17th-century France* (Tübingen: Narr, 2005).

Hughes, Alex, *Heterographies: Sexual Difference in French Autobiography* (Oxford: Berg, 1999).

Marshall, Bill, *Guy Hocquenghem: Gay Beyond Identity* (Durham, NC: Duke University Press, 1996).

Reader, Keith, *The Abject Object: Avatars of the Phallus in Contemporary French Theory, Literature and Film* (Amsterdam and New York: Rodopi, 2006).

Rees-Roberts, Nick, *French Queer Cinema* (Edinburgh: Edinburgh University Press, 2008).

Segal, Naomi, *André Gide: Pederasty and Pedagogy* (Oxford: Oxford University Press, 1998).

Segal, Naomi, *Consensuality: Didier Anzieu, gender and the sense of touch* (Amsterdam and New York: Rodopi, 2009).

Sheringham, Michael, *French Autobiography: Devices and Desires. Rousseau to Perec* (Oxford: Oxford University Press, 1993).

Thompson, Hannah, *Naturalism Redressed: Identity and Clothing in the Novels of Emile Zola* (Oxford: EHRC/Legenda, 2004).

Tidd, Ursula, *Simone de Beauvoir: Gender and Testimony* (Cambridge: Cambridge University Press, 1999).

Williams, James, *The Erotics of Passage: Pleasure, Politics and Form in the Later Work of Marguerite Duras* (Liverpool: Liverpool University Press, 1997).

Wilson, Emma, *Sexuality and the Reading Encounter: Identity and Desire in Proust, Duras, Tournier and Cixous* (Oxford: Oxford University Press, 1996).

Worton, Michael and Judith Still (eds), *Textuality and Sexuality: Reading Theories and Practices* (Manchester: Manchester University Press, 1995).

Part IV: The Place of Literature

9

Integrated Learning: Teaching Literature in French

Simon Gaunt and Nicholas Harrison

Initially we were to contribute separate chapters to this collection, one on pre-modern French Studies, another on the place of literature in French Studies today. We decided, however, to write this piece together in the belief that the two questions are intimately related, on several levels (at least for UK universities, on which we shall focus). In practice, pre-modern studies in university French programmes are to a significant extent literary studies; and such pressures as exist to move away from pre-modern areas are closely linked to wider pressures to move away from literature of any era. Much of this chapter is concerned with the sources of pressure, which are multiple and sometimes murky. To put it more positively, though, we want to suggest that there are still good reasons to study French/francophone literature, and that the reasons for studying contemporary francophone film, say, are fundamentally similar to the reasons for studying medieval poetry.

According to survey results reported in Michael Worton's 2009 *Review of Modern Foreign Languages Provision in Higher Education in England*, undertaken for HEFCE, 'By far the most widely-reported trend was a move towards a greater emphasis on contemporary cultural studies – including film studies, contemporary literature and "area studies"'.[1] Trends in teaching and research are closely linked and the RAE 2008 *Sub-panel Overview Report* for French noted that: 'The relatively low numbers of specialists in the fields of linguistics, medieval studies, Renaissance and seventeenth-century studies continue to be a cause of concern.'[2] The report expressed regret that 'appointments seem to be failing to

---

1 Michael Worton, *Review of Modern Foreign Languages Provision in Higher Education in England* (London: HEFCE, 2009), p. 25, § 124, online resource consulted 25 November 2010.

2 Higher Education Funding Council, For England. *RAE 2008 Subject Overview Reports. Panel M, UOA 52, French* (London: HEFCE, 2009), p. 6, online resource, consulted 25 November 2010.

keep pace with retirements' for the medieval period,[3] that although 'the demographic reduction of the French Renaissance, noted in 2001, has stabilised', nonetheless, 'fewer than 20 national departments submitting to the 2008 French sub-panel have Renaissance specialists',[4] and that for the seventeenth century 'even some large departments are without a specialist'.[5] This chapter airs some possible reasons for this trend.

Shortly after relaying respondents' remarks on the tendency towards contemporary cultural studies, the Worton review notes: 'several respondents noted the need to find an appropriate and attractive balance for students between linguistic and cultural content, whilst other felt challenged by the perceived need to ensure that their subject remains "relevant"'.[6] Three crucial ideas are encapsulated here: the question of what is attractive, or believed to be attractive, to students; the question of what is relevant (to students' lives, to society, etc.), or believed to be relevant; and the relation of language study to other dimensions of the discipline/degree programme.

The question of attractiveness is tied to what is taught in French classes in schools. In this respect, as in all others, there are notable variations and disparities within the UK school system, but in general the school curriculum has gone further than universities in the move towards contemporary cultural and area studies in French, as well as placing a greater emphasis on communication skills. Whatever the reasons for that shift, it has done nothing to prevent the decline of French at A level; indeed, it is not impossible that it has been a factor in that decline. Another difficulty here (perhaps inherent, to some extent, in the transition between school and university, or between basic and advanced language study, but arguably exacerbated by the current syllabus) is the fact that whereas those who *do* choose to study French at A level and beyond are often those who are particularly interested in language study as such, language study seems to be what puts off many students who might otherwise flourish in other dimensions of a languages degree – whether those dimensions are literary or not. The very high recruitment rates for English A level and English degrees offer a sharp contrast with French; on that basis, it would seem that literary studies are very attractive to large numbers of good students. Could more of them be diverted into a French degree if they saw it as an opportunity to study literature at a high level?

The issue of 'attractiveness' comes into play on other levels. First, there is the question of which university and which programme to choose, for those who have decided to study French. There is tremendous variety, in terms of different combined degrees and of differences

3 *RAE 2008 Subject Overview Reports*, p. 8.
4 *RAE 2008 Subject Overview Reports*, p. 9.
5 *RAE 2008 Subject Overview Reports*, p. 9.
6 Worton, *Review*, p. 25, § 127.

between French programmes. Some students will no doubt try to weigh all these options carefully, but numerous factors with little direct connection to the syllabus come into play. Many students will be strongly influenced by a university's general prestige, its location, and its ranking in league tables. In most universities that are strongly positioned in these general terms, those running French programmes continue to have the luxury of selecting from among straight-A students, and they are likely to be in a stronger and more confident position when it comes to designing a syllabus of whose merits students can be convinced after, rather than before, they arrive. Second, there is the question of the choices students are offered once they do arrive. Choice is important, but in any programme it will be determined by the expertise of staff and then modulated by demands of coherence, balance and intellectual progression. A crucial consideration here is that new students are not well placed to take an informed decision about they want, given that large parts of the university syllabus will have had no forerunner in the topics studied at school.

In our experience, it is certainly possible to convince students that courses in literature, including pre-modern literature, are every bit as interesting and rewarding as courses on non-literary topics. When we survey our incoming students at King's College London, most have never studied French literature before (8 out of 9 in one recent first-year group, the exception being a student educated in France), and only a minority have studied pre-modern literature even in English (4 out of 9 in the same group). Students for whom literature is new tend to be worried that they will be disadvantaged in relation to students who have done literary A levels, but that is not our experience.[7] Most new students assume initially that they will concentrate where possible on options in cinema, contemporary society, history and politics, along with modern literature. In practice, after their first year, many opt entirely for literary courses, and many for pre-modern courses. What produces the change in their attitudes is an introductory survey course that includes literary texts from the Middle Ages through to the twenty-first century, a course that is taught in small groups by all staff with literary research interests. The decision to make this course compulsory, along with other aspects of curriculum design, rests on a collective conviction that a literary syllabus with chronological depth remains intellectually valid and enriching in the twenty-first century. It means too that, as we continue to appoint scholars of pre-modern literature to teaching posts, those scholars have the opportunity to teach in their fields of expertise: on the

---

7   We are thinking here not only of students' success on literature courses at university, but also, prior to that, of admissions decisions (at Cambridge, where we both worked previously, as well as at King's). The latter point is also worth emphasising in relation to another trend at the level of schools, where literary study as part of a language course has become increasingly associated with the private sector.

compulsory survey course and, more importantly, on options at higher levels, including MA; which in turn can lead, through PhD supervision, to the renewal of the discipline and the profession.

Crucially, study of the distant past is not identified solely with specialist interests; all staff are involved equitably in delivering a curriculum that reflects the department's full range of research interests. The assumption behind this is that all students gain from exposure to pre-modern texts, even those who will go on to specialise in modern literature or non-literary fields, in later undergraduate years or as graduates. Studying pre-modern culture is thus presented as a vital part of the discipline of French in the first year; and it is something that most students come to see as worthwhile and attractive.[8]

The question of 'relevance' is another where a lot depends on perception. It is linked to 'attractiveness', and to employability. Many people will assume automatically that a degree in the social sciences or the hard sciences is more 'relevant', and a greater asset on the employment market, than a degree in literary studies. As it happens, however, among non-vocational degrees, languages offer some of the very best employment prospects.[9] To what extent graduates of any non-vocational degree use their subject-specific skills in subsequent employment is harder to gauge, but our assumption would be that across all jobs taken by all such graduates, many of the necessary skills are transferable, and the connections to the undergraduate syllabus mostly indirect (how many geography graduates, say, work as geographers?). All of this suggests that there is no particular reason to address the issue of 'relevance' in terms of French degrees, languages degrees, or even literary studies; indeed (given that there seems little prospect of a HEFCE review of English literature provision in higher education), there is something disingenuous about the idea that relevance is a particular problem for

8 We have recently carried these principles through to the new second year of our undergraduate programme, in which most options, from a smaller range than before, are now literary and transhistorical. One, called *The Idea of France* (online resource, consulted 9 August 2010), begins with the *Chanson de Roland* and ends with *Le Chagrin et la pitié*, drawing substantially on material from Pierre Nora's *Les Lieux de mémoire*; it is designed to appeal to students of literature, but also to students on our European Studies programme, which has an orientation towards political science. Joint honours students (i.e. most of our students) have a free choice among these modules; single honours students are required to study pre-modern as well as modern literature. In their final year and at MA level, students have a free choice of modules, which are tied closely to staff research interests.
9 According to the Higher Education Statistics Agency, unemployment rates for new graduates in languages are lower, at 8.9 per cent, than for a wide variety of other subjects including social studies (9.5 per cent), maths (10.1 per cent), business (10.6 per cent), physical science (10.6 per cent), engineering and technology (13.1 per cent), and computer science (17 per cent); from *Destinations of Leavers of Higher Education in the United Kingdom for the Academic Year 2008/09*, online resource, consulted 9 August 2010.

university modern languages provision. Rather, alongside questions about the teaching of French in schools, the pertinent questions are much wider ones about the nature and purposes of education, especially non-vocational education.

This is not the place to pursue these questions in any depth, but, with regard to our immediate topic, we would note that we consider the idea that contemporary literature or popular culture is inherently more 'relevant' than older literature simplistic. If what you are interested in is, say, contemporary French attitudes to 'race', there are clearly good reasons to approach the topic historically. Moreover, one could argue that to understand the French (for whatever purpose, including doing business with them) one needs to understand how they have been educated; which includes the fairly traditional literary education that remains an essential component of the baccalaureate and is inextricably linked to a certain notion of Frenchness. On another level, however, it is possible to reach an informed view about attitudes to 'race', to stick with that example, without taking a detour via literature (or song, etc.) of any era. A crude or narrow notion of 'relevance' will tend to lead you out of the arts and humanities altogether, and towards such areas as the (mythologised) quest for a cure for cancer or pollution-free energy, rather than towards contemporary cultural or area studies. A serious discussion of this issue would need, then, to encompass a critique of the very notion of 'relevance', and such characteristics of current political discourse as an over-emphasis on 'the national interest' or the economic benefits of a degree (or indeed the extra-educational 'impact' of research).

Particularly with regard to the perceived (ir)relevance of pre-modern studies, those last points may seem too abstract or too negative, especially for the purposes of dealing with university managers. But another argument that may carry more weight with them, and that is more concrete (if somewhat circular conceptually), relates to the assessment of research quality. The RAE's benchmarks of excellence encouraged UK academics to think of their work in an international context.[10] This suggests that it is appropriate, when we consider what makes for excellent, well-rounded research communities and curricula in the discipline of French, to look to international points of comparison. Thinking of the decline, in the UK university sector, in research on, and in the teaching of, pre-modern literature, as reported by the RAE sub-panel in French, one might ask, then, whether there has been a comparable decline in the best French departments elsewhere in the world.

10 The quality profiles are defined in Higher Education Funding Council for England, *Quality Profiles: Introduction to the RAE 2008* (London: HEFCE, 2009) online resource, consulted 9 August 2010. The top ranking (4*) was defined as 'Quality that is world-leading in terms of originality, significance and rigour'; the definition of 3* was 'Quality that is internationally excellent in terms of originality, significance and rigour but which nonetheless falls short of the highest standards of excellence'.

One obvious point of comparison here might be France, but the stakes in France are different from those in countries where French is not the (or a) national language. A better point of comparison is the USA. Quite apart from the connections and similarities between the UK's and the USA's relation to French, the prevalence of US universities in all international league tables leaves no doubt as to their pre-eminence, or at least, their perceived pre-eminence. For instance, in the Times Higher Education-QS World University Rankings 2009, eight out of ten of the top universities in the humanities are in the USA (Harvard, Berkeley, Yale, Princeton, Stanford, Chicago, UCLA, and Columbia; the other two are Oxford and Cambridge).[11] There are no subject-specific tables comparable to UK RAE quality profiles, but US ranking tables of research universities throw up a very similar cast of characters.[12] If we then survey the profile of research and teaching in French of the top US universities, we find that all those universities with French programmes still undertake research and teaching across the full chronological range of the discipline, indeed, are actively committed to the very areas that seem to be in decline in the UK. One might even argue that in practice, for various reasons, high quality is strongly associated with this very range.

To a significant extent the same can still be said of the UK, despite the decline in pre-modern studies. According to the rankings produced through analysis of the results of RAE 2008, all of the top 15 French departments in the UK preserve pre-modern literature. Indeed, for most of these departments, it is a very significant element in their research and teaching profile, at least according to their self-presentations online. Furthermore, according to the ranking tables produced on the basis of the RAE 2008 quality profiles, the highest ranking university to teach no pre-modern literature at all comes in about half way down the list, with most of the universities that concentrate exclusively on the modern and contemporary periods in the bottom quartile.[13]

Having presented this argument in fairly strong terms, we should add some riders. First, we do not want to overstate our confidence in league

---

11 See *Times Higher Education-QS World University Rankings 2009. Arts and Humanities* (London: TSL Education Ltd, 2009), online resource, consulted 9 August 2010.

12 See, for example, Elizabeth Capaldi *et al. The Top American Research Universities: 2009 Annual Report* (Tempe, AZ: The Center for Measuring University Performance, 2009), p. 8, online resource, consulted 9 August 2010, where the top 10 universities overall are listed as Harvard, Yale, Stanford, Princeton, MIT, the University of Michigan at Ann Arbor, Northwestern, Columbia, the University of Texas at Austin and Chicago.

13 We realise that not all tables give exactly the same rank order. For convenience we refer to the THE's rankings in French on pp. 11–12 of its 'Table of excellence', see 'RAE 2008, The results', *Times Higher Education* (18 December 2008), online resource, consulted 9 August 2010. The top 15 departments are: Aberdeen, St Andrew's, Cambridge, Durham, Exeter, Kent, King's, Leeds, Manchester, Nottingham, Oxford, Reading, Sheffield, UCL, Warwick. Of these 13 employ medievalists and 13 early modern specialists; only one of these institutions has no specialist in an earlier field.

tables, including those produced by the RAE. Second, as we have already implied indirectly in discussing 'attractiveness', many factors other than the syllabus, or the range and quality of research to which it is tied, may affect the rankings.[14] Third, a fair amount of research in French Studies (for example, film, cultural studies, linguistics and contemporary area studies) was not submitted to the French RAE sub-panel but to other panels, such as European studies. Some might argue that the French sub-panel's quality profiles suggested a degree of prejudice in favour of literary studies. However, its report makes it clear that a great deal of work in non-literary fields was also submitted to it in 2008, while the tone of the report hardly suggests any prejudice against non-literary subjects.[15] So, sticking with the possibility of RAE success as an argument that may carry weight, and without pretending to have explored the issues fully here, we want to emphasise that the implication of the panel's remarks on pre-modern studies was that the quality of research in the discipline of French *as a whole* will be severely compromised if the national decline in chronological depth in literary study is not halted (and indeed reversed). To put it another way, in terms that go beyond the RAE, the quality profiles in French as a whole seem to suggest that research in *all* areas of the discipline is qualitatively improved by being embedded in a broad sense of the discipline that continues to embrace and promote its full chronological range.

We do not intend this to be an argument against models of the discipline that do not foreground literature. Indeed, the internal variety of French is something to celebrate and there are several ways of embedding research and teaching in a wider and deeper context. Our own experience suggests that even literary researchers in predominantly literary departments will find that some of their main interlocutors and sources of inspiration come from outside anything one might call French Studies. This variety and interdisciplinarity is reflected in most degree programmes, too: in our own institution, the predominantly literary degree programmes in French run alongside, and overlap with, programmes including comparative literature, European studies and film. Many European studies students take literary options, and many French students take options in history and politics.

---

14 The capacity to recruit PhD students, for example, which feeds into research assessment and is seen as a ready indicator of research quality in many other subject areas (both for individual researchers, and for the subject area as such), is not a reliable indicator in French, where the pool of prospective students is small and where contingencies such as a university's location and its student exchange and funding mechanisms have a proportionately larger effect.

15 See *RAE 2008, Subject Overview Reports*, pp. 10–11. The fields listed are text and image studies, film studies, modern French thought, philosophy and theory, francophone and postcolonial areas, French linguistics, political, historical and social studies.

Part of the point here is that even relatively traditional French pro-grammes have been far from static in recent decades. We have spoken so far of certain circumstantial pressures promoting change, but the sources of change have been intellectual, too. Most departments that once concentrated on 'French literature', meaning canonical metropoli-tan literature, have expanded into areas including film, 'theory', history and francophone/postcolonial cultures, even if they have remained attached to literary studies to a significant degree. Both terms in the phrase 'French literature' have come under scrutiny: the centrality of France and French culture to French programmes – and indeed to francophone culture – has been challenged (which complicates an 'area studies' model, too), and there has been growing scepticism, in French Studies as in English studies, about the historical foundations of liter-ary study, which include nationalism and its fetishisation of the relation between a 'national' literature, the 'national' language, and national genius.[16] That sort of theme cries out to be examined historically, but the pressure to expand the syllabus geographically and conceptually has often taken resources away from earlier periods, even where this has not been a deliberate policy.

In that broad and heterogeneous context, perhaps the only thing still holding 'French' together as a discipline has been the integral place given to language learning. That too may be unsettled, however. For one thing, many of those teaching area studies courses have been trained in other disciplines (history, political science and so on) and may be unwilling, and even ill-equipped, to contribute to (or invest intellec-tually in) language teaching as such. For another, from the sceptical perspective outlined above, the association between language study and literary study (and nationalism) suddenly appears a kind of historical accident, as does a certain Eurocentricity.[17] At this point, intellectual arguments may converge with contingent pressures around the funding of home/EU undergraduates, the high level of overseas student fees, and the linguistic limitations of most 'JYA' (Junior Year Abroad) students, to produce momentum towards 'world literature' courses, say, or other

---

16 Classic treatments of this topic include Antoine Compagnon, *La Troisième République des lettres* (Paris: Seuil, 1983), and George Steiner, 'To civilize our gentlemen', in *Language and Silence: Essays 1958–1966* (London: Faber & Faber, 1967), pp. 75–88. In relation to the French Studies context today, the latter now appears at once prescient and old-fashioned.

17 This Eurocentricity starts with the traditional emphasis in the UK on French above any other foreign language. The arguments for protecting and promoting French may include France's geographical and cultural proximity, but are also pragmatic: it would be very difficult for the teaching of Chinese, say, to become generalised, given the need for a critical mass of willing learners and of teachers at all levels; and a focus on Chinese rather than French or any other language would remain restrictive and, in key respects, equally arbitrary.

'content' modules in which the prerequisite of foreign language learning is dropped.[18]

We come back, then, to the third point we identified at the start – the question of the relation of French language learning to other dimensions of the degree. We suggested that although many UK students are put off French by the prospect or experience of language learning, those students who do want to take French degrees are generally keen on the language-learning dimension of the degree; for most prospective students, we would suggest, it is the predominant attraction. This is one of the reasons why it is easy to put excessive or simplistic emphasis on the importance of the 'attractiveness' of the 'content' side of the degree to prospective undergraduates. (Others on which we have touched include general issues of prestige, which are tied up in complicated ways with research and research assessment.) The same goes for 'relevance', with regard to prospective students and to prospective employers: as noted earlier, languages degrees are, if anything, often considered more relevant than other degrees in arts and humanities (more than English, say, although English is a much more popular degree); and relatedly, language graduates have a strong record when it comes to getting jobs. The relative success of language degrees in these regards is doubtless less to do with the specific syllabus, of whatever sort it may be, than with language skills, allied with the maturity and independence students gain during their year abroad.

What arguments remain, then, for continuing to study literature, and to link language study to literary study, as part of a French degree – or of some French degrees? The background arguments, we suggested, are fundamentally general ones about the attractions and benefits of a non-vocational degree in the arts and humanities, or, more generally still, of any non-vocational education. In our more specific case, one part of the argument would necessarily turn on the question of the intellectual and cultural value of literary tradition and of literature as such, a topic we cannot hope to pursue here but on which there has been a renewed proliferation of work in recent years. In this respect, any crisis of confidence in French literary studies again needs to be understood in a much wider academic and socio-cultural context.[19] Another part of

18 For further discussion of the tensions between the intellectual ambitions of 'world literature' and its foreign-language underpinnings, see Nicholas Harrison, 'Life on the Second Floor', review article on *Comparative Literature in an Age of Globalization*, ed. Haun Saussy, *Comparative Literature* 59 (2007), 332–48. Similarly, the intellectual and comparative ambitions of some recent scholarship on earlier literature are compromised by limited linguistic range and Anglocentrism in the Anglo-American academy; see Simon Gaunt, 'Can the Middle Ages be postcolonial?', *Comparative Literature* 61 (2009), 160–76.

19 Recent work on this topic in English includes Marjorie Garber, *A Manifesto for Literary Studies* (Seattle, Washington: Washington University Press, 2004); J. Hillis Miller, *On Literature: Thinking in Action* (London: Routledge, 2002); Eli Park Sorensen, *Postcolonial*

the argument would turn on the pedagogical richness of literary texts, linked with their constitutive ability always to be about something other than themselves, to introduce us compellingly to perspectives different from our own (from different cultures, from different eras), to make us think again about things we take for granted. And another part of the argument, which would apply to languages degrees more strongly than to English degrees, would turn more specifically on their linguistic sophistication and variety. Ideally, a university programme in French will facilitate a productive dialectic between language learning and the objects that it makes accessible and that support it, objects whose riches deepen as one's knowledge of the language deepens, and which deepen that knowledge.[20]

That way of putting things may seem grandiose or old-fashioned, but a similar idea can be expressed in more contemporary terms. The European Union's policy is to promote multilingualism; it aims for a situation (a distant dream in the UK) in which every EU citizen can speak at least two foreign languages in addition to his or her mother tongue. In practical terms, it recommends content and language integrated learning (CLIL), which involves teaching a curricular subject through the medium of a language other than that normally used.[21] The EU multilingualism website gives the example of history lessons being taught in English in a school in Spain; and states that: 'CLIL is taking place and has been found to be effective in all sectors of education from primary through to adult and higher education. Its success has been growing over the past 10 years and continues to do so.' Ten key benefits of integrated learning are listed, including the way it 'develops multilingual interests and attitudes', 'increases learners' motivation and confidence in both the language and the subject being taught', and 'develops intercultural communication skills'. All of these benefits could be associated with literary study, and some – 'builds intercultural knowledge and understanding', or 'provides opportunities to study content through different perspectives' – read almost like descriptions of the things a French teacher may hope literature can do.

Studies and the Literary: Theory, Interpretation and the Novel (Basingstoke: Palgrave Macmillan, 2010); Michael Wood, *Literature and the Taste of Knowledge* (Cambridge University Press, 2005). In French, it includes Antoine Compagnon, *La Littérature pour quoi faire?* (Paris: Collège de France/Fayard, 2007); Dominique Maingueneau, *Contre Saint Proust ou la fin de la littérature* (Paris: Belin, 2006); William Marx, *L'Adieu à la littérature: histoire d'une dévalorisation, XVIIIe–XXe siècle* (Paris: Minuit, 2005); Jacques Rancière, *Politique de la littérature* (Paris: Galilée, 2007); Tzvetan Todorov, *La Littérature en péril* (Paris: Flammarion, 2007); Alain Viala, *La Culture littéraire* (Paris: PUF, 2009).

20 One important element of this 'deepening' can be the historical study of language through literary texts, in that learning how to read earlier forms of French undoubtedly improves a student's grasp of modern French.

21 See 'Language Teaching: Content and language integrated learning', *European Commission: Multilingualism* (n.d.), online resource, consulted 9 August 2010.

Bibliography

Compagnon, Antoine, *La Littérature pour quoi faire?* (Paris: Collège de France/Fayard, 2007).
Compagnon, Antoine, *La Troisième République des lettres* (Paris: Seuil, 1983).
Garber, Marjorie, *A Manifesto for Literary Studies* (Seattle, Washington: Washington University Press, 2004).
Gaunt, Simon, 'Can the Middle Ages be postcolonial?', *Comparative Literature* 61 (2009), 160–76.
Harrison, Nicholas, 'Life on the Second Floor', review article on *Comparative Literature in an Age of Globalization*, ed. Haun Saussy, *Comparative Literature* 59 (2007), 332–48.
Hillis Miller, J., *On Literature: Thinking in Action* (London: Routledge, 2002).
Maingueneau, Dominique, *Contre Saint Proust ou la fin de la littérature* (Paris: Belin, 2006).
Marx, William, *L'Adieu à la littérature: histoire d'une dévalorisation, XVIIIe–XXe siècle* (Paris: Minuit, 2005).
Nora, Pierre, *Les Lieux de mémoire*, 3 vols (Paris: Gallimard, 1997).
Park Sorensen, Eli, *Postcolonial Studies and the Literary: Theory, Interpretation and the Novel* (Basingstoke: Palgrave Macmillan, 2010).
Rancière, Jacques, *Politique de la littérature* (Paris: Galilée, 2007).
Steiner, George, 'To Civilize our Gentlemen', in *Language and Silence: Essays 1958–1966* (London: Faber & Faber, 1967), pp. 75–88.
Todorov, Tzvetan, *La Littérature en péril* (Paris: Flammarion, 2007).
Viala, Alain, *La Culture littéraire* (Paris: PUF, 2009).
Wood, Michael, *Literature and the Taste of Knowledge* (Cambridge University Press, 2005).
Worton, Michael, *Review of Modern Foreign Languages Provision in Higher Education in England* (London: HEFCE, 2009), available at www.hefce.ac.uk/pubs/hefce/2009/09_41/ (consulted 25 November 2010).

Websites

Capaldi, Elizabeth, *et al.*, *The Top American Research Universities: 2009 Annual Report* (Tempe, AZ: The Center for Measuring University Performance, 2009), available at http://mup.asu.edu/research2009.pdf (consulted 9 August 2010).
'Language Teaching: Content and Language Integrated Learning', *European Commission: Multilingualism* (n.d.), available at http://ec.europa.eu/education/languages/language-teaching/doc236_en.htm (consulted 9 August 2010).
'Module 2010–11 5AAFF252 *The Idea of France*' (London: King's College, London, 2010), available at www.kcl.ac.uk/schools/humanities/depts/french/ug/current/second/mod1011/f252.html (consulted 9 August 2010)
Higher Education Funding Council for England, *Destinations of leavers of Higher Education in the United Kingdom for the academic year 2008/09*, available at www.hesa.ac.uk/dox/pressOffice/sfr148/sfr148_table_3.pdf?v=230810 (consulted 9 August 2010).
Higher Education Funding Council for England, *RAE 2008 Subject Overview Reports. Panel M, UOA 52, French* (London: HEFCE, 2009), available at www.rae.ac.uk/pubs/2009/ov/ (consulted 25 November 2010).
Higher Education Funding Council for England, *Quality profiles: Introduction to the RAE 2008* (London: HEFCE, 2009) avalable at www.rae.ac.uk/results/intro.aspx (consulted 9 August 2010).
Times Higher Education, 'RAE 2008, The results', Times Higher Education (8 December (2008), online, available at www.timeshighereducation.co.uk/Journals/THE/THE/18_December_2008/attachments/RAE_2008_THE_RESULTS.pdf (consulted 9 August 2010).
Times Higher Education-QS World University Rankings 2009: Arts and Humanities (London: TSL Education Ltd, 2009), available at www.timeshighereducation.co.uk/hybrid.asp?typeCode=422 (consulted 9 August 2010).

10

Oxford, Theatre and Quarrels

Alain Viala

Oxford University's French subfaculty occupies a rather unusual position in the network of French Studies in the UK: the size of the department, the collegiate structure of the university, and certain of its very specific traditions all contribute to this singularity. But in recent years this department has, like so many others, undergone a series of necessary changes; some of them welcome and others less so. Certain of these changes will doubtless require development in the coming years: it is these changes that form the subject of this chapter.

It begins with a rapid overview, rendered absolutely necessary by the singularities mentioned above. But the function of this quick sketch, which does not claim to be exhaustive, is largely to provide a background for two proposals, addressed in the two subsequent sections. In keeping with the spirit of this volume, this is not an attempt to present a complete survey of the activities of the department; rather the aim is to focus on specific case studies. The two evoked here concern the early modern period, which is one of the sectors most beset with worries for the future. It should be emphasised that this is merely one viewpoint: both the overview and the choice of examples are clearly based on the author's (or the authors')[1] own experience, and represent only his (or their) opinion. Equally, the resulting suggestions are simply intended to provide material for wider reflection.

Overview

The French subfaculty at Oxford comprises more than 30 postholders (31 or 35, including the specialists in French linguistics, who are also attached to the linguistics faculty). To this we add college lecturers, a

---

1 This chapter was written by Alain Viala, with the help of information and opinions from Helen Swift and Rowan Tomlinson concerning the 'pre-modern'.

peculiarity of the Oxford collegiate system[2] (their number can vary, but only within certain limits, and the current total stands at 18), junior research fellows, and visiting professors and researchers occupying set posts.[3] In all, then, a faculty of somewhere in the region of 60 people involved in teaching and research. The size of the department enables it to cover every period of literature (from the medieval to the present day), and a whole range of specific themes (including womens' studies, francophone studies and cinema).

In terms of students, the department attracts around 200 new undergraduates each year. Of fifty or so graduate students, about fifteen follow the MSt programme, while the others are preparing DPhils. The precise number of new undergraduates is determined by the number of places available in each college, with the collegiate structure playing a major regulatory role.[4] These days the number of candidates greatly exceeds the number of available places (to give an approximate idea, only one in two interview candidates, already pre-selected based on their applications, is ultimately accepted.) Quantatively then, French at Oxford is not threatened by a crisis in falling rolls.

To round off this brief description, it is important to mention, alongside an important and very active language centre, two particular resources.[5] The first is the Maison Française d'Oxford (MFO). Its main purpose is to host French researchers (12 young researchers for periods of one year, and 4–6 senior Centre National de la Recherche Scientifique (CNRS) researchers for two or three years), some of whom are also attached to the subfaculty. In addition, the MFO houses a library and projection room, as well as providing a venue for seminars and conferences. The second resource is the Voltaire Foundation. Though mainly occupied with philological work (the edition of the complete works of Voltaire) and publication, the foundation also contributes to the research life of the university through the Oxford Besterman Centre for the Enlightenment (OBCE).

Undergraduates are therefore offered lectures, seminars and/or tutorials on all areas of literary history and French intellectual life, while graduates can attend both the seminars specifically aimed at the MSt programme, and three research seminars on the medieval, early modern and modern periods.

2   Not included in this total, despite the importance of their contribution, are the lecteurs and lectrices, who spend only one academic year in Oxford.
3   This last refers to the researchers at the Maison Française d'Oxford – see later in this chapter – and to a link with the Sorbonne-Nouvelle, which provides for one visiting professor.
4   Places are also regulated according to the principles governing the study of double specialisms – French and another language, or French and another discipline.
5   This is without even mentioning libraries (the Bodleian and the Taylor Institution), which represent enormous resources.

But we should move away from this purely descriptive view, to avoid giving the impression that everything is going wonderfully in the best of all possible Wonderlands. Now the ecstatic postcard must give way to a more nuanced sketch, which is far richer in contrasts. These contrasts are the result of both financial and qualitative problems.

In qualitative terms, the loss of French's pre-eminence as a modern foreign language in the UK has had well publicised consequences. As a result, the level of French among new undergraduates is very uneven. Catch-up summer schools have recently been set up as a way of partially addressing the problem; but – and this is one of the first points at which financial and qualitative issues come together – the financial crisis is already threatening the very existence of these sessions.

The same qualitative issues, along with a general trend towards the study of the contemporary (and the illusion that today's language is 'less difficult' plays a large role here) contribute towards the strong teaching bias in favour of the modern – the nineteenth and particularly twentieth centuries. This period, for example, eats up more than 55 per cent of potential teaching staff. This situation has two consequences. The first is largely positive. Since the start of the twenty-first century, there has been a sustained effort towards the creation of posts in new specialist areas: cinema and francophone studies are on very solid ground. The second consequence is more problematic. Certain sectors are finding themselves stripped to a bare minimum, in particular the medieval and the start of the early modern period.

These issues are doubly important: on a national level, not all universities are able to offer teaching in these specialities, and on an intellectual level, the implications are enormous. A medieval post has recent become vacant through retirement, but there is no guarantee that it will be re-filled. The fear that this engenders is not negligible, and it is therefore worth stopping for a moment to explore this area of French Studies.

Specialists in the medieval and early modern have taken it upon themselves to defend their periods with great energy. The medievalists have created a specific website.[6] Without repeating in detail what is described elsewhere in this collection, it should be noted that the pre-modern period is particularly suited to encouraging young people to study modern languages at a university level. This might seem strange and incongruous, given that this period lacks any obvious 'direct relevance'. However, students seem to be open to all sorts of new explorations of literary culture when they arrive at university, in part because they have so little exposure to literature in the secondary school syllabus. In sessions with 14- to 18-year-olds, particularly in the context of the 'Aimhigher' programme, their first encounters with images taken

---

6   Available at http://users.ox.ac.uk/~fmml0059/OFOx1.htm (consulted 1 November 2010).

from medieval manuscripts, or with Renaissance poetry, have proven to provoke lively discussion on various aspects of cultural diversity. Similarly, in certain US universities, the medieval *chanson de geste* (and particularly *La Chanson de Roland*) is used as a way of approaching the question of the 'culture shock' currently being experienced between the Western world and the Middle East; between Christianity and Islam. The growth in printing and textual dissemination seen in the late fifteenth and sixteenth centuries – what scholars have recently called the 'early modern information overload' – offers further suggestive points of comparison with cultural changes occurring in our modern, digital age.

Furthermore, literature from the pre-modern period can provoke reflection on some of the fundamental questions in literary culture: the idea of the author, the relationship between the author and his audiences, the circulation of texts, early steps in philology; influence, imitation, originality, and so on. It is certainly not a question of simply stepping backwards in time (which is not without intrinsic value: there is a lot to be said in favour of history for history's sake), but rather of appreciating the intellectual import of creating a 'prehistory'; even more so if this prehistory avoids the trap of teleology. In fact, this sort of study allows us to analyse not only the roots of literature, but also the roots of intellectual history and the history of humanity: an example might be the pre-history and the birth of the idea of dualism, of which traces appear in texts that are not easily classed as *either* 'literary' *or* 'philosophical'. The pre-modern period, then, is particularly suited to courses aiming at a transverse view of culture; addressing themes like the relationship between literature and the visual arts, or female writers in France, or the history of the concept of 'moi'.

It also provides a wealth of potential for interdisciplinary research – an area which is as fruitful as it is attractive to funding bodies. In Oxford this is evidenced by the group entitled 'Voices in Medieval French Narrative' (literature and linguistics), as well as a network of scholars working on 'Text and Image in Medieval French Culture' (literature and art history), both enterprises funded by British Academy grants. Similarly, a conference on 'Method and Variation: Narrative in Early Modern French Thought' (literature and philosophy) received funding from the Leverhulme Trust.

Finally, early texts can provide an important contribution to theoretical reflections in the literary field – for example, in terms of the theorisation of the role of the author or artist; a topic that has been the subject of several workshops and research seminars in Oxford.

It is clear that these evolutions in the study of the modern, and these new initiatives in the pre-modern, are all part of a move towards a position which the sub-faculty has been aiming to adopt for several years, which might be summarised with the formula: 'Literature and ...' (cinema, society, philosophy, history, the arts ...). The aim is to re-invigorate the linguistic and literary dimensions of French Studies by situating them in the context of contemporary thought, society, arts, and cultural and intellectual life in general. Language and literature both benefit, since this approach highlights their central role in the construction of an individual culture. Of course, in order to proceed along these lines, students need to be provided with knowledge bases to which they have not previously had access. This has resulted in the provision of classes and seminars (for undergraduates and MSt students) in French history and cultural history.[7]

All of this serves to demonstrate the importance of providing ever more varied courses, at a time when student numbers are consistently high, but staffing numbers, far from increasing, are instead threatened with cuts. It is little wonder that pressure has continued to build, and combined with a climate in which economic worries are common currency, the resulting atmosphere is not what we might call calm.

In these circumstances, there is no better action than to invest! In the Oxonian context, since the number of undergraduates can hardly increase, it is instead the graduate students[8] and researchers who can and should attract the bulk of new initiatives and innovations. Here, we will limit ourselves to a brief examination of two examples. Both concern the early modern period, in part because this is the area most known to the author of this chapter, but also because of the dynamism currently displayed by this area in Oxford.[9]

In Favour of more Theatre

Oxford University has no theatre studies department. However, every spring the colleges play host to a wealth of productions, in various languages including French, directed, performed and produced by the students themselves. Since there are also three town theatres, there is something of a paradoxical contrast between such a potentially intense theatrical life, and the absence of any specific academic provision. A paradox, though, in which this absence might in fact be viewed as positive: if there were indeed a university department devoted to the theatre, might it not constitute too much of a drain on both the energies of participants and on the audience, thereby impoverishing the general

---

7 For the moment, these lectures concentrate on the Ancien Régime. It would be helpful if the history department were to offer support in this area, but such an offer is so far not forthcoming, despite the fact that French departments are often asked to provide language teaching for students on other courses. On the teaching of history, see my article 'The Importance of being Endogenous', in *Teaching the Early Modern Period*, ed. D. Conroy (forthcoming, Dublin).

8 The number of graduate students can and must increase.

9 Though this is not to diminish research activity on the Modern period, which Leverhulme scholarships and British Academy Fellowships have recently brought to the fore.

dynamic? In this framework, it seems possible that the French department could have a role to play.

The theatre plays a very significant role in French literature and culture, both in the present, and throughout history. The French 'classics' *par excellence* are playwrights, and for a long time theatre specialists have made up an important part of the teaching body, most notably those specialists in early modern 'classics' like Molière and Racine. However, changing teaching profiles in the department have tended to weaken the role of this area of French Studies. It needs to be reactivated – an enterprise that is already in progress, but which requires more development. In fact, the theatre provides a way of working on texts and on larger cultural phenomena (music, sets and costumes, social questions). Students' reading or even performance of the texts has a hugely beneficial effect on their language, since visual and corporeal signs combine with verbal meaning to make the latter both more meaningful, and more accessible.

The first logical step towards reviving theatre studies is to look at the whole as a single reality – that is, as much performance as text. In this vein, alongside a corpus of prescribed authors (Molière, Racine), Oxford now offers a 'special subject' entitled 'Dramatic Theory and Practice, 1605–1660'. Furthermore, undergraduates also have access to a course on theatre history, from the medieval to the Revolution, which focuses as much on venues, troupes and staging as it does on themes and aesthetics.

Other universities around the country have already developed initiatives along these lines, and are consequently more advanced, but at least efforts are being made in the right direction. Indeed, a second major target area is that of graduate studies. Efforts here are already bearing fruit, with success both at MSt level (one popular special subject focuses on Early Modern French Theatre) and at a doctoral level (with five DPhils currently in progress, at the time of writing). The topic is being approached from all angles, covering its whole history: from 'classical' drama (Molière) to contemporary theatre (the theatre in a postcolonial context); from the careers of authors (Goldoni in France) to those of directors (Peter Brook and Ariane Mnouchkine). Furthermore, all possible dimensions are being explored. This is an important point: the underlying question is whether doctoral students are purely engaged in an exercise of reproduction; the repetition of their superiors' career paths, or whether, instead, their training can equally prepare them for jobs outside the academic sphere. The gamble has paid off in one case: a student in the final stages of his thesis has just accepted a job in professional theatre, which is an important sign. The fate of French Studies is also largely dependent on its ability to provide routes into various other sectors, at the highest level.

At the heart of French Studies, the theatre is an area that offers very real potential. It goes without saying that the theatre occupied – indeed, still does occupy – a significant position in the history and cultural life of

France. But more than this, France has long represented a centre whose rays have reached far beyond the borders of the country itself. (This is, of course, said without making any sort of value judgement – while the writer of this chapter is a veteran of productions of Molière, and has spent many years working on Racine, he is no less a fan of Shakespeare and the RSC, of Faustus, Goethe and Lopez; there is, then, no question of reviving any sort of 'Racine vs Shakespeare' debate.) Today, through the networks born of decentralisation, and through the recognised role of this art in the fabric of national culture (the 2003 strikes by part-time theatre workers testified this), the theatre is a crucial part of the 'exception française'. It might be termed a sensitive spot in the study of French culture.

This raw nerve has also, for a long time, been the focus of some of the UK's most talented researchers. To give a few prime examples – and without, regretfully, being able to give a complete historical bibliography – we might cite work on the history of venues and troupes (the Théâtre Guénégaud as analysed by Jan Clarke, or the Copiaux by Henry Phillips), the history of the *mise en scène* (including David Bradby's recent monograph) and vast documentary collections (the website CESAR, conceived by Barry Russell). The theatre, then, not only offers a particularly rich teaching object, nor does it merely provide one of the best access routes into understanding a society, but *here, this* theatre is particularly prominent. Anyone who has studied Clausewitz knows that the best strategies are those that reinforce one's strong points. French Studies, then, would do well to look to the reinforcement of such a strong point as the theatre. The initiatives described above are part of this logic; but they remain limited, and should be taken further.[10] However, without giving any more detail on this example, we move on to pose similar questions about a second case.

The second example is that of a research programme based on Quarrels. Why Quarrels? Because the literary, artistic, intellectual and cultural histories of France are rife with them. This list of adjectives is a good indicator of the extent to which this curious object of study also fits well into the model 'Literature and ...' evoked above, with a vast range of related fields: literature and the arts, but also science, religion, philosophy. It suggests, furthermore, that the word 'quarrel' is a convenient, but potentially provocative summary. The preponderance of words like debate, dispute, conflict, polemic, controversy, but also confrontation, even 'battle' or 'war', indicates that the phenomenon is as complex as it is omnipresent. To take this linguistic exercise a bit further: in the list of the most celebrated cases in France – the *Querelle des Femmes*, la *Querelle du Cid*, the quarrel of the ancients and moderns,

10 Oxford University's Cameron Mackintosh Chair is open to both actors and directors, and the French subfaculty has requested that on one occasion it should be reserved exclusively for a French candidate.

la Querelle des Bouffons, la *Querelle de la Nouvelle Critique* – we always find the word 'quarrel'. *La 'Bataille' d'Hernani* employs a different term (and even this is really an episode in the quarrel of the classics and the romantics). And the use of different terms is by no means the same in other European languages: this is clear in the English 'Quarrels', and even more in other language where another root is used ('Querela' is replaced by 'pelea', 'lite', 'streit'.) It is possible, indeed, that this is a peculiarity of the French language and culture.

We might then put forward the hypothesis that the literary field, and indeed the wider cultural field, achieved particularly early definition in France, with central powers intervening significantly in the constitution of institutions corresponding to these emerging fields (such as the national Academies). Similar tensions and struggles contributed to the construction of the social field, which itself acted as a sort of theatre in which these issues were played out. Furthermore, since France occupied a dominant position in Europe, at least from the mid-seventeenth century to the mid-nineteenth century (and even as far as the mid-twentieth century in literary and artistic terms), French quarrels had a particularly wide impact (for example, the 'Battle of the Books'). This is, then, a potentially rich subject of study.

Even more so, of course, because literature is always at the centre of conflicts – either as their subject, or as their means of communication. Therefore, the epistemological challenge of this sort of research is to bring out the central, even crucial role of texts in these collective debates; and in so doing, highlight the centrality of the humanities in the understanding of fundamental social truths. Today's world is rife with controversies – the media laps them up, and even if necessary creates them. An understanding of the history of 'quarrels', then, is also useful, because is allows us to define the models and the different interests that gave birth to this practice. This has consequences for literary and cultural studies, as well as in the domains of sociology and communication.

In 2008, having established the idea of the quarrel as an object of interest, some initial explorations took place. A group was formed, based at the OBCE, which hosted the first study day, entitled simply 'Quarrels.'[11] The OBCE has since organised a conference at the MFO (on quarrels in theatrical institutions, from the seventeenth to the nineteenth century), as well as several other seminar sessions. Much of this work has been undertaken in collaboration with other research groups, particularly the GRIHL (Groupe de recherches interdisciplinaire sur l'histoire du littéraire, Ehess-Paris III). This initial phase has led to the formulation of a more formal project, which will provide three 'pillars' on which to base further work. The first of these consists in arriving at a definition of the

---

11 This initial study day was organised by Kate Tunstall, the Programme Director of the OBCE.

phenomenon itself. The study day 'Quarrels' revealed that a 'querelle' (from the Latin *querela*; complaint, taking to court) assumes a model in which one party accuses another of having treated them unjustly, the other responds, and the debate is taken before an authority which is called upon to pass judgement: this authority might be an institution (for example the Academy), a political power, or most often (and implicitly, always), the public. The formulation of such a general model allows us to see that this phenomenon exists in every field (science, law, religion and philosophy, as well as literature and the arts). It also highlights the importance of comparisons between France and the countries with which it is in direct contact. The second pillar is the creation of an inventory and history of quarrels in France. And the third is the creation of a similar, comparative inventory. Lists of terms (particularly important in a language department), of quarrels, and of bibliographical information, will be compiled in databases that will immediately be made available both to the academic community, and the wider public.[12]

The implementation of these various strategies will result in what might be termed a project 'in 3D'. In Oxford itself, this is a collaborative project between colleagues in the French department, but it also draws in other European languages and other disciplines (history, philosophy, history of art, musicology, law). This range has made French the hub of a network that takes in all of the humanities. The project also brings together colleagues from other universities. This dimension is international, for it includes collaborations with other countries: with France, obviously, but also outside Europe. All this has requires recourse to the appropriate funding bodies: the Arts & Humanities Research Council (AHRC), the ANR in France, and the European research fund. At the time of writing, the ANR has made a significant contribution,[13] the application to the AHRC is under consideration, and the application to Brussels is in preparation. The project, then, is well into phase two: its methodical realisation.

There is a long and rich tradition of French Studies in the UK, and their present is alive with research of the highest level (some of which has been mentioned above). Why, then, the discussion of this project at Oxford? Aside from the fact that the description of a research structure is always going to provide interesting information, and possible exchanges or even collaborations, this chapter also aims to highlight an important aspect of the future of research in French Studies. This project raises at least four issues (four ... a contravention of the rules of the French *dissertation* as they are so widely employed in the texts of quarrels ...).

---

12 For the moment, this project focuses on the early modern period, but the intention is that in a further phase it should extend to the Modern period (as certain examples cited above imply).

13 Awarded for a programme of comparative analysis between France and Great Britain, co-organised with Alexis Tadié (Paris IV).

The first issue is the collective nature of this project, a practice that is nowhere near as widespread as it should be. It is not a case of diminishing or stunting individual research; on the contrary, through the creation of a space for exchange and collaboration, the work of individuals can be invigorated. In a department like Oxford's, the number of colleagues makes this a lot easier, but this is not the case everywhere: we must be sure to make the most of this advantage. The second issue, linked to the first, is the project's interdisciplinarity. Working with colleagues in other languages, and especially from other disciplines, is clearly stimulating and, most importantly, it brings to the fore the areas of knowledge that are ours alone: that is, linguistic and literary skills (exchanges with philosophers are even more interesting when they bring out their different approaches and abilities in this regard). This, then, requires that the area of French Studies be considered as a single entity, in which expert advice can be sought from specialists in different areas, thereby limiting the need to rely on superficial or vague contextualisation. A third issue, of a different scale, is that of the involvement of graduate students and Post Docs in this wider enterprise. And here again, the aim should not be merely the reproduction of a career path: working on quarrels, debates, disputes and controversies can also lead to involvement in the world of communication, in the media, and in public and political life in the widest sense.

The fourth issue deserves its own paragraph. Not because it represents a particularly original idea but, on the contrary, in the name of reiteration. Essentially, the suggestion already made about theatre in the preceding section also applies here: it is important to make the most of your strong points. And it would seem that France was the European, even the world champion in quarrels, not necessarily in idealistic debates, or in internal conflicts or even civil wars, but in confrontations through the means of discourse and publication. As we well know – at least since Perelman, but even since long before, since Aristotle – debate in words is the best way for a society to give a space to conflict, and thus avoid recourse to tests of strength or bitter battles. France is far from serving as an example, much less as a model, in this sense, however, it does provide a privileged field of observation, and particularly rich material for reflection.

This reiteration leads us towards a conclusion. The term 'strategy' has already been used twice, and is worth using once again. The aim of this volume is effectively to imagine the future. This can be done in two ways: either by assuming the prolongation of the present state of affairs, or by envisaging change. A strategy – when the notion is not reduced to the hackneyed sense of a selfish calculation – is a way of seeing the future in terms of change. French Studies, exposed to erosion, worn down by financial crises, and perhaps even by a crisis of confidence, cannot bet on a long and unchangingly stable future.

We have seen that the 'Quarrels' project relies on the fact that France was a particular centre of such activities; a 'strong point' of the phenomenon. It therefore provides more and better material for reflection than can be found elsewhere. This is attractive – to students, researchers, and funding. The choice lies, then, between chasing after fashionable trends, or instead finding a trend within our own area of research. The fashion may be for 'societal' questions – the emerging trend in a world dominated by languages and cultural references other than French (today these are anglophone, but tomorrow?) – and this area may, in the short term, attract certain advantages and certain talented people. But. this is only a short-term plan. *Passée la fête, adieu le saint,* and once a fashion is *passée,* then *adieu* to the new jobs. This conforms entirely to the structure of a world in which capitalism triumphs, in its brutal quest for short-term profit. However, the intellectual interest, which clearly also translates into professional interest, resides in projects with a much longer time scale: in French Studies, these are projects that focus on the fundamental questions; on what France and its history can tell us in the long term.

That said, this is not an attempt to preach any particular lesson. Not least because everyone knows that Oxford French occupies an unusual position with regard to other institutions. At the same time, we should not harbour any illusions: though French at Oxford might be healthy in some respects, it is also threatened by the crisis, by the loss of funding, and by increasing job instability. The aim here is simply to present certain facts, and to put forward some suggestions for general reflection. If two areas have received particular attention – the theatre and the development of research on a subject like quarrels – it is because of a conviction that, in the face of the short-term calculations of cynical capitalism, the real economy of knowledge is one which revitalises literature by situating it in a whole network of practices; which cultivates a language by investigating the peculiarities of its culture; which, in order to move ahead into the future, delves deep into the past. The pre-modern and early modern periods can therefore play a major role today. Those of us who work in these areas cannot afford to adopt a defensive, inward-looking stance, but must rather be open, and operate an offensive strategy. We must emphasise that the present is fuelled and shaped by a long history: this stance makes the most sense from a professional point of view in our own little world, but also makes a positive ethical contribution to society in general.

11

Defining (or Redefining) Priorities in the Curriculum when the Good Times have Flown

William Burgwinkle

'Where are French Studies going in this era of financial constraints and cut-backs?' This is a question that is posed repeatedly in the media as the bad news about budget cuts and falling enrolments filter out from schools and universities around the UK. Our first response is to shout out to anyone who is listening that of course university language courses are useful, necessary and enriching and that of course we should be encouraging students to pursue them in ever larger numbers. Governmental decisions in the past decade have ensured that our numbers are dropping – confirming what all the language professionals consulted back in 2003 predicted[1] – but in 2010 they were dropping in step with massive cuts in funding and that produces a very worrying scenario of self-fulfilling prophecy.[2] Questions about where we are going in French Studies can always prompt a useful reflection on just what we do and how we do it but this time those questions are no longer simply heuristic or solely posed for the purpose of intellectual debate.[3] When the role of the arts and humanities in a liberal education is being challenged on a regular basis and language learning becomes a political and ideological football lobbed from one party's court to another, it is really up to us, the practitioners, to intervene, arbitrate and set the tone of the discussion.

The problem is, of course, that there is no one single answer, and no point in expecting consistency or consensus from the wide variety of

---

1 The UK Labour government instituted a change in 2004 stipulating that at age 14 students could henceforth drop all foreign language study.

2 The crisis in language enrolments received a great deal of media attention in the autumn of 2010; as A-level results were reported in the British press it became clear that French fell out of the top 10 subjects tested that year, for the first time since A levels had been offered. See for example: Alan Garner, 'The Language Crisis in British Schools', *The Independent* (25 August 2010), online resource, consulted 25 August, 2010; and Angela McLachlan, 'Are we heading towards a language crisis in our schools?', *The Times* (17 May 2010), online resource, consulted 25 November 2010.

3 One author who has taken on the topic recently is Robin Adamson in her book, *The Defence of French: A Language in Crisis?* (Bristol: Multilingual Matters Ltd, 2007).

institutions in which French language, literature and culture are taught. Yes, we admit that language learning is in a crisis; yes, we can assert that French continues to matter; and yes, we might even admit that the traditional curriculum seems not to have been working for all students in an age in which increased emphasis is placed on transferable skills; but that does not mean that there is any one solution or any one approach that will suit all departments. As each university in the UK faces the upcoming academic year and the looming research excellence framework (REF) review (now set for 2013–14), we will all be looking to provide answers to some of these questions and, most importantly, to prepare a defence of those responses to our institutions and their administrative watchdogs. This will all happen, of course, just as the conflict between curricula and administrative expectations is heating up: what we do and what others think we do can sometimes be startlingly different. When education is expected on a regular basis to justify its raison d'être – whether that be phrased in the language of 'products' and 'client satisfaction' from the administrative point of view or 'intellectual integrity' and 'relevance' from the perspective of colleagues and students – it is imperative that we re-examine our strengths and our aims and be clear about what the study of languages, linguistics, literature and film does for our students and for the intellectual climate of the society that supports it.

One natural response to the current crisis is to say that we have all been there before, that the 1970s' economic crisis and the 1980s' cuts to public spending matched or exceeded the current dire prognosis; but the fact remains that we are facing not just a challenge to our staffing and curriculum this time but a more profound question about our future viability and existence as a discipline. While it is clear that French as a language will continue to be taught and studied, the looming fact is that attainment of that end – proficiency in the French language – can be accomplished, admittedly with uneven results, through enrolment in language academies, private language schools and overseas courses. What distinguishes such language courses from what we do in university courses? We might as well admit that language learning is almost never put forward, in and of itself, as the major purpose of a university language department. Fluency and the ability to operate in the language might be one of the major goals of such programmes in the UK but it remains only a part of the larger goal that we set ourselves. That goal includes, as well, what we call cultural fluency, analytical ability and sensitivity to the patterns in historical evolution that have made France 'France' and French 'French'. Broader issues are usually behind our curricular decisions, issues that put to use our own training as language, literary and linguistics scholars and, in many cases, cultural historians as well.

We are now asking ourselves whether French Studies will continue to play in the next decade the role that it has played over the past hundred or so years, a period in which an education in French also served as a primary vehicle for the transmission of the rich heritage of continental thought and philosophy that is too easily overlooked in the UK. Will it continue to be through French Studies that students are introduced to political theory and cultural studies, as is still often the case? Will it remain the purview of French departments to pass on to new generations the role that the romance languages have played in the development of the English language and of British culture? Or has the growth of Spanish, Portuguese and Italian impinged already so much on French's hegemonic role in the secondary schools that that hegemony is no longer any more than a fiction or fading fantasy? As secondary language education becomes ever more sidelined by student choice – choice that is too often presented before the available options are presented or understood – and the curriculum shrinks to match a decreasing array of expectations, are universities to become glorified language schools in which students learn to talk about, but not necessarily analyse, contemporary ethical and political events and the changes in intellectual style that may have led indirectly to the development of those events? Is French to become simply a subsection of European studies, a mere cog in the ideological machine of liberal thought? Or will its traditional reputation for cultural transmission and inter-disciplinarity – see how frequently the teaching of French has in the past century veered into the areas of art history, cuisine, architecture, linguistics, political thought, revolutionary politics, nationalism, colonialism – carry the day and survive the current crisis?

It will be certainly be clear from my framing that my take on this issue is hardly objective and probably not particularly balanced. The only answers that are really useful and pertinent these days are those that are informed by personal experience – by our own institutional practices, curricula and expectations. While it is easy to say that French Studies will survive and continue to prosper because France itself will weather the storm, it is nonetheless the case that the status of the French language continues to evolve in the world, as English, and soon Chinese, begin to dominate industry and research; and French leadership in the arts is challenged continually by the politics of the European Union and the rebirth of regional identities. If French is seen by some as less than crucial to the business skills of some UK students, it remains nonetheless at the forefront of intellectual enquiry in many areas of intellectual endeavour and these areas have expanded, not shrunk, in the past decade. The future of French Studies in UK might even be said to be primarily interdisciplinary, in the sense that French thought continues to interest and sometimes even to dominate discussions of sociology, contemporary philosophy, anthropology and suchlike.

While French Studies have often been used as an umbrella under which discussion of broader questions in university studies have been addressed – for example, intellectual history, popular culture, the growth of nationalism, political theory – this is largely because the French Studies community has continued to embrace those topics as part of its mission. We have seen it as part of our task of transmitting a vision of the future that the future be grounded firmly in the accomplishments of the past and that any understanding of a language and a culture requires historical and literary sensitivity to that culture's accomplishments. When pressures were exerted in the past decades to trim our offerings and conform to a business model, French departments refused to be sidelined simply as service providers, repositories of predigested cultural production useful only for establishing student credentials.

I think that most of us would maintain that French Studies in the twenty-first century must continue to embrace this historic mission and then expand it. We must foreground the interdisciplinary nature of our subject area and remain open to examining and questioning our own inclusiveness, and that of French speakers around the world, as the boundaries between political entities and language communities become more porous and the question looms of what it means to be French or francophone in the electronic age. One way for universities to move in that direction – and again, I am speaking from my privileged position in a large department of French at a very selective university – is to turn our attention back to the origins of French identity and the French state and simultaneously to look at how those definitions, those self-definitions, have both limited and expanded that sense of identity and inclusiveness. In other words, we should be looking to the evolution of the notion of 'Frenchness' (or 'Francness', when talking about the twelfth and thirteenth centuries) and how it has developed over the past 1000 years before turning to the contemporary, postcolonial period in which notions of Frenchness sometimes depend more on language use than on nationalism and on places far beyond the reach of Paris and the French state.

My insistence on the Middle Ages, the evolution of French identity and the complications that have arisen in that regard in the postcolonial era do not constitute an attempt to obfuscate or complicate the question of the future of French Studies – quite the opposite. It seems quite obvious to me that in those two eras, at either extreme of French vernacular language history, we encounter moments in which representation of French identity was at its most porous and amorphous. Looking closely at these two periods, the medieval and the postmodern, allows one to examine a world that was every bit as challenging and dangerous and hopeful as anything that the postmodern world has to offer and to seek some wisdom from the superimposition of these time periods. These are worlds in which languages themselves are under assault, as Latin is becoming French and creoles intersect with the language of the metropolis; in which colonialist ventures are either beginning or changing shape completely, and ethnic differences are ultimately of secondary importance and often overshadowed by religious and political affiliations.

In this sense, the medieval and the postmodern mirror one another, offering counsel to those who feel themselves threatened by difference and its representation within social formations, or by the domination by a single unified state. The Middle Ages offer the vision of a world that is post-Empire (Roman and Carolingian) but pre-nation. We might speak regularly about France and England in the twelfth century but what we really mean by those terms is the lands that would later become France and the lands that would later become England. Feudalism, for all its faults, does not count centralisation, conformity and absolute intolerance of difference among them. Despite our modern-day (especially cinematic) insistence on the bleak social terrain of the medieval world – the misery of the poor and the scapegoating of the outsider – there is little evidence to support the view that such practices were anywhere near as extensive as in the twentieth century. Much medieval literature displays no such scapegoating of the religious and ethnic other while it is difficult to imagine much more misery than that among the industrial working class at the turn of the twentieth century.

Even people of religious and ethnic difference were often integrated within urban populations in the medieval world, often, no doubt, in a circumscribed manner but one which still left the individual free to make his or her living and participate in some sense in a community. Money was not standardised in the Middle Ages; languages were not standardised; and political loyalties were often as fickle as the wind. Despite the differing circumstances and milieux of the thirteenth and twenty-first centuries, the very fact of holding within the self several different notions of identity (i.e. one could be simultaneously French, Gascon and Cathar) is not so unlike the mixed identities of French-speaking, multi-ethnic populations from *outremer* former colonies.

On the political level, these sorts of identities, always conflicting, however much they seem resolved, were particularly volatile as the French King Philippe Auguste began to centralise his administration and assert his rights to a new form of kingship that would upset the traditional aristocracy; and some of that struggle can be intuited from readings of the literature of the period and the language used to discuss issues of belonging and political sovereignty. From the appearance of the first texts in written French, the saints' lives of the tenth and eleventh centuries, French was a language that seemed terribly aware of its cultural capital and the prestige associated with it. Charlemagne's ninth-century empire, the first post-Roman empire to unite a large part of Western Europe and reintroduce classical learning to the Christian court, left in its wake a deep respect for all things associated with his name and realm. As the official defender of the papacy, his legacy was weighty and that responsibility remained with the 'French' until well into the twelfth century and occasionally beyond.

The simmering tension between Constantinople and Rome, the rival capitals of the Roman empire, was exacerbated by the crowning of Charlemagne as Holy Roman Emperor in the year 800. Though the Byzantines were too weak militarily to fulfil their obligations as defenders of the Roman empire, they nonetheless resented the usurpation of that role by the Franks. The arrival of the Seljuk Turks in the eleventh century and the Byzantine appeal to Rome for help served as a boost to French royal claims of being the secular arm of the spiritual centre of Rome; and the pro-eminence of the Francs in the crusades of the twelfth and thirteenth centuries – even though it is never entirely clear what the significance of the term 'Franc' really entails – meant that France had perhaps higher status even than the Holy Roman Empire, the supposed heir of the Carolingian legacy. By the time that the *Chanson de Roland* was committed to parchment in the late eleventh century, notions of France and of Frenchness were already up for grabs. The royal domain of France in 1100 represented little more than a sliver of its current political form, yet the author(s) of the *Roland* returns again and again to an imaginary construct which he calls France and which incorporates all of the lands with which 'France' trades, from which it recruits its armies, and in which one finds local nobility who owe feudal allegiance to the French King. See, for example, Roland's boast that with his trusty sword, Durendal, he has conquered:

> E Anjou d Bretaigne,
> Si l'en conquis e Peitou e le Maine;
> Jo l'en cunquis Normendie la franche,
> Si l'en cunquis Provence e Equitaigne
> E Lumbardie et tresute Romaine,
> Je l'en cunquis Baiver e tute Flandres
> E Buguerie e trestute Puillanie,
> Costentinnnoble, dunt il out la fiancé,
> E en Saisonie fait il ço qu'il demandet;
> Jo l'en cunquis e Escoce e Irlande,
> E Engletere, quë il teneit sa cambre;
> Cunquis l'en ai païs e teres tantes,
> Que Carles tient ki ad la barbe blanche.

(The Anjou and Brittany / and I conquered for him the Poitou and the Maine; / and I conquered for him Normandy the proud, / and I conquered for him Provence and the Aquitaine / and Lombardy and Emilia Romagna, / I conquered Bavaria and all of Flanders for him / and Bulgaria and all of Poland; / Constantinople, which owed him fealty, / and Saxony, where he does as he wishes; / I conquered for him both Scotland and Ireland, / and England that he held within his personal domain; / I conquered for him so many lands and countries, / over which Charles with the white beard now rules.)

This inclusiveness, while naturally suspect politically, is revelatory of the traditional language politics of the early Middle Ages and of the rise of the landed aristocracy. In a period in which nations did not yet exist, an age before the boundaries of highly centralised political units, the fluid identities and the languages used in any of these lands are consequently less firmly tied to political allegiances. French, for example, was throughout the Middle Ages a language of culture and learning but also a language of commerce; and it was used widely throughout the lands with which its speakers came into contact. Throughout the Mediterranean, from Naples to Sicily, Majorca to Moorea, Venice, Genoa and Lombardy, French was present not necessarily as the first language of the people, the language of family relations, but as a second language, a language of commercial and political communities, a language that expanded the realm of the possible and the expected. 'France dulce', the favoured epithet of the Roland epic is infamously unspecific: to what does it refer? The land of the Franks? The land in which Charlemagne once reigned? The kingdom of the Capetians or the Merovingians before them? Western Christendom? Or perhaps the lands in which French is spoken and understood, as first or second language, a land touched by both Christian culture, the mix of Frankish and Roman music, ritual, food and language? As Charlemagne mourns over the dead body of his beloved son or nephew, Roland, he expresses his greatest fears for his empire, while subtly distinguishing between France and his other realms:

> Morz est mis niés, ki tant me fist cunquere.
> Encuntre mei revelerunt li Seisne
> E Hungre e Bugre e tante gent averse,
> Romain, Puillain e tuit cil de Palerne
> E cil d'Affrike e cil de Califerne;
> Puis entrerunt mes peines e suffraites.
> Ki güïerat mes oz a tel poëste
> Quant cil est morz ki tuz jurz nos cadelet?
> E! France dulce, cum remains or deserte!

(My nephew is dead, who conquered for me so many lands. / Now the Saxons will rebel against me / And the Hungarians and Bulgarians and many other contrary and belligerent peoples, / The Romans, the Apulians and the whole hoard from Palermo / and the Africans and those from Califerne; / then my pains and sufferings will revisit me; / who will lead my army with such force / when the one who always lead it has fallen dead? / Ah, sweet France, how alone you stand, deserted on this day!)

What emerges from this isolated example, but also from the abundant mention of the Franks throughout the crusading period, is the fact that France remains a fantasy as well as a political entity. It signifies an ideological concept, and an unstable one at that, which intersects with Western Christendom and new notions of secular power but without sealing the porous boundaries that separate them. Charlemagne yearns to solidify his power and his empire, to draw the map of Europe according to his own yearnings; but in this moment of high emotion, the disintegration that he feels at the unravelling of his family and his army is not limited to the personal alone. His empire, the world of the Francs, is already in the process of disintegration.

In many ways, such a state of affairs should strike us as rather more familiar than not. As is already abundantly clear from the momentous events of the first decade of the twenty-first century, the overlap between the local and the global can only ever be incomplete, partial and unstable. The more the advocates of globalisation and the spread of democracy proclaim its inevitable ascent and their final victory over barbarism, tribalism and obscurantism; and the more the effects of globalism are noted on everything from language use and fast food to media, propaganda and fashion; the more local identities emerge as newly valorised, fetishised even, and recognised as essential, invaluable, and worth fighting for.

There has been no more potent fertiliser of local identity in Europe than the spread of the European Union, and no more potent ingredient in local, political identities around the world than the claims of the global net. Clearly, this presents a challenge to nationalisms around the globe and even to nationalistic identities in favour of a larger umbrella identity that exists in parallel to the local; but local and linguistic pocket identities continue to prosper in parallel with these ideologised identities and they present an ever larger challenge to the supposed eventual victory of the global economy. Surely the French speakers of Martinique, Morocco or La Réunion, while imaging themselves part of a larger concept of Frenchness, share comparatively little with the *banlieusards* of Paris or the farmers of the Auvergne. Yet this broadened notion of community, fed by common linguistic roots, is one of the ways in which we could look at a globalised French Studies of the twenty-first century, a French Studies that takes as its focus the roots, development and future of a French-speaking world – a French Studies that goes beyond the borders of France and Québec and that stretches from the ninth to twenty-first centuries.

How do such issues feed into curriculum change in universities? When secondary schools have almost universally given up literary study as a vestige of the past, too difficult and too narrow culturally for today's students, it is up to the universities to turn back to literary studies, by which of course I mean textual studies, studies that emphasise how language communities represent their links and allegiances to the past. Gone are the days when we argued over high and low culture and claimed greater moral resonance for one over the other. *Un Prophète*, Jacques Audiard's 2008 film, is every bit as literary as Zola and the French *fabliaux* as vulgar as any episode of *Little Britain*. Both are indispensable for discussing a broadened view of French identity and both should find their place in university curricula. Some university programmes might take it upon themselves to go back to the roots of local identities in France or *outremer*, to examine how these language communities developed in response to the cultural milieux around them and their rapport with a master narrative of French linguistic and historical development; another might look at France itself and split that political entity into the local communities out of which it developed and into which it might again one day dissolve. The response I am advocating, in other words, is to look to the archaeological and the local, the underpinnings of the nation and the sense that Frenchness is somehow irredeemably other than Germanness or Italianness or Englishness, and tied strongly to language use.

Admitting my biases as a medievalist, I would advocate reaching out to all of the areas in which French identity took shape, in which it presented itself as a comprehensive body of knowledge and social practice, and from which some have been excluded and others incarcerated. In terms of curriculum and departmental planning, this means studying history, but from a critical perspective, watching for what Michel Foucault called the epistemological breaks and charting their influence on the national, artistic and linguistic identity that emerged. One byproduct of such study is increased emphasis on the usefulness of French, not only for business, economics and politics but for understanding the world outside of France that has been touched by French, including the United Kingdom, North America, Southeast Asia, and most of all, Africa and the Middle East. It means looking at France as if in a Petri dish, as a laboratory specimen that contains all of the necessary ingredients for measuring social change, religious upheaval, political experimentation, social engineering, racial harmony (or disharmony), rural and urban interpenetration and philosophical radicalism.

If this sounds as if I am advocating a move to a medieval, postcolonial and film studies curriculum, that is not exactly the case, but it would be very accurate to say that I think those particular areas are of the greatest interest in 2010–11, along with intellectual history generally. This does not mean that I think we should reformulate our curricula to focus on these subjects – though these are areas in which French thought and identity and all they imply are brought to the fore – but that those three areas should not be shunned in the rush to cut budgets and supposedly appeal to students' tastes. All three merit the particular attention of departments who are interested in developing a wider view of what French has meant and means, and how it continues to play a silent role in processes of cultural abrasion and adaptation. I am at Cambridge and clearly have the advantages of a long history of institutional support, a large number of colleagues, a good intake, and a selective admissions policy. This is nothing to apologise for but should instead allow us to design a curriculum of our own making, without excessive worry about what is being done elsewhere. As we go into a process of curriculum revision, I am particularly aware that the issues discussed will be on the table at every working party meeting and will make their way into whatever proposals we forward to the School and University and I am further aware that this is a very good thing.

In these curricular discussions, we have decided to stay with what to some would seem a traditional curriculum for our second-year options –

papers involving coverage of historical periods of literature and thought (including film) and a separate paper in linguistics. If this is traditional, however, it could also seem radical in that it does not correspond to the choices that many universities have made. This is not problematic, for us or for them, and often reflects different funding decisions as much as philosophical divergence. In most institutions, financial cuts have made it necessary to trim course offerings and combine modules in ways that require a new paradigm for looking at the issues that I have been raising and there is no reason to think that students who have not been exposed to a historical presentation of French culture will be any less prepared for research in French Studies than those who have. Nonetheless, I believe that a radical change to curriculum should involve a radical change to the curriculum's aims, whether in terms of finance, research or personnel, and our decisions have not, so far, been driven by such an imperative. Instead, we will be working toward a new set of final-year offerings that will build on the solid base of the historically-oriented focus of the second-year papers, in order to look at issues that arise outside the paradigm of chronological development. Reading Marie de France's *Lais* alongside viewings of Vadim's *Liaisons dangereuses* then makes sense in a way that might not be possible without that background, in the same way that looking at crusader texts and the Iraq war or Sade and Catherine Breillat can only be enhanced by pointing out their differences as well as their similarities, based on a solid understanding of the periods in which they were created and the language in which they appear.

Bibliography

Adamson, Robin, *The Defence of French: A Language in Crisis?* (Bristol: Multilingual Matters Ltd, 2007).

Garner, Alan, 'The Language Criris in British Schools', *The Independent* (25 August 2010), available at www.independent.co.uk/news/education/education-news/the-language-crisis-in-british-schools-2061211.html (consulted 25 August 2010).

McLachlan, Angela, 'Are we heading towards a language crisis in our schools?', *The Times* (17 May 2010), available at www.timesonline.co.uk/tol/life_and_style/education/article7128793.ece (consulted 17 May 2010).

Part V: The Place of Linguistics in French Studies Today

12

French Linguistics Research and Teaching in UK and Irish HE Institutions

Wendy Ayres-Bennett, Kate Beeching, Pierre Larrivée and Florence Myles

Introduction

The research and teaching of French linguistics in UK higher education (HE) institutions have a venerable history; a number of universities have traditionally offered philology or history of the language courses, which complement literary study. A deeper understanding of the way that the phonology, syntax and semantics of the French language have evolved gives students linguistic insights that dovetail with their study of the *Roman de Renart*, Rabelais, Racine or the *nouveau roman*. There was, in the past, some coverage of contemporary French phonetics but little on sociolinguistic issues. More recently, new areas of research and teaching have been developed, with a particular focus on contemporary spoken French and on sociolinguistics. Well supported by funding councils, UK researchers are also making an important contribution in other areas: phonetics and phonology, syntax, pragmatics and second-language acquisition. A fair proportion of French linguistics research occurs outside French sections in psychology or applied linguistics departments. In addition, the UK plays a particular role in bringing together European and North American intellectual traditions and methodologies and in promoting the internationalisation of French linguistics research through the strength of its subject associations, and that of the *Journal of French Language Studies*. The following sections treat each of these areas in turn.

History of the French Language

There is a long and distinguished tradition in Britain of teaching and research on the history of the French language, particularly, but by no means exclusively, at the universities of Cambridge, Manchester and Oxford. Since at least the 1930s, British scholars have produced general single-volume histories of the language, which are excellent examples of research-informed works, which serve undergraduates and more advanced researchers alike; examples include Ewert, Price, Rickard and Posner.[1] These have been complemented by collections of texts, typically with commentaries, which illustrate the language at various points of its history; some, such as Studer and Waters, or Rickard,[2] focus on a particular period or century of the language's development, showing the diversity of its uses and its expansion into new domains, others, such as Ayres-Bennett, *A History of the French Language through Texts*, aim to trace the history of the language from the earliest extant texts to the present day. As in many other domains, British research in this area benefits greatly from bringing together in original ways the best research from the English- and French-speaking worlds. Recently this has led to an emphasis on socio-historical linguistics, a domain which is beginning to attract attention on the other side of the Channel. A notable example of this approach, which already underpinned – at least implicitly – some of the collected volumes of texts, is R. A. Lodge's *French: from Dialect to Standard*, which, unusually, has also been translated into French; further examples are the later work of Lodge, and Ayres-Bennett.[3] Another example of the marrying of different traditions is M. B. Harris's important work, *The Evolution of French Syntax*, which explored the extent to which French fits into typological models of language change; here too British work has been important in introducing such approaches to French colleagues.

Another particularly British focus has, unsurprisingly, been Anglo-Norman. Mildred Pope's *From Latin to Modern French*, which paid particular attention to the Anglo-Norman dialect, served generations of undergraduates in the twentieth century. Then there is the editing of Anglo-Norman texts: the emphasis here has similarly been to move beyond the traditional literary canon to give access to works on a range of subjects and styles, including falconry and medicine.[4] The most ambitious enterprise in this area is the Anglo-Norman dictionary and the

1   A. Ewert, *The French Language* (London: Faber & Faber, 1933); G. Price, *The French Language: Present and Past* (London: Edward Arnold, 1971); P. Rickard, *A History of the French Language* (London: Hutchinson, 1974); R. Posner, *Linguistic Change in French* (Oxford: Clarendon Press, 1997).

2   P. Studer and E. G. R. Waters, *Historical French Reader, Medieval Period* (Oxford: Clarendon Press, 1924); P. Rickard, *La Langue française au seizième siècle: étude suivie de textes* (Cambridge: Cambridge University Press, 1968); P. Rickard, *Chrestomathie de la langue française au quinzième siècle* (Cambridge: Cambridge University Press, 1976).

3   R. A. Lodge, *A Sociolinguistic History of Parisian French* (Cambridge: Cambridge University Press, 2004); W. Ayres-Bennett, *Sociolinguistic Variation in Seventeenth-Century France: Methodology and Case Studies* (Cambridge: Cambridge University Press, 2004).

4   T. Hunt (ed.), *Anglo-Norman Medicine*, 2 vols (Cambridge: D. S. Brewer, 1994–97); T. Hunt, (ed.), *Three Anglo-Norman Treatises on Falconry* (Oxford: Society for the Study of Medieval Languages and Literature, 2009).

associated Anglo-Norman hub (see below).[5] For much of the twentieth century historians of French were predominantly medievalists; and while this is less true today, Marnette's work shows how literary and linguistic approaches can be successfully combined.[6]

A final area perhaps worth singling out is work on the history of linguistic thought in France and the French-speaking world. Rickard's final collection of texts focused on seventeenth-century metalinguistic works,[7] as does Ayres-Bennett's project on the French *remarqueurs*,[8] while Sanders brings together work on Saussure.[9] Britain has also attracted leading scholars from other parts of the world to teach in its French departments: the Hungarian-born Stephen Ullman, author of important studies on the history and principles of semantics, worked in Glasgow, Leeds and Oxford, and today, Richard Waltereit, Pierre Larrivée and Maj-Britt Mosegaard Hansen, all leading experts in their fields, are helping to introduce a new generation of students to – in Price's terms – the French language, present and past.

Sociolinguistics

Alongside the distinguished tradition of French historical linguistics, new currents began to emerge during the 1970s and 1980s in a number of universities. From as early as 1968, academics at Essex University, led by Michel Blanc and Patricia Biggs, set out to complete their *Enquête Sociolinguistique d'Orléans*, a ground-breaking collection of tape-recorded sociolinguistic interviews collected with a view both to study the forms of everyday spoken interaction and as the basis for new methods of teaching contemporary spoken French. The tape-recorded interviews were transcribed and this corpus of interviews[10] is now an invaluable historical record of French in Orléans in 1968. Comparison of this corpus with more recent ones allows us to explore variation and

5 D. A. Trotter (ed.), *The Anglo-Norman Online Hub* (University of Aberystwyth and University of Swansea), online resource, consulted 25 November 2010; William Rothwell (ed.), *The Anglo-Norman Dictionary*, online resource, consulted 25 November 2010.

6 S. Marnette, Narrateur et points de vue dans la littérature française médiévale: une approche linguistique (Bern: P. Lang, 1998); S. Marnette, *Speech and Thought Presentation in French: Concepts and Strategies* (Amsterdam: John Benjamins, 2005).

7 P. Rickard, *The French Language in the Seventeenth Century: Contemporary Opinion in France* (Cambridge: Brewer, 1992).

8 See also W. Ayres-Bennett, *Vaugelas and the Development of the French Language* (London: Modern Humanities Research Association, 1987).

9 C. Sanders (ed.), *The Cambridge Companion to Saussure* (Cambridge: Cambridge University Press, 2004).

10 *ELICOP* (*Etude Linguistique de la Communication Parlée*), online resource, consulted 25 November 2010.

change in syntax and lexis. Indeed, there is a project underway, led by Olivier Baude, to replicate these sociolinguistic interviews in Orléans.[11]

In the following decades, a number of UK academics began to do research on sociolinguistic variation in French, and to teach in this area: Ager, Sanders, Ball, and Lodge *et al.* are excellent examples of this trend.[12] Anthony Lodge actively promoted sociolinguistics while he was at Newcastle University and a group of younger researchers, including David Hornsby (Kent), Nigel Armstrong (Leeds), Tim Pooley (London Met), Aidan Coveney (Exeter), Zoë Boughton (Exeter) and Kate Beeching (UWE, Bristol) has further developed the field and brought on PhD students investigating aspects of French sociolinguistics. There is a strong emphasis on phonological studies, such as Pooley, Coveney, Hintze, Pooley and Judge, and Hornsby,[13] but works also consider syntax and lexis,[14] regional varieties,[15] and semantic/pragmatic aspects.[16] A recent work which brings together sociolinguistic work by UK and French researchers is the collection of chapters edited by Beeching, Armstrong and Gadet.[17]

Researchers have typically collected corpora of spoken French, exemplified by the 1980s Beeching Corpus, which is available online,[18] and the corpus of oral narratives collected by Carruthers, soon to appear in the Oxford Text Archive.[19] This distinguishing feature of UK French sociolinguistic research following Anglo-Saxon empirical models has

11 *ESLO (Enquête Sociolinguistique à Orléans)*, online resource, consulted 25 November 2010.
12 D. Ager, *Sociolinguistics and Contemporary French* (Cambridge: Cambridge University Press, 1990); C. Sanders (ed.), *French Today. Language in its Social Context* (Cambridge: Cambridge University Press, 1993); R. Ball, *The French Speaking World: A Practical Introduction to Sociolinguistic Issues* (London: Routledge, 1997); R. A. Lodge *et al.*, *Exploring the French Language* (London: Arnold, 1997).
13 T. Pooley, *Chtimi: The Urban Vernaculars of Northern France* (Clevedon: Multilingual Matters, 1996); T. Pooley, *Language, Dialect and Identity in Lille* (Lewiston, NY: Edwin Mellen Press, 2004); A. Coveney, *The Sounds of Contemporary French Articulation and Diversity* (Bristol/Portland (Oregon): Elm Bank Publications, 2001); M.-A. Hintze *et al.* (eds), *French Accents Phonological and Sociolinguistic Perspectives* (London: CILT, 2001); D. Hornsby, *Redefining Regional French: Koinéization in Northern France* (Oxford: Legenda, 2006).
14 N. Armstrong, *Social and Stylistic Variation in Spoken French. A Comparative Approach* (Amsterdam/Philadelphia: John Benjamins, 2001); A. Coveney, *Variability in Spoken French. A Sociolinguistic Study of Interrogation and Negation* (Bristol/Portland (Oregon), USA): Elm Bank Publications, 2002).
15 M. Jones, *Jersey Norman French: A Linguistic Study of an Obsolescent Dialect* (Oxford: Blackwell, 2001).
16 K. Beeching, *Gender, Politeness and Pragmatic Particles in French* (Amsterdam/Philadelphia: Benjamins, 2002).
17 K. Beeching, N. Armstrong and F. Gadet (eds), *Sociolinguistic Variation in Contemporary French* (Amsterdam/Philadelphia: Benjamins, 2009).
18 K. Beeching (ed.), *Un corpus d'entretiens spontanés*, online resources, accessed 25 November 2010.
19 See also J. Carruthers, *Oral Narration in Modern French. A Linguistic Analysis of Temporal Patterns* (Oxford: Legenda, 2005).

been influential in promoting the study of the spoken language in France; Jacques Durand moved from Salford to Toulouse-Le Mirail and, along with Bernard Laks and Chantal Lyche, developed the *Phonologie du Français Contemporain* Project, whose website[20] charts and gives audio examples of varieties of French worldwide. Sonia Branca at Paris 3 has also followed this lead and began her Parisian French collection in the year 2000 with funding from the City of Paris. The project website[21] allows both researchers and students to hear samples of spoken Parisian French with soundfiles available online. Though the *Groupe Aixois de Recherche Syntaxique* also collected audio files with transcriptions, these are not easily accessible. In general, the corpus-based approach is a distinguishing feature of the UK tradition.

Phonology and Syntax

Although phonology and syntax are perhaps somewhat under-represented areas of French linguistics research in the UK, those who are engaged in it have made a considerable impact in their field. Ian Watson and Ros Temple (both at Oxford) study, respectively, developmental phonetics in French/English bilingual children and the interface between phonology and variationist linguistics. Mike Jones (Essex), Paul Rowlett (Salford) and J. C. Smith (Oxford) have made a strong international contribution to the investigation of theoretical syntax with particular reference to French, to which Rowlett and Jones apply a generative perspective under-represented in French-speaking Europe.[22] Interesting work, too, is being conducted on tenses by Emmanuelle Labeau at Aston,[23] and Janice Carruthers at Queen's, Belfast.[24]

Pragmatics

The linguistic field of pragmatics is arguably one which has its historical roots in the UK, stemming from Austin and Grice, along with Firth

---

20 *PFC (Phonologie du Français Contemporain)*, online resource, consulted 25 November 2010.

21 *Discours sur la ville; Corpus de Français Parlé Parisien des années 2000*, online resource, consulted on 25 November 2010.

22 See P. Rowlett, *The Syntax of French* (Cambridge: Cambridge University Press, 2007); M. A. Jones, *Foundations of French Syntax* (Cambridge: Cambridge University Press, 1996).

23 For example, E. Labeau, *Beyond the Aspect Hypothesis: Tense-Aspect Development in Advanced L2 French* (Bern: Peter Lang, 2005); E. Labeau and T. Saddour, *Tense Aspect and Mood in First and Second Language* (Amsterdam: Rodopi, forthcoming).

24 For example, J. Carruthers, *Oral Narration in Modern French. A Linguistic Analysis of Temporal Patterns* (Oxford: Legenda, 2005).

and Halliday, with their emphasis on 'context of situation'. Pragmatics in the European tradition is generally broader in scope than the narrower definition taken by, for example, Levinson, and both approaches are applied by researchers on French in the UK. These researchers apply pragmatic principles to the analysis of historical data,[25] or synchronic data.[26] This is a developing field with some promise particularly in the areas of semantic change and cross-cultural analysis (cf. Guillot's conference on this topic at the University of East Anglia in 2009, and her 2010 special issue of the *Journal of French Language Studies* on cross-cultural pragmatics). The emphasis on pragmatics and spoken interaction emanating from the linguistic tradition in the UK is mirrored in pockets of research in France, particularly in Lyon, originally in the work of Kerbrat-Orecchioni and currently in the multi-modal work of Mondada and Traverso.

Research on French Second Language Acquisition

Research on Second Language Acquisition (SLA) is a relatively new field of enquiry, which saw its origins in the UK with the work of Corder in Edinburgh in the late 1960s and 1970s. The field has developed extremely fast since then, and the initial dominance of research on the acquisition of English, still present today, has nevertheless slowly made way for the study of other languages, including French. Pioneers in this area were Richard Towell (Salford) and Roger Hawkins (Sheffield then Essex), whose large ESRC project in the mid-1980s contributed significantly to our understanding of the processes involved in the acquisition of French by university students.[27] Their focus was on the interaction

25 For example, K. Beeching, 'Politeness-induced Semantic Change: The Case of quand même', *Language Variation and Change* 17: 2 (2005), 1–27; R. Waltereit, Abtönung: Zur Pragmatik und historischen Semantik von Modalpartikeln und ihren funktionalen Äquivalenten in romanischen Sprachen (Tübingen: Max Niemeyer, 2006); M.-B. Mosegaard-Hansen and J. Visconti (eds), *Current Trends in Diachronic Semantics and Pragmatics. Studies in Pragmatics*, no. 7 (Bingley: Emerald, 2009).

26 Beeching, *Gender, Politeness and Pragmatic Particles*; M.-N. Guillot, 'Film subtitles from a Cross-cultural Pragmatics Perspective: Issues of Linguistic and Cultural Representation', *The Translator* 16: 1 (2010), 67–92.

27 R. Hawkins, 'The Contribution of the Theory of Universal Grammar to our Understanding of the Acquisition of French as a Second Language', *Journal of French Language Studies* 14: 3 (2004), 233–55; R. Hawkins and F. Franceschina, 'Explaining the Acquisition and Non-acquisition of Determiner-noun Gender Concord in French and Spanish', in P. Prévost and J. Paradis (eds), *The Acquisition of French in Different Contexts: Focus on Functional Categories* (Amsterdam: John Benjamins, 2004), pp. 175–205; R. Hawkins and R. Towell, 'Second Language Acquisition Research and the Second Language Acquisition of French', *Journal of French Language Studies* 2: 1 (1992), 97–123; R. Towell, 'Relative Degrees of Fluency: A Comparative Case Study of Advanced Learners of French', *International Review of Applied Linguistics in Language Teaching* 40 (2002), 117–50; R. Towell and J.-M. Dewaele, 'The role of Psycholinguistic Factors in the Development of Fluency Amongst Advanced Learners of French', in

between processing mechanisms and linguistic structure. Shortly after that, colleagues in Ireland (Vera Regan and, later, some of her students, Martin Howard and Isabelle Lemée) and in the UK (e.g. Jean-Marc Dewaele) put the study of sociolinguistic aspects of French SLA firmly on the international map, often in collaboration with colleagues on the other side of the Atlantic.[28] Their work included detailed studies of the acquisition of sociolinguistic variation in advanced learners of French, for example, *ne* deletion, the use of *tu/vous* or the optional liaison phenomenon. From the mid-1990s to date, a series of large projects led by Florence Myles and Rosamond Mitchell at the universities of Southampton and Newcastle gave rise to the creation of a large database of learner corpora of oral French, currently totalling over 3 million words (the *French Learner Language Oral Corpora*, FLLOC).[29] The database contains learner French from complete beginners to very advanced, as well as native controls, and each dataset contains soundfiles, raw transcripts and transcripts tagged for parts of speech, all available free of charge to the research community internationally. This resource is the first of kind and is used all over the world by research students and researchers, and has led to numerous publications on the SLA of French morphosyntax, vocabulary and discourse by the research team (e.g. Myles and David in Newcastle, Mitchell and Rule in Southampton, Marsden in York).[30] In

J.-M. Dewaele (ed.), *Focus on French as a Foreign Language: Multidisciplinary Approaches* (Clevedon: Multilingual Matters, 2005), pp. 210–39.

28 J.-M. Dewaele, 'The acquisition of sociolinguistic competence in French as a foreign language: An overview'. *Journal of French Language Studies* 14: 3 (2004), 301–19; J.-M. Dewaele (ed.), *Focus on French as a Foreign Language: Multidisciplinary Approaches* (Clevedon: Multilingual Matters, 2005); V. Regan, 'From Speech Community back to Classroom: What Variation Analysis can tell us about the Role of Context in the Acquisition of French as a Foreign Language', in Dewaele (ed.), *Focus on French*, pp. 191–209; M. Howard, 'The emergence and use of the plus-que-parfait in advanced French interlanguage', in Dewaele (ed.), *Focus on French*, pp. 63–87.

29 *French Learner Language Oral Corpora*, online resource, www.flloc.soton.ac.uk, consulted 25 November 2010.

30 For example, A. David *et al.*, 'Lexical Development in Instructed L2 Learners of French: Is there a Relationship with Morphosyntactic Development?', in H. Daller *et al.* (eds), *Vocabulary Studies in First and Second Language Acquisition: The Interface between Theory and Application* (Basingstoke: Palgrave, 2009), pp. 147–163; R. Mitchell, 'Rethinking the Concept of Progression in the National Curriculum for Modern Foreign Languages: A Research Perspective', *Language Learning Journal* 27 (2003); R. Mitchell and C. Martin, 'Rote Learning, Creativity and "understanding" in classroom foreign language teaching', *Language Teaching Research* 1: 1 (1997), 1–27; F. Myles, 'The Early Development of L2 Narratives: A Longitudinal Study', *Marges Linguistiques* 5 (2003), 40–55; F. Myles, 'From Data to Theory: The Overrepresentation of Linguistic Knowledge in SLA', in R. Towell and R. Hawkins (eds), 'Empirical Evidence and Theories of Representation in Current Research into Second Language Acquisition', *Transactions of the Philological Society* 102: 2 (2004), 139–68; F. Myles, 'The Emergence of Morpho-syntactic Structure in French L2', in Dewaele (ed.), *Focus on French*, pp. 88–113; F. Myles *et al.*, *Linguistic Development in Classroom Learners of French: A Corpus-based Study* (Amsterdam: John Benjamins, in prep.).

Aston, Emmanuelle Labeau has worked on the acquisition of tense and aspect in university learners of French,[31] and Marie-Noëlle Guillot at the University of East Anglia on the acquisition of pragmatics in English learners of French and French learners of English.[32]

This field is growing steadily, with UK scholars playing a leading role in its development internationally. Additionally, it is very popular with students, both undergraduates and postgraduates, and is attracting a good number of research students.

Research outside French Departments

It is not only in French departments or schools of modern languages, however, that French is a topic of interest to HE teachers and researchers. There are a number of French linguists in departments of linguistics, of education and of psychology. For example, in linguistics departments: Mike Jones (syntax) and Roger Hawkins (syntax; SLA) at Essex, Ghada Khattab (bilingual acquisition) and S. J. Hannahs (phonology) at Newcastle, Marilyn Vihman and Bernadette Plunkett (first language acquisition) and Damien Hall (sociolinguistics) in York, or Jean-Marc Dewaele (SLA) at Birkbeck.

In psychology departments, research is carried out on reading acquisition (Lynne Duncan, Dundee), visual processing of text (Alan Kennedy, Dundee), language processing (Alice Foucart, Edinburgh), to name but a few. French is also often one of the languages in large international projects investigating acquisition, bilingualism, processing, and so on.

In education departments in HE institutions, the study of French learning and teaching is often prominent, as French remains by far the most widely taught foreign language in the UK. For example, Ernesto Macaro at Oxford (teacher-learner interaction in the French classroom), Jim Coleman at the OU (many aspects of learning and teaching including the role of the 'year abroad'), Emma Marsden in York (various studies of French teaching and learning in secondary schools), or Ros Mitchell (Southampton; primary and secondary foreign language pedagogy).

This variety of institutional contexts and approaches is mirrored in the research grants which have been awarded to those working in French linguistics over the past ten years. While AHRC and Leverhulme grants tend to be awarded to colleagues working in French departments, ERSC grants have been much more diverse in topic (e.g. language processing, intercultural pragmatics, learning of French in UK classrooms) and in institutional association.

31 E. Labeau, *Beyond the Aspect Hypothesis: Tense-Aspect Development in Advanced L2 French* (Bern: Peter Lang, 2005); Labeau and Saddour, *Tense Aspect and Mood*.
32 M.-N. Guillot, Interruption in Advanced Learner French: Issues of Pragmatic Discrimination, *Language in Contrast* 9: 1 (2009), 98–123.

The Marriage of European and 'Anglo-Saxon' Intellectual Traditions

UK linguistics finds itself in a unique position, drawing on certain intellectual traditions and methodological approaches that are prevalent in Europe and on others which are often referred to as 'Anglo-Saxon' (mainly North American and/or British). It is thus in a strong position to act as a mediating force between traditions that may not otherwise benefit from each other's expertise. French linguistics in the UK is primarily distinguished by its talent for linking the study of internal mechanisms of language to external factors such as acquisition, variation, identity and change. In addition to the qualitative approaches to second-language learning, sociolinguistics and discourse analysis favoured by French colleagues, and their UK counterparts add the more quantitative approaches dominant in North-America, including French-speaking North-America.

Another area of leadership which derives from a particularly British spirit of empiricism is the development of outstanding scholarly resources for the study of language mechanisms in relation to individuals, history and society. The study of the lexicon is supported by world-class online tools. The extraordinary Anglo-Norman Hub led by David Trotter reminds one that French is very much part of the British heritage. The Hub has been instrumental in bringing about the recognition that Anglo-Norman, once dismissed by continental scholars as a bastardised version of French for obvious ideological reasons, is an important variety for the understanding of the history of French. It tells us about the internal organisation of medieval French, its lexicon, but also its syntax and its pragmatics, as well as social issues (medieval multilingualism, code-switching between French, English and Latin, English borrowings from French). The social and historical dimensions of medieval Britain are linked to the internal dimensions of French in corpora such as the online Anglo-Norman Correspondence Corpus[33] or the new *Narrations et Dialogues en français ancien: The Anglo-Norman Year Books Corpus.*[34]

Insights from pragmatics, coupled with a detailed study of such texts, can inform historical linguistics and the process of grammaticalisation: this is particularly well illustrated in recent work on negation typified by Larrivée.[35] The resources developed by Peter Ainsworth around Froissart, such as the latest *Online Froissart,*[36] illustrate possible synergies

---

33 *Anglo-Norman Correspondence Corpus*, online resource, consulted 25 November 2010.
34 *Narrations et Dialogues en français ancien: The Anglo-Norman Year Books Corpus*, online resource, consulted 25 November 2010.
35 P. Larrivée, 'The Pragmatic Motifs of the Jespersen Cycle. Default, activation and the history of negation in French', *Lingua* 120: 9 (2010), 2240–58.
36 *Online Froissart*, online resource, consulted 26 November 2010.

between language and literature studies. Such synergies can also be developed drawing on the corpora of everyday contemporary French language, which have been mentioned above. The research resources produced by UK French linguisticians show their attention to providing resources that are of relevance not only to internal linguistics, but also external linguistics, with an eye to synergies with literary and cultural studies, humanities and social sciences.

The International Impact of UK French Linguistics and its Subject Associations

As in most humanities and social sciences, linguistics is a discipline whose foci vary with the diverse communities to which it might be said to belong. The much needed mediating position of UK linguistics may well explain the relatively strong influence it exerts, given the comparatively small number of linguists concerned. The policy of internationalisation pursued by the *Association for French Language Studies* (AFLS),[37] for a number of years now, has reaped benefits both for the association itself and for the larger community of linguists of French, not only in France, but also in other French-speaking regions such as Switzerland, Belgium and Quebec. As in other disciplines, the small number of PhDs in French linguistics has made joint international PhDs a rare occurrence. However, a good number of French PhD candidates regularly attend the PhD session organised as part of the annual conference of AFLS; the *Atelier Doctorants* provides a unique forum for constructive discussion and feedback in a relaxed atmosphere. The alternation between Britain and French-speaking countries as the venue for the annual AFLS conference has helped build the international profile of UK French linguistics overall. AFLS was instrumental in the launch of, and remains closely affiliated to, the *Journal of French Language Studies*, one of the very few international journals that accepts submissions in both French and English.

Other associations have helped UK colleagues shape French linguistics. The most recent example is the *Société Internationale de Diachronie du Français*.[38] Led by Wendy Ayres-Bennett, the association aims to bring together an otherwise potentially somewhat disparate field. Whether the talent of UK French linguistics at bringing the international community together both socially and intellectually can be applied to develop more synergies with national colleagues in other disciplines of French Studies is certainly a challenge which is worth addressing.

37 *Association for French Language Studies*, online resource, consulted 15 November 2010.
38 *Société Internationale de Diachronie du Français*, online resource, consulted 25 November 2010.

Conclusions

The work of scholars in the UK in French linguistics is clearly having an important impact in shaping work in France and beyond and in providing major resources for future research. New opportunities for the funding of large-scale research projects, such as the current one on the French *remarqueurs* based in Cambridge,[39] or the French learner language projects based in Newcastle and Southampton[40] provide exciting opportunities for international collaboration. With an increasing emphasis on interdisciplinary work in the UK, linguistics will continue to play a central role in French departments since the study of language must remain at the heart of literary, social and cultural studies.

Bibliography

Ager, D., *Sociolinguistics and Contemporary French* (Cambridge: Cambridge University Press, 1990).

Armstrong, N., *Social and Stylistic Variation in Spoken French. A Comparative Approach* (Amsterdam/Philadelphia: John Benjamins, 2001).

Ayres-Bennett, W., *Vaugelas and the Development of the French Language* (London: Modern Humanities Research Association, 1987).

Ayres-Bennett, W., *A History of the French Language through Texts* (London: Routledge, 1996).

Ayres-Bennett, W., *Sociolinguistic Variation in Seventeenth-Century France: Methodology and Case Studies* (Cambridge: Cambridge University Press, 2004).

Ball, R., *The French Speaking World: A Practical Introduction To Sociolinguistic Issues* (London: Routledge, 1997).

Beeching, Kate (ed.), *Un corpus d'entretiens spontanés* (n.d.) (n.p.), available at www.uwe.ac.uk/hlss/llas/iclru/corpus.pdf (consulted 25 November 2010).

Beeching, K., *Gender, Politeness and Pragmatic Particles in French* (Amsterdam/Philadelphia: Benjamins, 2002).

Beeching, K., 'Politeness-induced Semantic Change: The Case of *quand même*', *Language Variation and Change* 17: 2 (2005), 1–27.

Beeching, K., N. Armstrong and F. Gadet (eds), *Sociolinguistic Variation in Contemporary French* (Amsterdam/Philadelphia: Benjamins, 2009).

Carruthers, J., *Oral Narration in Modern French. A Linguistic Analysis of Temporal Patterns* (Oxford: Legenda, 2005).

Coveney, A., *The Sounds of Contemporary French Articulation and Diversity* (Bristol/Portland (Oregon): Elm Bank Publications, 2001).

Coveney, A., *Variability in Spoken French. A Sociolinguistic Study of Interrogation and Negation* (Bristol/ Portland (Oregon, USA): Elm Bank Publications, 2002).

David, A. *et al.*, 'Lexical Development in Instructed L2 Learners of French: Is there a Relationship with Morphosyntactic Development?', in H. Daller *et al.* (eds), *Vocabulary Studies in First and Second Language Acquisition: The Interface between Theory and Application* (Basingstoke: Palgrave, 2009), pp. 147–63.

39 Under the direction of Wendy Ayres-Bennett. For more details, see *Observations and Remarks on the French Language,* online resource, consulted 25 November 2010.

40 *French Learner Language Oral Corpora,* online resource, consulted 25 November 2010.

152 · *Wendy Ayres-Bennett et al.*

Dewaele, J.-M., 'The Acquisition of Sociolinguistic Competence in French as a Foreign Language: An Overview', *Journal of French Language Studies* 14: 3 (2004), 301–19.

Dewaele, J.-M. (ed.), *Focus on French as a Foreign Language: Multidisciplinary Approaches* (Clevedon: Multilingual Matters, 2005).

Ewert, A., *The French Language* (London: Faber & Faber, 1933).

Guillot, M.-N., 'Interruption in Advanced Learner French: Issues of Pragmatic Discrimination, *Language in Contrast* 9: 1 (2009), 98–123.

Guillot, M.-N., 'Film Subtitles from a Cross-cultural Pragmatics Perspective: Issues of Linguistic and cultural Representation, *The Translator* 16: 1 (2010), 67–92.

Harris, M. B., *The Evolution of French Syntax: A Comparative Approach* (London: Longman, 1978).

Hawkins, R., 'The Contribution of the Theory of Universal Grammar to our Understanding of the Acquisition of French as a Second Language', *Journal of French Language Studies* 14: 3 (2004), 233–55.

Hawkins, R. and F. Franceschina, 'Explaining the Acquisition and Non-acquisition of Determiner-noun Gender Concord in French and Spanish', in P. Prévost and J. Paradis (eds), *The Acquisition of French in Different Contexts: Focus on Functional Categories* (Amsterdam: John Benjamins, 2004), pp. 175–205.

Hawkins, R. and R. Towell, 'Second Language Acquisition Research and the Second Language Acquisition of French', *Journal of French Language Studies* 2: 1 (1992), 97–123.

Hintze, M.-A. *et al.* (eds), *French Accents Phonological and Sociolinguistic Perspectives* (London: CILT, 2001).

Hornsby, D., *Redefining Regional French: Koinéization in Northern France* (Oxford: Legenda, 2006).

Hunt, T. (ed.), *Anglo-Norman Medicine*, 2 vols (Cambridge: D. S. Brewer, 1994–97).

Hunt, T. (ed.), *Three Anglo-Norman Treatises on Falconry* (Oxford: Society for the Study of Medieval Languages and Literature, 2009).

Jones, M., *Jersey Norman French: A Linguistic Study of an Obsolescent Dialect* (Oxford: Blackwell, 2001).

Jones, M., *Foundations of French Syntax* (Cambridge: Cambridge University Press, 1996).

Labeau, E., *Beyond the Aspect Hypothesis: Tense-Aspect Development in Advanced L2 French* (Bern: Peter Lang, 2005).

Labeau, E. and I. Saddour, *Tense Aspect and Mood in First and Second Language*, (Amsterdam: Rodopi, forthcoming).

Larrivée, P., 'The Pragmatic Motifs of the Jespersen Cycle. Default, activation and the history of negation in French', *Lingua* 120: 9 (2010), 2240–58.

Lodge, R. A., *French: from Dialect to Standard* (London: Routledge, 1993).

Lodge, R. A. *et al.*, *Exploring the French Language* (London: Arnold, 1997).

Lodge, R. A., *A Sociolinguistic History of Parisian French* (Cambridge: Cambridge University Press, 2004).

Marnette, S., *Narrateur et points de vue dans la littérature française médiévale: une approche linguistique* (Bern: P. Lang, 1998).

Marnette, S., *Speech and Thought Presentation in French: Concepts and Strategies* (Amsterdam: John Benjamins, 2005).

Mitchell, R., 'Rethinking the Concept of Progression in the National Curriculum for Modern Foreign Languages: A Research Perspective', *Language Learning Journal* 27 (2003).

Mitchell, R. and C. Martin, 'Rote Learning, Creativity and "Understanding" in Classroom Foreign Language Teaching', *Language Teaching Research* 1: 1 (1997), 1–27.

Mosegaard-Hansen, M.-B. and J. Visconti (eds), Current Trends in Diachronic Semantics and Pragmatics. Studies in Pragmatics, no. 7 (Bingley: Emerald, 2009).

Myles, F., 'The Early Development of L2 Narratives: A Longitudinal Study', *Marges Linguistiques* 5 (2003), 40–55.

Myles, F., 'From Data to Theory: The Over-representation of Linguistic Knowledge in SLA', in R. Towell and R. Hawkins (eds), 'Empirical Evidence and Theories of

Representation in Current Research in Second Language Acquisition', *Transactions of the Philological Society* 102: 2 (2004), 139–68.

Myles, F., 'The Emergence of Morpho-syntactic Structure in French L2', in J.-M. Dewaele (ed.), *Focus on French as a Foreign Language: Multidisciplinary Approaches* (Clevedon: Multilingual Matters, 2005), pp. 88–113.

Myles, F., 'Using Electronic Corpora in SLA Research', in D. Ayoun (ed.), *Handbook of French Applied Linguistics* (Amsterdam: John Benjamins, 2007), pp. 377–400.

Myles, F. *et al.*, *Linguistic Development in Classroom Learners of French: A Corpus-based Study* (Amsterdam: John Benjamins, in press).

Pooley, T., *Chtimi: The Urban Vernaculars of Northern France* (Clevedon: Multilingual Matters, 1996).

Pooley, T., *Language, Dialect and Identity in Lille* (Lewiston, NY: Edwin Mellen Press, 2004).

Pope, M. K., *From Latin to Modern French with Especial Consideration of Anglo-Norman Phonology and Morphology* (Manchester: Manchester University Press, 1934).

Posner, R., *Linguistic Change in French* (Oxford: Clarendon Press, 1997).

Price, G., *The French Language: Present and Past* (London: Edward Arnold, 1971).

Regan, V., 'From Speech Community back to Classroom: What Variation Analysis can tell us about the Role of Context in the Acquisition of French as a Foreign Language', in J.-M. Dewaele (ed.), *Focus on French as a Foreign Language: Multidisciplinary Approaches* (Clevedon: Multilingual Matters, 2005), pp. 191–209.

Rickard, P., *La Langue française au seizième siècle: étude suivie de textes* (Cambridge: Cambridge University Press, 1968).

Rickard, P., *A History of the French Language* (London: Hutchinson (1974).

Rickard, P., *Chrestomathie de la langue française au quinzième siècle* (Cambridge: Cambridge University Press, 1976).

Rickard, P., *The French Language in the Seventeenth Century: Contemporary Opinion in France* (Cambridge: Brewer, 1992).

Rothwell, William (ed)., *The Anglo-Norman Dictionary*, available at www.anglo-norman.net/gate/?session=S5309351274993467 (consulted 25 November 2010).

Rowlett, P., *The Syntax of French* (Cambridge: Cambridge University Press, 2007).

Sanders, C. (ed.), *French Today. Language in its Social Context* (Cambridge: Cambridge University Press, 1993).

Sanders, C. (ed.), *The Cambridge Companion to Saussure* (Cambridge: Cambridge University Press, 2004).

Studer, P. and E. G. R. Waters, *Historical French Reader, Medieval Period* (Oxford: Clarendon Press, 1924).

Towell, R., 'Relative Degrees of Fluency: A Comparative Case Study of Advanced Learners of French', *International Review of Applied Linguistics in Language Teaching* 40 (2002), 117–50.

Towell, R. and J.-M. Dewaele, 'The Role of Psycholinguistic Factors in the Development of Fluency amongst Advanced Learners of French', in J.-M. Dewaele (ed.), *Focus on French as a Foreign Language: Multidisciplinary Approaches* (Clevedon: Multilingual Matters, 2005), pp. 210–39.

Trotter, D. A. (ed.), *The Anglo-Norman On-line Hub* (Univeristy of Aberystwyth and University of Swansea), available at www.anglo-norman.net/ (consulted 25 November 2010).

Waltereit, R., *Abtönung: Zur Pragmatik und historischen Semantik von Modalpartikeln und ihren funktionalen Äquivalenten in romanischen Sprachen* (Tübingen: Max Niemeyer, 2006).

Websites

Anglo-Norman Correspondence Corpus, available at http://wse1.webcorp.org.uk/anglo-norman/ (consulted 25 November 2010).

Association for French Language Studies, available at www.afls.net (consulted 15 November 2010).

Discours sur la viille; Corpus de Français Parlé Parisien des années 2000, available at http://ed268.univ-paris3.fr/syled/ressources/Corpus-Parole-Paris-PIII/ (consulted 25 November 2010).

ELICOP, *Etude Linguistique de la Communication Parlée*, available at http://bach.arts.kuleuven.be/elicop/ (consulted 25 November 2010).

ESLO (Enquête Sociolinguistique à Orléans), available at www.univ-orleans.fr/eslo/ (consulted 25 November 2010).

French Learner Language Oral Corpora, available at www.flloc.soton.ac.uk (consulted 25 November 2010).

Narrations et Dialogues en français ancien: The Anglo-Norman Year Books Corpus, available at www1.aston.ac.uk/lss/research/research-projects/cycles-of-grammaticalization/ (consulted 25 November 2010).

Observations and Remarks on the French language, available at www.mml.cam.ac.uk/french/observations/ (consulted 25 November 2010).

Online Froissart, available at www.hrion-line.ac.uk/on-linefroissart/ (consulted 26 November 2010).

PFC (Phonologie du Français Contemporain), available at www.projet-pfc.net (consulted 25 November 2010).

Société Internationale de Diachronie du Français, available at www.sidf.group.cam.ac.uk/ (consulted 25 November 2010).

13

The Rise of Translation

Jo Drugan and Andrew Rothwell

Historical Introduction

As is now widely recognised, translation has played a major role at key historical periods in the development of national cultures and vernacular languages across Europe, with France being no exception. The terms *traduction* and *traducteur* were introduced into French in the sixteenth century by Etienne Dolet (1509–46), a humanist and translator regarded as the first translation theorist (and infamously burnt at the stake for a doctrinally deviant 'mistranslation' of Plato). Translation in the Renaissance, a preoccupation of the Pléiade poets as it was of Montaigne, served both to make Classical works available to a wider audience and to enrich the French language through the introduction of new vocabulary. French became the official language of the state in 1539, and increasing amounts of scientific, medical and technical work were translated from this time.

The *Belles Infidèles* of the seventeenth and eighteenth centuries (literary translations adapted and 'improved' to correspond to the moral and aesthetic models of the period) gave way to a new literalism and search for historical fidelity from the Romantic era onwards, with a particular emphasis on scientific writing in response to the growing internationalisation of science. Many twentieth- and twenty-first-century authors of French expression, including André Gide, Philippe Jaccottet and Yves Bonnefoy, have also been important translators, contributing to the increasing recognition of literary translation as a creative activity in its own right. Theorists writing in French, from Georges Mounin,[1] Jean-Paul Vinay and Jean Darbelnet,[2] to Antoine Berman,[3] Henri Meschonnic[4]

---

1   Georges Mounin, *Les Problèmes théoriques de la traduction* (Paris: Gallimard, 1963).
2   Jean-Paul Vinay and Jean Darbelnet, *Stylistique comparée du français et de l'anglais* (Paris: Didier, 1958).
3   Antoine Berman, *L'Épreuve de l'étranger* (Paris: Gallimard, 1984).
4   Henri Meschonnic, *Poétique du traduire* (Paris: Verdier, 1999).

and Daniel Gouadec,[5] and from Danica Seleskovitch and Marianne Lederer[6] to Daniel Gile,[7] have also made important contributions to both the theory of translation and interpreting and professional practice, in books which now figure prominently in the more 'academic' modules of translation studies programmes throughout the UK.

Literary translations were traditionally regarded in modern languages degrees as no more than cribs for students too ignorant or idle to read the original works, and university libraries generally refused to buy them for that reason. With the apparently long-term decline of language studies in the UK, however, departments are coming under pressure to use translations as a way of opening up their programmes to students from other disciplines who do not have competence in the foreign language. At the same time, the historical and contemporary role of translation as a vehicle of intercultural exchange and influence, and as a barometer for reception of the foreign, has been acknowledged by theorists and begun to be studied in practice, mostly at postgraduate level. Recent research has analysed multiple translations of the same work as evidence for what Walter Benjamin called, in 'The Task of the Translator' (1923), its *Nachleben*, or 'afterlife'.[8] A number of studies have shown not only that translators working in different periods have their own distinctive literary styles, but also that they read the source text differently, privileging some characteristics over others and resolving ambiguities in ways that can be characterised in terms of specific moral or ideological positions. While the different translated readings are undoubtedly all *potentially* present in the original, they often only surface and take shape as proposals of meaning during the complex decision-making process, which constitutes the act of translation. In other words, it is only the constraint of conversion into another language that actualises potential nuances, connections and interpretations, of which the monolingual native speaker may well not be aware.[9] Thus literary translation can be seen as not just an extension but also an enrichment of the critical tradition, and in the case of canonical authors whose works have been translated into several languages this opens up exciting possibilities for future multilingual projects which may in time add a new dimension to literary research.

5   Daniel Gouadec, *Profession: Traducteur* (Paris: La Maison du Dictionnaire, 2002).

6   Danica Seleskovitch and Marianne Lederer, *Interpréter pour traduire* (Paris: Didier, 1984).

7   Daniel Gile, *Basic Concepts and Models for Interpreter and Translator Training* (Amsterdam; Philadelphia: John Benjamins, 1995, revd edn, 2009).

8   Walter Benjamin, 'The Task of the Translator', in L. Venuti (ed.), *The Translation Studies Reader*, 2nd edn (London: Routledge, 2004), pp. 75–83, pp. 76–7.

9   See for instance Marilyn Gaddis Rose, *Translation and Literary Criticism* (Manchester: St Jerome, 1997) and Sarah A. Kennedy, *'The Masks of the Poet'. Charles Baudelaire's Petits Poèmes en Prose in English Translations: a Methodological Study* (PhD Dissertation: Swansea University, 2010).

Historically, however, the main place of translation in British universities has been as a language teaching and learning tool, with the avowed aim for the student of reading and writing the foreign language well enough to appreciate its literature. The emphasis was on acquiring an appreciation of style and on literary language, taught in a contrastive linguistics framework. Modern foreign language study was first made academically respectable by comparison with classics (where dead languages were learned as direct modes of access to their literatures) and English (which had legitimised study of the literature of a living language). The early days of the modern languages discipline around the turn of the twentieth century were marked by a concern to assimilate the literary canon, rather than with practical language learning or professional relevance. These disciplinary assumptions remained entrenched through the period after the Second World War and, although challenged by some of the 'new' universities and polytechnics of the 1960s with their emphasis on 'Business French', and so on, still dominate many traditional university BA programmes to this day, as well as much of the research agenda. When university student cohorts were a tiny elite, there was little need to worry about employability and skills: university was solely about intellectual training and languages graduates would readily find their niche as 'generalists' across a wide range of professions.

However, this changed with the 'massification' of higher education, first with the Robbins expansion of the 1960s, then under Margaret Thatcher in the 1980s and early 1990s and the Blair government more recently. Although much new literature has been written and literary study of French has repeatedly reinvented itself and built interdisciplinary bridges (critical theory, gender and queer studies, postcolonial literature, film studies etc.), it has long been evident that many UK undergraduates are disenchanted with the assumption that literary study is the goal of their degree, and increasingly ill-equipped to attain that goal. French literature has all but vanished from the A level experience of students outside the public schools, and language teaching has had to move away from the translation of challenging literary gobbets, towards a pragmatic focus on written and spoken communication with speakers of French, and knowledge of the countries in which they live. Demand from employers for graduates with a more identifiably vocational skill set has also combined with the widening participation agenda of social inclusion in higher education to push university language courses down this 'real world' route.

An extension of the same rationale has seen the recent introduction of translation studies as an undergraduate discipline (as in Spain or Germany, and to a lesser degree in France): our survey of provision in the UK found more than 20 such degree programmes with French, at 13 different institutions.[10] In such programmes, translation is treated

10 Universities and Colleges Admissions Service (UCAS).

not simply as a language learning tool but as a complex task governed by the type of text and the domain(s) in which it operates, the source and target cultural and economic environment, the purpose for which it is being translated and its presumed audience. This undermines any tidy distinction between 'general' and 'technical' language, as well as giving students a clear reason to research the linguistic, socio-economic and cultural background of the texts on which they are working. Alongside this integration of language, linguistics, translation theory and background research, such BA programmes typically also introduce students to aspects of translation technology, the translation industries and specialised skills such as interpreting.

Most of the translation studies programmes in the UK are, however, found at postgraduate level. Studentships for the 'first generation' of such programmes were provided by the Department of Trade and Industry, not the British Academy (which, until the advent of the Arts and Humanities Research Board in 1998, disbursed other arts-based awards). This corresponded to a perception that, while the nation undeniably needed a small number of vocational courses to produce translators and interpreters for business and the international organisations, the 'academic' focus of university higher-level languages programmes lay elsewhere. Arguably this division persists to the present day with the AHRC's separation of its masters studentships into 'Research Preparation' and 'Professional Preparation' streams. It is certainly visible in many UK universities in the uneasy cohabitation between academic languages departments and the translation programmes which have been grafted on to them, often delivered either by pressed men and women who would prefer to teach literature, or by external tutors (including professional translators) who are not regarded as 'proper academics'.

Such tensions are scarcely surprising: staffing in language departments has long been driven by the literary-cultural imperatives of the research assessment exercise (RAE) and its successor the research excellence framework (REF), which still has no place for translation and interpreting studies as disciplines in their own right. The interests and skills needed for a successful REF submission are significantly at variance with those required to train translators and interpreters, and to expect academics appointed as literary-cultural researchers to develop additional skills in technical translation, translation theory or language technology, when these are unlikely to lead to career-enhancing recognition on the research front, is asking a lot. Hence the continuing (though often disguised) literary and cultural orientation of many postgraduate translation programmes.

Despite this, recent government emphasis on impact and value for money in higher education has led to a higher profile and increased academic respectability for the professional-vocational stream of postgraduate languages education. So too has demand from graduates themselves, aware of the expanding opportunities for professional linguists in public and private sector organisations. Outstanding employability prospects have also (and paradoxically) conspired with a growing financial crisis in UK modern languages departments and the government's mechanism for funding student places, to boost recruitment to postgraduate translation programmes. While funded numbers of undergraduates are currently capped, there is no cap on the number of funded taught masters places; and unlike undergraduate fees, which until 2011 were set by government, universities were free to decide the level of their taught masters fees. When student demand coincides in this way with economic imperatives, it is no wonder that many 'top' universities have recently set up masters-level programmes in translation and/ or interpreting studies as a financial lifeboat for modern languages (a recent survey for the Institute of Translation and Interpreting identified no fewer than 83 masters courses in applied translation studies alone).[11]

In view of the continued steep decline in the number of qualified UK undergraduates coming through the system, it is perhaps unlikely that so many programmes can all prosper in the long term. However, the market is becoming increasingly sophisticated and differentiated, with programmes now specialising in high-value niche areas such as audiovisual translation, conference interpreting or software localisation. Many also seek to reach out beyond the UK market, to international students (translation out of English into Chinese and Arabic is now widely offered) and to those in continental Europe keen to gain their qualification in an English-speaking environment (the first UK masters programmes with a Bologna-compliant two-year structure designed for recognition across Europe are starting to come on stream). A natural extension of such initiatives is the translation masters by distance learning, with a potentially global market. In any event, the future place of French within these different initiatives seems assured.

Studying Translation with French in the UK Today

Unlike engineering or medicine, the translation industry is unregulated. In the UK, as in most of the world, anyone can claim to be a translator or interpreter. Sporadic attempts to control entry to the profession have foundered for various reasons, notably the virtual impossibility of requiring qualifications in this global industry. Many of the most experienced and respected translators 'learned by doing' and are understandably disparaging of claims that only those with formal qualifications ought to be allowed to practise. As translation studies scholar and translator trainer Anthony Pym has pointed out, 'Long-term university-level training is a

---

11 Survey conducted by Institute of Translating and Interpreting member, Charles Rothwell, for the ITI's Education and Training Committee, September 2010.

relatively recent phenomenon, mostly dating from the second half of the twentieth century and rising sharply in the late 1980s and early 1990s. That late development is why most practitioners, and indeed most translator trainers, have probably not received formal training of this kind.'[12]

How can we explain the apparent paradox of an open industry which anyone can enter and the recent rise of translation studies? Why pay substantial fees and devote anything from one to seven years to studying translation when you can simply declare yourself a translator and start practising? Why have specialist training programmes blossomed across the developed (and increasingly, the developing) world, and, more specifically, why do UK French degrees increasingly stress their translation content?

Increasing awareness of translation and corresponding student demand are partly responsible for these developments. The Internet age and globalisation have exposed growing numbers to translation, particularly the young, who are familiar with multilingual content through social networking, file sharing and MMO (Massively Multiplayer Online) games sites. Statistical machine translation (SMT) tools such as Google Translate[13] have made translation more accessible than ever before, enabled new forms of cross-language collaboration and caused a corresponding increase in awareness of translation more broadly. Technology lies behind the contemporary need for translator training in other ways, too: in addition to the translator's traditional linguistic proficiency, further skills and knowledge are increasingly necessary to work in today's industry. Many courses thus focus on adding skills, such as the ability to exploit Computer-Assisted Translation (CAT) tools (translation memories, terminology management databases) or subtitling software, manage complex multilingual localisation projects, translate for specific technical domains or post-edit machine translation output effectively. Not all languages graduates (or even translation students) will go on to work as translators or stay in the profession throughout their careers, but such training equips them for a wide range of future roles and is thus valued by employers and by students themselves.

The translation industry has witnessed phenomenal growth in the past two decades, even in the economic downturn. A recent large-scale European study estimated the annual compound growth rate at 10 per cent minimum during 2009–15, giving a European language industry valued at a 'conservative' 16.5 billion euros by the end of the period, with the 'real value' likely to be over 20 billion euros.[14] Languages

---

12 Anthony Pym, 'Translator Training'. Pre-print text for the *Oxford Companion to Translation Studies* (Oxford: Oxford University Press, 2010), online resource, consulted 28 August 2010.
13 *Google Translate*, online resource, consulted 25 November 2010.
14 Adriane Rinsche and Nadia Portera-Zanotti, *Study on the Size of the Language Industry in the EU*, online resource, consulted 27 May 2010.

students are increasingly aware of job opportunities in the field, and motivated to equip themselves with the skills needed to find work. And even if moves to restrict entry to the profession have proved fruitless, it is nonetheless true that in certain areas, qualifications are now essential. For instance, the European Union requires even freelance translators who work on a casual basis for the institutions to demonstrate they hold a relevant degree.

Given these developments, how is the study of French and translation organised in the UK today? The following overview is based on three surveys of universities accepting applications for entry in 2011, and online summaries of programme and module content. Sources were the Universities and Colleges Admissions Service (UCAS), the institutions' websites and specialist websites designed to help applicants select courses of study (e.g. Lexicool.com and Whatuni.com). An initial survey was performed in June 2008 for postgraduate-level study. This was updated in July 2010, when a survey of all undergraduate-level programmes (BA, BSc, Scottish MA) was also conducted. Translation studies was defined broadly to include programmes specialising in interpreting, localisation, subtitling or combinations of these. Niche programmes, such as those focusing on a particular text type, were also included.

In addition, a control group of undergraduate French degrees was surveyed. These courses did not specifically mention translation in their degree titles and were assessed to compare how far translation is integrated in non-specialist training. A representative range of UK institutions was included, including Russell Group and post-1992 universities. Course content was checked for references to translation. Where an institution offered undergraduate, postgraduate diploma or masters training, its website was checked for the availability of higher research training (PhD, DPhil, postdoctoral). Finally, staff research interests were surveyed for translation studies academics with French as one of their languages, where this information was available online.

Undergraduate degrees devoted to translation have been available since the 1970s in Scotland (Heriot-Watt) and late 1990s in England (Aston), but the prevailing view in the UK has been that translation and interpreting skills are best learned at postgraduate level. This view is usually based on the high-level linguistic skills, which are needed in at least two languages, and the world knowledge and experience on which translators and interpreters must be able to draw to work in specific domains. Traditional undergraduates are unlikely to have mastered both types of skills and knowledge. Indeed, even those institutions which offer undergraduate training often implicitly recognise that their graduates are not ready to practise without further study, as in the publicity for Salford's BA Modern Languages and Translation and Interpreting: 'In addition to the general wide-ranging opportunities afforded to graduates of languages degrees, this programme opens the way to postgraduate training and then to specific careers as professional in-house or freelance translators and interpreters, copywriters, lexicographers and terminologists.'[15] The preference for postgraduate training still dominates at many institutions, notably those with a tradition of postgraduate training (e.g. Bath, Imperial, Leeds, Manchester, Warwick). However, UCAS now lists thirteen institutions offering undergraduate courses in translating with French, including some at universities known for their masters courses (London Metropolitan, Salford, Surrey, Swansea, UEA, Westminster). Some of these institutions offer multiple undergraduate courses in translation so the total number of degree programmes is substantially higher, although it is not evident how many students actually register on these programmes, or even if they run every year.

Diversity is a strength of the UK university system. The tradition of student mobility has meant that students will usually relocate to attend the university offering the course closest to their interests, so even highly specialised courses have been viable. Unlike in many other countries, UK universities are relatively free to determine course content, subject to scrutiny by external reviewers and the requirements of professional bodies in some fields: in most disciplines, no national or regional authority dictates the curriculum. These traditions may be diluted in future by students choosing to live at home to save money, by cuts to universities' modern languages provision and by moves to coordinate programme content, such as the European Master's in Translation initiative.[16]

However, our research into the content of modules and programmes shows that diversity is more evident at postgraduate than at undergraduate level. In part, this relates to the higher number of postgraduate courses available. It is also linked to the different nature of the two levels of study, though. Because postgraduate courses start from the assumption that applicants have already mastered their languages and basic study skills (writing essays, giving presentations), they can be entirely devoted to specialisation in legal translation or sign language interpreting, for instance. In contrast, undergraduate programmes are constrained by the need to develop students' basic study skills and language skills, and must usually also include a period of residence abroad. The content of undergraduate training is thus relatively homogeneous. Virtually all of the undergraduate translation degrees rely on students taking credits in more traditional modern languages topics such as cultural studies, film, history, linguistics, literature or politics. One distinguishing feature is found in the year or term abroad: a higher proportion of the translation programmes require students to gain related work experience or some combination of study and work abroad, though many traditional

15 UCAS, August 2010.
16 *European Commission Translation: European Master's in Translation* (EMT), online resource, consulted 25 November 2010.

modern languages degrees do also offer this option. Finally, undergraduate translation degrees make the limit of their training ambitions clear through course titles such as 'Introduction to Translation'.

Undergraduate and postgraduate degrees in Translation with French differ in length, level and breadth. Are they also distinct from traditional modern languages degrees? Our snapshot of broader modern languages programmes implies this is not the case. Traditional degrees almost always require some translation, and most offer at least optional modules in interpreting too. The modular system adopted by most universities means that students who wish to specialise in translation can often take a similar range of courses to those enrolled on specialist degrees. For example, final-year students on the Portsmouth BA French Studies can take modules in interpreting, computer assisted translation and theory and practice of translation. An important difference may lie in the type of translation taught. The targeted degrees are more likely to specify text types relevant for careers in the language industries, such as technical or marketing texts. Traditional modern languages programmes typically fail to mention genre and many, if not most, still focus on broadly literary and journalistic texts. Regarding interpreting, traditional programmes rarely offer anything other than consecutive or liaison interpreting, whereas the newer degrees often focus on component skills, with targeted modules on note-taking, for example; they may also offer particular forms of professional interpreting (public service interpreting contexts, conference interpreting). The more traditional programmes also indicate related career paths for their graduates. For example, course documentation for the Cambridge BA Modern and Medieval Languages – (French) notes that, 'For a small number of graduates, the degree is more directly vocational: they become professional linguists (translators or interpreters), usually after further specialised training'.[17]

Most British graduates with French who progress to such further specialised training choose postgraduate courses in the UK, in part because they are rarely expected to work into their foreign language(s) professionally, so it makes sense to be trained to work into English. Small numbers do opt for internationally renowned qualifications abroad, such as those offered by the Institut Supérieur de Traducteurs et Interprètes (Brussels), the École de Traduction et d'Interprétation (Geneva), or the École Supérieure d'Interprètes et de Traducteurs (Paris) – some of which are taught in English. Fees at these institutions ranged from £415 to £920 in 2010; the latter figure was the total for a two-year master's. In contrast, UK fees for home/EU students on masters degrees at a representative sample of institutions ranged from £4,000 to £6,960 for one year's study.

---

17 *Cambridge University, Undergraduate Admissions, Modern & Medieval Languages*, online resource, consulted 2 September 2010.

There are dozens of general masters degrees in translation studies in the UK. All provide compulsory training in translation theory but differ in optional modules and expectations of hands-on translation practice. Perhaps surprisingly, many programmes do not require students to submit regular samples of their own translations for assessment, critical comment and feedback, even where they have degree titles such as 'Translation Practice' or 'Applied Translation'. Instead, students learn the history and theory of translation; their translations are only assessed if they choose particular modules, perhaps at the end of the year, when they may submit an extended translation, usually with a commentary. Some students do no practical translation exercises at all, instead spending the summer term on a dissertation. The rationale for this approach is usually that it permits students with less popular language combinations to learn about translation. Finding qualified tutors to run practical classes for one or two students is unlikely to be financially viable, but there is certainly demand for translators in these languages. Such courses include the Birmingham University MA in Translation and Language Technologies, the Surrey University MA Translation Studies, the UCL MA in Translation Theory and Practice, the UEA MA Applied Translation Studies, and the Warwick University MA in Translation and Transcultural Studies. Courses which do require hands-on translation practice are evidently restricted to students of languages in which staff can teach and provide feedback, something which limits their recruitment of international students and those with less widely studied languages. These include masters at the universities of Bath, Durham, Edinburgh, Leeds, London Met, Sheffield and Imperial College, London.

Although the number of translation masters programmes has mushroomed and the range of programme titles is wide, programmes can be divided into three groups, categorised by the approach they take to translation, programme specialisation or language combination. In the first group, we can distinguish between programmes which require hands-on practice and those which only study, describe and theorise about this practice. Another distinction in this group can be made between taught masters programmes – the overwhelming majority – and masters by research, which are available simultaneously at most institutions, though few list any current students or projects.

In the second group of programmes, those categorised by programme specialisation, we can observe the wide range available in the UK. Some programmes specialise in different genres (literary translation, medical/scientific/technical translation). Others focus on different media (web localisation, audiovisual translation). Increasing numbers of programmes are differentiated by the tools and technologies they teach (software localisation, translation memory, terminology management, project management). Interpreting masters may specialise in interpreting alone (conference interpreting, public service interpreting) or, more often, combine the study of translation and interpreting. A few highly specialised programmes (translation studies with TESOL, the history of translation in Scotland, translating children's literature) are also listed on institutions' websites, though again, these may run intermittently. The final group of masters programmes are those which offer particular language combinations. French remains one of the most common languages offered in the UK and is available as an option on almost all the masters surveyed here.

A complete survey of UK doctoral theses on topics related to translation with French is impossible. Many institutions do not provide details of individual students or theses, whether for reasons of confidentiality, infrequent website updates or because they currently have few or no registered students. In addition, PhD students in the field find a home in a bewildering array of departments. Students identified in our survey were registered in communication studies, comparative literature, computing, English language, English literature, French, linguistics, modern languages, and translation. Those studying translation with two languages, including French, are sometimes based in a different language department, if their main supervisor is located there.

Despite these limitations, the array of research topics found in our survey was impressive. The institution listing the highest number of doctoral students in 2010 is Manchester University, with '20–25 full-time students working on PhDs', though only one thesis title appears to be related to French Studies (a 'Bourdieusian' analysis). Most universities had more modest groups, typically around five registered students; and not all of these would include French. Initial numbers often looked higher but, on further investigation, these included former students who graduated some time ago.

Our survey found thesis topics in these broad areas:

1 Comparative linguistics
2 Comparative literary analysis: examining canonical texts in translation, comparing different translations of the same text, examining translation strategies for specific text types such as 'chick lit'
3 Corpus linguistics: that is, the study of large bodies, or corpora, of natural language. In translation studies, this usually involves parallel corpora, the comparative study of related corpora in two different languages. Both literary and non-literary corpora are studied
4 Interpreting: investigations of how to improve interpreter performance, comparative studies of interpreting scenarios, interpreting in specific contexts such as healthcare
5 Machine translation: that is, fully automatic translation. These theses usually examine technical aspects such as evaluating MT output and design
6 Pedagogy: translator training provision in different countries or regions, measuring the effects of different training and assessment techniques

7 Practical translation exercises: a few universities offer the opportunity to submit a long translation with associated commentary instead of a traditional doctoral thesis
8 Sign language interpreting: studies of training, comparative studies of sign languages and spoken/written languages
9 Sociological or political aspects of translation: translation and gender, translation of particular theorists, reception of translations
10 Subtitling and audiovisual translation
11 Terminology: classification, lexicography, preparation of specialist dictionaries or termbases with commentary
12 The history of translation: for particular language pairs or text types (e.g. religious texts)
13 The translation industry: the changing context in which translations are performed, translation and globalisation
14 Translating in specific contexts: in international organisations, volunteer translation
15 Translation technologies: critical studies of approaches to localisation, investigations of how contemporary tools affect translation output or workflow, or translators themselves
16 Translation theory: comparative studies of different schools, applications of theory to particular settings or texts
17 Translators: descriptive studies of leading translators, effects of translation tools or new contexts on translators (e.g. studies using eyetrackers, non-standard forms of French).

As PhD students are usually supervised by specialists in a related area, this list also gives a fair indication of current research 'hubs' and topics in translation studies research. Particular UK strengths are centred on applied translation, audiovisual translation, corpus linguistics, interpreting, technology and translation theory. Research-active groups of academics are found at the universities of Aston, Bath, Edinburgh, Heriot-Watt, Leeds, Manchester, Portsmouth, Roehampton, Salford, Surrey and Swansea, as well as at Imperial College and UCL. Manchester is also home to the leading specialist imprint, St Jerome.

Despite the diversity in programme content, a few emerging trends indicate that collaboration is increasing across the subject area. Nationwide initiatives, particularly the National Networks for Interpreting and Translation, Routes into Languages, the Languages and Linguistics Area Studies subject centre and CILT (the National Centre for Languages) have brought groups of academic partners together, whether to share teaching strategies or collaborate on research and outreach activities. This is likely to prove increasingly important in future as the full impact of the UK's crisis in language learning at school level affects undergraduate and postgraduate recruitment.

Bibliography

Benjamin, W., 'The Task of the Translator', in L. Venuti (ed.), *The Translation Studies Reader*, 2nd edn (London: Routledge, 2004), pp. 75–83.

Berman, A., *L'Épreuve de l'étranger* (Paris: Gallimard, 1984).

Gaddis Rose, M., *Translation and Literary Criticism* (Manchester: St Jerome, 1997).

Gile, D., *Basic Concepts and Models for Interpreter and Translator Training* (Amsterdam; Philadelphia: John Benjamins, 1995, revd edn, 2009).

Gouadec, D., *Profession: Traducteur* (Paris: La Maison du Dictionnaire, 2002).

Kennedy, S. A., *'The Masks of the Poet'. Charles Baudelaire's* Petits Poèmes en Prose *in English Translations: a Methodological Study* (PhD Dissertation: Swansea University, 2010).

Meschonnic, H., *Poétique du traduire* (Paris: Verdier, 1999).

Mounin, G., *Les Problèmes théoriques de la traduction* (Paris: Gallimard, 1963).

Pym, A., 'Translator Training', Pre-print text for the *Oxford Companion to Translation Studies* (Oxford: Oxford University Press, 2010), available at www.tinet.cat/~apym/on-line/training/2009_translator_training.pdf (consulted 28 August 2010).

Rinsche, A. and N. Portera-Zanotti, *Study on the Size of the Language Industry in the EU* (Brussels: European Commission Directorate-General for Translation, 2009), available at http://ec.europa.eu/dgs/translation/publications/studies/size_of_language_industry_en.pdf (consulted 27 May 2010).

Seleskovitch, D. and M. Lederer, *Interpréter pour traduire* (Paris: Didier, 1984).

Vinay, J.-P. and J. Darbelnet, *Stylistique comparée du français et de l'anglais* (Paris: Didier, 1958).

Websites

Cambridge University, Undergraduate Admissions, Modern & Medieval Languages, available at www.cam.ac.uk/admissions/undergraduate/courses/mml/ (consulted 2 September 2010).

European Commission Translation: European Master's in Translation (EMT), available at http://ec.europa.eu/dgs/translation/programmes/emt/index_en.htm (consulted 25 November 2010).

Google Translate, available at http://translate.google.com/# (consulted 25 November 2010).

Part VI: Theatre, Cinema and Popular Culture

14

Teaching and Research in French Cinema[1]

Phil Powrie and Keith Reader

Teaching and research in French cinema has developed rapidly in a relatively short time since the mid- to late 1970s. At that time, teaching was confined to the occasional course unit in a handful of universities, and research was only just starting to emerge from work aimed at cinephile rather than academic readerships. This chapter starts by considering the ways in which teaching has evolved over that time, and then gives an account of developments in research, with a strong focus on the UK, but also taking into account work done in France and the USA.

Teaching

We can make four key points about the teaching of French cinema in UK higher education institutions:

- There are about 60 staff teaching and researching French cinema, and these can be found both in departments of French and of film in UK universities.
- In both types of department, French cinema is frequently taught as part of broader film historical or thematic units, such as 'modern European film', 'film analysis', or 'gender in film'.
- Many units on French cinema are taught to non-French language specialists.
- Discrete units labelled as French cinema tend to be generic 'histories' of the French cinema or broad introductions, where the films studied can be very variable. Beyond that, the most frequent areas of study across all units, whether general cinema or specifically French cinema, and across the UK, USA and France, are the 1930s Poetic Realist

---

1 Parts of this chapter appear in Phil Powrie, 'Four decades of teaching and research in French cinema', in *Studies in French Cinema: UK Perspectives 1985–2010*, edited by Will Higbee and Sarah Leahy (Bristol: Intellect Press, 2010), pp. 353–71.

films (with a particular emphasis on Renoir), and The New Wave (with a particular emphasis on Godard).

Several of these points emerge from Keith Reader's account of teaching the subject in the following section. Since it is not always easy to disentangle the teaching of French cinema from the teaching of cinema more generally, it is worth giving a brief historical background for the latter.

Film studies emerged as a fledgling discipline towards the end of the 1960s, largely as a result of the expansion of the university system and the interrogation of the traditional disciplines. Cinephiles began to integrate the study of cinema in programmes of literature or fine art, generally as optional units within a broader curriculum. In France, the first of these was the University of Vincennes, later transferred to Saint-Denis as Paris 8,[2] much of the teaching being done by hourly-paid staff, generally people involved in the cine-clubs or cinema critics. It was only when universities began to make professorial appointments in film studies that it became possible to develop programmes in this area, and the study of French cinema naturally formed an important part of such programmes. The first of these was in Paris 3 (the Sorbonne nouvelle) in 1983.

A similar development occurred in the UK. Departments of film studies (or film studies combined with other disciplines such as television or theatre studies) were established early on in some of the 1960s universities, such as East Anglia, Kent and Warwick. Typically, film units were introduced before film programmes, and programmes were introduced well before the establishment of a department. In Exeter, for example, film teaching began in 1996, but the department of film studies was established by Susan Hayward in 2001; in Kingston, Keith Reader began teaching French cinema in 1975, a film programme was launched in 2001, and film was incorporated in a new School of Performance and Screen Studies, established in 2005.

Many anglophone universities do not have departments or schools of film studies and related disciplines, but rather, research-oriented groupings such as centres or institutes to which the postgraduate (and sometimes the undergraduate) study of film is attached. But in other universities, cinema is taught without the support of a separate department or significant research-based unit. Whether there is a school/department, a research centre or institute, or a looser programme structure, the study of film is often spread over a number of different disciplines, typically modern languages and English/American studies.

It is against this background that we can place the experience of one of the first colleagues to introduce the study of film in a French department, Keith Reader.

2 Michel Marie, *Guide des études cinématographiques et audiovisuelles* (Paris: Armand Colin, 2006), p. 27.

A Personal Account of the Development of French Film Studies by Keith Reader

I propose here to provide a brief overview of how the teaching of French cinema has changed in the 35 years since I first offered an undergraduate course in the area, at Kingston (now University, then Polytechnic). Cinema was one of four non-literary options offered to students following a single-honours degree in French, from among which they chose two, the others being Thought, Art and Politics. The course – originally devised by two colleagues, and amended as it went along – was *auteur*-based; the directors taught were (as I recall) Clair, Vigo, Carné, Renoir, Bresson, Godard and Resnais. Five of those six have figured more or less uninterruptedly in my teaching ever since, the exception being René Clair who is now a neglected if not altogether forgotten figure.

That bald summary already suggests some of the changes I seek to document and analyse here. The most obvious of these is that, in the mid-1970s, courses in French cinema were a rarity, whereas today virtually all departments offer some opportunity to study film. Sometimes this forms part of a dedicated module, sometimes films figure alongside literary and historical texts (thus, study of the Occupation and the Resistance may well involve viewings of *Lacombe Lucien* or *Le Chagrin et la pitié*). The idea that a post-1992 university could offer a primarily literature-based single-honours degree in French seems, at the time of writing, to belong in the area of academic science fiction. Moreover, the hegemony of the *auteur* paradigm in the study of cinema has long since been undercut by the development of star studies, so that in terms of theoretical approaches and availability of secondary-source material it is now possible to teach *Le Jour se lève* as both a 'Jean Gabin' and a 'Marcel Carné' film. One reason for the upsurge of interest in star studies is that it provides a more congenial paradigm for that sine (? cine) qua non of the contemporary humanities academy, gender, whose effects are nowadays felt in the construction of auteurist canons and syllabuses too. The course I taught all those years ago did not even offer the genuflection in the direction of Agnès Varda, which was almost all that would have been on offer in those days. Today, a director-based syllabus that did not include a single woman filmmaker would not survive five minutes' validation scrutiny.

These developments mirror changes, on the one hand, in the field of research, on the other in the humanities at large – especially but by no means exclusively literature. More specific to film studies is the immense, and massively beneficial, effect of technological change. Until 1988 or so, students would watch screenings of 16 mm copies of films as a group, which replicated the experience of going to the cinema, rather than watching television, but brought with it massive disadvantages. A technician was required to project the films, students who unavoidably missed a screening had no way of making up for it, and the expiry of rights meant that films were regularly withdrawn from distribution, often at very short notice, which made long-term syllabus planning somewhat difficult. Most infuriating of all, however, was the frequently execrable condition of the prints – often as much of a factor in the withdrawal of this or that film as questions of rights. I recall telling a group of students to pay particular attention to the image of the Cross which fills the screen at the end of Robert Bresson's *Journal d'un curé de campagne*, only to find that the crucial sequence was missing from the copy we had hired, which had shed its last few metres of celluloid.

The academic credibility of cinema was also not facilitated by the impossibility of being able to (re-)view a film as and when required. Students and researchers were of necessity reliant on secondary sources, published screenplays when these were available and notes taken during the screening – something which had not appeared to handicap André Bazin or Christian Metz but was often a problem for undergraduates. The very textuality of cinema, at least implicitly, was at issue here; were films entitled to be taken as seriously as books when they were so evanescent? The advent of VHS, first marketed in 1977 but not widely used in higher education until the 1990s, put paid to such concerns, along with the more practical problems referred to above. One major watershed was the regular issuing of new cinematic releases, and gradually of a back catalogue of classics, from 1990 onwards.

As important for educational institutions, however, was the setting up of the Educational Rights Agency (ERA) in 1989, which issued licences to colleges and universities to record films and other copyright material off-air for bona fide educational purposes. These two developments, technological and legal innovation working hand in hand, made the whole business of teaching film far more user-friendly and immeasurably broadened the range of material available to students and researchers, though there were – and still are – significant gaps. I was once told by the examinations officer that my setting of a question on Julien Duvivier's *La Belle Équipe* could potentially land me in court, for the film had not been screened on UK television since the setting up of the ERA and my copy thus had no right to exist. Certain important works were (from my perspective) issued belatedly on VHS and for a long time not broadcast on television, so that for years on end I was able to use Jean Renoir's *Le Crime de Monsieur Lange* only in a 'samizdat' off-air French TV recording – a major problem, as it turned out, given the poor quality of the film's sound and the exceptional quality and importance of its dialogue.

VHS was a quintessentially 1990s phenomenon, rendered all but obsolete in the new millennium by the advent of more durable and better-quality DVD copies. The first film to be issued on VHS by Artificial Eye – Raul Ruiz's Proust adaptation *Le Temps retrouvé* – came out in 1990, and the last – the Japanese Kitano Takeshi's *Zatoichi* – in 2004. VHS still has its uses, mostly for films that, for one reason or another, have not made the transition to DVD, and the ease of stopping a cassette at the precise point at which one wants to begin screening an excerpt is a positive advantage, but DVD is nowadays overwhelmingly the default format.

Such material concerns may appear as fripperies of little academic importance or intellectual interest, but they have played a vital part in the spread and development of film studies down the decades; nowhere more than in this area, at least in the humanities, has technological innovation exercised such an influence on course content. That influence, however, has in one important respect skewed the curriculum, for while any film given a cinematic release in these islands will shortly thereafter become available on DVD there is still a vast back catalogue awaiting issue, and that inevitably accentuates the drift towards the contemporary characteristic of literary and cultural studies across the board. One of the most important directors of the classic French cinema is undoubtedly Jean Grémillon, yet probably his greatest film, *Lumière d'été* of 1943, has never been available for purchase in any format, though it could briefly, many years ago, be hired on 16 mm. When that option disappeared I was able to show students an off-air French TV recording on VHS, but the sound and image quality was dreadful, and the copy, of course, had no subtitles, so that that and other major works of the pre-New Wave period such as Pierre Chenal's *La Maison du Maltais* or Julien Duvivier's *La Belle Équipe*, both available only sporadically on VHS via French Amazon, are effectively off-limits for teaching purposes.

This difficulty is exacerbated by the decline in modern languages student numbers, which forms a sombre context to the book of which this chapter is part. French cinema has been less affected in terms of course viability than many other areas – a result of the drift towards the contemporary mentioned above along with twenty-first-century students' arguably greater affinity with visual rather than literary culture (which is not of course to say that cinema cannot be both). Courses have also increasingly been opened to non-French specialists in a manner not, alas, available to, for example, *bande dessinée*, which is therefore more likely to be adversely affected – though not in my own department – by problems of French recruitment. In my university students of film studies and comparative literature (the former a relatively, the latter an extremely, recent innovation) not infrequently follow options in French cinema, which often brings a welcome broadening of perspective and contextual knowledge but has tended to limit the range of films that can be shown and of secondary material to which students have access. This situation is improving, thanks to the efforts of the British Film Institute and the excellent US Criterion collection which, for instance, in 2007 made Carné's *Le Quai des brumes* and *Le Jour se lève* available in subtitled form. French-issued DVDs nowadays often feature a range of subtitles, including in French for the hard of hearing – something that was rarely the case in their early days.

Two conclusions follow from the above points. One is that pre-Second World War, perhaps even pre-New Wave cinema increasingly occupies a position within what Bourdieusians would call the *champ* of French film studies analogous to that of say the seventeenth century in the literary curriculum – recognised as important, the focus as we show elsewhere in this chapter of high-quality research, but still a minority avocation compared to more recent work. There is, therefore, cause for at least some concern, as with earlier literary periods, about how its place is to be maintained, let alone strengthened, at a time of immense material pressure and dwindling recruitment to French degrees. The other is that the status of the filmic medium remains desolatingly vulnerable compared to its literary counterpart, despite the fact that since 1977 the Centre National du Cinéma has operated a *dépôt légal* system for French films. A great many important French films can be viewed only in the Bibliothèque de France or the Bibliothèque du Film in Paris; many, such as Jean Eustache's 1973 *La Maman et la putain*, are inaccessible even there. *La Maman et la putain*, which ranks among the very greatest of all French films, is the victim of a seemingly interminable rights imbroglio which means that it has never appeared on DVD except, fleetingly, in Japan, and the only VHS cassette – issued by Artificial Eye – is like gold dust. This is a scandalous situation – as scandalous as if no copies of, say, Georges Perec's *La Vie mode d'emploi* were available for purchase or even to consult in libraries. Making films available to students is no longer the lottery it used to be, and few will regret the days of mangled prints and last-minute withdrawal of copies; but questions of accessibility nevertheless continue to represent a problem.

Research

Where research is concerned, we can distinguish four broad periods, extending by decade from the 1970s onwards. The key year for academic research in French cinema studies was 1972, when the first American and French PhD theses on French cinema were awarded. Both countries saw a shift by the mid-1970s from cinephile publications to research-led publications. The New Wave was the most popular academic focus in the 1970s. For many, the defining book of that decade was James Monaco's influential study, *The New Wave: Truffaut, Godard, Chabrol, Rohmer, Rivette*. Godard was the major focus of the decade with several books by Americans,[3] and, in the UK, the British Film Institute's publication, *Godard: Images, Sounds, Politics* by Colin MacCabe *et al*. Godard has remained the most researched director in French cinema studies.

---

3   For example, Royal S. Brown (ed.), *Focus on Godard* (Englewood Cliffs: Prentice-Hall, 1972); Julia Lesage, *Jean-Luc Godard: A Guide to References and Resources* (Boston, MA: G. K. Hall, 1979).

The 1970s were not just focused on the New Wave, however. They also saw the establishment of Jean Renoir as an important figure in French cinema for anglophone academics, with a number of influential studies.[4]

The 1980s saw new developments. First, the number of theses awarded in the 1980s more than tripled to 80. Second, as well as the usual emphasis on the New Wave, there were three significant new emphases, mostly coming from the USA: francophone cinema, theory, and women directors. Third, and importantly for the UK, Ginette Vincendeau's 1985 thesis, on 1930s popular cinema, marks the start of the UK strand of French cinema studies, immediately preceded in 1984 by the first ever panel on French cinema at the French Studies conference, hitherto largely devoted to French literature. Fourth, although there were significant director studies in the decade, many of them on pre-1960 directors (Autant-Lara, Gance, Méliès, Ophüls, Renoir, Tati), a feature of the decade was that French and American academics turned their attention to French cinema history, with a number of books devoted to very specific periods,[5] especially the 1930s and early cinema.[6]

The 1990s was another step in the evolution of French cinema studies. First, there was an explosion of academic books in the first half of the 1990s, culminating in the centenary of the cinema in 1995. These were produced by journalists in France,[7] as well as by university-based academics.[8] But the USA also published some important books,[9] as

4 Raymond Durgnat, *Jean Renoir* (Berkeley: University of California Press, 1974); Leo Braudy, *Jean Renoir: The World of His Films* (London: Robson, 1977); Alexander Sesonske, *Jean Renoir: The French Films, 1924–1939* (Cambridge, MA: Harvard University Press, 1980); Christopher Faulkner, *Jean Renoir: A Guide to References and Resources* (Boston: G. K. Hall, 1979).
5 Freddy Buache, *Le Cinéma français des années 60* (Renens: 5 Continents/Paris: Hatier, 1987); Freddy Buache, *Le Cinéma français des années 70* (Renens: 5 Continents/Paris: Hatier, 1990).
6 Jean-Pierre Jeancolas, *15 ans d'années trente: le cinéma des Français, 1929–1944* (Paris: Stock, 1983); Raymond Chirat and Micheline Presle, *La IVe République et ses films* (Paris: 5 Continents/Hatier, 1985); Geneviève Guillaume-Grimaud, *Le Cinéma du Front Populaire* (Paris: Lherminier, 1986); Jonathan Buchsbaum, *Cinéma Engagé: Film in the Popular Front* (Urbana: University of Illinois Press, 1988); Richard Abel, *French Cinema: The First Wave, 1915–1929* (Princeton: Princeton University Press, 1984); Richard Abel (ed.), *French Film Theory and Criticism: A History/Anthology, 1907–1939*, vol. 1: 1907–1929 (Princeton: Princeton University Press, 1988).
7 Jacques Siclier, *Le Cinéma français*, vol. 1. *De La Bataille du rail à La Chinoise, 1945-1968*; vol.2. *De Baisers volés à Cyrano de Bergerac, 1968-1990* (Paris: Editions Ramsay, 1990); Pierre Billard, *L'Age classique du cinéma français: du cinéma parlant à la Nouvelle Vague* (Paris: Flammarion, 1995); Jean-Michel Frodon, *L'Age moderne du cinéma français: de la Nouvelle Vague à nos jours* (Paris: Flammarion, 1995); Jean-Pierre Jeancolas, *Histoire du cinéma français* (Paris: Nathan, 1995).
8 René Prédal, *Le Cinéma français depuis 1945* (Paris: Nathan, 1991).
9 Alan Williams, *Republic of Images: A History of French Filmmaking* (Cambridge, MA: Harvard University Press, 1992); Dudley Andrew, *Mists of Regret: Culture and Sensibility in Classic French Film* (Princeton: Princeton University Press, 1995). T. Jefferson Kline's *Screening the Text: Intertextuality in New Wave French Cinema* (Baltimore and

indeed did the 'first generation' of French cinema scholars in the UK. The much-regretted Jill Forbes published a major work, *The Cinema in France after the New Wave*, and Susan Hayward began the series on national cinemas she edits for Routledge with an ambitious revaluation of the whole of French cinema. Hayward and Vincendeau co-edited a key collection.[10]

The decade can be singled out for a second reason: there was a dramatic increase in the number of theses in French cinema, from 80 in the previous decade to 180 in the 1990s. Much of that increase occurred in the second half of the decade. Just over 100 of these were French, some 65 being American.

A new series devoted to French directors was launched in 1998, established by Diana Holmes and Robert Ingram for Manchester University Press, to which many established French cinema colleagues have contributed over the years. Manchester University Press also published Guy Austin's compact *Contemporary French Cinema: An Introduction*, in 1996, and there were several other volumes focused on particular periods.[11] There was an increasing trend away from the synoptic history prevalent in the 1980s towards extended essays on particular films.[12]

The new century ushered in new directions. The 1990s' trend of extended essays, often on individual films, was strengthened by the establishment of the journal *Studies in French Cinema*, in 2000, along with the Association of Studies in French Cinema and its annual conference. Work on French cinema was frequently being published in UK journals such as *French Cultural Studies*, and, to a lesser extent, *French Studies* and *Modern and Contemporary France*; but the establishment of *Studies in French Cinema* gave the community the chance to engage in a more sustained debate.

Closer ties between French and anglophone colleagues was a feature of the decade; a conference at the Ecole Normale Supérieure in Lyon in July 2004 brought together the French Association Française des Enseignants et Chercheurs en Cinéma et Audiovisuel, the US Society for Cinema and Media Studies (especially its French and francophone

London: The Johns Hopkins University Press, 1992) was a major revaluation of the New Wave, for example.

10 Jill Forbes, *The Cinema in France after the New Wave* (Basingstoke: Macmillan, 1992); Susan Hayward, *French National Cinema* (London and New York: Routledge, 1993; 2nd edn 2005); Susan Hayward and Ginette Vincendeau (eds), *French Cinema: Texts and Contexts* (London: Routledge, 1990; 2nd edn 2000).

11 Patricia Hubert-Lacombe, *Le Cinéma français dans la guerre froide: 1946–1956* (Paris: L'Harmattan, 1996); Emma Wilson, *French Cinema since 1950: Personal Histories* (London: Duckworth, 1999).

12 For example, Phil Powrie, *French Cinema in the 1980s: Nostalgia and the Crisis of Masculinity* (Oxford: Clarendon Press, 1997); Phil Powrie (ed.), *French Cinema in the 1990s: Continuity and Difference* (Oxford: Oxford University Press, 1999).

interest group), and the UK Association for Studies in French Cinema. Closer ties were also evident in published work, as several French scholars turned their attention to areas of the discipline previously associated with anglophone cinema studies, such as Geneviève Sellier, who has promoted gender studies in France.[13]

There were two key developments in the new century. The first of these is closely related to gender studies. Work on French stars in both the UK and France took off in the 2000s, with Vincendeau's magisterial essays on the French star system, *Stars and Stardom in French Cinema*, collecting work done over the previous decade. The second growth area was francophone and postcolonial cinema, broad surveys being complemented by more focused studies;[14] in a similar vein, Carrie Tarr, one of the first generation of scholars, collected and reframed material she had been publishing over a long period of time, and published a major statement on Maghrebi-French ('beur'), cinema, *Reframing Difference: Beur and Banlieue Filmmaking in France*.

Theses on French cinema increased again in this decade. Whereas there had been 180 for the whole of the 1990s, by the end of 2007 there were already 195. The number of UK theses grew in the 2000s; there had been nine in the 1990s, rising to 31 in the period 2000–2007. The trends were broadly similar to those of the 1990s, with some 40 theses devoted to the New Wave directors. Fifteen of the 40 theses involved work on Godard, who was the subject of a major international conference at the Tate in London in 2001. Work on the New Wave was complemented by other significant publications,[15] as well as volumes on Jacques Rivette[16] and Eric Rohmer,[17] both of them previously neglected.

13 Geneviève Sellier, *La Nouvelle Vague: un cinéma au masculin singulier* (Paris: CNRS, 2005); Noël Burch and Geneviève Sellier, *La Drôle de guerre des sexes du cinéma français: 1930–1956* (Paris: Nathan, 1996).

14 Lieve Spaas, *The Francophone Film: A Struggle for Identity* (Manchester: Manchester University Press, 2000); Roy Armes, *African Filmmaking: North and South of the Sahara* (Edinburgh: Edinburgh University Press, 2006); David Murphy and Patrick Williams, *Postcolonial African Cinema: Ten Directors* (Manchester: Manchester University Press, 2007).

15 Michel Marie, *La Nouvelle Vague: une école artistique* (Paris: Nathan, 2000); Richard Neupert, *A History of the French New Wave Cinema* (Madison, Wis.: University of Wisconsin Press, 2002); Naomi Greene, *The French New Wave: A New Look* (London: Wallflower Press, 2007).

16 Hélène Deschamps, *Jacques Rivette: théâtre, amour, cinéma* (Paris: L'Harmattan, 2001); Hélène Frappat, *Jacques Rivette, secret compris* (Paris: Cahiers du cinéma, 2001); Douglas Morrey and Alison Smith, *Jacques Rivette* (Manchester: Manchester University Press, 2009).

17 Jean Cléder (ed.), *Eric Rohmer: évidence et ambiguïté du cinéma* (Latresne: Le Bord de l'eau, 2007); Noël Herpe (ed.), *Rohmer et les autres* (Rennes: Presses Universitaires de Rennes, 2007); Derek Schilling, *Eric Rohmer* (Manchester: Manchester University Press, 2007); Keith Tester, *Eric Rohmer: Film as Theology* (London: Palgrave Macmillan, 2008).

Work on the 1930s was by contrast, and reflecting what Keith Reader writes above, considerably less extensive than in the 1990s, with barely half a dozen theses; this was to some extent compensated for by an important book on the period, Colin Crisp's *The Classic French Cinema: 1930–1960*, as well as several volumes on Renoir (including the lavishly illustrated biography by Faulkner and Duncan).[18]

Three new areas of interest emerged at the end of the last decade and during this decade, although they are as yet not reflected in significant thesis production: work on politically engaged cinema;[19] *le jeune cinéma*,[20] and the cinema of sensation – Martine Beugnet's *Cinema and Sensation: French Film and the Art of Transgression*.

In the middle of the decade there were two events that encapsulate the coming of age for academic work on French cinema studies. Vincendeau established the I. B. Tauris French Film Guides; this was preceded in 2004 by the British Film Institute's *The French Cinema Book*, by Michael Temple and Michael Witt, which brought together essays by a range of international scholars.

Conclusion

The distinguishing feature of UK-based scholarship where French cinema is concerned has been the gender paradigm, now being adopted by French scholars; and close attention paid to popular cinema, whether popular genres or stars, which has been less of a feature of research in France. The study of French cinema has never been so broad in its sweep, both in terms of its interests, and in terms of its two hundred or so researchers across the globe.

18 Christopher Faulkner and Paul Duncan (eds), *Jean Renoir: A Conversation with his Films 1894–1979* (Hong Kong/Köln/London: Taschen, 2007); Colin Davis, *Scenes of Love and Murder: Renoir, Film and Philosophy* (London: Wallflower, 2008); Charlotte Garson, *Jean Renoir* (Paris: Cahiers du cinéma/Le Monde, 2008).
19 Graeme Hayes and Martin O'Shaughnessy (eds), *Cinéma et engagement* (Paris: L'Harmattan, 2005); Laurent Marie, *Le Cinéma est à nous: le PCF et le cinéma français de la Libération à nos jours* (Paris: L'Harmattan, 2005); Martin O'Shaughnessy, *The New Face of Political Cinema: Commitment in French Film since 1995* (New York and Oxford: Berghahn, 2007).
20 Michel Marie (ed.), *Le Jeune cinéma français* (Paris: Nathan, 1998); Claude Trémois, *Les Enfants de la liberté: le jeune cinéma français des années 90* (Paris: Seuil, 1998); René Prédal, *Le Jeune cinéma français* (Paris: Nathan, 2002); Daniel Serceau, *Symptômes du jeune cinéma français* (Paris: Cerf/Corlet, 2008).

Bibliography

Abel, Richard, *French Cinema: The First Wave, 1915–1929* (Princeton: Princeton University Press, 1984).

Abel, Richard (ed.), *French Film Theory and Criticism: A History/Anthology, 1907–1939*, vol. 1: 1907–1929 (Princeton: Princeton University Press, 1988).

Andrew, Dudley, *Mists of Regret: Culture and Sensibility in Classic French Film* (Princeton: Princeton University Press, 1995).

Armes, Roy, *African Filmmaking: North and South of the Sahara* (Edinburgh: Edinburgh University Press, 2006). Translated into French by Françoise Rippe-Lascout and Marie-Cécile Wouters (Paris: L'Harmattan, 2006).

Austin, Guy, *Contemporary French Cinema: An Introduction* (Manchester: Manchester University Press, 1996).

Beugnet, Martine, *Cinema and Sensation: French Film and the Art of Transgression* (Edinburgh: Edinburgh University Press, 2007).

Billard, Pierre, *L'Age classique du cinéma français: du cinéma parlant à la Nouvelle Vague* (Paris: Flammarion, 1995).

Braudy, Leo, *Jean Renoir: The World of His Films* (London: Robson, 1977).

Brown, Royal S. (ed.), *Focus on Godard* (Englewood Cliffs: Prentice-Hall, 1972).

Buache, Freddy, *Le Cinéma français des années 60* (Renens: 5 Continents/Paris: Hatier, 1987).

Buache, Freddy, *Le Cinéma français des années 70* (Renens: 5 Continents/Paris: Hatier, 1990).

Buchsbaum, Jonathan, *Cinéma Engagé: Film in the Popular Front* (Urbana: University of Illinois Press, 1988).

Burch, Noël and Geneviève Sellier, *La Drôle de guerre des sexes du cinéma français: 1930–1956* (Paris: Nathan, 1996).

Burch, Noël and Geneviève Sellier, *Le Cinéma au prisme des rapports de sexe* (Paris:Vrin, 2009).

Chirat, Raymond and Micheline Presle, *La IVe République et ses films* (Paris: 5 Continents: Hatier, 1985).

Cléder, Jean (ed.), *Eric Rohmer: évidence et ambiguïté du cinéma* (Latresne: Le Bord de l'eau, 2007).

Crisp, Colin, *The Classic French Cinema: 1930–1960* (Bloomington: Indiana University Press, 1993).

Davis, Colin, *Scenes of Love and Murder: Renoir, Film and Philosophy* (London: Wallflower, 2008).

Deschamps, Hélène, *Jacques Rivette: théâtre, amour, cinéma* (Paris: L'Harmattan, 2001).

Durgnat, Raymond, *Jean Renoir* (Berkeley: University of California Press, 1974).

Faulkner, Christopher, *Jean Renoir: A Guide to References and Resources* (Boston: G. K. Hall, 1979).

Faulkner, Christopher and Paul Duncan (eds), *Jean Renoir: A Conversation with his Films 1894–1979* (Hong Kong/Köln/London: Taschen, 2007).

Forbes, Jill, *The Cinema in France after the New Wave* (Basingstoke, Hampshire: Macmillan, 1992).

Frappat, Hélène, *Jacques Rivette, secret compris* (Paris: Cahiers du cinéma, 2001).

Frodon, Jean-Michel, *L'Age moderne du cinéma français: de la Nouvelle Vague à nos jours* (Paris: Flammarion, 1995).

Garson, Charlotte, *Jean Renoir* (Paris: Cahiers du cinéma/Le Monde, 2008).

Greene, Naomi, *The French New Wave: A New Look* (London: Wallflower Press, 2007).

Guillaume-Grimaud, Geneviève, *Le Cinéma du Front Populaire* (Paris: Lherminier, 1986).

Hayes, Graeme and Martin O'Shaughnessy (eds), *Cinéma et engagement* (Paris: L'Harmattan, 2005).

Hayward, Susan, *French National Cinema* (London/New York: Routledge, 1993; 2nd edn 2005).

Hayward, Susan and Ginette Vincendeau (eds), *French Cinema: Texts and Contexts* (London: Routledge, 1990; 2nd edn, 2000).

Herpe, Noël (ed.), *Rohmer et les autres* (Rennes: Presses Universitaires de Rennes, 2007).

Hubert-Lacombe, Patricia, *Le Cinéma français dans la guerre froide: 1946–1956* (Paris: L'Harmattan, 1996).

Jeancolas, Jean-Pierre (1995), *Histoire du cinéma français* (Paris: Nathan).

Jenn, Pierre, *Georges Méliès cinéaste: le montage cinématographique chez Georges Méliès* (Paris: Albatros, 1984).

Kline, T. Jefferson, *Screening the Text: Intertextuality in New Wave French Cinema* (Baltimore and London: The Johns Hopkins University Press, 1992).

Lesage, Julia, *Jean-Luc Godard: A Guide to References and Resources* (Boston, Mass.: G. K. Hall, 1979).

MacCabe, Colin, et al., *Godard: Images, Sounds, Politics* (London: Macmillan/British Film Institute, 1980).

Marie, Laurent, *Le Cinéma est à nous: le PCF et le cinéma français de la Libération à nos jours* (Paris: L'Harmattan, 2005).

Marie, Michel, *La Nouvelle Vague: une école artistique* (Paris: Nathan, 2000). Translated by Richard Neupert as *The French New Wave: An Artistic School* (Malden: Blackwell, 2003).

Marie, Michel, *Guide des études cinématographiques et audiovisuelles* (Paris: Armand Colin, 2006).

Marie, Michel (ed.), *Le Jeune cinéma français* (Paris: Nathan, 1998).

Monaco, James, *The New Wave: Truffaut, Godard, Chabrol, Rohmer, Rivette* (New York/ Oxford: Oxford University Press, 1976).

Morrey, Douglas and Alison Smith, *Jacques Rivette* (Manchester: Manchester University Press, 2009).

Murphy, David and Patrick Williams, *Postcolonial African Cinema: Ten Directors* (Manchester: Manchester University Press, 2007).

Nacache, Jacqueline, *L'Acteur de cinéma* (Paris: Nathan, 2003).

Neupert, Richard, *A History of the French New Wave Cinema* (Madison, Wis.: University of Wisconsin Press, 2002).

O'Shaughnessy, Martin, *The New Face of Political Cinema: Commitment in French Film since 1995* (New York and Oxford: Berghahn, 2007).

Powrie, Phil, *French Cinema in the 1980s: Nostalgia and the Crisis of Masculinity* (Oxford: Clarendon Press, 1997).

Powrie, Phil (ed.), *French Cinema in the 1990s: Continuity and Difference* (Oxford, Oxford University Press, 1999).

Prédal, René, *Le Cinéma français depuis 1945* (Paris: Nathan, 1991).

Prédal, René, *Le Jeune cinéma français* (Paris: Nathan, 2002).

Schilling, Derek, *Eric Rohmer* (Manchester: Manchester University Press, 2007).

Sellier, Geneviève, *La Nouvelle Vague: un cinéma au masculin singulier* (Paris: CNRS, 2005). Translated by Kristin Ross as *Masculine Singular: French New Wave Cinema* (Durham: Duke University Press, 2008).

Serceau, Daniel, *Symptômes du jeune cinéma français* (Paris: Cerf/Corlet, 2008).

Sesonske, Alexander, *Jean Renoir: The French Films, 1924–1939* (Cambridge, Mass.: Harvard University Press, 1980).

Siclier, Jacques, *Le Cinéma français*, vol. 1. *De La Bataille du rail à La Chinoise, 1945–1968*; vol. 2. *De Baisers volés à Cyrano de Bergerac, 1968–1990* (Paris: Editions Ramsay, 1990).

Spaas, Lieve, *The Francophone Film: A Struggle for Identity* (Manchester: Manchester University Press, 2000).

Tarr, Carrie, *Reframing Difference: Beur and Banlieue Filmmaking in France* (Manchester: Manchester University, 2005).

Temple, Michael and Michael Witt (eds), *The French Cinema Book* (London: British Film Institute, 2004).

Tester, Keith, *Eric Rohmer: Film as Theology* (London: Palgrave Macmillan, 2008).

Trémois, Claude, *Les Enfants de la liberté: le jeune cinéma français des années 90* (Paris: Seuil, 1998).

Vincendeau, Ginette, *Stars and Stardom in French Cinema* (London and New York: Continuum, 2000).

Williams, Alan, *Republic of Images: A History of French Filmmaking* (Cambridge, Mass.: Harvard University Press, 1992).

Wilson, Emma, *French Cinema since 1950: Personal Histories* (London: Duckworth, 1999).

15

Popular Culture, the Final Frontier: How Far Should We Boldly Go?

David Looseley

This chapter is about the place of contemporary popular culture in French Studies.[1] Both '*populaire*' and 'popular' are of course problematic epithets, but I do not wish to encumber this particular discussion with matters of definition, important as they are at an epistemological level.[2] I therefore use 'popular culture' in its common English sense, refer-ring to contemporary industrialised forms and practices such as pop music, television, commercial cinema, pulp fiction, and so on, which reach a large, sociologically diverse audience. In French, such forms and practices have often been pejoratively referred to as *la culture de masse*, though this is changing, as with the rise of the term *culture médiatique* for example. '*Populaire*', meanwhile, has conventionally been reserved for traditional, 'folk' cultures, whether working class or peasant (though this too is changing). But in this conventional sense, *la culture populaire* is of a somewhat different nature and its situation within French culture, and French Studies, raises different issues, so it is not my main concern here.

Popular culture in the sense I have chosen has only recently become a focus of research in UK French departments, and its place in our discipline remains problematic. Of course, popular artefacts like youth magazines, BD, television programmes or songs have long been used in language teaching. As far back as 1967, when my own undergraduate studies in French began, I discovered Brel and Brassens not in an option on popular music, inconceivable in those days, but in a language-lab comprehension exercise. And over the next thirty years or so, study

---

1 In conformity with this volume's brief to discuss 'les études françaises' in the UK, and also for the sake of brevity, I refer throughout to 'French Studies', though it has become increasingly accepted that the discipline today should be known as French and Francophone (with or without the capital 'F') Studies.

2 A fuller discussion of the meanings of popular/*populaire* and the application of these meanings in a variety of French media will be available in D. Holmes and D. L. Looseley (eds), *Constructing the Popular in Contemporary French Culture* (provisional title) (MUP, forthcoming 2012).

of popular culture in the 'content' courses of French Studies degrees, as an object of textual analysis or criticism, remained exceptional. It is true that by 1997 I might have encountered Brel or Brassens in a *chanson* module somewhere. But I would have been likely to study them primarily as singing poets rather than as mass-cultural products of a powerful creative industry. Indeed, in France as in Britain, academic discourse until quite recently tended to present *chanson* as only meriting advanced study by virtue of its literary qualities.[3]

This absence of engagement with what is popular about popular culture is curious. Like the actors required to fight the Invisible Man in the 1950s TV series, UK French Studies has been energetically wrestling with itself for decades. Interrogating its ontology, it has quite rightly embraced a variety of neglected approaches to the academic study of French: gender and sexuality, politics and society, film, travel writing, autobiography, francophone or postcolonial writing, and more.[4] Yet the popular has not particularly been foregrounded in this interrogation, other than under cover of the postcolonial turn.[5] This relative neglect is, I believe, an Achilles heel, creating problems for the self-knowledge of UK French Studies, for its understanding of what it is and its ability to move forward. For example, we tend to make promiscuous use these days of the term 'cultural studies' to indicate that our teaching and research are 'interdisciplinary' – a buzzword of the higher education market in Britain at the moment. Yet I suspect that we do not entirely mean what cultural studies academics mean when they describe themselves in these terms. Admittedly, they too have trouble pinning down the full range of connotations of cultural studies today, because these are forever changing. Yet one only has to look at the numerous histories of cultural studies now available to observe that one of its first principles, and its core characteristic, as perceived by its theorists and practitioners has been its concern with popular culture – inevitably so, given its origins in the work of Richard Hoggart (1957), who founded the Birmingham School

---

3 See D. L. Looseley, *Popular Music in Contemporary France: Authenticity, Politics, Debate* (Oxford and New York: Berg, 2003), chapter 4. Bourdieu's comments on the social meanings of *chanson* in relation to education are illuminating in this context: see Pierre Bourdieu, *La Distinction: critique sociale du jugement* (Paris: Éditions de Minuit, 1979), chapter 1.

4 See Holmes in this volume.

5 The RAE 2008 sub-panel Overview Report at p. 11 (London: HEFCE, 2009) comes close to acknowledging this when it comments that the 'initial literary emphases in the [postcolonial] field are slowly adjusting to accommodate new research on a range of other forms and genres, most notably music, film and TV, and other manifestations of visual culture, including Bande dessinée (graphic novel)', online resource, consulted 1 January 2011. (The RAE is the research assessment exercise which takes place periodically as a means of basing future public funding for research in UK higher education institutions on the evaluation of its quality. In its latest form, it is called the REF: Research Excellence Framework.)

of Contemporary Cultural Studies in 1964, and of Raymond Williams (1958), whose statement that 'culture is ordinary' became a maxim.

This semantic misunderstanding between French Studies and cultural studies, which even the existence of a journal called *French Cultural Studies* has not fully resolved, goes some way to explaining a phenomenon I encountered for some years when trying to organise interdisciplinary research seminars in the context of the Popular Cultures Research Network: French Studies people do not always have much to say to cultural studies people, nor they to us. This, I suspect, is because both fields, despite any claims to the contrary, are actually quite territorial. Cultural studies has to a very large extent remained anglocentric; and French Studies still sees itself as primarily a language and literature discipline, so that what we tend to mean in practice by interdisciplinary cultural studies is the study of literature (ancient or modern)[6] and cinema (usually art-house) with the help of other disciplines: social sciences, philosophy, history of art, and so on.

Particularly revealing in this regard is the recent 'Overview Report' by the RAE 2008 sub-panel 52 on French in UK higher education,[7] where there is no sense at all of the popular as a recognised subset within the 'subject coverage'.[8] The word 'popular' appears only once in the sense that is relevant to our discussion, when the section on film studies correctly identifies among a number of significant new initiatives 'a critical reassessment of the relationship between popular and art-house traditions'.[9] 'Cultural studies' gets four mentions but, again revealingly, the best 'cultural studies-inflected work' is described as 'provid[ing] new perspectives on the literary field'. In truth, the report presents a *grille de lecture*, an interpretative grid: it takes for granted that French Studies consists by nature of a chronologically organised broadly literary menu with a couple of slightly perplexing side dishes: linguistics on the one hand and the conceptual doggy-bag of 'political, historical and social studies' on the other. And although after the chronological survey it does identify some cross-cutting themes ('text and image', 'modern French thought, philosophy and theory', and 'Francophone and postcolonial areas'), popular culture is not one of them. So why not?

Let me first be clear: this is not a question of apportioning blame. The report had to structure itself round the work being done and clearly a great deal of work is being done in literary areas. Its way of mapping the discipline also reflects the very real research dominance of Oxford

---

6   Under 'literature' I include, as the discipline traditionally has, the novel, poetry, drama and thought: those categories which give the term 'literature' its high-cultural connotation. I exclude, for example, popular fiction of mass appeal such as romance, detective or graphic novels, though of course such boundaries are never watertight.

7   HEFCE, Overview report, online resource, consulted 1 January 2011.

8   HEFCE, Overview report, pp. 8–11.

9   HEFCE, Overview report, p. 10.

and Cambridge and the language and literature model those universities perpetuate, which dates back to at least the nineteenth century
and was calqued on English and Classics.[10] Nevertheless, given the
conceptual and demographic changes in the discipline in recent years,
a different mapping was perfectly possible and might well have exposed
a significant research engagement with the popular, especially among
early-career academics. For example, the report refers to work on stars,
detective fiction, and popular film and music in the twentieth and
twenty-first centuries.[11] If from there one works backwards though the
century-based sections, adjusting our definitions of the popular to take
account of the differing socio-cultural and technological conditions,
one begins to notice work ranging from social history and photography
in the nineteenth century, to the interdisciplinary 'understanding of
different aesthetic media' in Renaissance studies, to anthropological approaches in medieval studies, and to the 'non-canonical' trends in both
early modern periods. Obviously, given the inevitable generality of the
report we cannot be certain that all such work would fit with the label
'popular', but the potential for bringing at least some of it together in an
alternative cross-cutting theme of this kind was none the less there. So
perhaps the problem is simply that we do not 'think popular'.

If so, I have a hunch that this is because, despite ourselves, the
contemporary popular lies outside our comfort zone. The implication of high-cultural excellence enshrined in the word 'literature' has
made us chary of station-bookstall 'fiction'. We have happily studied
art-house cinema for years but have not felt quite so comfortable with
popular film. And as I have already hinted, we are at ease with, say,
Brassens, or even a rapper like MC Solaar, because their verbal dex-
terity and historical allusiveness seem to call for a conventional literary
toolkit, allowing us to relate them to the troubadours or Villon. But
how do you solve a problem like Johnny? Or the *rappeuse* Diam's, or
'Star Academy'? Should we approach them as 'real-world' material for
topic-based language teaching, or as culture in the anthropological
sense, or as part of an area studies or '*civilisation*' curriculum? These
intersecting approaches have all been tried in recent years: for example
in the 'popular culture' component of AQA's AS level French syllabus
introduced in 2009, made up of cinema, music and fashion.[12] But, in an
effort to be value-neutral, such approaches eliminate what has been at
the very heart of French Studies, which is aesthetic analysis and critical
evaluation. This is the crucial theoretical question about how French
Studies should approach the popular.

---

10 See Holmes in this volume.
11 HEFCE, Overview report, p. 10.
12 AQA is the Assessment and Qualifications Alliance, the largest of the three English
    exam boards. AS level is a post-16 academic qualification representing half an A level.

It is actually a dilemma that cultural studies too has faced. Having decided quite early on (and a little too hastily in my view) that the aesthetic study of popular-cultural texts was a methodological dead-end, cultural studies in the 1970s and 1980s turned to reception. With the help of Michel de Certeau,[13] among others, it began examining how popular culture is reappropriated and subverted by its users. This is the 'creative consumption' argument. It has produced some important work but, as Simon Frith has suggested in a discussion of what he calls 'the value problem in cultural studies',[14] it also carries a negative implication regarding the popular. It implies that, unlike high-cultural forms which continue to receive close textual scrutiny as *production*, popular artefacts only merit academic attention as *consumption*; as if it went without saying that studying, say, a piece of popular music as an aesthetic artefact was pointless. As Frith points out, this is merely Adornism in disguise. It can perhaps be accounted for by the growing involvement in cultural studies of social scientists, just as the initial textual drift of cultural studies owed much to the humanities backgrounds of its founders. With some justification, social scientists, wearying of the 'textualism' produced under the influence of Barthes and poststructuralism, argued that such study isolated the text from sociological and political realities.[15]

French Studies, however, is textualist by both tradition and methodology. Indeed, the humanities more generally, it could be argued, need to find a way of 'doing' cultural studies that does not require us to become social scientists. More importantly, as Frith also insists,[16] the question of popular discrimination needs to be taken seriously: because 'the essence of popular cultural practice is making judgments and assessing differences' and because 'there is no reason to believe a priori that such judgments work differently in different cultural spheres'. He goes on:

> What I'm suggesting here is that people bring similar questions to high and low art, that their pleasures and satisfactions are rooted in similar analytic issues, similar ways of relating what they see or hear to how they think or feel. The differences between high and low emerge because these questions are embedded in different historical and material circumstances and are therefore framed differently....[17]

So my question is why should French Studies academics, schooled in critical evaluation and fully aware of the specific 'historical and material circumstances' prevailing in the countries they specialise in, avoid making such judgements or skirt the issue of how they are made?

13 M. de Certeau, *L'Invention du quotidien, vol. I: Arts de faire* (Paris: Gallimard, 1990).

14 S. Frith, *Performing Rites: Evaluating Popular Music* (Oxford and New York: Oxford University Press, 1998), pp. 3–20.

15 See A, Mattelart and E. Neveu, *Introduction aux cultural studies* (Paris: Découverte, 2003).

16 Frith, *Performing Rites*, pp. 16–17.

17 Frith, *Performing Rites*, p. 19.

It was this kind of question that led to the creation at the University of Leeds of the Popular Cultures Research Network (PCRN).[18] Set up in 2005–6, the PCRN has rapidly become an international, inter-disciplinary forum, bringing together over 100 scholars (and a small but growing number of practitioners) interested in popular culture. It is hosted by the Leeds School of Modern Languages and Cultures and was founded (not insignificantly, given the above dilemmas) by members of the Department of French. As a result, unlike in other popular culture groups in the anglophone world, francophone cultures are a major component. The French language is in fact present in two ways. First, there are French Studies academics in the four interdisci-plinary research clusters that the PCRN has so far generated: popular fictions; policy and the popular; popular music; and popular film and television. Second, the PCRN's international membership includes a significant number of native French speakers from a variety of disci-plines and locations. These include the well-known cultural sociologist Antoine Hennion (Ecole des Mines, Paris), Vincent Dubois, sociologist and political scientist at the Institut d'Etudes Politiques of the University of Strasbourg, and most significantly perhaps, the Centre de Recherches sur les Littératures Populaires et les Cultures Médiatiques at Limoges, an affiliated institutional member which collaborated with the PCRN on a major international conference at Leeds in April 2010 funded by the British Academy and the French Embassy, entitled 'Finding the Plot: On the Importance of Storytelling in Popular Fiction'.[19]

However, another important claim to originality is that the network is by no means focused exclusively on either French or other modern lan-guages. A high proportion of its members are from anglophone cultural studies, sociology, politics, philosophy, music, English, history, even law and education – disciplines which we in French at Leeds wanted to dialogue with in order to define and explore more thoroughly our claims regarding 'interdisciplinarity' and 'cultural studies'. Dialogue is in fact the overarching ambition of the PCRN. Since its inception, we have promoted an open, inclusive and evolving sense of what is meant by 'popular culture': hence, in part, the plural, 'popular cultures'. But the plural also underlines the need for modern language disciplines both to be aware of the well-established perspectives of anglophone cultural studies and to make inputs into, and where necessary change, those perspectives. Research in modern languages usually 'locates' popular cultures in various ways, rather than approaching them as stateless, global phenomena. It focuses particularly on their dynamic relation-ships with places and spaces in the form of nations, regions, localities and other communities with specific linguistic and cultural histories.

18 University of Leeds Popular Cultures Research Network (PCRN), online reources, consulted 1 January 2011.
19 *Finding the Plot*, online resource, consulted 1 January 2011.

We do not, then, privilege the anglophone world in the way cultural studies has tended to. But neither do we simply ignore that world and the processes of globalisation associated with it. Instead, the network promotes a polycentric conception of popular cultures in which the anglophone world features among the 'located' cultures the network is interested in, but in a creative and egalitarian exchange. This allows us to bring together diverse cultural histories and imaginations in the form of dynamic interdisciplinary encounters and to explore popular cultures in relation to the major preoccupations of cutting-edge research in the arts and humanities, the social sciences, and of course cultural studies.

But French Studies is also present in the network in its own right. A publication project has been launched involving members from Leeds and Southampton, who are working on a book edited by Diana Holmes and myself and due for publication by Manchester University Press in 2012.[20] This will be the first monograph to emerge as a direct result of the network's existence. It examines constructions of the popular in contemporary French culture via six case studies: the state, music, fiction, film, language and television. It is, then, about popular-cultural discourse, though the various contributors approach this orientation in different ways. At one level, discourse implies discussion and debate about the popular in those six case studies. But we are also interested in how discourses of the popular are embedded within cultural or aesthetic forms. Accordingly, an unusually diverse corpus of texts is used depending on the case study, including creative works and statements by their creators, polemical writing, political speeches, media debates, and linguistic debates and samples. In this way, the book aspires to be genuinely interdisciplinary by bridging the various branches of French Studies – linguistics, the arts, history and politics/area studies; and by questioning that high–low divide referred to earlier whereby highbrow artefacts are examined critically as production, while popular artefacts are only examined from the point of view of reception, sidestepping the issue of discrimination. Certainly, we do not claim at this stage to have come up with an overarching methodology for evaluating the popular; nor was this ever our aim. But given that the problem in French Studies has been knowing *how* to study the popular, it may be that starting with discourse proves a useful first step towards properly integrating the critical study of the popular into French Studies.

What I have just outlined is a research agenda. But what are the implications for teaching? My colleagues in the Leeds French department who have been involved in the network from the outset each teach popular culture in their own way in accordance with their own specialisms, notably linguistics, fiction and film. My own research and teaching have focused on popular music on the one hand, and on leisure, culture

20 Holmes and Looseley, *Constructing the Popular.*

and cultural policy on the other. I brought these dimensions together in a well-subscribed second-year undergraduate course (later a 20-credit module), entitled 'Aspects of Popular Culture in France since 1945'. The course description read as follows:

> The module aims to introduce you in the French context to some alternatives to 'high' culture by concerning itself with forms of cultural production which aspire to reach a large and sociologically diverse audience. Some notions of popular, mass and high culture since 1936 will be studied and a small selection of cultural products examined: popular music, *la chanson française*, and television. To introduce students to the diverse ways in which popular culture may be examined, a variety of approaches is adopted: historical, theoretical (to a small extent), sociological and textual.

In its early days, the course began with a set book designed to open up theoretical issues to do with mass, high and popular cultures in a six-week package called 'Notions of Popular Culture', by far the toughest part of the 20-week course (1.5 hours a week). Initially, I chose Barthes's *Mythologies*. Excellent though this was, it turned out to be too difficult as an introductory text for undergraduates unused to theorising even their own popular-cultural practices. I therefore replaced it with a very different text by Louis Dollot, *Culture individuelle et culture de masse*.[21] Although this never quite met my requirements either, it did at least provide students with a basic historical overview and with some theoretical perspectives to start them off. But I soon realised that it also served a quite different purpose. Here again, discourse was at the heart of the matter. The somewhat dry, aloof, value-laden prose in which the volume discussed 'mass-cultural' activities contrasted strongly with the intimately involved ways in which English-speaking students discourse about such activities. The clash proved illuminating and, for the students themselves, sometimes infuriating. Much more than just a required course text, then, the book became our first case study, tested against historical and institutional understandings of the popular, from the Popular Front's Léo Lagrange through Jean Vilar of the TNP to André Malraux and Jack Lang at the Ministry of Culture.

After this discursive baptism of fire, life got marginally easier for the students as we moved on to study the 'culture' itself in three further case studies: *la chanson française*, popular music more generally, and television in the contrasting forms of TF1's 'Star Academy' and the cultural channel ARTE. In all three case studies, the element of discourse remained central, so that students could be confronted not only with the artefacts themselves but also with the way they were rationalised and argued over. In the case of ARTE, for example, we examined the

---

21 L. Dollot, *Culture individuelle et culture de masse*. Series: Que Sais-Je (Paris: Presses universitaires de France, 1999).

aspirations of the channel, its programming and the debates surrounding its creation and evolution. But how did the option address the issue of critical evaluation? No doubt unsatisfactorily, but in two ways. Taking ARTE as an example again, the discourses we looked at were often evaluative ones, so that we were able to consider how such judgements were arrived at, what their underlying assumptions were and what we thought of them. Students were also expected to make use of the channel and develop their own evaluations in response to these vicarious judgements. Seminar time was thus taken up by the textual study of other people's views and the confrontation of these views with the students' own, to prevent the latter being purely subjective. Students were also urged to go beyond these preliminary discussions in the formal assessment via their own research.

The module, then, as with any traditional literature course, required them to read widely and to critically assess what they were studying. Paradoxically, perhaps, this made the module one of the more challenging but 'popular' of the second-year options, judging by student feedback. Indeed, one entertaining irony was that at the annual showcase event which the department held so that first-years could choose their second-year options, colleagues teaching literature would sometimes emphasise the elements of topicality and enjoyment in their modules while I would try to dissuade all but the stoutest of hearts by telling them that contemporary popular culture was all about intellectual challenge, historical perspective and heavy reading.

Other teachers would no doubt design a popular culture module differently – as might I if I had my time again. Nevertheless, the reasons for French as a twenty-first-century discipline to come to grips with contemporary popular culture in some form seem to me self-evident. Pragmatically, it attracts students, who are often looking – or think they are looking – for ways of avoiding 'literature'. More importantly, it helps them speak up in class (my lectures and seminars were mostly in French) because they feel on safer ground, even when confronted with difficult theoretical concepts. And it teaches them what a critical perspective can actually look and feel like in the familiar context of their own cultural practices, in a way that literature does not automatically do for those students who have experienced only audiovisual, dematerialised cultural practices before going to university.

Yet crucially, I do not in any way see popular culture, however contemporary, as literature's nemesis, though I am conscious that there are those who do. I myself studied, taught and researched literature for years before specialising in popular culture; and I am lucky to have taught in a department where this more recent specialism has been firmly embedded in, and relativised by, a set of other courses ranging from medieval writers and poets to the twenty-first-century novel. This has only confirmed my conviction that the study of popular culture is a bridge, not a bypass. As long as it retains the elements of textual analysis (including written sources) and historical three-dimensionality, as long as it is intellectually credible and challenging, I am convinced it can lead seamlessly into curiosity about other cultural outputs and value systems and eventually to a better understanding of them. I have known many students taking a mix of language, popular culture, literature/film and society modules who have made productive and occasionally stunning intellectual leaps across their diverse objects of study. How else can we help a generation steeped in global pop culture to understand what 'high' and 'low' actually mean?

As far as research and of course research-led teaching are concerned, it would seem equally self-evident that we should grapple with popular culture, whatever the conceptual and evaluative difficulties – at least, if we construe our mission in the UK higher-education system of today as being to arrive at a better understanding of French-speaking cultures, rather than only of 'literatures' that happen to be in French. If that is our mission, how can we hope to understand those cultures in the round if we ignore the cultural practices of the majority?[22]

Bibliography

Bourdieu, Pierre, *La Distinction:* critique sociale du jugement (Paris: Éditions de Minuit, 1979).

Certeau, M. de, *L'Invention du quotidien*, vol. I: *Arts de faire* (Paris: Gallimard, 1990).

Dollot, L., *Culture individuelle et culture de masse* (Que Sais-Je, Paris: PUF, 1999).

Donnat, O., *Les Pratiques culturelles des Français à l'ère numérique: enquête 2008* (Paris: Découverte/Ministère de la culture et de la communication, 2009).

Frith, S., *Performing Rites: Evaluating Popular Music* (Oxford and New York: Oxford University Press, 1998).

HEFCE, RAE 2008 sub-panel 52: French: Sub-panel Overview Report (London, Higher Education Funding Council for England (HEFCE), 2009), available at www.rae.ac.uk/pubs/2009/ov/ (consulted 1 January 2011).

Hoggart, R., *The Uses of Literacy: Aspects of Working-Class Life with Special Reference to Publications and Entertainments* (London: Chatto & Windus, 1957).

Holmes, D. and D. L. Looseley (eds), *Constructing the Popular in Contemporary French Culture* (Manchester, MUP, forthcoming 2012).

Looseley, D. L., *Popular Music in Contemporary France: Authenticity, Politics, Debate* (Oxford and New York: Berg, 2003).

Mattelart, A. and Neveu, E., *Introduction aux cultural studies* (Paris: Découverte, 2003).

Williams, R., 'Culture is Ordinary' (1958), reproduced in A. Gray and J. McGuigan (eds), *Studies in Culture: An Introductory Reader* (London: Arnold, 1997), pp. 5–14.

22 For evidence of what those majority activities are, and of the place within them of what I am calling 'popular culture', see O. Donnat, *Les Pratiques culturelles des Français à l'ère numérique: enquête 2008* (Paris: Découverte/Ministère de la culture et de la communication, 2009.

Websites

University of Leeds. *Finding the Plot*, available at www.leeds.ac.uk/french/events/findingtheplot.htm (consulted 1 January 2011).

University of Leeds Popular Cultures Research Network (PCRN), available at www.leeds.ac.uk/smlc/Popularculturesresearchgroup.htm (consulted 1 January 2011).

Part VII: Area Studies, Postcolonial Studies and War and Culture Studies

16

An Area Studies Approach in European and Global Contexts: French Studies in Portsmouth

Emmanuel Godin and Tony Chafer

In the 1970s, staff in the School of Languages and Area Studies (SLAS) at Portsmouth Polytechnic (as it was then) decided to develop a new type of language degree. At that time, the traditional model was the 'lang and lit' degree programme. Students who wanted to study languages were more or less obliged to combine the study of their chosen language(s) with the study of (mostly) the literary classics of that country. There were a few exceptions: York University, for example, offered programmes in language and linguistics, Salford and Bath specialised in translation, while Aston offered students the opportunity to combine language study with business administration. But the vast majority of language students took a 'lang and lit' degree.

It was against this background that Portsmouth, along with a small number of other UK higher education institutions, sought to break away from the traditional model and develop a new type of language degree – the 'language and area studies' degree programme – that would combine language study with the study of the history, politics, economy, society and culture of the country, or countries, in question. The new approach was to be resolutely multi-disciplinary and was essentially, but not exclusively, rooted in the social sciences.

Research-informed Teaching

The pioneers of this new approach recognised from the outset the importance of research. This was essential, first, for the develop-ment of an intellectual framework for the delivery of the new degree programmes. What were the implications of multidisciplinarity for curriculum development and delivery? Which were the key disciplines that should underpin an area studies approach and how could they be combined effectively? Was genuine interdisciplinarity, as opposed to multidisciplinarity, a possible and desirable objective within an undergraduate curriculum? These were some of the key questions that pioneers of the area studies approach sought to address. Second, there was a need for up-to-date, cutting-edge, interdisciplinary research to underpin and inform the teaching on these new degree programmes.

The *Journal of Area Studies* was launched in 1980 by staff in the School of Languages and Area Studies with these twin objectives: to provide a forum for theoretical reflection on the 'area studies approach' and an outlet for new empirical research in area studies. The journal sought to explain, theorise and legitimise this distinctive approach. Early articles stressed the importance of interdisciplinarity,[1] and above all, the need to integrate language and area studies.[2] As Eric Cahm put it: 'Since a modicum of knowledge of a foreign country is essential if one is to learn to speak its language convincingly, study of the country is an almost inevitable corollary of any but the most elementary language learning.'[3] The journal already advocated the study of 'extraneous forces', which were to become part of the fabric of life in a particular area, it encouraged comparative analysis and insisted that area studies research must be 'oriented towards current public issues' (as stipulated on the back cover of early issues),[4] and inform curriculum development.[5] This chimed with a critical, Marxist-inspired approach to the subject (see in particular the 'Presentation' of the second issue, autumn 1980). Moreover, a willingness to engage critically with theoretical and practical issues pertaining to the area studies approach remained a core feature of the journal, which regularly devoted articles and special issues that aimed at scrutinising and renewing its own principles.[6]

In the field of French area studies, 1980 also marked the launch by Eric Cahm and Tony Chafer of the School of Languages and Area

---

1   S. Holt, 'Purpose and problems of European Studies', *Journal of Area Studies* 4 (Autumn 1981), 1–3; J. Bramley, J. 'Analysis in Area studies', *Journal of Area Studies* 12 (Autumn 1985), 12–15.
2   J. C. Sager and P. M. Geake, 'The Role of Modern Languages in a Degree Course in European Studies', *Journal of Area Studies* 4 (1981), 4–8.
3   E. Cahm, 'Some Problems in the Teaching of Area Studies: The Portsmouth Experience', *Journal of Area Studies* 1 (1980), 6–8, p. 7.
4   See also M. O. Heisler, 'Area Studies: Cross Area Research and Policy Advice', *Journal of Area Studies* 1 (Spring 1980), 3–8.
5   J. Berryman, 'A Note on Social Science and Languages: Area Studies Programmes', *Journal of Area Studies* 5 (1982), 11–13.
6   See for example, M. Cornick and G. Salemohamed, 'Area Studies: Communication Skills and the Bricolage Practice', *Journal of Area Studies* 15 (1987), 22–3; I. Brulard, 'Comparativism in Interdisciplinary Studies', *Journal of Area Studies* 7 (new series) (1995), 114–27; E Godin, 'Language and Interdisciplinarity', *Journal of Area Studies* 11 (1997), 73–82. The journal continues to exist. From 1992 it was co-published by the universities of Portsmouth and Loughborough. It subsequently changed its name to *The Journal of European Area Studies* (1999) and then to the *Journal of Contemporary European Studies* (2002). It is now one of the leading academic journals in the field of area studies and is currently published by Taylor & Francis.

Studies in Portsmouth of *Modern and Contemporary France* as the journal of the Association for the Study of Modern and Contemporary France (ASMCF) (see in this volume the contribution by Professor M. Cross). Again the launch of the ASMCF reflected a desire to offer an original approach to French Studies. Portsmouth played an important role in the life of the association. *Modern and Contemporary France* was initially edited by colleagues at Portsmouth, which has continued to have a presence on the editorial board to this day. The journal continues to exist and has established itself as a major outlet for French area studies research. Colleagues from Portsmouth have frequently served on the executive committee of the association and Portsmouth has hosted several of the association's annual conferences: France from the Cold War to the New World Order (1994); The French Exception (2001) and France and the Mediterranean (2009).

The Development of French Area Studies

From the 1980s onwards, the area studies approach was to inform the work of many colleagues in the field of French Studies in places as diverse as Portsmouth, Loughborough, Aston, Wolverhampton, Sussex, Northumbria, Westminster and Bradford. However, major challenges to the area studies approach have emerged in recent years and this is reflected in the way French area studies has evolved at Portsmouth.

Acute theoretical questions have been ushered in by postcolonialism, Europeanisation and globalisation. These have led to challenges to the centrality of metropolitan France within French area studies and to a wider questioning of the possible delineation of what – and who – constitute the boundaries of French area studies. These theoretical uncertainties have been mirrored by practical choices and decisions made by students at Portsmouth: the number of students opting for a single honours degree in French Studies dropped significantly (until recently), whereas degrees combining French within a European or international dimension became much more popular. At the same time, at a national level, the overall number of students choosing to study a language degree declined: in order to survive some modules, such as French politics or French history, were offered to non-language specialists – for example, to students on history and politics degree programmes – thereby undermining what had until then been considered a constituent part of the area studies approach, as these modules could no longer be taught in French. Likewise, although French classes offered by the Institution-Wide Language Programme remained popular, they also reinforced the idea that languages could be taught independently from the culture(s) in which they were embedded. Yet, against the national backdrop of the decline of foreign languages in UK schools, French area studies in Portsmouth managed to remain a buoyant affair.

However, the nature of French area studies has been strongly re-defined in recent years by two key developments: evolving research agendas in French Studies, and, linked to this, a growing desire to re-contextualise French Studies in its wider European and global context. At the same time, as the employment market for graduates becomes more difficult, there is an increasing recognition of the need to improve the employability of graduates though enhanced interconnectedness between students' programmes of study and the world of work. Against this background, one of the strategies put in place in Portsmouth to address these challenges has been to develop a distinctive pathway in French and francophone studies, with a particular focus on Africa. Two key concerns have underpinned and guided the development of this pathway: that research should continue to inform both teaching and curriculum development and that the new degree programmes in French should maintain a level of integration between "the area" and the language studied.

'New' French Studies and the Research Agenda

French and francophone studies research form part of a larger research centre – the Centre for European and International Studies Research (CEISR) – and have made a major contribution to Portsmouth's research entry under the European studies rubric in successive UK research assessment exercises (RAE). This is a useful reminder that French Studies research is not always immediately visible when 'buried' under wider labels. However, belonging to a broader research grouping has proved to be an asset rather than a hindrance for a group of researchers whose interests mainly focus on the relations between France and its European and global contexts. Within CEISR, the work of the French and francophone research cluster is focused on two main areas. In the first, it is working on a reassessment of the legacy of French colonialism in terms of its impact both in the former French colonies and in metro-politan France. In the second, it studies the changing relations between France and the francophone world since political independence in the context of increasing globalisation of the world economy and culture. Members of the research cluster undertake work that is interdisciplin-ary in nature and that draws on the study of the history, culture and language of both metropolitan France and other francophone countries and regions of the world. Their research interests are focused on franco-phone Africa, where they have particularly strong links and where they also lead consultancy projects. Two recent research programmes will serve to exemplify the approach adopted by members of the cluster.

Recovering the motivations, experience and memory of Algerian and Senegalese veterans of the Algerian War through comparative and transgenerational oral history

This British Academy-funded research partnership investigates a little-explored aspect of the shared history of Algeria and Senegal: the participation of Senegalese soldiers in the French army during the Algerian War of Independence. Postgraduate students and young scholars in both African countries will be trained and equipped to carry out this oral history project among the older generation, with a particular focus on interviews in rural areas. This research will produce an oral archive accessible to all via the internet, and students and scholars will also be analysing some of the key themes that emerge from veterans' accounts under the guidance of the project leaders in the three countries. In the light of these interviews, a further central aim of this project is to reflect on how to conduct oral history in the African context, from both ethical and methodological perspectives, and, arising from this, to develop and provide training in the relevant skills for conducting such research.

The three-year programme (2009–12) is funded by the British Academy, through the UK-Africa Academic Partnerships Scheme. The aim of the project is not only to develop an oral history archive of veterans' accounts, but also to reflect collaboratively on methodologies for carrying out oral history in North and West Africa and to transfer this knowledge to postgraduate students in Algeria and Senegal. These students will then play an active role in developing the archive itself for the duration of the project and beyond.

A central activity of this partnership is a series of workshops in Senegalese and Algerian universities (Université Cheikh Anta Diop, Centre de Recherche Ouest-Africaine, Dakar and the University of Algiers and the Ecole Normale Supérieure in Bouzareah), bringing scholars from all three participating countries together with postgraduate students from the respective universities. Theoretical and methodological questions are discussed at these workshops, along with practical examples of oral history interviews. After these intensive workshops, postgraduate students and scholars in Algeria and Senegal will carry out oral interviews with veterans. These will be available as audio recordings and/or transcriptions on the partnership's website.

France and Britain in Africa since Saint-Malo

This three-year British Academy-funded research project (2007–10) aims to assess the extent to which the new policy of joint or 'bilateral' cooperation between Britain and France in sub-Saharan Africa, which was announced at the Franco-British summit in Saint-Malo in December 1998, has been implemented. The project is the product of a collaboration between colleagues from the CEISR in Portsmouth and the Department of European Studies at the University of Cardiff. It seeks to analyse the causal factors and constraints that have militated in favour of, and against, the introduction and implementation of this collaborative agenda, to examine whether this and similar 'bilateral' models can serve as a complement to traditional unilateral and multilateral approaches to Africa's challenges and to make policy recommendations to UK and French policy makers which would, if implemented, enhance Anglo-French cooperation in Africa. The research has been conducted in London, Paris, Brussels, New York, Dakar, Kinshasa, Abuja, Khartoum and Addis Ababa.

A key feature of the project is to explain how, following the debacle of its involvement in Rwanda and the Democratic Republic of Congo in the mid-1990s, France has moved away from its traditional unilateral approach to Africa, which in the military field had earned it the reputation of the 'gendarme' of Africa, towards a new focus on multilateralism. In a context of accelerating globalisation and under pressure in Africa from new powers such as China, successive French governments have also since the 1990s sought to move away from the traditional exclusive focus on the African '*pré carré*' (mainly ex-French colonies) and diversify French relations with Africa to encompass former British colonies such as South Africa, Nigeria and Kenya and former Portuguese colonies such as Mozambique. France has also sought to ensure that its interventions on the continent take place within a UN or EU framework and French African policy is increasingly mediated through the EU, often with support from the UK, as in the case of recent ESDP (European Security and Defence Policy) military missions in Africa.

With their transnational focus, these research projects can be seen at one level as significant contributions to redefining the boundaries of French Studies. In order to understand how France has developed and changed since the emergence of the 'age of empires' in the late nineteenth century, the study of France and French society have to be set in the context of their interactions with the francophone world, much of which – notably in Africa – was the direct product of the imposition of French colonial rule. In the late twentieth and early twenty-first century it has equally become imperative, in order to understand the evolution of France as a global power, to study the decline of France as a colonial power in a transnational and global context. A study of the 'Hexagon' that neglects these interactions with the wider world simply cannot make sense of the history, society, culture and politics of contemporary France.

From Research Agendas to the new MA Francophone Africa

As French Studies changes, there is a need for new types of specialist who can analyse and understand these changes. The greatest number of countries in the world in which French is the official language is in

Africa. Yet very little is known in the English-speaking world about the history, politics and society of those vast areas of the African continent that were previously under French colonial rule and that are today referred to under the generic term 'francophone Africa', largely because of the lack of language specialists who can work in francophone African studies. To address this gap there is a need to train students with the required language skills and knowledge base. This means restoring the links between languages and social science, to enable students to have access to archives, government reports and the French press, as well as to conduct interviews with key political, economic and social actors. Without such training, there will continue to be a lack of specialists who can interpret the cultural and political codes and meanings embedded in the language and have the interdisciplinary background necessary to make sense of these codes. It is hoped that the new MA Francophone Africa, to be launched in 2011, will also lead to more postgraduates undertaking PhD study in the francophone Africa field, as there are currently very few UK students currently applying to do a PhD in this area.

The new MA focuses exclusively on francophone Africa and provides students with an opportunity to study in depth France's relations with both French-speaking North Africa and sub-Saharan Africa. A key feature of the degree is that it incorporates a study of the history of the very different approaches to French colonial rule in each of these regions with an analysis of how this historical relationship has shaped – and continues to shape – contemporary relations between France and its former African colonies. France's rapidly changing relationship with both North and sub-Saharan Africa in the contemporary period and the impact of France's African empire on France today are also key areas of study. The MA's approach to francophone Africa will be informed by three distinctive intellectual approaches. The first will be comparative: the focus will not be on a particular nation or area, but will provide opportunities to examine connections and relationships across the whole of francophone Africa and between francophone and anglophone/lusophone Africa. Second, the course will study francophone Africa within a transnational context, underlining how Africans have engaged with, for example, decolonisation, nationalism, the Cold War, political Islam and globalisation. Third, the course will situate the region within its wider global context, with a view to analysing the singularity of the colonial and postcolonial experience of francophone Africa.

Curriculum Development at Undergraduate Level

There is a strong commitment to disseminate research results not only among our postgraduate but also our undergraduate students. As in many other departments, final year undergraduate students are offered modules which reflect the research interests of staff, such as 'Colonialism and the end of empire in North Africa and Sub-Saharan Africa', 'France in the World', or '*La France contemporaine* and the French model in a European and global context'. Such modules are supported by extra-curricular activities, such as study half days that bring together academic researchers, professionals and frequently also actors and witnesses to the events being studied. Feedback clearly indicates that students appreci-ate teaching that is embedded in research. In addition, the curriculum is also supported by larger events, such as international conferences (e.g. 2009: ASMCF Annual Conference: France and the Mediterranean; 2010: Conference to Mark the 50th Anniversary of the Year of Africa; 2012: 50 years of Algerian Independence).

Bringing language students together in the same classroom with those studying, for example, international relations or history, has been a chal-lenge. Driven by institutional rationalisation and the need to reduce the cost of delivering courses, there have nonetheless been some benefits. For example, while it has not been possible to maintain teaching in the target language, some elements of this have been retained through the use of a variety of texts and assessments depending on language competencies. At the same time, bringing together French Studies, European studies, international relations and history students has had a number of positive effects, with students making connections that they would otherwise in all probability not have made. This has also led to a more outward-looking curriculum, with students perceiving French Studies as being at the confluence of many other approaches. This 'problematisation' of French Studies is appropriate to, and in keeping with, the growing fluid-ity of the concept.

The Period of Residence Abroad

This 'redefinition' of French Studies is also supported by the period of residence abroad, with students being offered the opportunity to spend all or part of their year abroad in Senegal. The Dakar placement is unusual in that it comprises a combined study and work placement, with the exact balance between the two being negotiated to meet students' own interests. Portsmouth has a number of educational partnerships in Dakar, with the Université Cheikh Anta Diop, the Centre Africain d'Etudes Supérieures en Gestion, the Ecole Supérieure du Tourisme et de l'Enseignement des Langues and a bilingual pre-school, La Source Vive. It also has agreements with a local NGO for a placement in the health field and with an international NGO, Plan International, for a placement in their public relations and communication department.

The period abroad is assessed within the degree programme in terms of academic, cultural, intercultural, linguistic, personal and professional outcomes, with the language aspect situated in the full educational context of the study abroad. The period in Senegal is an intense learning experience – in the broadest sense – for students, as they adapt to the cultural and linguistic differences that they encounter. Yet no systematic study of the experience has so far been undertaken. A research project studying the long-term impact of the year abroad, in cultural, linguistic and employability terms, on students who have spent part of their period abroad in Senegal is therefore currently being undertaken by Tony Chafer (University of Portsmouth) and Jim Coleman (Open University). As John Canning has rightly pointed out, language degrees cannot – should not – be reduced to the acquisition of language skills: 'graduates with an intensive knowledge of the cultures and societies of specific countries and experience of living and working overseas develop attributes for employability that language skills alone cannot provide'.[7] This is, after all, what the area studies approach is striving to achieve.

Conclusion

The area studies approach provides a coherent framework within which French and francophone studies have been reconfigured over the past decade or so. Avoiding an exclusive focus on metropolitan France and adopting an approach that sets France and the French-speaking world in their international and European context have enabled French and francophone studies to be part of a wider research and curriculum agenda. Admittedly, the concept of French Studies has become more fluid and its delineation a major challenge, as Charles Forsdick explains in this volume. From an institutional perspective, managerial support has been forthcoming as French and francophone studies have made a crucial contribution to past European studies RAEs and provided flexible but coherent solutions to curriculum development in the field of European studies, international relations and development studies. One of the major challenges has been to maintain a strong link between area studies and language learning: this necessitates a degree of flexibility in the way the curriculum is delivered and the assessments are designed, which may sometimes run counter to higher education institutions' desire to rationalise provision. Here, it is essential that senior managers support language programmes, not simply as an added skill for students who are taking another subject, but as an integrated, multi-disciplinary programme that combines the attainment of advanced language skills with the acquisition of cultural competences. The number of universities offering modern language degrees in the UK has declined from 121 in 2002 to 67 in 2010, with the closure of language degree programmes being particularly marked in institutions that had broken the link

---

7   J. Canning, 'A Skill or a Discipline? An Examination of Employability and the Study of Modern Foreign Languages', *Journal of Employability and the Humanities* 3 (2009), online resource, consulted 23 May 2010.

between learning a language and understanding the social and cultural contexts in which it is spoken. The Portsmouth experience demonstrates the benefits of the area studies approach that considers language degrees as being firmly rooted in the social science and humanities disciplines.

Bibliography

Berryman, J., 'A Note on Social Science and Languages: Area Studies Programmes' *Journal of Area Studies* 5 (1982), 11–13.

Bramley, J., 'Analysis in Area studies' *Journal of Area Studies* 12 (Autumn 1985), 12–15.

Brulard, I., 'Comparativism in Interdisciplinary Studies', *Journal of Area Studies* 7 (new series) (1995), 114–27.

Cahm, E., 'Some Problems in the Teaching of Area Studies: The Portsmouth Experience', *Journal of Area Studies* 1 (1980), 6–8.

Canning, J., 'A skill or a Discipline? An Examination of Employability and the Study of Modern Foreign Languages', *Journal of Employability and the Humanities, Issue* 3 (2009), online resource, avaialble at www.uclan.ac.uk/ahss/ceth/files/JCanningArticle.pdf (consulted 23 May 2010).

Coleman, J. A., 'Residence abroad within language study', *Language Teaching* 30: 1 (1997), 1–20.

Cornick, M. and G. Salemohamed, 'Area Studies: Communication Skills and the Bricolage Practice', *Journal of Area Studies* 15 (1987), 22–3.

Godin, E., 'Language and Interdisciplinarity', *Journal of Area Studies* 11 (1997), 73–82.

Jahr, V. and U. Teichler, 'Employment and work of former mobile students', in U. Teichler (ed.), *The ERASMUS Experience. Major findings of the ERASMUS evaluation research* (Luxembourg: Office for Official Publications of the European Community, 2002), pp. 117–36.

Heisler, M. O., 'Area Studies: Cross Area Research and Policy Advice', *Journal of Area Studies* 1 (Spring 1980), 3–8.

Holt, S., 'Purpose and problems of European Studies', *Journal of Area Studies* 4 (Autumn 1981), 1–3.

Sager, J. C. and P. M. Geake, 'The Role of Modern Languages in a Degree Course in European Studies', *Journal of Area Studies* 4 (1981), 4–8.

17

French Studies and the Postcolonial: The Demise or the Rebirth of the French Department?

David Murphy

Introduction

Over the past two decades, we have witnessed what Françoise Lionnet has termed the 'becoming-transnational' of French Studies.[1] French and the other modern languages had originally been constructed as academic subjects around the framework of the nineteenth-century European nation-state but, as the primacy of the nation state has come to be challenged in the era of globalisation, this structure has been increasingly questioned by scholars working from transnational, global and postcolonial perspectives.[2] The prominent North American critic Lawrence Kritzman has been prompted to ask, in light of these developments, whether the very existence of French Studies is now in question:

> Can French Studies survive the death of the traditional idea of the nation, and the teleology of its progress? Does France's own identity crisis – the loss of its exceptional status, the progressive erosion of its role as an imperial messianic nation, its integration into the European community – endanger our own discipline of French studies?[3]

This chapter considers the specific challenge posed to previous conceptions of French Studies by the field's engagement with the specific 'transnational' form of questioning involved in the development of postcolonial teaching and research. Echoing Kritzman's questions cited above, it seeks it to explore whether the development of francophone postcolonial studies represents the demise or the rebirth of the French department.

---

1 Françoise Lionnet, 'Introduction', *Modern Language Notes* 118: 4 (Special issue: 'Francophone Studies: New Landscapes', edited by Françoise Lionnet and Dominic Thomas, 2003), 783–6, p. 784.

2 For a discussion of this process see Charles Forsdick, 'Between "French" and "Francophone": French Studies and the Postcolonial Turn', *French Studies* 49: 4 (2005), 523–30.

3 Lawrence D. Kritzman, 'Identity Crises: France, Culture and the Idea of the Nation', *SubStance* 76–7 (1995), 5–20, p. 19.

This is in no way to suggest that postcolonial studies scholars bear all the responsibility/deserve all of the credit (depending upon one's point of view) for the changes that French Studies has undergone as a field. The model of a modern languages curriculum based primarily on the study of the literature of the European nation from medieval times to the present had initially been challenged in the decades following the Second World War by scholarship seeking to develop sociological, historical, cultural studies and feminist approaches to metropolitan France. Writing in the late 1980s, Christophe Campos cast these developments as the fracturing of the coherence of an older model of French Studies: this coherence (if one can deem a subject as multifaceted as French to have ever possessed a strict coherence) was fractured further still when the study of France and Belgium's former colonial possessions began to challenge still further the previously dominant spatio-temporal model of French Studies. The rise of what was originally called 'Francophone studies' has opened up new trajectories for teaching and research and has permitted the development of innovative collaborative ventures within the changing landscape of the humanities. This chapter explores some of these new trajectories but also asks probing questions about just how fundamentally the subject of French Studies has changed in recent times. Has the development of a francophone postcolonial field genuinely transformed French Studies in irrevocable and profound ways?

From French and Francophone Studies to Francophone Postcolonial Studies

Before exploring these issues, it is necessary to examine precisely how the field has developed over the past few decades. The rise of 'francophone studies' initially took the form of an expansion of research interests, and more gradually of the curriculum, beyond the Hexagon to include the study of authors – and the process was, in its initial phase at least, solely literary – from Africa, North America and the Caribbean that were usually classified as 'francophone': thus began the ambiguous phase in the development of French Studies as a subject (particularly in North America) in which the epithet 'French and francophone' was increasingly deployed, in what has generally been cast as an inherently positive development (i.e. francophone studies is a 'good thing') without any significant questioning as to whether the use of the conjunction implied an optional extra or a fundamental complementarity that necessitated a reconceptualisation of the field. The necessity of such a reconceptualisation became ever more apparent as the loosely defined field of 'francophone studies' grew to incorporate a reassessment of metropolitan French history and culture as themselves inherently bound up in a series of transnational (if not always postcolonial) encounters.

The example of the Association for the Study of Caribbean and African Literature in French (ASCALF), founded in 1989, is emblematic of the evolution that the field has undergone. Founded by British and Irish scholars of metropolitan French literature who had discovered francophone writing in the 1970s–1980s (e.g. Roger Little, Peter Hawkins, Dorothy Blair, Patrick Corcoran, Bridget Jones), ASCALF fostered research into 'black' writing and provided a forum for emerging scholars who have since gone on to become leading figures in the field (e.g. Nicki Hitchcott, Dominic Thomas, Maeve McCusker). Gradually, scholars thus emerged whose doctoral research was focused explicitly on 'non-French' topics, and they in turn have brought through a new generation of doctoral students who take it for granted that the 'francophone' is an integral part of the field of 'French Studies'. Despite ASCALF's initial pragmatic decision to focus on 'black' writing, it became clear as time progressed that there was a need for a scholarly grouping that would include writing from other 'francophone' contexts (not least the Maghreb) and that would also provide a forum in which to discuss the postcoloniality of metropolitan France. By 2002, ASCALF had changed its title to the Society for Francophone Postcolonial Studies, thereby reflecting a desire both for a more radical transformation of the relationship between French and francophone studies, and also for a more sustained engagement with francophone material within what was, at that time, the predominantly anglophone field of postcolonial studies.

Charles Forsdick has outlined the strategic nature of this call for the creation of a francophone postcolonial studies, which stems from a profound dissatisfaction with the two more established fields that it attempts to bring together:

> The persistent assertion of Francophone Postcolonial Studies as a field of enquiry in its own right reflects a constructively critical strategy emerging from dissatisfaction with both the *monolingual* emphases of postcolonial criticism [...] and the *monocultural*, essentially metropolitan biases of French Studies.[4]

In essence, the emergence of a francophone postcolonial field was deemed necessary because French Studies had focused primarily on France while postcolonial studies had focused far too exclusively on English-language contexts. Engagement with postcolonial theory has thus been promoted by many scholars as a means of changing the nature of French Studies, while simultaneously situating French-language

---

4 Charles Forsdick, 'Challenging the monolingual, subverting the monocultural: the strategic purposes of Francophone Postcolonial Studies', *Francophone Postcolonial Studies* 1: 1 (2003), 33–41, p 36; my emphasis.

material within a comparative postcolonial framework.[5] If the epithet 'French and francophone' left room for doubt about the nature of the relationship between a supposed French core and a marginalised francophone periphery, the self-conscious act of field creation involved in announcing the birth of francophone postcolonial studies explicitly sought to place France itself within a postcolonial framework: the premise involved in such a gesture is that colonialism is not something that simply happened in faraway, 'exotic' places, it is in fact crucial to our understanding of France. Scholars of metropolitan French culture have long examined the relationship between France and Europe (e.g. modernism), as well as France and the USA (e.g. post-war consumerism), acknowledging the ways in which French culture has been renegotiated via its encounter with the Other. However, the extent to which France has been transformed by its relationship to its colonies has not until recently been deemed to be as self-evident. A very strong tradition of scholarship on colonial culture and travel writing had explored France's imagined vision of Asia, Africa and other parts of the world but such work did not always explicitly highlight (or in some cases even acknowledge) that these other cultures might have an impact on our understanding of France. The past two decades have produced a generally, if not universally, accepted recognition that understanding France also necessarily involves an attempt to understand the relationship between France and its former colonial possessions, as Kristin Ross so brilliantly argued in *Fast Cars, Clean Bodies*.[6]

Some of the most interesting research that has charted this postcolonial understanding of France has been the work of historians, often but not exclusively based in North America. Alice Conklin's *A Mission to Civilize* traces the complex interrelationship between colonial education policies from 1895 to 1930 and attempts in France to create a collective identity that would help the sometimes recalcitrant provinces to embrace

5   For examples of this critical engagement between Francophone studies and postcolonial theory, see Celia Britton and Michael Syrotinski (eds), 'Francophone Texts and Postcolonial Theory', special issue of *Paragraph* 24: 3 (2001); Charles Forsdick and David Murphy (eds), *Francophone Postcolonial Studies: A Critical Introduction* (London: Arnold, 2003); Charles Forsdick and David Murphy (eds), *Postcolonial Thought in the French-Speaking World* (Liverpool: Liverpool University Press, 2009). I do not want to give the impression that all scholars in the UK have adopted the epithet 'Francophone postcolonial studies'; indeed, some scholars, such as those involved in the *International Journal of Francophone Studies*, continue to view the term 'francophone' as useful in its own right without the qualification provided by 'postcolonial'. However, to my knowledge, no French Studies scholars in the UK have heaped the scorn on postcolonial studies that is to be found in the work of a North American counterpart Richard Serrano, author of the polemically titled *Against the Postcolonial: 'Francophone' Writers at the Ends of French Empire* (Lanham, MD: Lexington Books, 2005).
6   Kristin Ross, *Fast Cars, Clean Bodies: Decolonization and the Reordering of French Culture* (Amherst, MT: MIT Press, 1995).

a more uniform Republican identity.[7] In *The French Imperial Nation State*, Gary Wilder traces the development of a colonial humanism that departed from the policy of assimilation, and sought instead to value the complex, rich but fundamentally different cultures of the colonies.[8] Such thinking was in turn taken up by Aimé Césaire, Léopold Senghor and the Negritude 'movement' to justify their demands for equality without assimilation: in essence, Negritude sought to divorce French citizenship from adherence to a specific metropolitan form of French culture in ways that still seem radical today. Finally, Herman Lebovics explores in *Bringing the Empire Back Home* the complex ways in which colonial relationships and policies kept resurfacing in France in an unexpected fashion in the era of decolonisation: for example, repatriated colonial administrators were often given posts in the French provinces and were asked to reinforce regional ties to a Republican centre in ways that they had already done overseas.[9]

Many of these historians have also explicitly explored the implications of their research findings for the teaching of 'French' history, in ways that have profound resonance for French Studies scholars here in the UK. In two articles whose sub-titles illustrate the research and pedagogical agendas of their authors – 'Teaching French History as Colonial History and Colonial History as French History'; 'Citizenship, Colonialism, and the Borders of French History' – Alice Conklin and Laurent Dubois argue for the need to transcend national histories in order to explore the nation within a transnational, globalising framework.[10] France's engagement in what is often seen as the very recent development of a process of globalisation, in fact, began several centuries ago, and included involvement in the slave trade and colonial conquest. Dubois's work on the Haitian Revolution has charted the profound challenge posed by events in the Caribbean to the 'universal' values of the French Revolution: rather than being merely a faraway event 'inspired' by its French counterpart, the Haitian Revolution revealed the unspoken ethnocentrism of much Enlightenment thought. Indeed, some of the most exciting work in francophone postcolonial studies now being carried out by scholars on both sides of the Atlantic focuses on Haiti (Peter Hallward, Chris Bongie, Nick Nesbitt, Deborah Jenson, Rachel Douglas, Charles Forsdick), not solely as a 'faraway'

7 Alice Conklin, *A Mission to Civilize: The Republican Idea of Empire in France and West Africa, 1895–1930* (Stanford, CA: Stanford University Press, 2000).
8 Gary Wilder, *The French Imperial Nation State: Negritude & Colonial Humanism Between the Two World Wars* (Chicago, Ill: University of Chicago Press, 2005).
9 Herman Lebovics, *Bringing the Empire Back Home: France in the Global Age* (Durham, NC: Duke University Press, 2004).
10 Alice Conklin, 'Boundaries Unbound: Teaching French History as Colonial History and Colonial History as French History', *French Historical Studies*, 23: 2 (2000), 215–38; Laurent Dubois, 'La République Métissée: Citizenship, Colonialism, and the Borders of French History', *Cultural Studies*, 14: 1 (2000), 15–34.

francophone location worthy of interest in its own right but also as the site of a complex interrogation of profoundly French conceptions of Enlightenment and universality.

France and the Postcolonial

Although the preceding section cites the work of anglophone scholars in helping to develop a more complex 'postcolonial' understanding of French history and culture, this is in no way to deny the crucial role played by scholars in France in promoting similar concerns. In the literary sphere, we could cite the pioneering work of Bernard Mouralis or Charles Bonn, while in the social sciences, there is no shortage of candidates, from Michel Wieviorka to Benjamin Stora to Gérard Noiriel. However, the emergence of a 'postcolonial' field of research in France has proven contentious, particularly in the field of literary studies where there has been marked resistance to engagement with postcolonial theory. In their initial guise, in the early twentieth century, most French departments in the UK explicitly looked to France for scholarly models with which to shape the curriculum. This inclination to import French scholarly frameworks has of course evolved as French Studies, particularly in its broadly cultural studies phase of the last few decades, has come to promote the inherently ethnographic dimension of teaching the language and culture of another country to a predominantly British student audience. But what does it mean for francophone postcolonial studies research and teaching if the possibilities for collaboration with scholars in France are at times quite fraught? At the conference to mark the twentieth anniversary of the launch of ASCALF at the French Institute in 2009, it was remarked upon by many of those who had been there in the early years of the association that there had been a far greater French presence at ASCALF events throughout the 1990s. Does this mean that bridges between colleagues on either side of the Channel have been burned because of the 'postcolonial turn' of the past decade?

In the literary sphere, the possibility of dialogue between 'francophone' scholars in France and those scholars in the UK who explicitly place their work within a postcolonial frame remains quite a complex issue. In 2005, several members of SFPS were invited to participate in a symposium at the Sorbonne, under the promising title of 'Etudes littéraires francophones et notion de "postcolonial": perspectives croisées'. Although the event did produce some 'perspectives croisées' (exchange of perspectives), these were less in evidence than the 'tirs croisés' (crossfire) of rival critical fields deeply suspicious of one another.[11] However,

---

11 The papers from the 2005 Sorbonne event are collected in a special issue of *Francophone Postcolonial Studies*, 4: 2 (2006).

there are signs that relations have evolved in recent times, for in March 2010, Daniel Lançon and Claude Coste hosted a far more productive event, entitled 'Perspectives européennes des études littéraires francophones', in Grenoble. This conference drew together scholars from France, the UK, Belgium, Holland and Germany in a genuine attempt to gain a sense of the institutional and methodological frameworks that informed our different approaches.

While a certain French antipathy to postcolonial studies was still in evidence, it was far less pronounced than five years previously, and the very nature of the event lent itself to a realisation that behind epithets such as 'francophone' and 'postcolonial' one often finds profoundly similar work. Indeed, individual scholars, working in their own particular area of expertise (e.g. Sub-Saharan Africa, Algeria, Québec) had continued to collaborate with like-minded scholars in France throughout what one might mischievously call the 'Cold War' period of relations between 'francophone' and 'postcolonial' studies scholars. Equally, the notion of French literary scholars' resistance to postcolonial studies was never complete, as is witnessed by the pioneering work of Jean-Marc Moura and Jacqueline Bardolph.[12]

The main change that had occurred between 2005 and 2010 was that France had by the latter date developed its own public and academic debate on the postcolonial. Indeed, it is now commonly accepted that 2005 marked the entry of the term 'postcolonial' into public and academic debate in France: this *année charnière* saw the launch of the *Appel des Indigènes de la République*, the *loi du 23 février 2005*, the November riots in the suburbs, and the publication of the controversial edited volume, *La Fracture coloniale*. Equally, key works of postcolonial theory, such as Edward Said's *Culture and Imperialism*, Homi K. Bhabha's *The Location of Culture* and Dipesh Chakrabarty's *Provincializing Europe* have all now been translated into French,[13] thereby permitting a more sustained engagement in France with aspects of postcolonial thought. (Much of the so-called 'resistance' to postcolonial studies in France may in fact be attributable to this previous linguistic divide.)

Previously perceived as an alien 'Anglo-Saxon' concept, the 'postcolonial' has now become the subject of intense critical debate in France, one that has at times been quite rancorous. On the one hand, scholars such as those associated with the historical collective ACHAC (Association pour la Connaissance de l'histoire de l'Afrique Contemporaine) have claimed that 'nous sommes entrés qu'on le veuille

---

12 Jean-Marc Moura, *Littératures francophones et théorie postcoloniale* (Paris: PUF, 1999); Jacqueline Bardolph, *Études postcoloniales et littérature* (Paris: Champion, 2002).

13 Edward Said, *Culture and Imperialism* (New York: Knopf, 1993); Homi K. Bhabha, *The Location of Culture* (London: Routledge, 1994); Dipesh Chakrabarty, *Provincializing Europe* (Princeton, NJ: Oxford: Princeton University Press, 2000).

ou non dans la postcolonie',[14] and have warmly embraced postcolonial studies as a way of reframing and reconceptualising debates on Empire and its multiple legacies.[15] On the other hand, eminent scholars such as Jean-François Bayart condemn postcolonial studies as 'un carnaval académique': it is the latest trend, a bandwagon on to which misguided scholars have scrambled – 'une stratégie de niche de la part de cher-cheurs en quête d'une part du marché académique'.[16] Bayart views postcolonial studies as inherently flawed and its practitioners as either deeply misguided or flagrantly opportunistic (or both).

The polarised nature of the debate in France concerning the value or otherwise of postcolonial theory does not necessarily augur well for greater collaboration with postcolonial studies scholars in the UK but at the very least this debate has produced a greater understanding of the institutional frameworks within which scholars are working. What is perhaps most remarkable about the French postcolonial debate is that it has largely been situated within the social sciences rather than within the predominantly literary or 'representational contexts' that have marked its development in the anglophone academy. In many ways, postcolonial theory in France has 'travelled', in Edward Said's sense: unmoored from its original context, it has managed to take on new forms and new mean-ings, and the UK-based francophone postcolonial scholar occupies an important position in charting these 'travels', capable of acting as a *passeur* between the two contexts.

The Demise or the Rebirth of the French Department?

The work of the many scholars associated with SFPS, as well as the success of the renowned *International Journal of Francophone Studies*, edited by Kamal Salhi at the University of Leeds, are just two of the most visible examples of the explicit engagement with francophone post-colonial material that is now part and parcel of the activities of most French departments in the UK. But just how central is francophone postcolonial material to the field of French Studies? Most departments in the UK now have a member of staff with some form of non-French, 'francophone' specialism, although regrettably this still cannot be

---

14 Nicolas Bancel, 'De la colonie à la postcolonie', *Cultures Sud: revue des littératures du Sud* 165 (2007), 6–11, p. 11. Trans: we have entered, like it or not, into the era of the postcolony.

15 See also, Pascal Blanchard and Nicolas Bancel (eds), *Culture postcoloniale, 1961–2006: Traces et mémoires coloniales en France* (Paris: Autrement, 2006).

16 'Jean-François Bayart, *Les Etudes postcoloniales: un carnaval académique* (Paris: Karthala, 2010), p. 37. Trans: a niche strategy on the part of researchers looking for their share of the market.

declared to be the norm: Karen Gould's depiction of the 'francophone hire' to be found in the North American academy (i.e. the single member of staff expected to cover the entire francophone world in their teaching), may well resonate with some colleagues on this side of the Atlantic.[17] Although a certain unspoken level of 'resistance' to francophone post-colonial studies may well exist in UK academia, I cannot think of an explicit British counterpart to the North American scholar Sandy Petrey, who has repeatedly, in a series of publications, criticised what he views as the breakdown of a coherent model of French Studies based on the study of metropolitan French literature across the centuries. (It should be noted that Petrey is even more critical of cultural studies approaches than he is of francophone studies.) For Petrey, francophone studies is a form of 'Francophobic inquiry',[18] which reveals a profound dislike of France and an almost morbid interest in the dark side of its history.

A more nuanced reading of the situation in the UK may be found in Lawrence Kritzman's self-mocking observation that scholars of French of his generation in the USA are still informed by 'a certain idea of France':[19] attracted to the subject through a profound attachment to the language and culture of France, many French Studies scholars may inevitably presume that a metropolitan conception of France should occupy centre stage in the field. Consequently, the vision of a normative version of French Studies actively policing the spread of francophone postcolonial material does not really ring true, although there still remains a perception in certain quarters that France is what French scholars *do*, even if the situation is, in reality, in a constant state of evolution.

It seems fair to say that, despite the changes that have taken place in recent decades, the Society for French Studies (SFS) and its journal, *French Studies*, retain a privileged position for many in the UK as the most representative organs available to the field (which is not to say that all French Studies scholars in the UK would agree with such a judge-ment). In this context, it is intriguing to analyse the content of *French Studies* over the period 2006–10 in order to assess the space occupied within it by francophone postcolonial material. At first glance, one could argue that there is little in the way of 'francophone' material in the more traditional sense of articles examining work by artists/scholars from former French/Belgian colonies: in 2006, there was one article on Abdelkébir Khatibi; in 2007, there was a piece on Frantz Fanon; and 2009 saw two the publication of two articles, a general piece on Creole in the Caribbean, and one on the writer and theorist V. Y. Mudimbe.

17 Karen Gould, 'Nationalism, Feminism, Cultural Pluralism: American Interest in Quebec Literature and Culture', *Yale French Studies* 103 (2003), 24–32.
18 Sandy Petrey, 'Language Charged with Meaning', *Yale French Studies* 103 (2003), 133–45, p. 135.
19 Lawrence D. Kritzman, 'A Certain Idea of French: Cultural Studies, Literature and Theory', *Yale French Studies* 103 (2003), 146–60.

A glance at the table of contents over the same period of another prominent journal, *French Cultural Studies*, itself the product of an earlier questioning of the focus of French Studies, initially reveals a far more prominent position accorded to francophone material: there are articles on Tahar Ben Jelloun, Azouz Begag/Linda Lê, Leïla Sebbar, Ben Jelloun/ Abdelwahab Meddeb, Edouard Glissant and Abdellatif Kechiche, as well as a special issue on representations of the Rwandan genocide.

A core difference that explains the disparity in coverage between these two publications is surely to be found in their remits: *French Cultural Studies* focuses by and large on the 'modern' period of post-Revolutionary France, whereas *French Studies* attempts to provide historical coverage stretching back to the medieval period. (Although still primarily focused on literature, *French Studies* also attempts to find space for 'cultural' material, in an acknowledgement of those other challenges to previous conceptions of the field cited above.) However, a more nuanced reading of the contents of both publications reveals a similar engagement with what might be considered a postcolonial agenda in relation to metro-politan French culture: to put it more bluntly, we should not look for the postcolonial purely by tracking down the foreign-sounding names. So, if we look again at *French Studies* from 2006 to 2010, we find articles on Le Clézio, Holocaust and Empire, representations of the Algerian war, and François Maspero; equally, *French Cultural Studies* features a range of articles with a postcolonial focus: there are pieces on Michael Haneke's *Caché*, the *Exposition anti-coloniale* of 1931, the Quai Branly museum, Marie Cardinal, and there is even a special issue on 'Writers, Intellectuals and the Colonial Experience'.

It is equally noticeable that francophone postcolonial material now regularly appears in 'general' postcolonial studies journals – *Journal of Postcolonial Writing, Interventions, Postcolonial Studies, Third Text* – as well as journals focusing on specific geographical contexts, such as the Caribbean (*Small Axe*) and Africa (*Research in African Literatures*). What all of these examples reveal, I believe, is the extent to which 'French' and 'postcolonial' concerns are now intermingled, and, just as French Studies journals open up space for postcolonial material, what were previously almost exclusively anglophone postcolonial studies journals are finding space for work on French-language material. Essentially, French Studies and francophone postcolonial studies should not be seen as rival fields, nor can one be subsumed as a subfield of the other; rather they constitute a set of overlapping frameworks interested in the study of French language and culture that tie our work into new and evolv-ing configurations. For example, my colleague Bill Marshall argues in *The French Atlantic* for an exploration of modes of minor Frenchness within the transnational framework of an emerging 'Atlantic studies'.[20]

20 Bill Marshall, *The French Atlantic: Travels in Culture and History* (Liverpool: Liverpool University Press, 2009).

Elsewhere, within anglophone postcolonial studies, the emergence of a francophone postcolonial field has helped to foster explicitly comparative projects, which open up the possibility for highly innovative teaching and research collaborations in the future.[21] Far from having exhausted the postcolonial paradigm, it would appear that the major task of creating an interdisciplinary and comparative postcolonial studies has barely even begun, and French Studies scholars have a major part to play in this.

Conclusion

In a time of great change and uncertainty, as 'autonomous' French departments increasingly become a thing of the past, merging into larger schools that group together the other modern languages, as well as a wide range of arts/humanities subjects, it can be tempting and perhaps inevitable to read change as 'decline' or 'betrayal'. However, for all the changes that reek of crass managerialism, there are many others that are, in terms of our teaching and research, welcome expansions of the traditional remit of French Studies within the university. Of course, the potential for change to be carried out in productive ways will differ greatly from one institutional context to another. Thus, while it is possible that French Studies engagement with the postcolonial will open up exciting research trajectories, changes in teaching and the curriculum may be harder to achieve in some institutions.

Francophone postcolonial studies may not be as entrenched within the academy as is sometimes thought but nor is it the outsider that it once was. Its relative success now poses difficult questions in a context of falling staff numbers on most French programmes. For the development of francophone studies, the logic of which seems to demand an ever-growing geographical coverage, has coincided with a period in which many language departments have suffered cuts in staffing. As we now enter what may be a protracted period of profound budget cuts and retrenchment, departments are likely to be asked to make difficult choices between maintaining geographical coverage of a wider francophone world and maintaining historical depth in their coverage of metropolitan France, and this will require important strategic thinking by all of us in the field. The French department as it was once known is now dead, or at least dying, subsumed into larger structures but a revised and, in some respects, reinvigorated French Studies still survives. It was not postcolonial studies that killed the French department and nor will it be responsible for the death of French Studies; on

---

21 See John McLeod (ed.), *The Routledge Companion to Postcolonial Studies* (London and New York: Routledge, 2007), and Prem Poddar *et al.* (eds), *A Historical Companion to Postcolonial Literatures: Continental Europe and its Empires* (Edinburgh: Edinburgh University Press, 2008).

the contrary, the postcolonial has played an important part in transforming what we mean by French Studies, and it has tied the field into a new set of academic partnerships that will continue to evolve in the years to come.

Bibliography

Bancel, Nicolas, 'De la colonie à la postcolonie', *Cultures Sud: revue des littératures du Sud* 165 (2007), 6–11.

Bardolph, Jacqueline, *Études postcoloniales et littérature* (Paris: Champion, 2002).

Bhabha, Homi K., *The Location of Culture* (London: Routledge, 1994).

Bayart, Jean-François, *Les Etudes postcoloniales: un carnaval académique* (Paris: Karthala, 2010).

Blanchard, Pascal and Nicolas Bancel (eds), *Culture postcoloniale, 1961–2006: Traces et mémoires coloniales en France* (Paris: Autrement, 2006).

Britton, Celia, and Michael Syrotinski (eds), Francophone Texts and Postcolonial Theory', special issue of *Paragraph* 24.3 (2001).

Campos, Christophe, 'Le français dans les universités britanniques', *Franco-British Studies* 8 (1989), 69–108.

Chakrabarty, Dipesh, *Provincializing Europe* (Princeton, NJ; Oxford: Princeton University Press, 2000).

Conklin, Alice, *A Mission to Civilize: The Republican Idea of Empire in France and West Africa, 1895–1930* (Stanford, CA: Stanford University Press, 2000).

Conklin, Alice, 'Boundaries Unbound: Teaching French History as Colonial History and Colonial History as French History', *French Historical Studies* 23: 2 (2000), 215–38.

Dubois, Laurent, 'La République Métissée: Citizenship, Colonialism, and the Borders of French History', *Cultural Studies* 14: 1 (2000), 15–34.

Forsdick, Charles, 'Challenging the monolingual, subverting the monocultural: the strategic purposes of Francophone Postcolonial Studies', *Francophone Postcolonial Studies* 1: 1 (2003), 33–41.

Forsdick, Charles, 'Between "French" and "Francophone": French Studies and the Postcolonial Turn', *French Studies* 49: 4 (2005), 523–30.

Forsdick, Charles, and David Murphy (eds), *Francophone Postcolonial Studies: A Critical Introduction* (London: Arnold, 2003).

Forsdick, Charles, and David Murphy (eds), *Postcolonial Thought in the French-Speaking World* (Liverpool: Liverpool University Press, 2009).

Gould, Karen, 'Nationalism, Feminism, Cultural Pluralism: American Interest in Quebec Literature and Culture', *Yale French Studies* 103 (2003), 24–32.

Kritzman, Lawrence D., 'Identity Crises: France, Culture and the Idea of the Nation'. *SubStance* 76–7 (1995), 5–20.

Kritzman, Lawrence D., 'A Certain Idea of French: Cultural Studies, Literature and Theory', *Yale French Studies* 103 (2003), 146–60.

Lebovics, Herman, *Bringing the Empire Back Home: France in the Global Age* (Durham, NC: Duke University Press, 2004).

Lionnet, Françoise, 'Introduction', *Modern Language Notes* 118: 4 (Special issue: 'Francophone Studies: New Landscapes', edited by Françoise Lionnet and Dominic Thomas, 2003), 783–6.

Marshall, Bill, *The French Atlantic: Travels in Culture and History* (Liverpool: Liverpool University Press, 2009).

McLeod, John (ed.), *The Routledge Companion to Postcolonial Studies* (London and New York: Routledge, 2007).

Moura, Jean-Marc, *Littératures francophones et théorie postcoloniale* (Paris: PUF, 1999).

Petrey, Sandy, 'Language Charged with Meaning'. *Yale French Studies* 103 (2003), 133–45.

Poddar, Prem, Rajeev Patke and Lars Jensen (eds), *A Historical Companion to Postcolonial Literatures: Continental Europe and its Empires* (Edinburgh: Edinburgh University Press, 2008).

Ross, Kristin, *Fast Cars, Clean Bodies: Decolonization and the Reordering of French Culture* (Amherst, MT: MIT Press, 1995).

Said, Edward W., *Culture and Imperialism* (New York: Knopf, 1993).

Said, Edward W., 'Traveling Theory', in Edward W. Said, *The World, The Text and The Critic* (London: Faber & Faber, 1984 [1983]), pp. 226–47.

Said, Edward W., 'Traveling theory reconsidered', in Edward W. Said, *Reflections on Exile and Other Literary and Cultural Essays* (London: Granta, 2000 [1994]), pp. 436–52.

Serrano, Richard, *Against the Postcolonial: 'Francophone' Writers at the Ends of French Empire* (Lanham, MD: Lexington Books, 2005).

Wilder, Gary, *The French Imperial Nation State: Colonial Humanism and Negritude between the Two Wars* (Chicago, Ill; London: University of Chicago Press, 2005).

18

The Development of War and Culture Studies in the UK: From French Studies, Beyond, and Back Again

Nicola Cooper, Martin Hurcombe and Debra Kelly[1]

The place of France and French/Francophone Studies in the development of 'War and Culture Studies'

France provides a particularly complex and fascinating object of analysis for any investigation into the impact of war on modern and contemporary cultural production and cultural history, having been at war for almost fifty years of the twentieth century. This impact is characterised by radically different experiences and memories of the two world wars, and further complicated by enduring legacies of those wars, and of subsequent, brutal colonial wars. An understanding of the impact that the experiences of these different types of war have made on French cultural, social and political identity is essential for the broader analysis of developments in France throughout the twentieth and into the twenty-first centuries, and indeed its role in European and global affairs. The study of France, then, has played a pivotal role in the development of 'war and culture studies' in the UK over the last two decades or so for a number of reasons that are explored in this chapter.

What do we mean by 'war and culture studies'? This chapter first considers more generally the 'cultural turn' in war studies in recent decades, and then looks specifically at the work of the Group for War and Culture Studies (GWACS) and its contributing scholars in developing a particular approach to the relationship between war and culture during conflict and its aftermath in the twentieth and twenty-first centuries. Why should the study of war be of such interest to scholars in the humanities and to students and researchers in French and Francophone Studies in particular?

---

1 With additional research by Caroline Perret, Group for War and Culture Studies and *Journal of War and Culture Studies* of the Research Office at the University of Westminster.

Elaine Scarry, in her seminal text *The Body in Pain*,[2] has demonstrated that the 'structure of war' and what she terms 'the structure of unmaking' are one subject. It is obvious that war (and, in Scarry's analysis, torture) is an act of destruction and 'entail[s] the suspension of civilization' (and are somehow the opposite of that civilisation); less obvious is that:

> They [war and torture] are in the most literal and concrete way possible, an appropriation, aping and reversing of the action of creation itself. Once the structures of torture and war have been exposed and compared, it becomes clear that the human action of making entails two distinct phases – making-up (mental imagination) and making-real (endowing the mental object with a material or verbal form) – and that the appropriation and deconstruction of making occur sometimes at the first and sometimes at the second of these two sites.[3]

War unmakes and the artist, writer, poet, composer makes; this is essential for human survival since: 'we make ourselves visible to each other through verbal and material artefacts'.[4] The cultural production of France in the twentieth and at the beginning of the twenty-first centuries has frequently been a response, implicitly or explicitly, unconsciously or consciously, to the experience of war whether in written texts, visual culture, or popular culture. Many twentieth-century Western cultural 'touchstones' in the representation of the war experience as soldier, civilian, victim or perpetrator are French in origin, or were created in France – from Henri Barbusse's novel *Le Feu* (1916), Jean Renoir's film *La Grande Illusion* (1937), Jean Fautrier's '*Otages*' series of sculptures and paintings (mid-1940s), to the more recent international publishing successes of Irène Némirovsky's novel *Suite française* (2004) and the diary of Hélène Berr (2008) – and including, of course, Picasso's iconic *Guernica* (1937), whose presence in the form of the tapestry which normally hangs in the United Nations building in New York remains a powerful reference point for contemporary wars.

These are just a rather haphazard handful of examples amongst a myriad of others that spring immediately to mind. In the act of war the reality is that the human may be destroyed, but what remains is nonetheless intensely human. The imagination (which 'makes up' and then in the case of cultural production 'makes real'), reacts to the impact of war. It may flourish at those moments, of which war is one, when the state tries to close ideas down. It allows us to enter into the minds and deeds of those who are abhorrent to us, and into experiences that we have not known, but desire to understand.

2 Elaine Scarry, *The Body in Pain: the Making and Unmaking of the World* (Oxford: Oxford University Press, 1985).
3 Scarry, *The Body in Pain*, p. 21.
4 Scarry, *The Body in Pain*, p. 22.

Indeed, at this historical moment in the West, although we are at war, few of us know war, as Val Williams has pointed out:

> Few of us have any real experience of the war zone. Our comprehension of war comes instead from what we have read and what we have seen [...]. What we make of war emerges from our memories of words and images constructed for us by a hugely diverse collection of journalists, photographers, filmmakers and artists.[5]

To which we can add writers of all sorts, poets, novelists, dramatists, essayists, autobiographers and biographers, across the spectrum of cultural production. To talk of the positive aspects of war remains taboo. We know, however, that they do exist, not least in terms of technological and medical developments, which are then sometimes used for greater social benefit. But war is also good for the economies of some countries to the detriment of others, for arms dealers, for exploitation of every sort. As will be discussed, two specifically UK-based (although both have a very international dimension) groups of scholars have made a significant contribution to the development of war and culture studies. The collective and individual work of the GWACS and the *Journal of War and Culture Studies* (JWACS) considers in what ways the act of creation (understood in the largest sense of the word) seeks, if not to reverse, then to give imaginative form to the act and effects of war, its consequences and its aftermath, thereby ensuring that the human remains visible, that form is given to an experience and is 'objectified in language and material objects',[6] that is to say, in cultural artefacts that are the marks, traces, legacy of human experience.

War Studies and the 'Cultural Turn'

Culture has espoused war as a major topic. And significant canons of aesthetic interpretation in literature, film and the visual arts have emerged throughout the twentieth century.[7]

For many years, the study of war was confined to specialist academic departments dealing primarily in military history. War studies meant the study of great leaders, their tactics and strategies; the changing face of conflict which came with the advent of evolving technologies and weapons of war; or a detailed focus on operations, logistics and specific campaigns. War studies was the preserve of a very specific set of specialist historians and often had clear links with the military and

---

5 Val Williams, *Warworks: Women, Photography, and the Iconography of War* (London: Virago Press Ltd, 1994), p. 9.
6 Scarry, *The Body in Pain*, p. 255.
7 Williams, *Warworks*, p. 17.

political establishment. 'Doing War Studies' was a gendered and elitist pursuit, and its pedagogy and research were often used to train and inform military personnel.[8]

As with many other fields of study, war studies underwent a dramatic diversification during the last couple of decades, one to which some commentators have been keen to attach the term 'cultural turn', which has elsewhere been applied to the developments across the arts and humanities that sprang from the emergence of 'cultural studies' in the 1960s. The emergence of social, cultural and gender history meant that many historians began to ask new questions about the place and role of war in society. The great military leader and his battle plan were displaced as the central interest of studies of war, and were replaced by a broadened focus on the 'ordinary' experience of war: oral histories came to the fore; the experiences of both soldiers and civilians were made more central to our understanding of war; and the roles of women in wartime were no longer eclipsed. These newer approaches to war studies effectively broke down the rigidly upheld boundary constraints that had confined war to military historians. New interdisciplinary perspectives challenged and recentred the discipline.

Indeed, war studies broadened to the point that it was no longer the preserve of historians. War was no longer viewed as a solely military and political phenomenon, but one which should, to be understood fully, be viewed also through social and cultural perspectives. The study of the cultures of war – of how war is mediated in literature, art, cinema, exhibitions, television, and so on; and, indeed, how cultural production impacts upon war itself – have displaced the centrality of 'history' to war studies. Within the academy, research on war studies is now undertaken across an extremely diverse range of disciplines: modern languages, sociology, media studies, literary studies, art history, fine art, cultural studies, memory studies and gender studies. At the same time, this has brought an expansion of the 'primary material' of war studies: film, television, photography, song, theatre, poetry, letters, postcards, diaries, school curricula, posters, landscapes, architecture, and more. These approaches have changed the methodology of war studies. For what this diversity shows is that the impact of war on individuals and on nations is perhaps most fully understood only through the adoption of a form of 'cumulative' history. While the framing of the events of war within a traditional historical narrative provides a necessary scaffold, the real bricks and mortar of understanding war and its impact comes through the accumulation of disparate and often competing interpretations and responses to war. To this end, we have witnessed the proliferation of studies engaged with popular cultures, literary cultures and visual

8 See also the position piece on this subject by Martin Evans, University of Portsmouth, in the *Journal of War and Culture Studies* 1: 1 (2007), 47–51.

cultures; sensory responses to war, the memorialisation of conflict, the semiotics of war, its rhetoric and propaganda; the topographies, landscapes and architectures of war; and the foregrounding of the mental processing of war, and how those processes affect and inflect responses towards future conflict.

The extent and legacy of the cultural turn in the study of war can be discerned in the volume of literature published in both French and English in the last quarter of a century. As far as France is concerned, initial focus was turned predominantly to the Second World War. The reason for this is perhaps obvious; a military history alone of France's experience of that conflict could never do justice to a war that infiltrated all aspects of national life. This was, after all, total warfare and a war that was fought out not only in the military opposition of the Allies, the Free French and the Resistance, on the one hand, to the German occupier, Vichy and the collaborators, on the other, but in those political, social and cultural spheres that are the territory of war and culture studies. Heroic narratives of resistance that had dominated the 1950s and 1960s had been subsequently challenged and corrected by social and political histories of collaboration published in the 1970s (such as that offered by Robert Paxton).[9]

Arguably, however, it was only with the analysis of cultural collaboration initiated in the 1980s that the full extent of collaboration, but also of resistance, as national phenomena became truly apparent. While the social and political histories challenging what had become the myth of *La France résistante* originated predominantly in the English-speaking academic community, the cultural turn in Second World War studies gained momentum, principally through the work of Henry Rousso and his 1987 study *Le Syndrome de Vichy de 1944 à nos jours*, whose influence extends across the Channel. What begins here, then, is a dialogue between the French and English-speaking academic communities around the subject of France's Second World War, a dialogue that leads to a vast range of studies of French film and literature published in both languages since the late 1980s. Two examples of English-language milestones include Margaret Atack's *Literature and the French Resistance*, and Alan Morris's *Collaboration and Resistance Reviewed*. Moreover, to gauge this dialogue, we need only consider, for example, the number of works dedicated to the literature of Patrick Modiano, one of those writers associated by Rousso with the *mode rétro* of the 1970s responsible for shattering the complacent image of a nation that had been told for too long that it need feel no shame over its war.

What is noticeable about many of these studies, from Martine Guyot-Bender and William VanderWolk's *The Occupation and Other Histories in the Novels of Patrick Modiano* to John Flower's *Patrick Modiano*, is

---

9   Robert O. Paxton, *La France de Vichy 1940–1944* (Paris, Le Seuil, 1973).

that they are often bilingual. Another remarkable feature of this dialogue is the use that British scholars have made, and continue to make, of French philosophers' engagement with the phenomena of collective and individual memory in the late twentieth and twenty-first centuries – an engagement which, in the cases of Michel de Certeau and Paul Ricœur, for example, stems in part from the encounter with, and memory of, war in the French context. The same process can also be seen to be at work in recent French and English language studies of the First World War. Here too war has been increasingly understood not just in terms of strategy and the geo-politics of the early twentieth century – the focus of many early studies – but as an experience that, like its successor, also penetrated the social and cultural spheres of national life.

Once again, the work of French cultural historians was crucial in introducing a cultural turn to the study of this particular conflict. Stéphane Audoin-Rouzeau's 1986 study *Les combattants des tranchées* was the first study to cast the common infantryman not only as an authoritative historical source, but, through the production of trench journals, as an active cultural agent and no longer the passive victim of a war popularly conceived as militarily mismanaged. Similarly, the work of Annette Becker was, and continues to be, groundbreaking in its analysis of the material culture of that same conflict.

Once again, a dialogue was established from the 1990s not only between French scholars, but between French, francophone and English scholars, particularly in relation to the study of the literature of the First World War. The works of the Belgian scholars Luc Rasson and Pierre Schoentjes, along with that of the Swiss academic, Jean Kaempfer, complement earlier studies such as John Cruickshank's *Variations on Catastrophe*, and more recent works by scholars active in the Group for War and Culture Studies – for example, Martin Hurcombe, *Novelists in Conflict: Ideology and the Absurd in the French Combat Novel of the Great War*, and Alison Fell, *Les Femmes face à la guerre / French and francophone women facing war*; Alison Fell and Ingrid Sharp, *The Women's Movement in Wartime: International Perspectives, 1914–1919*; and a special double issue of *Minerva: Women and War* (Spring and Autumn 2007). Indeed, the contribution of British scholars to the study of French cultures of the First World War, and Fell's recent work in particular, have served to open up the experience of the war, incorporating the study of what is usually designated non-combatant experience, revealing the voices of those who are traditionally excluded from narratives of war, particularly those of women whose experience of, and part in, the war were often downplayed in post-war France,[10] and questioning the very notion of combat as an exclusively male domain itself.

---

10 See also Alison Fell, 'Gendering the War Story', *Journal of War and Culture Studies* 1: 1 (2008), 53–8.

The Genesis and Development of the Group for War and Culture Studies: from the Site of France to Comparative Perspectives

In the UK the approaches developed by GWACS and its participating scholars in research seminars, conferences and publications focusing on France formed the working methods for future developments as its work expanded into a comparative cultural approach. Its early publications, Valerie Holman and Debra Kelly's *France at War in the Twentieth Century. Propaganda, Myth and Metaphor* (containing a chapter by Nicola Cooper); and Debra Kelly's *Remembering and Representing the Experience of War in Twentieth-Century France*, established both the breadth (the First and Second World Wars and colonial wars) and the methodologies of the group's work. Marie-Monique Huss's pioneering study of the place of the postcard in the First World War which included a comparison across France, Germany and Britain, *Histoires de famille 1914–1918. Cartes postales et culture de guerre*, was also the subject of a public exhibition at the Historial de la Grande Guerre, Péronne (Somme). The GWACS's place of origin in the academic environment of French and francophone literary, linguistic, and cultural studies (rather than in a department of history, for example), is essential to its approaches and methodologies in the analysis of the impact that war has had on cultural production and cultural identity, on the relationships between war and culture during conflict and its aftermath, and on the forms and practices of cultural transmission in time of war. With its genuinely interdisciplinary approach and its emphasis on culture in the sense of 'cultural artefacts', the group's innovative work is seen by scholars in the field as having revolutionised the study of the cultural history of war in the modern and contemporary world through its approach based on concepts of representation, memory and identity.

The Group for War and Culture Studies was established at the University of Westminster, London in 1995.[11] The original aim of the group was broadly to undertake and promote research into the relationships between war and culture, and its focus was France and francophone countries in the twentieth century. The initial announcement of the group's establishment, and a call for interested researchers to make contact, exceeded all expectation, with some 200 scholars from 14 countries around the world indicating their interest in those early days. Frequent requests to participate in the group's activities came from those working in what came to be called the field of war and culture studies, but whose expertise and interest was in geographical and cultural areas other than France.

---

11 The founding members of the GWACS were academic staff of the School of Languages: Ethel Tolansky (whose idea it was to focus on the relationship between war and culture and to establish the research group), Hilary Footitt, Marie-Monique Huss, Riccardo Steiner, Alan Morrison, Valerie Holman (First GWACS Research Fellow), and Debra Kelly (who has been the group's Director since 2000).

It soon became clear that it was both illogical and intellectually narrow to focus solely on France, and that although the experiences of France and francophone countries constituted a valuable case-study, the analysis of war cannot be confined to one cultural area, for obvious reasons, and was indeed undesirable from a scholarly point of view. At its annual conference in 2000, which that year took as its theme 'Legacies of War: Mourning and Beyond', the GWACS further developed the interdisciplinary approach that had guided its work on France, continuing to foster interdisciplinary work by specialists in cultural history, literary studies and all forms of visual studies, and extended its geographical coverage to include France's main allies and adversaries throughout the twentieth century, while retaining its distinct emphasis on cultural history and cultural production as significant forces that have shaped the experience, representation and memory of war. A comparative approach, which at this conference covered France, Spain, Britain and Germany, quickly showed itself to be the most productive, insightful and stimulating, and has produced some of the group's strongest and most original work. Key aspects of the group's work continue to be the relationship between war and culture during conflict and its aftermath, the forms and practices of cultural transmission in time of war, the analysis of the impact of war on cultural production, on cultural identity and on international cultural relations. The sites and experiences of France and of francophone geographical areas continue, however, to play a pivotal role in these approaches.

The core of the group's work, seminars, annual conferences and the preparation of resulting publications was originally based in London, with participants coming from around the UK and other countries to participate there (its activity is extensive and can be consulted in full at the group's website).[12] In 2000, the GWACS also established a second research site at the University of Bristol.[13] This was followed by the organisation of a series of one-day symposia, and the first of these considered 'The Figure of the Soldier' across the Russian, French and francophone, Spanish, German (East and West) cultural areas, again in the spirit of extending the geographical scope of the group's work. Its annual conferences have taken as their themes areas such as myth and propaganda; memory and the representation of war; legacies of war; humour as a strategy in war; war, narrative and the idea of 'nation'; visual

---

12 *The Group for War and Cultural Studies*, www.history.ac.uk/war-and-culture, consulted 8 February 2011.

13 Dr Martin Hurcombe and Professor Nicola Cooper who became members of the Steering Group at that time were then both based in the French Department at the University of Bristol, and founded the *Journal of War and Culture Studies* with Debra Kelly. Dr Hurcombe has remained at Bristol, while Professor Cooper is now the Director of the Callaghan Centre for the Study of Conflict, Power, Empire at the University of Swansea.

cultures of war; intellectuals and war; the body at war; and symposia and other events in London and Bristol have considered subjects such as violence and language; war, art and medicine; war, community and the visual; and women and war.

The *Journal of War and Culture Studies*: France within International Perspectives

In 2008 another milestone was reached in the development of war and culture studies in the UK, with the founding of the *Journal of War and Culture Studies* (JWACS). The subject of war and its impact on world cultures is potentially vast and the JWACS has a broad but clearly defined research field, taking as its principal focus the relationship between war and culture in the twentieth century, and into the twenty-first, primarily in Europe but not excluding other areas involved in conflict, although these should retain a focus on their relationship to Europe, and therefore necessarily to France. The journal's remit is constructed so as to be clear enough to ensure coherence, while remaining broad enough to attract the best and most innovative work with the aim of developing further the field of war and culture studies, as the GWACS has done since its inception. Its first issue published a series of position papers written by members of the editorial board and represents a cross-section of views concerning the *état présent* of war and culture studies in the first decade of the twenty-first century.

With its additional three full-length articles, this issue provides an overview of what is meant by 'war and culture studies'. Areas covered include: the relevance of the First World War and its paradigmatic status as an interpretative framework for understanding subsequent conflicts, and the debates around the notion of 'war culture', particularly in France; the complex relationship between film and memory by which the national collective memory is mediated by film rather than necessarily by lived experience; two different conceptions of the Spanish Civil War, the Spanish and the international, and the possibilities of a new understanding of that conflict in recent cultural production; a history of war documentary-making, offering some critical insights into issues of production and authenticity; an analysis of memorial culture showing how apparently static monuments are subject to both interpretational and geographic change; the significant emergence of gender studies into the study of war and the emerging trends in which two previously distinct areas now combine productively; and the argument for placing aesthetics at the heart of war studies when the bifurcated nature of the study of war has hampered synergies and prevented a full understanding of war, which is precisely what the *Journal of War and Culture Studies* seeks to counter.

Among the three full-length articles in this first issue, also authored by members of the editorial board, France remains very present: the phenomenon of battlefield collection by both combatants and non-combatants (apparently differently motivated, but finally both converging as a way of negotiating collective loss) is analysed; the Occupation years are revisited in a reading of texts and films that articulate the French experience of being neither at peace nor at war, resulting in recurrent themes of guilt, sin and shame; and, finally, issues around France as colonial power are also revisited in the study of the contemporary representation of war with an analysis of Bouchareb's film *Indigènes / Days of Glory*, providing a postcolonial critique of the film and relating its creation to a strong European trend of memory activism and its effect on national memory and governmental policy.

The themes of the subsequent volumes of the JWACS to date mainly build on the work of recent conferences: 'The Body at War', 'War and Visual Culture' (2008); 'Intellectuals and War', 'The Figure of the Soldier', and 'The Spanish Civil War' in its international dimensions commemorating the seventieth anniversary of the end of that war (2009). 'War, Culture, Technology'; 'Performance and War' (2010). Future volume themes include: 'Masculinities at War'; 'National Memory and War', a further treatment of 'The Body at War', 'Reporting War', 'Traces of War', and a review of post-9/11 cultural production on the tenth anniversary of the attack on the World Trade Center. The introduction of a 'Varia' issue in each volume and occasional varia articles in individual issues from 2010 onwards aims to ensure that the group and the journal remain abreast of new trends and research in war and culture studies as they develop. As far as France is concerned, researchers have, to date, covered subjects as diverse as (for example): André Mare and the Cubist *camoufleurs* of the First World War; the use of soldier *gouaille* and the construction of the legend of the *poilu*; French collaborators who fought for the Nazis as members of the Legion of the French Volunteers against Bolshevism and their portrayal in literature and films; Romain Rolland and the rejection of pacifism; Mauriac, Vaudoyer, the Académie française and the Occupation; photography and the French exodus of 1940; visual representations of the combatant's body in interwar France; war, wounds and remembrance in the work of Nina Bouraoui and Leïla Sebbar. As a whole, therefore, this research continues to find new ways of approaching a diverse range of the experiences of the First and Second World War and colonial wars.

Conclusion: War and Culture Studies / French Studies / Cultural Studies: Beyond France and Back Again?

How, then, has war and culture studies affected the discipline of French Studies? It is clear that it has provided a rich seam of new research that is far from having yet been exhausted. Some might argue, however, that the emphasis on war and culture detracts from the integrity of

French Studies, and there is no doubt that French scholars often find themselves deployed by their institutions to other departments and disciplines – notably history in the case of war and culture studies, but also film studies, for example, and even comparative literature. It is nonetheless an area of study which continues to fascinate and engage students at both undergraduate and postgraduate levels. It teaches them a range of interdisciplinary skills by allowing them to extend their critical and analytical skills across a range of disciplines.

To provide evidence of the ongoing and developing contributions of war and culture studies with reference to France, we end on a brief – and certainly not exhaustive or systematic – overview of recent publications in this area. A rapid search of the British Library catalogue for the last five years on 'War', 'Twentieth century' and 'France' turns up around 360 entries; of these more than 50 may be considered to be 'cultural' in their approach, written in both French and English. As in the *Journal of War and Culture Studies*, both world wars and colonial wars, especially Algeria, continue to produce new research. And if we look at 2009/2010 publications – 2010 being a year which commemorates the seventieth anniversary of de Gaulle's arrival and the founding of the Free French in London, the Blitz and the Battle of Britain, and which therefore lends itself to interest in perhaps more traditional historical and political studies, and to the British view of the Second World War – we also note (once again among many other possible examples): Alan Riding's *And the Show Went On: Cultural Life in Nazi-Occupied Paris*; Jo McCormack's *Collective Memory: France and the Algerian War (1954–62)*; Carine Bourget's *The Star, the Cross and the Crescent: Religions and Conflicts in Francophone Literature from the Arab World*; Patricia Lorcin and Daniel Brewer's *France and its Spaces of War: Experience, Memory and Image*; Charles Glass's *Americans in Paris: Life and Death under Nazi Occupation*; Robert Paxton's *Archives de la vie littéraire sous l'Occupation: à travers le désastre;* Kirrily Freeman's *Bronzes to Bullets: Vichy and the Destruction of French Public Statuary 1941–1944*; Jean-Pierre Azéma *et al.*'s *Otages de guerre: Chambord 1939–1945*; and Annette Becker's *Guillaume Apollinaire, une biographie de guerre, 1914–1918–2009*. Apparently well-trodden paths are therefore approached anew, and new areas for investigation are constantly found.

Our understanding of the war experience will be most productively enhanced when we further narrow the gaps between the military, technical, political, social, historical and cultural study of war. War is an extremely complicated phenomenon and we still need to develop more adequate cross-disciplinary frameworks within which to analyse warfare. Now that war and culture studies is firmly on the map – figuratively and literally – that is the next challenge, and France and the French experience will necessarily feature prominently in that work.

Bibliography

The Group for War and Cultural Studies, online resource, available at www.westminster. ac.uk/schools/humanities/research/french/group-for-war-and-cultural-studies (consulted 4 February 2011).

Atack, Margaret, *Literature and the French Resistance: Cultural Politics and Narrative Forms, 1940–1950* (Manchester: Manchester University Press, 1989).

Azéma, Jean-Pierre *et al.*, *Otages de guerre: Chambord 1939–1945* (Versailles: Art lys / Domaine national de Chambord, 2010).

Audoin-Rouzeau, Stéphane, *Les combatants des tranchées* (Paris: Armand Colin, 1986).

Becker, Annette, *Guillaume Apollinaire, une biographie de guerre, 1914–1918–2009* (Paris: Tallandier, 2010).

Bouchareb, Rachid (dir.), *Days of Glory* (Algeria/France: Tessalit Productions, 2006).

Bourget, Carine, *The Star, the Cross and the Crescent: Religions and Conflicts in Francophone Literature from the Arab World* (Lanham, Md: Lexington Books, 2010).

Cruickshank, John, *Variations on Catastrophe: Some French Responses to the Great War* (London and New York: Oxford University Press, 1982).

Fell, Alison, *Les Femmes face à la guerre / French and Francophone Women Facing War* (New York: Peter Lang, 2009).

Fell, Alison, 'Gendering the War Story', *Journal of War and Culture Studies* 1: 1 (2008), 53–8.

Fell, Alison and Ingrid Sharp (eds), *The Women's Movement in Wartime: International Perspectives, 1914–1919* (Basingstoke: Palgrave, 2007).

Fell, Alison and Ingrid Sharp (eds), of *Minerva*, special double issue *Women and War*. 1: 1 and 1: 2 (2007).

Flower, John, *Patrick Modiano* (New York: Rodopi, 2007).

Freeman, Kirrily, *Bronzes to Bullets: Vichy and the Destruction of French Public Statuary 1941–1944* (Stanford, CA: Stanford University Press, 2010).

Glass, Charles, *Americans in Paris: Life and Death under Nazi Occupation* (New York: Penguin Press, 2010).

Guyot-Bender, Martine and William VanderWolk, *Paradigms of Memory: the Occupation and Other Histories in the Novels of Patrick Modiano* (New York: Peter Lang, 1998).

Holman Valerie and Debra Kelly (eds), *France at War in the Twentieth Century. Propaganda, Myth and Metaphor* (Oxford: Berg, 2000).

Hurcombe, Martin, *Novelists in Conflict: Ideology and the Absurd in the French Combat Novel of the Great War* (New York: Rodopi, 2004).

Huss, Marie-Monique, *Histoires de famille 1914–1918. Cartes postales et culture de guerre* (Paris: Noesis, 2000).

Kelly Debra (ed.), *Remembering and Representing the Experience of War in Twentieth-Century France* (Lampeter: Mellen, 2000).

Lorcin, Patricia, and Daniel Brewer, *France and its Spaces of War: Experience, Memory and Image* (Basingstoke: Palgrave Macmillan, 2010).

McCormack, Jo, *Collective Memory: France and the Algerian War (1954–62)* (Lanham, Md: Lexington Books, 2010).

Morris, Alan, *Collaboration and Resistance Reviewed: Writers and 'la Mode rétro' in Post-Gaullist France* (Oxford: Berg, 1992).

Paxton, Robert O., *Archives de la vie littéraire sous l'Occupation: à travers le désastre* (Paris: Tallandier/IMEC, 2010).

Paxton, Robert O., *La France de Vichy 1940–1944* (Paris, Le Seuil, 1973).

Riding, Alan, *And the Show Went On: Cultural Life in Nazi-Occupied Paris* (London: Gerald Duckworth and Co., 2010).

Rousso, Henry, *Le Syndrôme de Vichy de 1944 à nos jours* (Paris: Le Seuil, 1987).

Scarry, Elaine, *The Body in Pain: the Making and Unmaking of the World* (Oxford: Oxford University Press, 1985).

Williams, Val, *Warworks: Women, Photography, and the Iconography of War* (London: Virago Press Ltd, 1994).

Part VIII: Adventures in Language Teaching

19

French Studies at the Open University: Pointers to the Future

Jim Coleman and Elodie Vialleton

> Part-time study is an obvious way for students to carry on earning while learning, keeping costs down and providing alternative routes into education. Part-time students now make up one third of all undergraduates. Giving a fairer deal to part-time students could raise our skills base and improve social mobility while actually saving the Government money. (David Willetts, now Minister for Universities and Science)[1]

At the Open University, French is taught by the largest but least conventional department of languages in the UK. Numbers of language students are now approaching 10,000 a year, which translates into over 3,000 full-time equivalent student (FTEs) numbers. In terms of recruitment, whether actual students or FTEs, the Open University is also the largest French department in the UK. This chapter describes our distinctive and innovative approach to teaching French, and our related research activities. It opens by setting language learning in the context of supported distance education, and concludes by proposing wider inter-university collaboration in the context of globalising higher education and falling UK interest in degree-level language study.

Principles of Supported Distance Learning at the Open University

By the time the Open University (OU) moved into languages, it had already demonstrated the effectiveness of supported distance learning, and its ability to help large numbers of disparate and geographically

---

1   David Willetts, *Policy Review* 23 January (2010), online resource, consulted on 25 November 2010.

scattered students to achieve their educational ambitions. The OU's mission has always been distinctive: being open to people, places, methods and ideas brings challenges unfamiliar to conventional, residential universities. Social inclusiveness means that around 10,000 of the OU's students are disabled in some way, while around 2,500 are in prison without access to computers and the internet. Soldiers in Afghanistan or diplomats on overseas postings face distractions very different from those of traditional, full-time students, and learners without a readily available peer group to provide advice and mutual reassurance require distinctive forms of support, whatever their domain of study.

The OU's courses are open to all, including those unable or unwilling to participate in tutorials, so the quality and nature of the learning materials are more important than in traditional universities. All of the many functions fulfilled in the classroom by the teacher are therefore met by incorporating the 'teacher's voice' in the materials themselves, which are created and repeatedly revised through developmental testing and external review before being made available to students. In a face-to-face classroom, the occasional gaffe or muddled explanation can easily be retrieved, but this is not the case where a print run of several thousand is involved, and explains in part why delivering distance higher education requires high upfront investment. It also explains why OU courses are widely regarded as an international benchmark, and frequently pirated or photocopied by other institutions. All materials result from a team effort: multiple inputs ensure consistent quality (and perhaps a rather unvarying 'voice') across courses, and although individual and even idiosyncratic ideas may well be adopted, it is no place for prima donnas.

Course books – which remain central to the OU's approach to supported distance learning – are complemented by audio, video and computer-based materials, and the module's website brings together all the resources provided within the Moodle VLE (Virtual Learning Environment). Through this single access point, students can see and hear the teaching and assessment materials, use other internal and external resources, and participate in asynchronous and synchronous networking with their tutors and fellow students. The discussion forums, both for individual tutor groups and for the whole course, compensate to an extent for the lack of campus-based classmates. Requiring no more than clear ground rules and occasional light-touch monitoring, such forums attract thousands of posts and provide demonstrably effective peer support and encouragement. At Christmas 2009, students on L192 Beginners' French even organised an online French pantomime.

There are no admission requirements for OU courses, although plentiful advice and – for languages – tasters are available. Consequently, student profiles are very much wider than in conventional, residential universities where mature students remain the exception. Students tend to be older – although the fastest growing sector is under-25s – and while many already hold a degree-level qualification, many others have no experience of post-compulsory or higher education.[2]

Not only are all tutorials optional, but they are also infrequent: the model allows only some 20 hours of group tuition for each module. Tutors, all of whom receive extensive initial and ongoing professional development, also provide very detailed individual feedback on compulsory scheduled assignments throughout the course. Samples of each tutor's formative and summative assessment are regularly monitored to ensure that criteria are respected, and that supportive and accurate feedback is provided in an equitable way. Where any module has a population of several hundred (Beginners' French typically attracts 1,400 students a year), such quality assurance is essential.

Despite a recent move to encouraging students to aim at a degree or other qualification, rather than just successful completion of the current module, recruitment and registration still apply only to a single module. Many enrol just for the learning, rather than its certification, and there is no automatic sequence or progression. Whereas, in conventional universities, the vast majority of students, once launched on a particular pathway, will dutifully follow it for the next three or four years, the OU needs to devote considerable attention and resources to both initial recruitment and to retention: only a positive learning experience will lead a student to complete the current module and register for the next. With 70 per cent of OU students in full-time employment, motivation and persistence on their part and effective teaching and support on ours are essential to keep them studying. In some respects, our role is akin to adult education or university language centres: not every student is seeking a formal qualification, many are following a course for interest or pleasure and have no intention of taking it further, and numbers are higher at lower levels. However, this does not mean that courses are not challenging, and the inclusion of content alongside language skills puts OU language courses in the same category as specialist rather than non-specialist provision in other universities.

French at the Open University

The four French modules which the OU currently offers (described in Table 1) attract some 3,500 students a year, all of whom are part-time and distance taught. The modules, which take students from beginner to degree level over four years of study, integrate the four language skills with the study of contemporary culture and society in France and the French-speaking world.

---

2 J. A. Coleman and C. Furnborough, 'Learner characteristics and learning outcomes on a distance Spanish course for beginners', *System* 38: 1 (2010), 14–29.

Table 1 *French modules available at the Open University*

Module Code	L192	L120	L211	L310
Title	*Bon Départ*	*Ouverture*	*Envol*	*Mises au point*
Level	Beginners	Intermediate	Upper intermediate	Advanced
CEFR	A2	B1	B2	C1
Credits	30	30	60	60
Dates	Nov–Oct	Feb–Oct	Feb–Oct	Feb–Oct
Duration (Teaching)	11 months	8 months	8 months	8 months
Current cost	£480	£480	£1165	£850
Qualification	Certificate in French		Diploma in French	

In addition to the distance courses, all students may take LXR122 *Action in French*, a one-week residential school at Caen University for beginners, false beginners and intermediate learners, which earns 10 credits. A compulsory residential school in Caen is embedded in the upper intermediate module; students who are unable to travel take part in an online 'Alternative Learning Experience' which delivers the same learning outcomes.

Two principles which operate from the start are:

- development of all four language skills
- integration of language skills with 'content'.

This means that those who complete courses up to and including degree-level (L310) will have a knowledge of French language and the society and culture of contemporary France comparable to those from any other UK university: external examiners confirm that this is the case, and indeed that OU students frequently attain higher levels in both linguistic and cultural domains. The learning outcomes for L310, for example, include academic writing, critical and analytical skills, and intercultural competence, while the six themes are:

- *History*: The end of the French Empire; a profile of General de Gaulle; Revolution and republicanism
- *Multicultural France*: Interviews with the writer Azouz Begag; an exploration of secularism (*Laïcité*) and its role in French identity; immigration and identity through the prism of literature
- *The media*: The regional daily *Sud Ouest* – production and presentation of the news; French radio, listener participation, consumer issues; television, the internet, globalisation, and celebrity culture.
- *The arts in France*: The influence of *la bande dessinée* in France; the national *Fête de la musique*; the state of the Arts

- *Science and technology*: The *Cité des sciences et de l'industrie,* science and the public; a profile of two French oceanography museums; scientific endeavour the French way
- *Expression and identity in the French-speaking world*: The literatures of Québec; the Caribbean and French-speaking Africa; the French-speaking world.

Successful completion of the two Level 1 modules (L192 and L120) currently leads to the award of a Certificate in French. Adding the Level 2 and Level 3 modules (L211 and L310) earns a Diploma in French. No Single Honours degree is offered, but students can obtain the BA (Honours) in Modern Language Studies by achieving 360 credits across two languages (which may include English). With the OU, students can attain a degree, at today's prices, for below £5,000, despite the impact of the previous government's withdrawal of state funding for students pursuing an equal or lower qualification (ELQ) than they already hold.

The Pedagogy

OU French modules make selective use of technological tools adapted to particular skills and learning outcomes, and offer a combination of independent study and support through work with peers and tutors.

Like almost all OU courses, the French modules are delivered through blended learning. Study materials are composed of a blend of media (course books, CDs, DVD-ROMs, a dedicated website), which allows students to learn and practise each of the four skills through the most appropriate medium, and which helps to accommodate a variety of learning styles and study preferences and provides more choice. For example, books are preferred for text-based activities, and they are easy to carry around, DVD-ROMs are used to deliver materials based on audio clips and videos without requiring fast internet access to download them, while an online environment gives more flexibility to provide activities based on mixed media and up-to-date news, content and tools. The module website brings together all the components of a module in a format that is accessible from any computer or mobile device with internet access, and gives students access to communication tools. It is therefore also the space that forms a virtual community by bringing students together and allowing them to interact in real time or asynchronously, either for social purposes or to work together.

Indeed, one of the main challenges of learning a language independently and at a distance is the acquisition of skills which depend on interaction. This is achieved through the use of technology. Asynchronous online activities are designed to get students to take part in collaborative tasks in French. For example, in the upper intermediate French module, each thematic unit includes a number of optional group tasks which students perform in a discussion forum. They get to write a film review collaboratively, or to collect and organise arguments and examples together before writing an individual essay. These tasks do not take place in real time and they are written tasks, but they do enable students to practise using French structures to share or ask for information and to negotiate meaning. The use of teleconferencing in all OU French courses adds an extra dimension by allowing students to practise these skills in real time and in speaking. Activities for synchronous and asynchronous online tasks are carefully designed as an integral part of a module. Some are meant to be used by groups of students working autonomously, and some are led by tutors as part of the tuition. Students are also free to use teleconferencing and discussion forums on their own as part of peer-support groups to support each other, to practise their speaking skills or just to chat.

While most of the students' work is done independently, its success depends on the strong student support available. In this the role of the associate lecturers, who act as individual tutors to OU students, is instrumental. They deliver tutorials, some of which take place face to face and some online through teleconferencing. They also support their tutorial group in tutor group discussion forums, which are used as virtual asynchronous classrooms to bridge the gap between tutorials. Finally, they provide individualised support by phone or email and through the extensive feedback sent to students about each of the frequent compulsory assignments that punctuate the course of a module.

Research

When it comes to research, French is integrated with the other foreign languages (German, Spanish, Italian, Chinese, Welsh, English for academic purposes) now offered by the OU. A strategic decision was taken in 2001 to focus the research effort of the Department of Languages on a single domain. Although many individuals have published, and a few continue to publish, in areas related to cultures and literatures, the predominant output has been on foreign language learning. Given the long-standing OU expertise in distance education, and in particular in how new technologies are most effectively used in support of learning and teaching, it was natural to focus principally on e-learning, or online learning of languages. And while research also continues in areas such as study abroad, intercultural narratives, language motivation in UK secondary schools, and the Common European Framework of Reference for Languages, the largest body of research, with around 200 publications since 2001, has been devoted to computer-mediated communication (CMC), both within language learning and as a generic domain, including online cultures, multimodality and new research methodologies.

Many of the issues addressed by the Open Languages Research Group – including overcoming distance in language learning, good pedagogic practices, autonomy and self-management, affect, new technologies within a socio-cultural paradigm, alternative tools and affordances, anxiety and motivation in online conferences, and tutor training – have recently been summarised by Coleman and Furnborough,[3] in an article which also shows that the same learning outcomes can be achieved by online tuition as through face-to-face classes. New initiatives seek to establish, from online tutorials, a digital corpus of spoken learner language.

International recognition of Open Languages in this increasingly important area of research has been evidenced by invited plenaries and peer-reviewed contributions to conferences across the world. In RAE 2008, given the continued absence of an Applied Linguistics Sub-panel, language research was submitted as part of a 77-strong cross-Faculty entry to Education, which saw the OU's Centre for Research in Education and Educational Technology (CREET) ranked third among educational research centres in the UK.

Much of the CMC research, while underpinned by educational and applied linguistic theory,[4] feeds directly into teaching, where languages are among the most innovative departments at the OU. Since language learning depends on tutor–student and student–student interaction, lessons learned in French or other foreign language classes can be transferred to any course where tuition relies on interaction. Cross-language cooperation means that an initiative taken by a single language course can be implemented at scale across all languages and levels, benefiting all 10,000 language students.

This may be one reason why language courses repeatedly feature, in the annual survey, among those evincing highest levels of student satisfaction across the whole OU, which has itself been in the top three UK universities each year since the National Student Survey was launched in 2005.

Appreciation of the OU's approach to the learning of languages and cultures is also evidenced on an international scale. Sample units are made available free of charge both via OpenLearn,[5] which passed one million visitors in January 2010, and via *iTunesU*.[6] The OU was globally the first university to achieve 20 million iTunes downloads, a total which had reached 24 million by August 2010.[7] The top four 'tracks'

3 Coleman and Furnborough, 'Learner Characteristics'.
4 J. A. Coleman *et al.*, 'Collaboration and interaction: The keys to distance and computer-supported language learning', in G. Levine and A. Phipps (eds), *Critical and Intercultural Theory and Language Pedagogy* (Boston, MA: Cengage Heinle, in press), pp. 161–80.
5 *OpenLearn*, online resource, consulted 25 November 2010.
6 *The Open University on iTunesU*, online resource, consulted 25 November 2010.
7 *The Open University on iTunesU: Impact*, online resource, consulted 25 November 2010.

are beginners' Spanish, French, Chinese and German, with two further language units in the top ten downloads.

The Future: A Worsening Climate

In the context of cuts in higher education funding, which are anticipated to be greater than any experienced since the Great Depression of the 1930s, it is unrealistic to think that French Studies will be immune from change. Among conventional universities, there has existed a widely used but tacit distinction between 'selectors' – those institutions whose reputation guarantees more applicants than the places available – and 'recruiters', who need to actively attract enough students to fill their places. At disciplinary level, the distinction hardly operates: those with substantial French programmes are virtually all selectors, and most (with Portsmouth a signal exception) from the Russell Group. Unprecedented pressure on places for 2010 admission and government funding constraints herald an era when, overall, demand substantially exceeds supply. But there is little reassurance for languages in general and French in particular.

Back in 2000, the Nuffield Report on Languages already found that 'University language departments are closing, leaving the sector in deep crisis'.[8] That same year, 347,007 students took a French GCSE, and 18,221 a French A level. Since then, while overall modern languages numbers have fallen by 9.4 per cent at A level and 38.4 per cent at GCSE, French has plummeted by 24.0 per cent and 48.8 per cent respectively. The 2009–10 declines alone are, at 3.4 per cent and 6.0 per cent, showing no sign at all of levelling off. Yet, as Michael Worton has noted, and despite the continuing closure of courses and departments, the university modern languages sector is not behaving as if it were in a critical position, but clinging to past sectarian divisions of language, specialism, foundation date or position in league tables rather than working together to maximise chances of surviving or even thriving.[9]

French cannot afford to ignore the political climate in the UK, which remains hostile to languages.[10] Indeed, the coalition government elected in 2010 is arguably pursuing an even more strictly monolingualist agenda than its predecessor – as evidenced by the immediate scrapping of the Diploma in Languages and International Communication and the abandonment of Sir Jim Rose's recommendation for compulsory language

8 The Nuffield Foundation, *Languages: The Next Generation* (Milton Keynes: English Company (UK) Ltd, 2000).

9 Michael Worton, *Review of Modern Foreign Languages Provision in Higher Education in England* (Bristol: HEFCE, 2009), online resource, consulted 8 August 2010.

10 J.A. Coleman, 'Why the British do not Learn Languages: Myths and Motivation in the United Kingdom', *Language Learning Journal* 37: 1 (2009), 111–27.

provision in primary schools. These actions contradict Willetts's call for students to undertake study abroad and to offer more language skills. Referring to a recent report by the Confederation of British Industry in 2010, he said: 'British companies want to export abroad but one of the problems they raise with us is that British students don't have foreign languages and an experience of living in another country.'

Modern languages at university level in the UK are already an élitist subject, and in conventional universities further socio-economic concentration appears inevitable. While we recognise that many of our own students are also drawn from privileged sectors of society, the OU's critical education and social inclusion philosophy requires that we challenge such a situation.

We have already stressed the need to challenge the simplistic messages of the media.[11] Press coverage of Deputy Prime Minister Nick Clegg's use of Dutch, Spanish and German in June 2010 is, sadly, typical of the media construction of multilingualism as freakish, problematic and unnecessary. In *The Times*, Roger Boyes recalled that Edward Heath's use of French 'was held against him' for 'trying too hard to please the foreigners', that Tony Blair 'thought it wise to play down any linguistic skill' and that, for UK politicians, speaking other European languages is taboo in case it suggests 'politically unsound interest in European integration'.[12] Kate Connolly in the *Guardian* mentioned his spokeswoman's German nationality, and portrayed Clegg's use of German to Germans not as natural or courteous, but as sneaky: 'There's no better way to flatter a German than to speak his or her tongue.'[13]

Connolly implies that Clegg's linguistic skills result not from choice and long-term effort, but from the serendipity of a Dutch mother, a Spanish wife, a school trip to Munich and working as a ski instructor in Austria. Sarah Sands in the *Independent* takes the same tack: 'Clegg is more connected to European blood lines than the Royal Family.'[14] She recognises that 'a mastery of foreign languages is regarded by most of us with admiration – and suspicion', and even argues that: 'The Philistinism towards foreign languages is bad enough. Worse is the sense that it is boastful and somehow unpatriotic to use a foreign language.' Unfortunately, she undermines her own argument with the statement that 'there is no need for an English person to learn another language'. The usual xenophobic verbs stand in for speaking a foreign language: for Sands, 'Clegg gabbled about the mist in Berlin', while Paul Moss on

11 Coleman, 'Why the British do not learn Languages'.
12 Roger Boyes, 'Nick Clegg's Mastery of German Breaks Down Walls in Berlin', *The Times* (11 June 2010).
13 Kate Connolly and Giles Tremlett, 'Nick Clegg: The Gift of the International Gab?', *The Guardian* (12 June 2010).
14 Sarah Sands, 'Clever Clegg Minds his Languages – All Six of Them', *The Independent* (13 June 2010).

the BBC's *World Tonight* spoke of Clegg 'jabbering away with the locals in their own language'.[15]

Beyond occasional lip service, there is no real evidence that government will challenge the widespread, if fallacious, beliefs that 'English is enough' and that language study is an irrelevance. If there is some evidence that some adults and undergraduates in non-language disciplines continue to recognise the importance of languages, the continuing shrinking of the pool from which specialist undergraduates are drawn shows no sign of slowing.

The Future: New Models of Higher Education

In July 2010, the current Universities Minister, David Willetts, and Business Secretary, Vince Cable, referred rather dismissively to the 'Club Med' model of conventional universities, where comfortably-off students who have mostly just left secondary education look to a single provider to offer the full spread of education, accommodation and other facilities in a highly intensive, once-in-a-lifetime experience, not without elements of a holiday village.[16] They explicitly support a more diverse provision which includes part-time and lifelong education. Shortly after his election, the Prime Minister, David Cameron, chose the OU as the venue for a speech on change and modernisation, citing it as an example of 'the success that change and modernisation can bring':

> Respected the world over, you are a demonstration that in this country, yes we have some of the best old universities in the world, but also some of the best innovation in the world such as we have through The Open University.[17]

Subsequently, in July 2010, the OU's Vice-Chancellor was one of four to accompany Cameron, Willetts and Cable on a major mission to India. It can come as no surprise if government in future backs a different model of higher education, incorporating distance, online and/or part-time elements.

The globalisation and marketisation of higher education are equally inescapable. Bill Gates echoed the UK ministers in suggesting that higher education, 'except for the parties, needs to be less place-based'. He claimed in August 2010 that, within five years, 'place-based learning

---

15 Paul Moss, speaking on BBC Radio 4 *The World Tonight* (12 June 2010).
16 Rosa Prince, '"Club Med" University Experience is Over', *The Daily Telegraph* (20 July 2010).
17 'David Cameron Keynote Speech at OU Library', *Open University News* (26 May 2009), online resource, consulted 25 November 2010.

will be five times less important than it is today'.[18] Gareth Williams, Emeritus Professor at the Institute of Education Centre for Higher Education Studies, also believes 'higher education may increasingly be delivered via distance learning'.[19]

As the 2001 benchmark statement on modern languages,[20] and a recent guide to university teaching in modern languages,[21] spelt out, and the 2009 Worton Report reiterated,[22] French is part of a very diverse sector, embracing literary, cultural, film and linguistic studies, as well as providing language training and cultural insights to both a dwindling number of specialists and a growing number of non-specialists. Like religions, languages have historically focused much more on what divides them than on common interests. At a time of monolingualism and budget cuts, it behoves us all to look at ways of working together more effectively for the good of all.

Departments face a choice between sitting complacently like shipwreck survivors in a lifeboat, with the strongest eating the weakest from time to time as numbers dwindle, or taking action at a political, societal and pedagogical level. Currently, too many disdain to argue publicly and to decision makers the practical value (dare one say 'impact'?) of studying languages. Few challenge the media messages that English is enough and that other languages are a problem rather than a resource. And collaborative teaching initiatives are few and far between, despite examples such as *Netzwerk Deutsch*, a beginner's German course based on OU learning materials and offered by a number of partner universities.

The OU has real and recent experience of the value of working together, and collaborates through choice and not necessity. It has unparalleled expertise in distance learning, in online tuition, in managing synchronous and asynchronous computer-mediated communication, in training colleagues to teach online, and in delivering quality learning at scale and worldwide. We welcome from colleagues anywhere proposals which might protect and enhance national provision of French in higher education.

18 Bill Gates, 'Bill Gates on In-person vs. Online Education', *Techonomy Conference, Lake Tahoe, California* (6 August 2010), online resource, consulted 25 November 2010.

19 John Morgan, 'The Heat is on: Official Hints that Cuts Could Rise to 35%', *Times Higher Education* (12 August 2010), p. 6.

20 Qualification and Assesment Authority (QAA), *Honours Degree Benchmark Statements: Languages and Related Studies* (London: QAA, 2007), online resource, consulted on 25 November 2010).

21 J. A. Coleman and J. Klapper (eds), *Effective Learning and Teaching in Modern Languages* (London: Routledge, 2005).

22 Worton, *Review*.

Bibliography

Boyes, Roger, 'Nick Clegg's Mastery of German breaks down Walls in Berlin', *The Times* (11 June 2010).

Cameron, D., Keynote speech at OU Library', *Open University News* (26 May 2009), available at www3.open.ac.uk/media/fullstory.aspx?id=16186 (consulted 25 November 2010).

Coleman, J. A., 'Why the British do not Learn Languages: Myths and Motivation in the United Kingdom', *Language Learning Journal* 37: 1 (2009), 111–27.

Coleman, J. A. and C. Furnborough, 'Learner Characteristics and Learning Outcomes on a Distance Spanish Course for Beginners', *System* 38: 1 (2010), 14–29.

Coleman, J. A. and J. Klapper (eds), *Effective Learning and Teaching in Modern Languages* (London: Routledge, 2005).

Coleman, J. A., R. Hampel, M. Hauck and U Stickler, 'Collaboration and interaction: The keys to distance and computer-supported language learning', in G. Levine and A. Phipps (eds), *Critical and Intercultural Theory and Language Pedagogy* (Boston, MA: Cengage Heinle), pp. 161–80.

Confederation of British Industry (CBI), *Stronger Together: Business and Universities in Turbulent Times* (CBI: 2010), available at http://highereducation.cbi.org.uk/uploaded/CBI_HE_taskforce_report.pdf (consulted 25 November 2010).

Connolly, Kate and Giles Tremlett, 'Nick Clegg: the gift of the international gab?', *Guardian* (12 June 2010).

Gates, Bill, 'Bill Gates on In-person vs. Online Education', *Techonomy Conference, Lake Tahoe, California*, 6 August (2010), available at www.youtube.com/watch?v=p2Qg80MVvYs&feature=player_embedded (consulted 25 November 2010).

Morgan, John, 'The heat is on: official hints that cuts could rise to 35%', *Times Higher Education* (12 August 2010), p. 6.

The Nuffield Foundation, *Languages: The Next Generation* (Milton Keynes: English Company (UK) Ltd, 2000).

Policy Review (23 January 2010) available at www.policyreview.co.uk/articles.php?article_id=70 (consulted 25 Novmeber 2010).

Prince, Rosa, '"Club Med" University Experience is Over', *Daily Telegraph* (20 July 2010).

Qualification and Assesment Authority (QAA), *Honours Degree Benchmark Statements: Languages and Related Studies* (London: QAA, 2007), available at www.qaa.ac.uk/academicinfrastructure/benchmark/honours/languages.pdf (consulted on 25 November 2010).

Sands, Sarah, 'Clever Clegg minds his Languages – All Six of Them', *Independent* (13 June 2010).

Worton, Michael, *Review of Modern Foreign Languages Provision in Higher Education in England* (London: HEFCE, 2009), available at: www.hefce.ac.uk/pubs/hefce/2009/09_41/ (consulted on 8 August 2010).

Websites

OpenLearn, available at http://openlearn.open.ac.uk/ (consulted 25 November 2010).

The Open University on iTunesU: Impact, available at http://projects.kmi.open.ac.uk/itunesu/impact/ (consulted 25 November 2010).

The Open University on iTunesU, available at http://www.open.ac.uk/itunes/ (consulted 25 November 2010).

20

Opportunities and Challenges of Technologically Enhanced Programmes: Online and Blended Learning at King's College London

Dominique Borel

Background

Blended learning, a mix of face-to-face and virtual interactions, and online courses have been developed at the Modern Language Centre (MLC) at King's since 2004. They are a key component of the department's strategy for fostering autonomous learning both within credit-bearing language courses, and for students enrolled on non degree-language programmes, while adhering to Quality Assurance Agency (QAA) criteria and promoting academic excellence. Incorporating an e-learning dimension into existing face-to-face programmes, and designing specific online material and courses has been a deliberate policy choice, both in support of the college's own strategic plan, and in the desire to enhance the learning experience of students. Although the level of involvement in blended learning and online programmes varies across the college, some departments have already established a global reputation in delivering innovative online programmes, examples being King's Dental Institute[1] and the Department of War Studies.[2]

The projects undertaken by the MLC were entirely college funded through a succession of bids, and benefit from the support of a dedicated e-learning team within the MLC, including coordinators and a part-time technician. In addition, and perhaps to an unusual extent, a majority of MLC staff have an interest in technologically enhanced teaching methodology, and have been particularly responsive in taking up training opportunities in this area.

Of relevance to this paper, is the online MA/PGDip in French Language and Culture,[3] developed and taught in collaboration with the

---

1   *Ivident, International Virtual Dental School*, online resource, consulted 1 December 2010.
2   MA, 'War in the Modern World' (WiMW), online resource, consulted 1 December 2010.
3   Online MA/PGDip in French Language and Culture, King's College London, online resource, accessed 1 December 2010.

Department of French at King's, Pedagogical Grammar for French,[4] French for Medics,[5] a blended learning course for students and practitioners of medicine, and the Languages and Communicative Skills self-access programme, providing undergraduate and postgraduate students with access to wide-ranging online resources at all levels in French as well as Arabic, German, Italian, and Spanish.

Online MA/PGDip in French Language and Culture

This pioneering programme – according to our research, we believe this is the only truly entirely online postgraduate degree in both French language and content in the UK – was launched in October 2009. We believe that it is an excellent example of good practice at a time when establishing partnerships between traditional research-based higher education (HE) language departments and skills-focused language centres remains tentative across the UK.

In his HEFCE-funded *Review of Modern Foreign Languages Provision in Higher Education in England*,[6] Professor Michael Worton states:

> There would seem to be many areas in which pedagogical and intellectual collaboration between Language Departments and Language Centres would prove productive and HEIs should encourage the development of such synergies. There is also an urgent need for an open dialogue between MFL Departments and Language Centres that recognises the unique role that each can play in creating an identity and a profile for MFL in HE.[7]

And further:

> Universities need, where appropriate, to address the tensions that can exist between MFL Departments and Language Centres, ensuring that there is parity of esteem for both, and with a commitment to building a culture of collaborative development for languages provision.[8]

As in the case of all other e-learning developments by the MLC, the selection of courses on offer is based on building well-established areas of strength and specialisation within the host institution. For example, French Pedagogical Grammar provides online support to trainee teachers enrolled on King's PGCE (Ofsted have graded the King's

---

4   Pedagogical Grammar for French, King's College London, online resource, consulted on 1 December 2010.
5   French for Medics, King's College London, online resource, consulted 1 December 2010.
6   Michael Worton, *Review of Modern Foreign Languages Provision in Higher Education in England* (London, HEFCE, 2009), online resource, consulted 1 September 2010.
7   Worton, *Review*, p. 30.
8   Worton, *Review*, p. 35.

College London Postgraduate Certificate in Education (PGCE) with a Grade 1 'outstanding'). French for Medics offers a bespoke post-A Level blended learning course to students of King's School of Medicine, one of the oldest medical schools in the UK.

In the case of the MA/PGDip, both the French Department's Research Assessment Exercise rating (it was ranked second nationally in the most recent RAE, with the great majority of its research rated as 'world-leading' or 'internationally excellent') and the MLC's expertise in language provision on both credit-bearing and external courses provided an ideal opportunity for synergy.

Course format

The MA/PGDip is designed for students with an advanced level of French who are seeking to perfect their French language skills and to pursue higher-level study of French literature and culture. The MA includes a substantial research element in the form of a dissertation, whereas the postgraduate diploma can be gained by taking only the taught modules.

All modules include full tutorial support and interaction, delivered via the King's virtual learning environment (VLE) online. Students and tutors interact in several ways – for example, through written feedback on work submitted and presentations, through voice recordings (for the oral module), through chat rooms. The course is delivered online, via Blackboard. The language modules include tests on speaking, through the use of the latest, innovative technological resources such as Skype and Elluminate, providing a virtual environment for conducting seminars and oral examinations.

Teaching is divided into six two-week thematic blocks, each subdivided into a number of related topics. For each block, students are required to read the introductory text written by the tutor on each topic (the virtual equivalent of a lecture or seminar introduction), and to study the set reading/viewing for that topic. Apart from a number of set texts, which students are expected to buy, all other material is provided online.

At the end of the two-week block, one or two students (depending on overall numbers) are required to post a short written presentation on each of the topics, by a given date. All students are then expected to respond to these presentations and participate in discussion via the message board. The tutor logs on at prearranged times to respond, clarify, summarise and raise further questions for discussion, and then to close the discussion at a given point. Students are given individual tutorial support and essay guidance via email.

Students opting for the full MA are required to take four language modules and two content modules (Literature and Visual Arts, and Literature and Classicism), each worth 20 credits. They must also complete a 60-credit 10,000 word dissertation.

Of paramount importance, as in all e-learning programmes, is the need for flexibility. In the case of the MA/PGDip this is reflected in the timescale for delivery and for completion. Students can choose to enrol on a part-time basis (at present, we expect virtually all students to be part-timers), either in September or January, with a minimum of one module per year. The overall maximum completion period is six years. Alternatively, students can enrol on the entire MA programme in September of any academic year and complete it in one year, excluding time devoted to the final dissertation. We currently have no full-time students, and do not expect many in future. It is also possible for suitably qualified students to take individual modules or groups of modules with no commitment to complete the PGDip/MA. Key administrative procedures such as enrolment, examinations, monitoring of attendance, require the services of an admissions tutor, departmental administrators, a programme supervisor and a technician.

Year 1 Review

For this flagship programme, which is still being piloted, student and staff feedbacks are crucial. Useful suggestions made in this first year, relating especially to workload and choice of technological tools, have been acted upon ahead of the 2010–11 enrolment session. A key issue, that of the efficiency in central administrative and financial services roles when registering students' academic progression, and fee payment, requires further improvement. In their paper entitled 'Strategies for Embedding e-Learning in Traditional Universities: Drivers and Barriers', Kay MacKeogh and Seamus Fox, state:

> In effect, e-learning is not just the responsibility of academics; administrative support units are key facilitators, including the Learning Innovation Unit, Library, Student Services, Computer Services, Registry, Finance, Human Resources etc. For e-learning to flourish, all systems must interact to ensure that there are no blockages or inhibitors.[9]

From a statistical point of view, it is fair to point out that our sample responses are modest in number at this stage, and may not be sufficient to form a definitive opinion. Out of 43 initial enquiries by potential students, from as far afield as Alaska, Columbia, France, Great Britain, Malaysia and Saint Lucia, six firm offers were made (four of these were for the MA), and three additional January enrolments were received. Interestingly, reasons for enrolment were far ranging, from professionals seeking enhanced career prospects, specialists involved in lifelong

9 Kay MacKeogh and Seamus Fox, 'Strategies for Embedding e-Learning in Traditional Universities: Drivers and Barriers', *Electronic Journal of e-Learning* 7: 2 (2009), 147–54.

learning of languages, such as mid-career French teachers, and in the case of the language modules, PhD students – a recognition that even students with good BAs or even MAs in French can keep improving their French, and recognise this themselves.

Student Feedback

Overall, students evaluated the programme content and staff feedback very positively, commenting on how constructive the latter had been, and describing the relationship with the lecturers as extremely supportive. The opportunity for online 'live' discussion forums was especially appreciated. Access to online material varied in signal quality and speed, but this was not singled out as a major problematic issue, which may reflect students' familiarity with technology in general. As Amanda Jefferies and Ruth Hyde remark in their paper on the Joint Information Systems Committee (JISC) funded project at the University of Hertfordshire:

> the authors now suggest that for many HE students, technology has become a ubiquitous part of their lives to the extent that they may own or access regularly multiple items of personal technology that are used interchangeably for learning and leisure, including their computers and their MP3 players.... In her Foreword to Beetham and Sharpe's, *Rethinking Pedagogy for a Digital Age*, Diana Laurillard commented that: 'Education is in an interesting phase between its 'ICT-free' past and its 'ICT-aware' future.' This phase may only be valid for a short time more as the pace of technological change accelerates and the effects of ICT and their influence on the provision for schools and universities are felt throughout the UK education sector. Research conducted since January 2007 by among other organisations, Educause (Oblinger and Oblinger, 2007) and ECAR (Caruso and Salway, 2007) has highlighted that the generation of 18-year-olds entering HE as undergraduates at the end of the first decade of the twenty-first century is both more technically knowledgeable and confident than any previous intake of students and that they generally have very high expectations of what technology might be available to them and how they could use it to access their learning.

Satisfaction with improved language skills and a high motivation rate were also prominent in the overall feedback.

From the outset we were aware both of the need to create a learning community, and of the fact that prospective students who are unfamiliar with interactive e-learning are likely to worry about this issue in particular. We met that challenge by building a high degree of interactivity, of various forms, into the modules, thanks to the commitment of the teachers. In light of student feedback, and being aware that students, too, are at different points on the path from an ICT-free past to an

ICT-aware future, we have added an induction week for the 2010–11 session in order to introduce the programme to students formally, to ensure they are equipped with the necessary technological skills, to provide them with clear guidelines on administrative procedures, and to help develop a fruitful dynamic to encourage student participation in discussions. This is crucial in a situation where distance makes establishing successful relationships between students, and between students and teachers, much more challenging.

Staff Feedback

Although a proportion of academics may be increasingly aware of the added-value of technology in supporting learning, studies also indicate some concern that the practice may detract from students' need to develop more traditional research skills, such as critical thinking and analysis. Given the ground-breaking nature of the online MA – a postgraduate programme entirely taught through distance learning – a certain level of anxiety was felt by all involved. Both the language and content modules had to be written from scratch in less than a year, owing to timetable constraints. The project is a triumph of collaborative effort, and it is fair to say that its success is due to a large extent to the determination of staff in both departments, not only to complete the material in time, but also to undertake technical training where necessary, despite being placed under pressure. A large proportion of MLC staff already had experience in technologically-enhanced material design and teaching, whereas many colleagues in more traditional research departments are still relatively unfamiliar with alternative delivery formats – though that situation is changing quite rapidly.

In her paper entitled 'Learning Submarines: Raising the Periscopes', Gilly Salmon states:

> Most e-moderator recruits come from face-to-face teaching where they may have relied quite heavily on personal charisma to stimulate and hold their students' interest. It is a big change to make when switching to online. Even teachers who are used to developing distance learning materials need to explore how online materials can underpin and extend their teaching. Conversely, students used to the paradigm of teacher as the instructor may expect a great deal of input from the e-moderator. This can be very time consuming and unsatisfactory for both. The e-moderator must explain his or her role at the start, to reduce the chances of unreasonable expectations arising.[10]

---

10 Gilly Salmon, 'Learning Submarines: Raising the Periscopes' (Open University Business School and United States Open University, 2007), online resource.

With hindsight, one key recommendation, to ensure the successful launch of such projects, would be to ensure a realistic time frame for adequate preparation, module design and for identifying staff training needs well in advance.

The administrative processes involved in online programmes warrant special attention. One year on, our review pointed to the need for improved clarity and simplicity of administrative procedures and, above all, harmonisation with the centralised procedures operated by the host institution. Given the small, almost experimental nature of the programme at this stage, administrators in both departments are able to liaise and work closely together in order to prevent duplication and confusion. An ongoing dialogue between departmental and central administrative services, and with academic stakeholders is also crucial.

Very limited time was made available for advertising the course and much support was provided by external agencies, not least the Institut Français in London, who provided very useful contacts in the form of mailing lists to similar organisations worldwide. Both departments made ample use of their website facilities and of their networks in promoting the programme as widely as possible, despite a very limited advertising budget. We are hopeful that, eventually, the programme will expand through word of mouth recommendations, as is often the case in such situations.

It became clear that the most challenging aspect of the project in the first term proved to be staff workload. There were two reasons for this: first, the need for staff to familiarise themselves with new technologies and, second, the frequently unmanageable, unrealistic expectations on the part of both students and staff regarding working patterns. Research illustrates that a perception of loss of control over access to tutors appears to heighten anxiety levels in students engaged in online programmes. However, with an improved understanding of the aims and objectives by term two, the student–staff contact ratio had been reduced to a more realistic level. One of the induction session key points for the coming year will be to help clarify expectations and define and agree student–staff contact time.

None of the difficulties described in this section were surprising, given the innovative character of the programme, and should be kept in perspective when considering the (hopefully) long-term investment to which the two departments in question have committed themselves, in addition to the benefits to students worldwide who would not traditionally have had access to such programmes. In conclusion, despite initial and inevitable challenges, staff motivation and enthusiasm remain intact, and participants are keen to build on lessons learnt so far.

Pedagogical Grammar

This blended learning course, designed by the MLC and aimed at prospective teachers of modern foreign languages (novice teachers of MFL interested in the methodology of teaching grammar and teacher training colleges/organisations) offers a variety of online resources intended to improve subject knowledge, reflect on methodology and enable discussion of techniques for teaching French, German and Spanish grammar. The programme consists of ten hours of face-to-face sessions, plus access to online resources and teaching methodology, The course is taught collaboratively to students of the Postgraduate Certificate in Education (PGCE) in modern foreign languages at the Department of Education and Professional Studies (DEPS) at King's, which was recently awarded a grade 1 'outstanding' by Ofsted. The PGCE programme is an initial education route to becoming a qualified teacher in secondary schools. Topics include:

- teaching grammar
- teaching vocabulary
- error correction
- teaching pronunciation
- using authentic materials to teach culture.

The modules can easily be integrated into teacher education programmes (e.g. PGCE, MA or Certificate in Teaching Modern Foreign Languages) and can be used in a blended-learning environment or as stand alone.

The course exists in three bilingual versions: French/English, German/English and Spanish/English. Participating students engage in critical reflection of their own practices, beliefs and knowledge. Each of the six modules is divided into interactive, collaborative and self-study sections comprising brainstorming and discussions, presentation and practice, assignments and feedback.

Tools provided within the VLE allow course leaders to devise a programme to suit a given curriculum, to communicate with students, to provide individual and collective feedback, to monitor students' progress, to collect quality assurance and student satisfaction data. Students have ample opportunity to practise and improve their reading, writing and oral language skills.

French for Medics

The aims and objectives of this blended learning module are as follows:

- to prepare students for the diploma French for Medics, 'Diplôme de Français Médical', delivered by the Chamber of Commerce and Industry of Paris

- to allow students to familiarise themselves with the health environment in a French context
- to develop oral presentation skills in a medical context
- to enable students to develop medical writing techniques (for letters, medical reports, etc.).

Teaching is communicative and includes brief lectures, video or audio material, discussions, workshop activities in small groups and student presentations. Classes are conducted exclusively in French.

In an article in the *BMA News*, dated 21 November 2009, a student following the programme endorsed the benefit of such specialist courses which equip doctors to work abroad, in that particular instance in Rwanda. In terms of widening participation and enhanced employability, it seems clear that for such resources to be available entirely online would have a significant impact. Offering a blended learning version of French for medics is therefore a step in the right direction, but developing the current format into an online course remains a prime objective, subject to funding being forthcoming.

Student Feedback

Feedback on the course delivery has been overwhelmingly positive, with an average overall level 5 ranking. Of particular interest to the students was the vocational dimension of the course, and students referred in particular to specialist vocabulary, which was useful in view of their choices of overseas careers. In addition, students of medicine enrolled on the 40-hour face-to-face course are able to access content, videos and interactive exercises while on three-week internship placements, hence the crucial role of the online dimension.

Language and Communication Skills Online Project

In 2009, the MLC received college funding to develop an entirely online bank of resources in five languages: Arabic, French, German, Italian and Spanish for King's VLE:

The aims and objectives of the project were as follows:

- to develop and improve King's students'/staff language and communication skills in five key languages
- to provide a detailed index of quality online language resources for self-access, dedicated to the needs of King's students and the research community
- to promote the use of e-learning and help students to communicate and collaborate through language learning, thus creating a learning community in line with the College Strategic Plan.

Currently KCL, not uniquely, offers no interactive online language resources designed for independent learning. Students and staff wishing to develop, maintain or improve their linguistic competence are not always able to attend language classes, either because of the academic demands of their core subjects or because they cannot afford the additional cost of fees charged for language classes. This project offers solutions to both problems.

The development of e-learning and study skills in subject-specific contexts are key targets in the current King's School of Humanities Learning and Teaching Strategy Action Plan. Online materials allow students and staff to study with maximum flexibility in terms of pace and location, and promote self-evaluation. The online resources can provide immediate feedback and exposure to different types of self-assessment, thus targeting students' individual learning styles and preferences.

This new initiative keys into the college's increasing international focus, and fits well into the overall college strategy of developing more international/collaborative degrees and e-learning resources. The additional resources are not only an added incentive for overseas students, but also offer greater international prospects for home students. By improving their language proficiency, communication skills and intercultural awareness, students will increase their international employability. The proposal is in line with the Bologna Process, which aims to create a European higher education area to make HE more compatible, competitive and more attractive for European and international students.

Another benefit of the project, designed to serve all learning communities at King's via the use of technology, is its sustainability. Once established and running, the project will require only occasional and minimal interventions to ensure that appropriate and high quality resources continue to be provided.

As well as a detailed index of relevant online language resources at various levels and for a range of skills, access to specialist e-learning courses and modules designed by the MLC – that is, Spanish for Medics (Beginners) and Arabic (Beginners) – diagnostic tests to check students' initial language level, personal learning logs/e-portfolios for setting up an individual syllabus and monitoring individual progress have all been made available. Tools (e.g. forums, chats, blogs, wikis, Wimba voice tools, Skype) for collaborating with peers and creating a learning community have been incorporated, as well as questionnaires and surveys designed to monitor students' feedback and usage. Postgraduate students engaged on both taught programmes and research can also benefit from an academic skills section, including practical tips for successful interviews, and a series of intercultural awareness training presentations.

Conclusion: E-learning Programmes in French Language and Culture, a Vision of – and for – the Future?

From our own experience, the online and blended innovations are clearly beneficial from an institutional perspective, in that they contribute to internationalisation, from a departmental point of view, in that they extend the range of modes of delivery, expand the range of offerings, and also feed into staff motivation and departmental synergies.

The benefits and challenges of incorporating blended learning elements into face-to-face courses, and of developing e-learning programmes, have been well documented. In their research paper *Building the Future: Students' Blended Learning Experiences from Current Research Finding*, Amanda Jefferies and Ruth Hyde state:

> Embedding an e-learning culture across an institution inevitably takes time…. The incoming generations of students now expect to have e-learning access and support for their courses and praise its benefits…. Furthermore, academic staff are expected to be trained and able to use the available technologies as noted by Ellis and Goodyear (2010, p. 44). Sharpe et al (2009) have commented that: 'There is a related need for staff development so tutors can be confident models and knowledgeable guides.' This point is further reinforced by Beetham et al (2009) 'Tutors are still insufficiently competent and confident with digital technologies for learning, despite evidence that learners are strongly influenced by their example'.[11]

Among the MLC's e-learning projects, the online MA has proved the most challenging in terms of introducing a truly innovative course in a traditional institution where face-to-face taught programmes are still very much the norm, and where pass rates are crucial. This chapter has already referred to some of the difficulties involved, but now focuses on the benefits.

Not perhaps a primary aim of the programme, but a key factor attested by the unorthodox profile of student intake in 2009–10, is the opportunity for lifelong learning. The diversity in intake, not only with regard to students' geographical background, but also of their socio-economic make-up, clearly reflected the advantages of a truly flexible learning format. Over and above flexibility in time and location and the provision for self-paced learning, students responded to the opportunity afforded, recognising career-enhancing benefits.

Applications were received from professionals who, hitherto, had not accessed higher education, either by choice or through circumstances.

---

11 Amanda Jefferies and Ruth Hyde, 'Building the Future: Students' Blended Learning Experiences from Current Research Findings', *Electronic Journal of e-Learning* 8: 2 (2010), 133–40.

On page 11 of the Final Report of *The Digital Divide – Barriers to E-learning*, by The Australian Institute for Social Research,[12] 'increased access to learning, improved student attitudes to learning, opportunities to interact internationally and gain a global understanding of complex issues, study opportunities that remove the need to travel or move away from home or are otherwise not affordable, encouragement of students to self-regulate their learning', listed among the recognised benefits of using the medium of ICT, would apply here. A second, indirect, key benefit is the way in which staff involved in the teaching of the MA content and language were prompted to reassess their own methodology and to introduce an increased degree of creativity in their delivery. In their paper *Strategies for Embedding E-learning in Traditional Universities: Drivers and Barriers*, the authors state:

> In response to a series of questions aimed at identifying factors which would increase or decrease motivation to adopt e-learning, it appears that the potential to reach new students and experiment with new technologies rank highly as motivating factors, whereas factors likely to decrease motivation are more pragmatic, relating to inadequate technical support, time, and recognition of the work involved.

Interestingly, although motivation for the use of technologically enhanced delivery varied among colleagues involved in the project, and was perceived by a minority as an obstacle rather than an asset, it fair to say that it has inspired a genuine interest in innovative delivery formats in general, and an appetite for developing opportunities to engage students in lively and motivating activities focused on autonomous language learning. In the report, *Digital Divide*, the authors state:

> Despite the inherent flexibility of online delivery, unless its pedagogy is addressed, it can itself present a barrier to learning instead of removing many of the barriers inherent in offline or traditional learning…Technology does not cause learning. As an instructional medium online technologies will not in themselves improve or cause changes in learning. What improves learning is well-designed instruction …*Jasinski (1998)*

Measuring learning outcomes through clearly defined appropriate pedagogical aims and objectives has remained a priority. Although staff have embraced the new possibilities offered by technological applications, academic programmes such as the online MA must continue to fulfil their role, namely to reward students with the right level of qualifications, to ensure QAA criteria continue to be met, and that King's reputation is not in any way compromised.

---

12 *The Digital Divide – Barriers to E-learning*. Final Report presented to Digital Bridge Unit, Science Technology and Innovation Directorate (DFEEST) (Australia: Australian Institute for Social Research, University of Adelaide, April 2006).

Given that one of the college's strategic priorities is for a policy of technological enhancement to be defined within the next ten years, allowing for a clear strategy for implementation in both undergraduate and postgraduate curriculums, such pioneering projects will help change attitudes, and create a more favourable and more receptive climate, which will impact on eventual reviews of teaching and research deliveries.

From a collaborative point of view, the project has been entirely successful and an inspiration. One of its key strengths has been the excellent working relationship between MLC staff and colleagues from the French department, at all hierarchical levels, and not least between those crucial partners, namely the departmental and central administrators. To my mind, this factor is as important as any requirement for adequate technological support or appropriate methodologies.

All such projects will of course actively support King's internationalisation efforts, especially the most recent MLC innovation, the Language and Communication Skills Project. All are potentially of interest to overseas undergraduate and postgraduate students, and may be an added incentive in attracting research students. Six out of ten French for medics students cited the fact that languages are on offer as having influenced their choice of university.

Regular monitoring by means of meetings and progress reporting ensured that the online MA was implemented in line with requirements. However, as with all pilot schemes, areas for improvement, already referred to, were identified. Although both staff and students experienced some technology-related problems, on the whole these were minor and easily dealt with. There may be several reasons for this: the MLC works in close collaboration with King's Information, Services and Systems (ISS), which are able to provide the MLC with day-to-day support in technology-related matters. In addition, as mentioned previously, the MLC enjoys the benefits of its own dedicated technologist who helps maintain all blended learning and e-learning programmes.

From the learner perspective, literacy and IT skills and aptitude for self-direction, being confident and motivated to participate in online learning have also been identified as potential barriers to effective learning online learning. The level of technical support available has a significant influence on the impact of these learner-based attitudes (Cashion and Palmieri: 2002). ... A key finding of research is the need for professional development to enable RTOs to maximise online learning and delivery (Guthrie: 2003; Sawyer: 2004). (*The Digital Divide – Barriers to E-learning*)

In addition to technological support, staff training ensured the appropriate level of skills development on the part of those delivering the programme. Apart from college-wide training sessions, the MLC offers technology refresher courses to its staff and to colleagues from other departments. Once again, it is a tribute to colleagues involved in these projects that they recognised their own training needs and addressed them accordingly.

Last, but not least, we must consider the issue of cost. When taking into account content development, staff time and labour, technological support and roll-out costs, investing in e-learning is not a cheap option. The medium to long-term benefits can only be measured once sufficient numbers of students have enrolled and once the staff–student ratio has been more economically balanced. On this particular issue, it is still too early to reach any decisive conclusions as regards the online MA.

To summarise, in our experience, blended learning and e-learning have added value to the delivery of our French programmes in the ways indicated here. As with all pioneering endeavours, though, much will need to continue to be evaluated before a final assessment is made. As regards the MA/PGDip, remaining concerns pertaining to administrative procedures, to long-term sustainability, to student numbers, will need to be reviewed at a later stage, and will require fuller discussion. Key questions have emerged: can administrative processes be sufficiently harmonised to ensure that procedures operate efficiently? Can costs be kept down? These are just some of the incidental but important questions that have arisen so far, and which will undoubtedly continue to concern us.

For now, we have embraced the experience wholeheartedly and found it extremely stimulating, not least in the way online delivery challenges preconceived ideas and encourages creativity. The projects we have developed can be used as templates, and applied in suitable contexts. One additional key benefit of online programmes, as we see it, is that their development and implementation keep the teaching of French language and culture at the forefront of lively and vital debates.

Bibliography

BMA News (21 November 2009).

The Digital Divide – Barriers to E-learning. Final Report presented to Digital Bridge Unit, Science Technology and Innovation Directorate (DFEEST) (Australia: The Australian Institute for Social Research, University of Adelaide, April 2006).

Jefferies, Amanda and Ruth Hyde, 'Building the Future: Students' Blended Learning Experiences from Current Research Findings', *Electronic Journal of e-Learning* 8: 2 (2010), 133–40.

MacKeogh, Kay and Seamus Fox, 'Strategies for Embedding e-Learning in Traditional Universities: Drivers and Barriers', *Electronic Journal of e-Learning* 7: 2 (2009), 147–54.

Beetham, Helen and Rhona Sharpe (eds), *Rethinking Pedagogy for … e-Learning* (London: Routledge, 2008).

Salmon, Gilly, 'Learning Submarines: Raising the Periscopes' (Open University Business School and United States Open University, 2007), available at http://oubs.open.ac.uk/ gilly (consulted 1 September 2010).

Tschirhart, Cecile and Elena Rigler, 'London Met E-packs: A Pragmatic Approach to Learner/teacher Autonomy', *Language Learning Journal, Journal of the Association for Language Learning* 37: 1 (2009), 71–83.

UK Department of Education and Skills, *Languages Review* (28 February 2007).

Watson, David and Michael Amoah (eds), *The Dearing Report, Ten Years on* (Bedford Way Papers, London: Institute of Education, University of London, 2007).

Worton, Michael, *Review of Modern Foreign Languages Provision in Higher Education in England* (London: HEFCE, 2009), available at www.hefce.ac.uk/pubs/hefce/2009/09_41/ (consulted 1 September 2010).

Websites

French for Medics, King's College London, available at www.kcl.ac.uk/schools/humanities/depts/mlc/ugrad/modules/modules/french/frm5.html (consulted 1 December 2010).

Ivident, International Virtual Dental School, King's College London, available at www.ivident.info (consulted 1 December 2010).

MA, 'War in the Modern World' (WiMW), Kings College London, available at www.kcl.ac.uk/schools/sspp/ws/grad/programmes/wimw (consulted 1 December 2010).

Online MA/PGDip in French Language and Culture, Kings College London, available at www.kcl.ac.uk/schools/humanities/depts/mlc/elearn/mafrench.html (consulted on 1 December 2010).

Pedagogical Grammar for French, Kings College London, available at www.kcl.ac.uk/schools/humanities/depts/mlc/elearn/pedgram.html (consulted on 1 December 2010).

21

French Studies and Employability at Home and Abroad: General Reflections on a Case Study

Maryse Bray, Hélène Gill, Laurence Randall

Ten years ago, the teaching of French in British universities was in decline. Five years ago it was in peril throughout the land, with many French departments closing. As an academic subject, French nose-dived in terms of student recruitment figures, the discipline apparently destined to be confined to a branch of classics in Russell Group institutions. It was at risk from extinction in the former polytechnics where it became threatened even as a subsidiary subject in its market-friendly incarnation as Business French. To many, the choice was stark but clear – stake all on French for Business or die.

But for some, even this solution was either too little or too late to save the day, with the result that the subject was phased out as a meaningful part of their undergraduate provision from the early 2000s, as a string of French and modern languages departments and sections were closed, or disappeared into merged subject areas where languages – let alone French – seldom featured in the title. Yearly, members of surviving French departments would gather at the French Institute to watch a *film d'art et d'essai* and lament the situation – and the bleak outlook. Meanwhile, out in the wider British higher education debate, the main justification for this debacle was 'jobs'. With globalisation, the world was set to trade and to communicate in English. Europe was losing its appeal as a trading partner in favour of emerging markets to the East. It was now deemed a luxury to keep languages on the syllabus for the over 14s, with the possible exception of Mandarin Chinese.

Fortunately, the gloomiest forecasts have not been verified by the turn of events, and in 2010 the situation has largely recovered in those French departments that remain. Even the more vulnerable post-1992 institutions now recruit full cohorts and the emphasis has shifted to the need not to overshoot the recruitment targets set by the Department of Business, Innovation and Skills. Former polytechnics have even upgraded their A-level entry requirements. For the first time in lecturers' memory, some may not resort to 'clearing' to make up their numbers of entrants – and the reason behind this undreamt-of reversal of fortune?

The answer paradoxically is once again jobs, or rather employability, the new corporate education 'buzz word' coined during the years of trouble to improve job prospects for humanities graduates, that became the order of the day. Across many institutions it has sparked a number of ingenious initiatives to make French and other languages attractive once again to new cohorts of hard-headed school-leavers with strong career aspirations.

The Employability Imperative

Thus for some years, the question of student employability has been at the top of the agenda for universities, for employers (who frequently berate their new graduate employees' poor vocational skills),[1] and for students themselves, who are saddled with debt and therefore keen to get onto the work ladder. Finding work is indeed their foremost preoccupation, ahead of the actual spending power they may achieve once gainfully employed. This is especially the case for students from disadvantaged backgrounds for whom, in the words of Phillip Brown, Professor of Social Sciences at Cardiff University: 'the primary motivation does not reflect an expression of personal freedom and intellectual curiosity because it is secondary to the requirements of the competition for a livelihood'.[2]

In *The Mismanagement of Talent*, a book he co-authored with Anthony Hesketh,[3] Brown identifies two ideal types of candidates to employability: the purists – winning a competitive advantage in a meritocratic race where individual achievement reflects innate capabilities, effort and ambition; and the players – who understand employability as a positional game of how to win a competitive edge in a congested job market.

The case for developing employability across all disciplines is also supported by the Bologna Declaration (1999) and, in the UK, by a number of studies and reports such as the Leitch report (2006) or even, a decade earlier, Lord Dearing's 1997 report recommending that higher education (HE) establishments enable students to monitor, build and reflect on what it terms their personal development portfolio (hence the acronym PDP, although personal development per se was not the heart of the matter). A direct consequence may have been the creation of the Centre for Recording Achievement (CRA). A successor to earlier projects sponsored in the early 1990s by the then Department

1 Jack Grimston, 'Top Firms Forced to Reject "Barely Literate" Graduates', *Sunday Times* (1 August 2010).

2 Phillip Brown, 'When Merit Means Nothing', *Times Higher Education Supplement* (20 July 2007).

3 Phillip Brown and Anthony Hesketh, *The Mismanagement of Talent: Employability and Jobs in the Knowledge Economy* (London and New York: Oxford University Press, 2004).

of Employment, this body advises a range of FE and HE institutions as well as the HE Funding council. The CRA defines itself as: 'a national network organisation seeking to promote the awareness of recorded achievement and action planning processes as an important element in improving learning and progression throughout the world of education, training and employment'.[4]

As such, it is particularly operative for us in university languages departments. Faced with a predicted decline from 2012 in the number of 18- to 19-year-olds applying to universities – while by 2020 almost half the workforce is anticipated to be made up of graduates – academic linguists, in their endangered departments, have been feeling the need to engage ever more closely with employers. At the same time, we like to stake a claim on our vocation to produce languages graduates with the intellectual and critical powers to take on a range of careers, rather than to train them for a specific line of work where French, if needed at all, will play an all but instrumental role. In other words, our aim is not to train but to educate our students: 'It is a myth to believe that, in higher education, business-facing activity and academic rigour are mutually exclusive.'[5]

Fine words indeed, and a relief to all teachers of French weary of being told on the airwaves that declining French verbs is now an out-moded activity, which blocks timetable space desperately needed for more vocational subjects such as IT or marketing studies. 'Tutors must critically reflect on their role in maintaining education as personal trans-formation' chimed in two months later an article entitled 'Having, Being and Higher Education'.[6]

In this context employability, in a variety of guises, became an in-creasingly pressing imperative in the entire tertiary sector, but more especially in 'new' universities, which have a large proportion of students who are second-generation arrivals in this country. Many, in addition, are the first in their family's history to go to university. It is therefore as part of an active widening participation agenda that many of them introduced, in the mid-2000s, a sometimes tightly integrated, sometimes 'bolted on' personal, academic and career development pro-gramme. What follows is a case study of one such effort carried out at the University of Westminster.

4 CRA (Centre for Recording Achievement), 'Mission statement' (2010), online re-source, accessed 1 October 2010.

5 Gill Nicholls, 'Academic Rigour can most Certainly do the Business', *Guardian* (26 May 2009).

6 Mike Molesworth, Elizabeth Nixon and Richard Scullion, 'Having, Being and Higher Education: The Marketisation of the University and the Transformation of the Student into Consumer', *Teaching in Higher Education* 14: 3 (2009), 277–87, online resource, consulted 1 October 2010.

The Career Management Skills (CMS) Strategy at Westminster

CMS has now run successfully at Westminster over two full academic years. At department level we organise interactive workshops designed to help students enhance their transferable skills. Most, if not all, already have competences that would make them employable, but by and large, they do not know how to put them forward to a potential employer. At the workshops, they are presented with folders containing sets of practical exercises designed, for example, to enhance communication skills. To tackle these, they need to demonstrate their potential as communicators in a given professional setting. Other exercises simulate employment situations: going through a CV planner, evaluating strong and weak points from another person's CV, and so on. In the final year of the course, workshops focus on a student's interview skills: how to value, present and emphasise the general graduate skills they have acquired as language specialists to an employer who may (or may not) request French language fluency in the job description. Students are later invited to debate these issues, and to put their ideas to practice by taking part in semi-directive mock interviews. Workshops also reflect on past experience by alumni, such as the recent graduate of modern languages (French/English literature) who was offered a job with Routledge publishers within two days of being awarded her degree.

To round up the workshops, students are invited to enter a culture of reflective practice, leading to a live e-portfolio: each is given a reflective log sheet to complete and hand in at the end of each semester. Log sheets then feed into a summative e-portfolio where a student will input their CV, record of skills acquired doing their French Studies and their work experience, if any. This portfolio thus contributes to ensure our students are equipped at the end of their course in order to find employment.

Prizes and Networking Events

At Westminster we are fortunate in having an external sponsor for our current CMS drive: a Hong-Kong based entrepreneur who subsidises yearly CMS prizes across all languages. Every year those students who submitted the best reflective log sheets at each level are awarded £150 plus an award certificate handed out at a special CMS award ceremony.

Another feature was the launch in 2009 of an employer networking event, which attracted over 80 undergraduate students. Sixteen employers engaged in fields ranging from banking (Credit Suisse) to hospitality (The Langham Hotel) were invited to assist our students in getting a concrete idea of where their modern languages degrees may lead, beyond obvious prospects such as translation work or a teaching career. This networking event is now set to become a yearly fixture.

Student Feedback and Future Prospects

The impact of the CMS scheme is assessed via questionnaires asking students to evaluate the workshops and to point out what activities, in their view, should be added to the current programme. Focus groups are also organised where students are able to discuss what worked and what did not. They are, in addition, required to write reflective practice reports at the end of each CMS module. Typical responses would include (from a final year French and Chinese student): 'I am a mature student and have had experience of completing application forms. Yet this course widened my thinking. It has encouraged me to reassess my past experiences, and to see how I can use these to match job specifications.'

Alongside organised channels of feedback, students also send impromptu letters, and, of course, the very content of their e-portfolios is in itself valuable feedback. Staff involved in career management teaching hold end-of-year review meetings. Moreover, CMS lecturers consult and give feedback to each other on an ad-hoc basis in order to respond as pointedly and flexibly as possible to the requirements of individual student cohorts as they vary from year to year.

In devising all these workshops, meetings and various events, collaborative work is carried out with the career advice centre. There are future plans to enhance the scientific base of the scheme by launching international comparative research projects which could be funded by high-profile firms in the UK. The intention could be, for example, to study employability across frontiers starting from a sample made up of three European universities – one located in the UK, one in France and another in Spain. The aim would then be to investigate the ways in which employability is embedded in the curriculum in these institutions, and to report on what can be learned from it in the UK.

Embedding Employability Skills in the Curriculum

Before Career Management Skills were formalised at Westminster, long before the Dearing Report had even been published, teachers of languages realised our students' potential for employment. The problem was that these students generally found their transferable skills hard to pinpoint and articulate in a way that would 'speak' to future employers, and the chief aim of the CMS programme is to close this opportunity gap. There is another gap, however, that also needs bridging: the hiatus between the teaching provision itself and the world of work. This is best done, we would argue, by embedding professional knowledge and competence in the curriculum, rather than offering it as an add-on, or as an afterthought.

By the mid-2000s, the word began to spread even beyond teaching circles that some academic subjects challenged vocational degrees in their role in developing their students' readiness for employment. Thus the study of languages – especially 'hard' languages such as French, with its reputedly complicated syntax and grammar – was ripe for a reappraisal as a provider of high quality job applicants. Beyond linguistic skills, moreover, the study of French history and literature, with assorted research and the need to access sources written in the original language, develops precisely the intellectual skills and attributes sought by most employers. These range from the most practical, such as time-management or communication in more than one language, to the more demanding, such as critical thought, the construction of argument, and intercultural skills. Our students of French know this too, even if too often in a nebulous kind of way. There is a need, therefore, for them to sharpen and to cultivate these skills and attributes not only in order to secure interviews but to function as young professionals in the workplace. And so the need to bridge the gap remains.

Westminster is clearly not alone in coming to this realisation. There are, however, huge variations between institutions in how employability is rolled out, as well as some controversy on the validity of such programmes within academic degrees. Thus Gary Day from De Montfort University in Leicester is quoted as saying that PDP 'is about getting [students] to conform to certain targets, not to think for themselves'.[7] Frank Furedi, Professor of Sociology, University of Kent and another outspoken detractor of PDP, has called it an empty gesture.[8] This has not been the line taken at Westminster, where it has never been the sole remit of central career services acting on government guidelines to alert languages students to the professional uses of their field of study. Employability for French Studies undergraduates has strongly influenced course design, its early implementations pre-dating the CMS initiatives described above. Today, as a result, employability is a two-pronged integrated approach: CMS *and* an innovative *filière* in the curriculum, known as French in Action. Ultimately, our main claim for pioneering action in this matter rests on how employability has become embedded in the undergraduate course design and in the subject provision with the Language in Action strand. This was achieved without the need to lessen or dilute the cultural content – let alone replace it with a French for Business pathway.

The French in Action Strand at Westminster

At the latest validation of our undergraduate programme, a series of incremental applied language modules was introduced, known as the Languages in Action strand. These modules are not designed to be 'an instrumentalist or a utilitarian servant of a pure mercantile economy,

7 Harriet Swain, 'Debate is about to get Personal', *Times Higher Education Supplement* (14 July 2006), online resource, consulted 1 October 2010.
8 Swain, 'Debate', 2006.

however.[9] On the contrary, they follow a rigorous task-based academic curriculum, informed by the QAA guidelines on work-based learning. They aim to develop students' ability to use their language and graduate skills within professional contexts. They develop independence, responsibility, commitment and ability to work to a brief.

The French in Action strand forms a third of the French provision during each year when our students are in London – one module in each semester of each year. For ex-beginners, Language in Action modules bear the title *Language in Practice*. For those students starting the course post A level, they are called, more ambitiously, *Language for Work*. French in Action modules run alongside two other strands on the course: language development (devoted to second language acquisition) and area studies. They are incremental in terms of language competence, and articulated on a student's corresponding level of French language.

This provision dovetails with the CMS scheme because of its professional tenor and format. Meanwhile, an hour-long workshop from the career skills provision is timetabled as part of the French in Action programme each semester to seal the connection between the two. Thus the professional content of the French in Action workload is, in a way, sanctioned by its implication in the wider CMS scheme, while the latter is not perceived by the student as an add-on, peripheral to the French Studies focus of the course. This ensures both schemes are incrementally embedded across three years, a defining feature inscribed in the learning aims and objectives of each French in Action module. This claim, put to the test each academic year, is thus open to scrutiny by successive validation and revalidation panels and their external assessors.

Employability and Residence Abroad

The most direct, effective and enjoyable boost to languages students' competences is, without doubt, the opportunity to reside and function in the country where their language of study is spoken. Exposed to the native speaker's idiom and to the peculiarities of the local culture, the French Studies undergraduate morphs into a new creature, quite unlike the fresher who entered Level 4 with brand new A levels, or the admittedly more assured second-year orals candidate. Residence abroad tutors and other staff remark on the phenomenon, finding that returnees are more mature, that they have 'found themselves', and look ahead to their professional futures with greater confidence than those who graduate on the three-year degree. Indeed, the year abroad, regardless of whether it includes a work placement, has been demonstrated to have a positive impact

---

9   Thomas Docherty, 'Being a Humble Servant to Business will be a Disaster for Everyone', *Times Higher Education Supplement* (4 June 2009).

on the employability of the new graduate.[10] Beyond its immediate effect in helping statistics on ex-students in work a year after graduation, it is seen to inform professional choices in later life, and to impact on alumni's earning power: French graduates with experience of residence in France or in a francophone country tend to make more money five or ten years into their working lives than those who did not take up the opportunity.

The secret of the year abroad is total immersion, delivering, where it genuinely is 'total', a range of benefits far beyond mere language competence. These benefits are gained not only through verbal exchange, but through complex social interaction channels, both formal and informal. At individual student level, these patterns can follow different trajectories, some of more benefit to the subject's future employability than others. On closer examination, most students go through three successive phases of socialisation in the target culture, giving ground for the elaboration of a 'three circles' theory.[11] The first circle is made up of fellow English-speaking students with whom they tend to stick on arrival; the second comprises other non-French native speakers, and locals – such as the teaching staff, shopkeepers and other passing acquaintances – with whom they have limited linguistic exchanges; the third and most beneficial circle consists of French people of any age with whom the year abroad student has repeated in-depth and meaningful interaction. Most studies on the year abroad recommend a French-speaking boyfriend or girlfriend, though a work placement boss and a set of colleagues do just as well in language terms, and far better in familiarising the student with the world of work in France and at home. They will acquire the skills that are instrumental to the job; they will also be able to reflect on the utility of these skills with a view to future employment.

Coleman points out that for a stay abroad to be entirely successful, there needs to be a centrifugal dynamic whose momentum accelerates the closer a student's activities move to this inner circle. Sadly, some struggle even to access the second circle. It is clear, however, that a work placement while abroad is the quick route to achieving immediate and complete immersion. British Council teaching assistantships to French *lycées*, institutionally sponsored work placements and approved private internship agreements are all, in principle, equally valuable, and Erasmus today facilitates this route into student mobility. What is more, a work placement report complete with the employer's appraisal is an appealing solution to the thorny problem of assessing and sanctioning the year abroad.

10 Anthea Lipsett, 'Graduates Who Have Studied Abroad More Appealing to Businesses', *Guardian* (16 October 2008),
11 Jim Coleman, 'What is the Year Abroad for? Insights and Principles to Inform Assessment', presentation given at the conference 'Assessment of the Year Abroad in Modern Language Degrees', University of Bath (25 June 2010), online resource, consulted on 1 October 2010.

Placements Abroad on the Three-year Degree

The year abroad used to be an integral part of the modern language degree at British universities. More recently, however, increasing cultural and financial pressures have combined to turn it into an escapade too far and, too often, an unaffordable expense for many undergraduates, who find it hard enough to make ends meet while in their home institutions. With the arrival, since the start of the century, of a wave of students in that category, institutions have had to innovate, and look for means of offering, to students on their language degrees without a year abroad, the opportunity to study or to work abroad during the generous stretches of time that lie fallow between the teaching terms.

Currently, Westminster is conducting a new pilot project of work placements in France. In 2009–10, seven of our students of French took part, six of them second-year students. The work placements were all situated in Montluçon in the Massif Central, but varied in their range of activities: one placement was at the local *Institut Universitaire de Technologie* (IUT); one student was employed at the town hall, another worked in a secondary school during the month of June. Two others worked during the summer months at the tourist office and at a conference centre, while the only first-year student involved in this pilot was an intern with a local estate agent. Interns were visited by a member of staff during their work placements and feedback was very positive. Not only did the quality of their spoken and written French language reportedly improve tremendously, but organising their stay, local travel, and finding accommodation via CROUS (Centre régional des œuvres universitaires et scolaires) also contributed to a wide range of transferable skills.

Setting up this pilot demanded rigorous preparation, with a lot of input and personal focus from a member of the French staff who is native to Montluçon. Thanks to this privileged, direct approach, every prospective employer was originally visited to assess feasibility in terms of the company's needs and of the capability of the students, who all happened to be ex-beginners. The operation's success depended on matching these parameters; failing to do so would preclude repeating it in future years, let alone expanding the scheme locally and further afield.

The internships involved the second-year students in a wide variety of tasks. In the Communications Department of the Montluçon Town Hall, our student (on a combined French and Spanish degree) translated their website from French into Spanish. In the IUT (a branch of the University of Clermont-Ferrand), she was asked to translate their website from French into English. At Athanor, a conference centre, the two interns also translated their website, while the estate agents used their intern to do administration work and visit properties set to be put on the market. In the tourist office, the placement involved translating a leaflet and conducting surveys. In the case of a student whose native language was not English, she was assigned a peer mentor from the French final year at Westminster who went over her translation. We received excellent feedback both from employers and students.

Gone are the days, therefore, when the period of residence in France was a 'year off' when the student was out of sight and out of touch, picking up the language and culture in the way of an educated amateur. As we have seen, French Studies departments have travelled a long way since modern languages and skills training for employment were described as polar opposites. The experience described at Westminster is but one of many, as universities get to grips with the employability issue and find that the benefits are multiple. It may not be by chance that the improved take-up of French Studies places in British universities appears to have coincided with this new awareness, at least chronologically. Successful employability schemes integrate personal, academic and career development in their brief. Appropriately devised, they enhance a student's self-belief, self-confidence and understanding of the world of work. They turn young undergraduates into professionals in the making.

Bibliography

Brown, Phillip, 'When Merit Means Nothing', *Times Higher Education Supplement* (20 July 2007).

Brown, Phillip and Anthony Hesketh, *The Mismanagement of Talent: Employability and Jobs in the Knowledge Economy* (London and New York: Oxford University Press, 2004).

Coleman, Jim, 'What is the Year Abroad for? Insights and Principles to Inform Assessment', presentation given at the conference 'Assessment of the Year Abroad in Modern Language Degrees', University of Bath (25 June 2010), available at www.bath.ac.uk/education/research/conferences/info.html (consulted 1 October 2010).

CRA, 'Mission Statement' (2010), available at www.recordingachievement.org (consulted 1 October 2010).

Docherty, Thomas, 'Being a Humble Servant to Business will be a Disaster for Everyone', *Times Higher Education Supplement* (4 June 2009), available at www.timeshighereducation. co.uk/story.asp?sectioncode=26&storycode=406815 (consulted 1 October 2010).

Grimston, Jack, 'Top Firms Forced to Reject "barely literate" Graduates', *Sunday Times* (1 August 2010).

Lipsett, Anthea, 'Graduates Who Have Studied Abroad More Appealing to Businesses', *Guardian* (16 October 2008).

Molesworth, Mike, Elizabeth Nixon and Richard Scullion, 'Having, Being and Higher Education: The Marketisation of the University and the Transformation of the Student into Consumer', *Teaching in Higher Education* 14: 3, (2009), 277–87, available at www. informaworld.com/smpp/section?content=a911692220&fulltext=713240928 (consulted 1 October 2010).

Nicholls, Gill, 'Academic rigour can most certainly do the business', *The Guardian* (26 May 2009), available at www.guardian.co.uk/education/2009/may/26/gill-nicholls (consulted 1 October 2010).

Swain, Harriet, 'Debate is about to get personal', *Times Higher Education Supplement*, 14 July 2006), available at www.timeshighereducation.co.uk/story.asp?storyCode=204321 &sectioncode=26 (consulted 18 August 2010).

22

Sartre in Middlesex, De Beauvoir in Oxford: The Contribution of the ASMCF to the Study of France

Máire Fedelma Cross

Founded in 1979, the ASMCF offers an unrivalled multidisciplinary forum for those involved in teaching and research on all aspects of France since 1789. The Association's worldwide membership brings together scholars, researchers and graduate students in disciplines ranging from history and the social sciences to philosophy, education, politics, language, literature, media studies and the arts.[1]

The Association for the Study of Modern and Contemporary France (ASMCF) sees its contribution to promoting knowledge of France mainly, but not exclusively, through the area studies approach, which is broadly the study of the country including its political system, history, geography and general culture integrated with its language. That area studies is now a key term alongside languages and culture in the definition of French Studies is testimony to the achievements of the ASMCF and recognition of its place in the research and teaching of French.[2] The ASMCF has the largest membership of all the area studies associations in the umbrella group UKCASA.[3] It has three main areas of activity: the annual conference, publication of the journal, and support for local and regional research groups. This chapter sets out to explain the growth of the association during the expansion of French teaching in higher education.

---

1 Cited in the frontispiece of the Association's journal, *Modern and Contemporary France* 18: 2 (May 2010).
2 The Subject Centre for Languages Linguistics and Area Studies (funded by HEFCE), online resource, consulted 12 November 2010.
3 UKCASA (United Kingdom Council for Area Studies Associations) is a council made up of area studies associations in the UK. Its aims are: to promote, support and defend area studies programmes at both undergraduate and postgraduate level, to develop a collaborative community among area studies associations and practitioners and to promote interdisciplinary research and teaching about specific regions of the world; online resource, consulted 12 November 2010.

The reason for the creation of a French area studies association lies in the name: the emphasis is on the study of twentieth-century and present-day France. This is evinced from the manner in which the journal and annual conferences are organised. Using the term area studies is useful to distinguish the ASMCF from the Society for French Studies – an older learned society which has as its journal *French Studies*.[4] The two organisations share an interest in postcolonial studies, gender studies and in French intellectual ideas, equally influential in the broader fields of critical theory and philosophy in the humanities and social sciences. When the association was founded some academics questioned the scholarly worth of topics other than literature in French Studies. ASMCF members sought to convince colleagues that:

> Students learn to talk about something in an analytical way, preferably in the foreign language as they get better at it, and in a number of registers. [...] we should not worry whether they are discussing literature, verse or contemporary France – they are all equally relevant. The point is that students learn to operate using their foreign language across a number of areas, developing a thinking and analytical register, not just practising colloquial chatter.[5]

Why did the association expand when it did? Two waves of expansion of student numbers in higher education, first in the late 1960s and early 1970s, and then in the late 1980s and early 1990s, opened up the possibility for the creation of new French courses and new combinations of subjects. The first wave saw the spread of area studies as common practice in French teaching and research, the second the fusion of the new methods that had developed in polytechnic and new university French departments, together with the expertise of staff such as in the older university sector teaching French in politics, history and geography departments and where the literature content was being adjusted to provide diversity in French courses. In the first wave of expansion the association contributed to the recognition of the value of integrating research and teaching through a topic-based approach in the target language that is now current practice. In the second wave it

---

4   During the same period French Studies underwent a transformation by recasting its traditional sphere of literature to include a wider cultural studies remit. With its membership largely in French departments from Oxford, Cambridge, London and the old universities, the scope of *French Studies* is still distinct from that of the approach of the ASMCF as its range covers all periods from the medieval to the present day, but not without some overlap, since it includes work on French and francophone literature and thought, theatre, film, media and cultural studies, linguistics of French and French language studies.

5   Siân Reynolds, quoted in Jennifer Birkett and Michael Kelly (eds), *French in the 90s: A Transbinary Conference, July 1991* (Birmingham: Birmingham Modern Languages Publications, 1992), p. 45.

successfully consolidated its membership across the old and new university institutions and increased its visibility dramatically in research and quality publications. The staunch support of founder member Douglas Johnson, the association's first president, and historians Ralph Gibson and Maurice Larkin, geographer Hugh Clout, politics specialists Peter Morris and David Bell, all outside French departments, was crucial at this time.

The first wave of expansion in French teaching also saw the need for new course materials. There is a close connection between two innovative texts published for teachers and students and the founding of the association. Eric Cahm, then at Reading University, produced a collection of source texts on France since 1789 and then three other Reading French staff, David Hanley, Neville Waites and Pat Kerr, published a concise survey of France since 1945.[6] These books reflected the importance attached to examining France's specificity as well as problematic issues in French society and were to bear the hallmark of the association's approach. They were followed by others too numerous to mention here.[7]

It is no coincidence that, together with Peter Morris from Nottingham University and his colleagues Brian Jenkins and Tony Chafer in Portsmouth Polytechnic, now Portsmouth University, Eric Cahm as head of the School of Languages and Area Studies, was one of the leading lights in the creation and running of the journal. Through his specialism of Third Republic history with a particular interest in the Dreyfus affair, and like other founding members such as David Bell, Brian Darling and Jolyon Howarth, he was able to network in France on the association's behalf to persuade French scholars to participate in conference activities. Sociologist Brian Darling from North London Polytechnic was for a long time the secretary of the association and was a generous host for the thrice-yearly Saturday committee meetings in London during the first twelve years of the association's life. Alec Hargreaves's pioneering

---

6 Eric Cahm, *Politics and Society in Contemporary France 1789–1971* (London: Harrap, 1972), translated as *Politique et société : La France de 1814 à nos jours* (Paris: Flammarion, 1977); D. L. Hanley, A. P. Kerr and N. H. Waites, *Contemporary France: Politics and Society since 1945* (London: Routledge and Kegan Paul, 1979, 2nd edn, 1984). Jill Forbes and Nick Hewlett; with François Nectoux and Anne Reymond, *Contemporary France: Essays and Texts on Politics, Economics, Society* (Harlow, Essex: Longman, 1994). The roll-call of honour of other academics who contributed key texts includes historian and faithful conference delegate Maurice Larkin, author of *France since the Popular Front: Government and People, 1936–1986* (Oxford: Clarendon Press, 1988). Also in history, Rod Kedward and Siân Reynolds, from the politics departments, David Bell, Anne Stevens, Vincent Wright, Jack Hayward and Raymond Kuhn, all added gravitas to the association through their support during its early years.

7 See Forbes *et al.*, *Contemporary France*. Like many textbooks on contemporary France which date quickly, this edition was revised and republished (Harlow: Longman, 2001). See also Jolyon Howorth and George Ross (eds), *Contemporary France: A Review of Interdisciplinary Studies* (London and New York: F. Pinter, 1987) and subsequent works of the same title by the same editors.

work on immigration in France was also groundbreaking in the study of French society.[8] Claire Duchen, Gabrielle Parker, Siân Reynolds, Anne Stevens, Máire Cross, Maggie Allison, Diane Holmes and Sheila Perry were among the women present in committees and in conference sessions, ensuring that feminism and gender questions in France were given prominence. Indeed, from the outset the association has always striven to be inclusive and sensitive to parity in its internal organisation and in its choice of topics in scholarly matters, as can be seen from Appendices 2 and 3. In addition to the founding editors, Eric Cahm, Peter Morris, Brian Jenkins and Tony Chafer, those who played a major editorial role have been Martyn Cornick (University of Birmingham), Raymond Kuhn (Queen Mary University of London) and currently Jackie Clarke (University of Southampton).

The ASMCF grew during the democratisation of higher education from which came the requirement of a different type of graduate in French, expected to have knowledge of contemporary issues in society, flexibility of thinking and an ability to solve problems in a foreign language. With the increasing involvement of the UK in the European Community, and judging by the continuous success rate in employment of language graduates, these skills were especially appreciated by employers in both the public and private sectors. The first wave of the expansion of French teaching therefore saw the curriculum development of area studies in higher education and the second wave saw its widespread adoption. This was only made possible with the creation of a new generation of teacher both in the higher education sector and in schools when the A-level syllabuses were diversified to teach society topics such as those listed in Appendix 1. From the available pool of graduates of French with a PhD in literature applying for teaching jobs from the early 1970s higher education institutions, most had to quickly become trained into teaching area studies and then researching an aspect of contemporary France, thereby stimulating the demand for an association that would facilitate their tasks.

A further stimulus to the growth of the ASMCF is that since its founding meeting in 1979, members have seen an increase in the recognition of the value of research in all higher education institutions whereas previously it was the preserve of the older universities. Where subjects were previously taboo, they now have their legitimacy. Thirty years ago anything literary, or prior to 1945, was not considered relevant in some departments of the polytechnic sector in the first years of expansion, in the same way that the study of authors representing movements such as feminism that later sprouted gender and LGBT studies

---

8 Alec G. Hargreaves, *Immigration, 'Race' and Ethnicity in Contemporary France* (London: Routledge, 1995).

were not necessarily present on the curriculum of the older universities.[9] The ASMCF has given colleagues confidence to challenge established notions of French research and has enabled the existence of a collective identity of research in aspects of contemporary France. Throughout the past thirty years, it has provided a very necessary forum for showcasing their research into France and, increasingly the francophone world.

The topic style of A-level French was of benefit to the expansion of the ASMCF. The conferences and associated groups attracted A-level French teachers and many of the items in the early *Newsletter* and *Review* were geared to this readership. A further stimulus to the popularity of the annual conferences and regional meetings was the fact that until economic constraints affected spending levels in universities, funding to attend conferences was possible, thereby enabling academics to attend conferences as staff training events. In addition, putting on sampler courses for sixth formers and offering day courses for A-level teachers was a significant part of the role of the association in the earlier decades of its existence: for instance, a two-day residential course for teachers on area studies was offered by Portsmouth staff in July 1983 and, similarly, when this author organised one-day conferences at Newcastle Polytechnic in 1989 and 1990 there were over 80 teachers present, whose training costs were funded by their local education authorites.[10]

Politically and professionally, therefore, the association's roots are embedded in an international, interdisciplinary and contemporary approach of the 1980s generation of successful language departments in polytechnics, particularly Portsmouth, Wolverhampton, Newcastle, Coventry, Cambridge Technical College, Kingston, Middlesex, North London and Oxford Brookes, or to the class of 'new' universities created in the 1960s such as Aston, Sussex, Surrey, Loughborough, Bath and Ulster, which teamed up with staff in some of the older universities (Birmingham, Leeds, Nottingham, Reading, Newcastle), which were developing their BA and MA programmes on the area studies model. By the time of the second wave of expansion the traditional mould of French through literature had been broken, enabled by the integration of language teaching with content.

The vast majority of the membership in the first years was in the UK. There is now a healthy geographical spread in other English-speaking countries, especially North America where our nearest sister journal is

9   See the work of David Drake who taught in Middlesex University, served as President of the United Kingdom Society for Sartrean Studies (UKSSS), member of the Editorial Board of *Sartre Studies International* and of *Modern and Contemporary France*, and Elizabeth Fallaize, a founder member of the association's sub-group, Women in French and a pioneer in the 1980s in women's writing who became the first female fellow of St John's College, Oxford in 1990 then professor of French at the university, and in 2005 its pro-vice-chancellor for education.

10 Máire Cross (ed.), *La Société Française: French Teachers' Conferences Papers* (Newcastle: Newcastle Polytechnic, 1991).

probably *French Politics, Culture and Society*, although since our journal *Modern and Contemporary France* has not limited itself to politics, one could argue that we have a complementary readership. An indication of the strength of scholarly collaborations and associations is that the same era has seen the creation of a UK-based French history association, the Society for the Study of French History and its journal *French History*.[11] The French language association AFLS, the nineteenth-century studies association Society of Dix-neuvièmistes and its journal *Dix-neuf*,[12] and the continued flourishing of the Society for French Studies,[13] means that the ASMCF is just one of many associations that thrived during this period.[14]

Diversity in the study of France is now a major feature but the growth was not without tensions among members of the profession. It was not simply a division between 'traditionalists' and 'innovators' in language teaching, or between literary and non-literary specialists in content teaching. The interdisciplinary approach of necessity relies on fluid links between departments and disciplines which can wither very easily if not nurtured by a sympathetic university environment. Recently, as a result of the diminishing supply of applicants to study languages, pioneering institutions have seen their language departments close or reduced to institution-wide language service departments, among them Wolverhampton, the University of the West of England, Sussex and Surrey.

How did the Association fulfil its mission of making visible the new identity of French area studies and group colleagues who might otherwise have been isolated? Three main areas of activity have all contributed to its success: the annual conference, publication of the journal and support for local and regional research groups.

The majority of the ASMCF conferences have been held in England. It was not until 1999 that a conference was held in Wales. Thanks to a cross-Channel collaboration with CRECIB, a similar association, but not by any means a natural bedfellow, Paris was the venue in 2003.[15] The year 2011 sees the conference venue in Scotland for the first time and we have yet to be approached by members in Ireland to host one there. The conferences have offered three days of intense lectures and discussion, many in French and led by the experts in the questions from France. Invited guests over the years have included, Edgar Pisani, Pierre Bourdieu, Juliette Minces, Hervé Hamon, Régis Debray, Madeleine

11 Society for the Study of French History, online resouce, consulted 16 November 2010.

12 Society of Dix-neuvièmistes, online resource, consulted 25 November 2010

13 Society for French Studies, online resource, consulted 25 November 2010.

14 Association for French Language Studies, online resource, consulted 25 November 2010.

15 A key figure in France who facilitated cross-Channel connections until his death in early 2010, François Poirier hosted the Paris conference. Founder and president of the European Network for British Area Studies he played a leading role in the SAES (Société des anglicistes de l'enseignement supérieur).

Réberioux, Roland Cayrol, Christine Bard, Michel Dreyfus, Hervé Le Bras, Patrick Champagne, Marc Abeles and Françoise Thébaud.

For the journal, librarians in Newcastle and Portsmouth distilled material on the vast numbers of topics and in every review number from 1987 there was a list providing a keyword search tool, now migrated to an online service. A chronology of main events offered a quick digest of recent developments on the political and economic fronts.

The association's publication, which began as a newsletter, has evolved from being a teaching tool with announcements on future events, a book service for speeding up the purchase of French publications and a reading guide for authentic materials, to a high-class internationally rated research journal. Search tools and library resources have always been a feature of the journal with a view to assisting staff to access authentic materials on France.

Since it became a commercially produced journal in 1990, there has also been a shift in the kind of articles published. The range published in the quarterly journal is now much more eclectic. The choice of subject matter reflects not so much a change of approach but rather is a reflection of what is happening in France. The coming of age of the Fifth Republic has meant that there is less space allocated to formal political institutions, elections and parties. Just as in France, there have been intense debates on identity and inequalities, so too do they feature in our journal issues and conference topics.

The association was founded just prior to the arrival of internet communication, of satellite media communications, online availability and e-mails. From the typewriter that produced the early newsletters, the association's members have not been slow to take advantage of new outlets for disseminating their work. The latest development is a move to podcasting: the plenary sessions of the 2010 conference held in Nottingham Trent University made available online have had a spectacular success, possibly because of the apposite theme of France and the Crisis.[16]

The journal *Modern and Contemporary France*, currently selling very well to overseas university libraries on subscription, and the published conference proceedings, reach out to those in French for whom research-led teaching is a priority. The web page is increasingly vital as a showcase and means of communication that can lead to international networking. Since its inception, opportunities for long-distance research collaboration have increased and our journal is more widely read in North America. At the same time, francophone area studies are a key feature of our activities. The cross-Channel contacts that members have built up within and beyond the Hexagon have matured into francophone studies as exemplified by the Franco-African studies research group in

16 La France et la Crise, online resource, consulted 25 November 2010.

Portsmouth which is part of the Centre for European and International Studies Research (CEISR), a major interdisciplinary centre for research on Europe, its diasporas and its relations with the wider world.[17]

Regional and sub-groups of researchers are regularly sponsored by the association, the most recent being the North-West Regional ASMCF Group. Women in French (WIF) was founded in 1988; the French Media Research Group was started in 1995 as the Northern Media Research Group (NMRG) by Hugh Dauncey and Geoff Hare, then both in the School of Modern Languages, Newcastle University and Sheila Perry, then at the School of Modern Languages, University of Northumbria, now at the University of Nottingham. A group of postgraduates meets regularly at their annual meeting. We consider that the association has a vital role to play in encouraging the next generation of French research-teaching staff. In addition, we have representation on national bodies and subject groups relating to area studies and modern languages (including AUPHF, UCML and UKCASA) and through them we have been involved in the current national debate on the teaching of foreign languages in education at all levels.

Conclusion

The study of French is long established in the UK and Ireland and, compared to other EU countries, the subject here enjoys considerable disciplinary diversity and strength thanks to the influence of societies. The ASMCF is the only interdisciplinary society that can network with colleagues outside languages departments in fields such as history, sociology, philosophy, politics and media studies who work on aspects of France's rich philosophical and cultural traditions. However, future directions for French need to be planned carefully in order to ensure the healthy diversity of the discipline of French nationally, a health that will be reflected in effective language learning in schools and viable numbers of undergraduate and postgraduate linguists receiving excellent teaching delivered by specialists in the discipline, and the continuing vibrancy of French Studies research.

Although there is a decline in the number of staff teaching in language departments compared to the peak of the early 1990s, the quality of the research has not diminished: on the contrary, the topic of contemporary France has spawned hundreds of scholarly works in research and as teaching aids, all striving to explain the specifics of French society and its evolution in past decades, an enormous subject. The international reputation of the association has grown exponentially; the

17 University of Portsmouth, Centre for European and International Studies Research (CEISR), online resource, consulted on 25 November 2010.

interdisciplinary approach is firmly embedded in French degree programmes. Of course, the association cannot profess to have a monopoly on interdisciplinarity but it can rightly claim to be its breeding ground: no French department can survive without running courses on contemporary France.

The association's fortunes will depend on the destiny of its membership which, in turn, depends on the direction French area studies research and teaching takes. We have seen in the past decade that if there is a drop in student numbers, university senior management may be tempted to close departments just as it also had the power to expand courses. The demand-led policy-making drive, which dictates how subjects in university thrive, is currently in direct conflict with the knowledge that the current shortage of language skills is a handicap for the British economy. The skills that the area studies approach developed in the 1980s are exactly what employers required then, and still do: a combined knowledge of the country's contemporary position and of the language.

The survival of language departments where French is taught is bound up with government education policy on the future of languages. Academics in French have also been closely involved in HEFCE initiatives (*Routes into Languages, Links into Languages*) to reverse the decline in the numbers of students taking French at school. The future of French area studies will depend on the commitment of university policy makers to sustain an international dimension to their curricula. That future will also depend, crucially, on how policy makers in the UK address the challenges arising from the contraction in student numbers in languages.[18] Deskilling in languages is also having a severe effect on postgraduate studies as highlighted by the British Academy's 'Language Matters' report of January 2009. This provides evidence of a mismatch between supply and demand in languages skills for research and reflects on the consequences of this mismatch. The humanities and social sciences fields are encountering difficulties associated with increasingly monolingual research students. Strengthening links between languages and area studies, on the other hand, is a sure way of promoting interdisciplinarity, multilingual ability of graduates and the international standing of researchers in humanities and social sciences. The presence of studies on Sartre in Middlesex and on De Beauvoir in Oxford symbolises the groundbreaking work of the association's members and the vibrancy of its impact that should be allowed to flourish for many years to come.

---

18 Matthew Reisz, Michael Worton and Glyn Hambrook, 'Foreign Talk isn't Cheap – it's Priceless', *Times Higher Education Supplement* (21 October 2010), pp. 34–41. Currently, Mike Kelly is proposing to start of a five-year campaign: 'Speak to the future: The campaign for languages', to improve public perception of the value of languages. The relevance of such a campaign to French area studies is crucial.

Appendix 1: Sample of the type of topics that are taught in French A-level courses in secondary education:

- **Media**: Television; advertising; communication technology
- **Popular culture**: Cinema; music; fashion/trends
- **Healthy living/lifestyle**: Sport/exercise; health and well-being; holidays
- **Family/relationships**: Relationships within the family; friendships; marriage/partnerships
- **Environment**: Pollution; energy; conservation
- **The multicultural society**: Immigration; integration; racism
- **Contemporary social issues**: Wealth and poverty; law and order; impact of scientific and technological progress
- **Cultural topic from target language-speaking region/community**: A period of twentieth-century history; work of a writer/director/architect/musician/painter

Appendix 2 Special issues of *Modern and Contemporary France*

Date	Theme	Guest editor(s)
18: 4 2010	Women in French Politics	Rainbow Murray
18: 2 2010	Empire and Culture Now	Mary Gallagher and Douglas Smith
17: 4 2009	The Sarkozy Presidency	Philippe Marlière and Joseph Sarka
16: 4 2008	The Fifth Republic at Fifty	Ben Clift
16: 2 2008	1968: Forty Years After	David Drake and Keith Reader
15: 3 2007	Youth Cultures in the Fifth Republic	Wendy Michallat and Chris Tinker
15: 1 2007	French Cinema: 'Transnational' Cinema?	Carrie Tarr
14: 3 2006	Gays and Lesbians in Contemporary France: Politics, Media, Sexualities	Renate Günther and Owen Heathcote
14: 1 2006	France / Asias	Charles Forsdick, Alex Hughes and Bill Marshall
13: 3 2005	Political Communication in the Fifth Republic	Raymond Kuhn
13: 1 2005	France and Africa in the Global Era	Gordon Cumming and Rachael Langford
12: 3 2004	Intellectuals and Ideas in France	Christopher Flood and Nick Hewlett
12: 1 2004	New Voices in French Politics	Joanna Drugan, Jim House and Sarah Waters
11: 3 2003	Tradition and Modernity in Rural France	Hugh Clout and Marion Demossier
11: 1 2003	Cultural Practices and Policies: Democratisation Reassessed	Philip Dine and David Looseley
10: 4 2002	France and Algeria, 1962–2002: Turning the Page?	Alec G. Hargreaves
10: 3 2002	The Jospin Government 1997–2002	Alistair Cole
10: 1 2002	Debating and Implementing Gender Parity in French Politics	Sandrine Dauphin and Jocelyne Praud

9: 3 2001	France and Globalisation	Mairi Maclean and Susan Milner
9: 1 2001	France – History and Story: Identity in France	Paul Rowe and Martyn Cornick
8: 4 2000	Napoleon's France: History and Heritage	Malcolm Crook and John Dunne
8: 3 2000	Representing Paris	Alison S. Fell and Chris Tinker
8: 1 2000	The Right in France	Catherine Fieschi
7: 3 1999	Media in France	Raymond Kuhn and Sheila Perry
7: 1 1999	Gendering the Occupation of France	Hannah Diamond and Claire Gorrara
6: 3 1998	Sport, Culture and Society in Modern France	Hugh Dauncey and Geoff Hare
6: 2 1998	'Croppy Lie Down!': Unruly Elements or Unclaimed Messages of the Past	Máire Cross
5: 4 1997	Sociology and Anthropology in Twentieth-Century France	Christopher Johnson
5: 2 1997	La fin du dirigisme?	Vincent Wright
4: 4 1996	France and Black Africa	Tony Chafer
3: 4 1995	Challenges to French Social Policy in the 1990s	Jan Windebank
3: 2 1995	1945–1995: Fifty Years of Universal Suffrage	Máire Cross
2: 2 1994	The Algerian War	Charles Giry-Deloison and Alec G. Hargreaves
1: 4 1993	Cities	Eleonore Kofman
1: 2 1993	Political Scandal in France	Brian Jenkins and Peter Morris

Appendix 3 Conference History of the Association from 1980 to 2010

Date	Theme	Venue	Publication
2010	La France et la Crise : bilan et perspectives, ruptures antécédents	Nottingham Trent University	Follow-up website (see note 16)
2009	France and the Mediterranean	Portsmouth University	Emmanuel Godin and Natalya Vince, *France and the Mediterranean: International Relations, Culture and Politics* (Oxford: Peter Lang, 2011)
2008	Constructing French Identity/Identities	University of Manchester	Barbara Lebrun and Jill Lovecy (eds), *Une et divisible?: Plural identities in Modern France*, Modern French Identities 90 (Berne: Peter Lang, 2010)
2007	Mapping France	University of Reading	Articles
2006	Liberté, Egalité, Fraternité: the Concept of Rights in Modern and Contemporary France	University of Sheffield	
2005	Forces for Radical Social Change in France Today	Loughborough University	
2004	Discourse, Persuasion and Public Perception in France	University of Surrey	
2003	France and Britain: Cross-influences, Mutual Representations, Comparisons	Paris	
2002	At the Border: Margins and Peripheries in Modern France	University of Glamorgan	Henrice Altink and Sharif Gemie (eds), *At the Border: Margins and Peripheries in Modern France* (Cardiff: University of Wales Press, 2008)
2001	La France Exceptionnelle?	University of Portsmouth	Tony Chafer and Emmanuel Godin (eds), *The French Exception* (Oxford: Berghahn, 2004) updated: Tony Chafer and Emmanuel Godin (eds), *The End of the French Exception? Decline and Revival of the 'French Model'* (Basingstoke: Palgrave Macmillan, 2010); Brian Jenkins (ed.), *France in the Era of Fascism: Essays on the French Authoritarian Right* (Oxford: Berghahn, 2005)

Year	Title	University	Publication
2000	Shifting Frontiers of France and Francophonie	University of Leicester	Yvette Rocheron and Christopher Rolfe (eds), *Shifting Frontiers of France and Francophonie* (Berne: Peter Lang, 2004).
1999	Reinventing France: Towards the New Millennium	University of Cardiff	Susan Milner, Nick Parsons (eds), *Reinventing France: State and Society in the Twenty-First Century* (Basingstoke: Palgrave Macmillan, 2003).
1998	The Fifth Republic Forty Years On: Actions, Dialogues and Discourses	University of Bradford	Maggie Allison and Owen Heathcote (eds), *Forty Years of the Fifth French Republic: Actions, Dialogues, and Discourses* (Berne: Peter Lang, 1999).
1997	France: Fin(s) de Siècle(s)	University of Liverpool	Kay Chadwick and Timothy A. Unwin (eds), *New Perspectives on the Fin de Siècle in Nineteenth- and Twentieth-Century France* (Lampeter: Edward Mellen Press, 2000).
1996	France: The Mitterrand Era in Perspective	Royal Holloway	Mairi MacLean (ed.), *The Mitterrand Years: Legacy and Evaluation* (Basingstoke: Palgrave Macmillan, 1998).
1995	France: Population and People	University of Northumbria at Newcastle	Máire Cross and Sheila Perry (eds), *Population and Social Policy in France* (London: Frances Pinter Publishers, 1997); Sheila Perry and Máire Cross (eds), *Voices of France: Social, Political and Cultural Identity* (London: Frances Pinter Publishers, 1997).
1994	France: From Cold War to the New World Order	University of Portsmouth	Tony Chafer and Brian Jenkins (eds) *France: From the Cold War to the New World Order* (Basingstoke: Palgrave Macmillan, 1997).
1993	France: Violence and Conflict	University of Sheffield	Janice Windebank, Renate Günther (eds), *Violence and Conflict in the Politics and Society of Modern France* (Lampeter: Edward Mellen Press, 1995); Janice Windebank, Renate Günther (eds), *Violence and Conflict in Modern French Culture* (Sheffield: Sheffield Academic Press, 1994).
1992	France: Nation and Regions	University of Southampton	Mike Kelly and Rosemary Bock (eds), *France: Nation and Regions* (Southampton: University of Southampton and ASMCF, 1993).
1991	France: Social and Cultural Identity	University of Nottingham	Rosemary Chapman and Nicholas Hewitt (eds), *Popular Culture and Mass Communication in Twentieth-Century France* (Lewiston NY, Lampeter: E Mellen Press, 1992).
1990	France and Europe	Wolverhampton Polytechnic	Khursheed Wadia and Stuart Williams (eds), *France and Europe* (Wolverhampton: ASMCF Books, 1993).
1989	War and Society in 20th-Century France	University of Bath	Michael Scriven and Peter Wagstaff (eds), *War and Society in Twentieth-Century France* (Oxford: Berg, 1991).

Year	Title	Institution	Reference
1988	Beliefs in France	University of Loughborough	Martyn Cornick (ed.), *Beliefs and Identity in Modern France* (Loughborough: European Research Centre, Department of European Studies, Loughborough University, 1990).
1987	May '68 Twenty Years On?	University of Reading	David L. Hanley and A. P. Kerr (eds), *May '68: Coming of Age* (London: Routledge, 1989)
1986	France: Image and Identity	Newcastle Polytechinic	Jeff Bridgford (ed.), *France: Image and Identity* (Newcastle upon Tyne: Newcastle Polytechnic Products, 1987).
1985	France and Modernisation	University of Aston	John Gaffney (ed.), *France and Modernisation* (Aldershot and Brookfield, VT: Avebury, 1988).
1984	France and the World	University of Nottingham	Peter Morris and Stuart Williams (eds), *France in the World* (Association for the Study of Modern and Contemporary France, 1985).
1983	Equality and Inequalities	University of Leeds	Peter Morris (ed.), *Equality and Inequalities in France: Proceedings of the Fourth Annual Conference of the Association for the Study of Modern and Contemporary France* (Association for the Study of Modern and Contemporary France, 1985).
1982	Socialism in France	Wolverhampton Polytechnic	Stuart Williams (ed.), *Socialism in France from Jaures to Mitterrand* (London: Pinter, 1983).
1981	France in the New Era	University of Loughborough	
1980	Elites in France	University of Aston	Jolyon Howorth and Philip G. Cerny (eds), *Elites in France: Origins, Reproduction and Power* (Basingstoke: Palgrave Macmillan, 1982).
1979	Inaugural Meeting	University of Aston	

Bibliography

Birkett, Jennifer and Michael Kelly (eds), *French in the 90s: A Transbinary Conference, July 1991* (Birmingham: Birmingham Modern Languages Publications, 1992)

Cahm, Eric, *Politics and Society in Contemporary France 1789–1971* (London: Harrap, 1972), translated as *Politique et Société: La France de 1814 à nos jours* (Paris: Flammarion, 1977).

Cross, Máire (ed.), *La Société Française: French Teachers' Conferences Papers* (Newcastle: Newcastle Polytechnic, 1991).

Forbes, Jill, *et al.*, *Contemporary France: Essays and Texts on Politics, Economics, Society* (Harlow: Longman, 1994).

Hanley, David L., *et al.*, *Contemporary France: Politics and Society since 1945* (London: Routledge and Kegan Paul, 1979 [2nd edn, 1984]).

Hargreaves, Alec G., *Immigration, 'Race' and Ethnicity in Contemporary France* (London: Routledge, 1995).

Howorth, Jolyon and George Ross (eds), *Contemporary France: A Review of Interdisciplinary Studies* (London and New York: F. Pinter, 1987).

Larkin, Maurice, *France since the Popular Front: Government and People, 1936–1986* (Oxford: Clarendon Press, 1988).

Reisz, Matthew, Michael Worton and Glyn Hambrook, 'Foreign Talk isn't Cheap – it's Priceless', *Times Higher Education Supplement*, 21 October 2010, pp. 34–41.

Websites

Association for French Language Studies, available from www.afls.net/ (consulted 25 November 2010).

La France et la Crise, available from http://lafranceetlacrise.com/ (consulted 25 November 2010).

Society for the Study of French History, available from www.frenchhistorysociety.ac.uk/ (consulted 16 November 2010).

Subject Centre for Languages Linguistics and Area Studies, available from www.llas.ac.uk/ areastudies.html (consulted 12 November 2010).

Society for French Studies, available from www.sfs.ac.uk/ (consulted 25 November 2010).

Society of Dix-neuvièmistes, available from www.sdn.ac.uk/ (consulted 25 November 2010).

UKCASA (United Kingdom Council for Area Studies Associations), available from www. ukcasa.ac.uk/membership.html (consulted 12 November 2010).

University of Portsmouth, Centre for European and International Studies Research (CEISR), available from www.port.ac.uk/research/ceisr/ (consulted 25 November 2010).

23

Culturetheque: A New Tool for French Culture

Laurence Auer

On 27 May 2010, the central project of the centenary celebrations of the Institut français du Royaume-Uni was unveiled: a digital platform called Culturetheque. The response of the French Institute in South Kensington, London to the new challenges posed by the digital revolution was to launch a new tool, which was unprecedented both in the UK and in France.

Culturetheque offers French culture at home, on the Internet, for free, in an accessible and user-friendly way: books to read online, films to watch online, podcasts of conferences and live retransmissions. Culturetheque is not a simple online platform to learn French, nor is it a research website; rather, it is a tool with French resources for anyone in the UK who is interested in French culture and would like to know more about French painters, authors, events, and so on. The content online is changed regularly, providing privileged access to a selection of carefully chosen content, with commentaries in English and a strong focus on everyday life, such as travel, cooking, fashion, or books.

The Genesis of 'Your Digital Institute'

The project was initiated in January 2009 by the head of the Mediathèque. First of all, the 80,000 books in the Institut's beautiful wood-panelled library were being consulted less and less, notably by students who now chose to use the Internet rather than go into the library. Also, there has been a significant decline since 2004 in the number of young people taking GCSE French, diminishing from 300,000 to 170,000 in 2010; and only 13,850 students took A level French in June 2010, a decline of over 3 per cent compared to 2009.

The first aim of Culturetheque was therefore to attract a new public, one interested in French films and books, but who would not, or could not, travel to the French Institute or engage with any Alliance Française. Culturetheque aimed also to create a community of younger members who are used to accessing content on the Internet. Our goal was therefore to offer a wider range of exciting and entertaining cultural content to a broader range of users.

However, the concept of Culturetheque remains true to the vision which led Marie d'Orliac, an enterprising young French woman, to create the French Institute in London in 1910 and then to go on to create other institutes in Liverpool, Manchester, Bath, Bristol, and elsewhere. One hundred years after she began her pioneering work, her founding idea that culture and language are intertwined and that the best way to learn French is to fall in love with its literature, music and films has proved to be still valid.

For the team at the Institut français, it was also a challenge to create a tool with which to attract new audiences. No such tool existed in any of the 150 French Institutes around the world, so intensive work had to be done between the various departments in order to work across the boundaries between different specialisms and to combine cinema and debates, French lessons and theatre.

Culturetheque was officially opened by the French ambassador, Maurice Gourdault-Montagne and Gabriel de Broglie, member of the Académie Française and Chancellor of the Institute of France, who through their presence and their speeches gave French government legitimacy to this new way of spreading French culture abroad.

Mr de Broglie had some reservations about the neologism, Culturetheque, which does not fit with his vision of the precise and elegant use of the French language. I therefore had to justify it by reference to the creativity of the British developers and marketing team who recommended the term 'Culturetheque' as conveying contemporary chic. As with that other neologism, Bistrothèque, they argued that it is a 'cool' and trendy term which evoked both Frenchness and the cutting edge.

Culturetheque: A Multiplicity of Changing Contents

The new digital platform offers more than 5,000 e-books in French, constituting the first French digital library in the UK. Contemporary novels are available alongside great French classics, as well as many essays on French society, travel books, cookery books, and resources allowing users to find out more about studying in France.

Culturetheque also offers a great deal of audio-visual content (audio books and films): there are 500 French documentary films on major issues, such as climate, ecology, immigration and religion. Furthermore, nearly 250 recordings of conferences held at the Institut since 1967 are available online. The greatest names in French philosophy and literature as well as cinema all feature on Culturetheque. The contributors include Etienne Balibar, Julia Kristeva, Michel Butor, Patrick Chamoiseau and Pierre Boulez. The oldest historical recording dates from 1939.

The Institut has also digitised its outstanding collection of rare books dating from the seventeenth and eighteenth centuries, including, for example, an edition dating from 1788 of *Le Paysan parvenu* by Marivaux and the first translation into French of *The Arabian Nights*. Furthermore, many tools for learners of French are available online, such as podcasts specially designed by the Institut and the Alliance Française in Glasgow; again, these are all available free to all users.

Can Culturetheque become the *Nouvelle Heloïse* of the twenty-first century? Can this new cultural and educational platform create a new community of members? The evidence is clear: in the first three months alone, 4,000 web users had used the site, with an increase of 20 per cent per week; 16,000 pages were watched in this period, with 75 per cent of the users located outside London. Membership rose from 400 in May 2010 to 1,200 in September 2010.

It is too early to decide whether all of our objectives have been met. However, there are many points in favour of Culturetheque. First of all, the cost of the platform is low with regard to the cost of web rights or design and development: in creating it, we were careful to evaluate its potential efficiency in the long term.

A second point is that Culturetheque must regularly renew its content in order to attract an ever larger audience; in particular, it should include feature movies on a regular basis. Impact of contemporary and historical affairs can be measured by the fact that to mark the anniversary of General de Gaulle's appeal to the Free French on 18 June, 1,000 people watched the movie during the 10 days that it was accessible on Culturetheque. Future plans include the possibility of watching French films, with a full online programme, in parallel with the programmes offered at the Cine Lumière of the French Institute.

Third, the Institute hopes that this platform will be an effective support tool for learners of French. Podcasts aimed at those beginning to learn French are currently being produced in partnership with the Alliance française in Glasgow. Another initiative is an online web competition operating throughout the year on the theme of 'Your France in the UK', whereby schools and web users will be invited to send short films, shot on their mobiles or digital cameras.

A Culturetheque community will be developed through Twitter and events such as online concerts, and there are plans to use smartphone applications and digital readers to enlarge the number of users.

So is the innovative Culturetheque an answer to the declining numbers of French language learners in the UK? It cannot do this all on its own, but it does offer a variety of resources for its community of those who are interested in French culture and the French language. If Culturetheque achieves a wide take-up, it can become an empowering collaborative tool for all Francophiles in the UK. I am sure that 100 years after she created the l'Université des Lettres françaises, Marie d'Orliac would see Culturetheque as an appropriate renewal of French creativity and dynamism in the UK.

Appendices. Addresses to
the *Future of French Studies* Conference,
12 February 2010

Appendix 1

Opening Speech. A Vast and Dynamic Field of Research and Teaching

HE M. Maurice Gourdault-Montagne
Ambassador of France to the UK

Professor Michael Worton,
M. le Sous-Directeur du Français, Ministry of Foreign and European Affairs,
Ladies and Gentlemen, Professors of French Studies and representatives of academic associations and societies of French Studies.

Friends,

French Studies in the UK covers a vast range of research. It includes, of course, French and Francophone literature from the Middle Ages until the present day, but it also includes research on theatre, cinema, the media and cultural studies; French linguistics and studies of the French language; medieval and modern Occitan language, politics in France and in Francophone countries and the sociology and history of those countries. Researchers in French Studies also do important research in postcolonial studies, gender studies, and studies of philosophy and French thought. Additionally, the discipline makes a significant contribution to research in comparative literature and to our understanding of the relationship between literature and the other arts (for instance, on word and image interactions). Other important areas covered by French Studies are translation and the development and analysis of the pedagogy of the French language.

The results of the Research Assessment Exercise 2008 give a very positive picture of research in French Studies at the national level. Out of 33 French Studies units assessed, 17 obtained a ranking that put them in the 3★ and 4★ quality levels (i.e. 'internationally excellent' or 'world-leading').

A Subject None the Less in Difficulties

Paradoxically, in spite of the overall excellent quality of French Studies, there is an ongoing decrease in the number of students studying French and a decrease in the number of posts available for teachers and researchers. Over the past decade, the number of both undergraduate and postgraduate students has declined. The 1990s began with a record demand for the study of languages at undergraduate level, with French being the language most sought after. However, since then, there has been an ongoing decline in the learning and languages in general. The number of students of French has decreased, although less so than that of students of German, for example: indeed, in recent years, the number of students studying French has more or less stabilised. The number of students studying Spanish has dramatically increased over the same period, but now seems also to be stabilising, and other languages (for example, Chinese and Arabic) are increasingly popular.

In large part, the place of French in universities depends now more than ever on government policy regarding primary and secondary schools. Many academics are actively engaged in organisations and initiatives which aim to stem the decline of French and other foreign languages in schools. The maintenance and the effective management of French departments depends also, I believe, on the extent to which the administration of higher education institutions takes an active approach to the fostering of modern languages. It is admirable that many staff in French departments are involved in the initiatives of the Higher Education Funding Council for England to staunch the drop in the number of school pupils taking French in secondary schools, and I am delighted to meet representatives of these initiatives here today. The future of French Studies, both in French Studies departments and in the interactions that French Studies has with other subjects (for example, comparative literature, cinema studies, history and politics), will depend on the way in which French departments meet the challenges posed by the changes in the UK's student population. Access to foreign language study should be regarded as a priority in education at the national level. We need also to remember that the decline in language skills has a significant impact on postgraduate studies, as was made clear in *Language Matters*, the report published by the British Academy in January 2009. Humanities and social sciences departments are encountering ever greater difficulties arising from the monolinguism of British doctoral students.

French Studies, a Vibrant Subject

French Studies has been established for a very long time in the UK, and it is renowned for its diversity, as well as enjoying a considerable national and international reputation – and, indeed, French Studies has had a considerable influence on the development of other university subjects. The number and the quality of the societies and organisations in which many of you are involved has had, and continue to have, a significant impact on the level of modern language students in the UK, both undergraduates and postgraduates, and these students all benefit from the excellent teaching by specialists and from the vibrant research of UK French Studies.

I want to reassure you that our embassy is committed now and in the future to support all of your activities as best we can, be these of your university departments or of your associations in which you are involved. I trust that this conference will be a great success, and give my special thanks to Professor Michael Worton for his involvement with this organisation.

Appendix 2

A View from France

Jean-Paul Rebaud

Monsieur l'Ambassadeur,
Professor Michael Worton,
Ladies and gentlemen, Professor of French Studies

Dear Colleagues,

I am both delighted and honoured to be here in the prestigious building of the British Academy and to speak at the opening of your conference on French Studies in the UK, which has been organised by the French Embassy and University College London, as part of the celebration of the centenary of the French Institute in London. Of all the events organised to celebrate this centenary, this conference is undoubtedly the one which delves deepest into the history of the cultural representation of France in your country and also the one that focuses most on one of the most exciting aspects of our Franco-British relations.

In historical terms, we can, I think, place our exchanges today under the tutelary image of Marie d'Orliac, who a century ago, founded the Universitè des Lettres Françaises, a prefiguration of the French Institute in London. We are also reminded here of the origin of cultural diplomacy in France, which celebrated its own centenary last year. Indeed, it was in 1909 that the Quai d'Orsay created a 'Service des Oeuvres', which was responsible in particular for the support and organisation of French schools abroad, for cultural exchanges, and for the first French institutes opened in the main European capital cities with the help of French universities.

The French Institute in London was linked to the University of Lille, and the institutes in Madrid and Lisbon were later linked to the universities of Toulouse and Bordeaux. The idea at the time was to offer higher education courses mainly in literature and the social sciences to foreign students and researchers. Such courses enabled French universities to strengthen the existing relationships and to forge new relationships with their counterparts in other countries, and to organise exchanges between teachers, researchers and students. This initiative thus revitalised and gave new directions to both the teaching of, and research into, French language, literature and civilisation. The discussions at this conference will no doubt tell us much about the role played by the Institut français in London in the development of French Studies in the UK, in your universities, and more generally, in British intellectual circle.

I said that French Studies is at the heart of Franco-British relationships, just as is the case in other countries with which we have special intellectual and cultural affinities. I would add that French Studies is bound up with something which is sometimes considered somewhat out of date, and which we still call 'francophilia'.

I am not an Anglicist, but I used to be a Brazilianist, and I understand how much personal, passionate commitment to the chosen foreign country is felt by the professional languages specialist and I am certain that true critical analysis of a foreign culture tells us as much about the individuals doing the analysis and about the public opinions of their country as it does about the country that is being scrutinised.

I would thus invite you to reflect on the idea that, while French Studies, of course, offers pertinent analyses of French and francophone cultures, it also probably reveals a great deal about the British psyche. It is therefore for your francophilia that I would like first of all to thank you. As you will imagine, francophilia is something of which the French people are rather fond. Caught between a reputation for arrogance which some people are prone to pin on us, and a defeatism fuelled by the idea of an inexorable decline, we are happy to be loved for who and what we really are by those who know us well, that is to say you, specialists of France and French culture. However, we also feel that your francophilia takes a more reasonable form on that found in the past in, for example the Hispanic countries, where the 'afrancesados' showed an excessive enthusiasm for French ideas and in fact, this 'idolatry' has over the years given way to indifference or even aggression towards us. That is certainly not the case here.

In more objective terms, the analytical scrutiny of France by UK French Studies has long demonstrated its acuity and originality. The emblematic study of the *History of French Passions*, by Theodore Zeldin is one of the UK's most spectacular achievements, but it is by no means the only one. What is most striking in the British case is, in fact, the extraordinary diversity of approaches and fields of interest. Nothing or next to nothing that our country has known in terms of major political and cultural phenomena or in significant societal developments one can be impressed by the list of learned societies and associations of specialists in the UK which are interested in our history, our literature, the French language and the culture of francophone countries. Naturally, I am not going to draw any specific conclusion from these few remarks. That is the point of today's conference, which will be assessing your own work and that of your predecessors. However, you know that we shall be listening carefully and that for a very long time we have done our best to support the activities of your departments.

We are very attentive to the changes in academic policies in your subject areas. We know that these changes can be a cause of concern for you, but we know also that the move from the purely literary and historical approach to an educational approach that takes into account professional and socio-economic outcomes is unavoidable. We must prepare for it.

In 2003, 2005 and 2009, we organised in Paris a series of conferences on the future of French Studies departments in European universities (some of you may well have taken part in these conferences). The operational conclusions which we drew from these meetings show some significant trends. The first of these is that there is no point in despairing over the decrease in the number of your students and the reduction of professional opportunities available to them. These decreases are in no way ineluctable, as long as new curricula and pedagogies are developed. The future belongs to multidisciplinary approaches which combine several core subjects (e.g. language and lay; language and management; literature and translation; linguistics and education sciences, etc.), in order to prepare students for the new jobs which increasingly require several competences, and (this is essential for academic courses specialising in the study of foreign countries) which must include an international dimension, this being even more important, given the impact of globalisation. The multi-disciplinary approach is essential not only in academic education and training, which are the primary aims of university degrees, but also in the fields of research and doctoral studies. The notion of a subject area functioning as a single unit in isolation from other subjects is no longer viable. The Bologna reform process and the creation of a European space for higher education also facilitate the mobility of teachers/researchers and scientific and scholarly exchanges. In the humanities and social sciences, these exchanges are, of course, of particular interest and usefulness for disciplines focusing on foreign countries.

Our second conclusion concerns the training of teachers of French in secondary education, a traditional mission of universities. Especially in Europe, the promotion of multilingualism has become an absolute necessity if we are to create a union of truly European citizens. The learning of European languages must be the glue that holds this new citizenship together, and it is for this reason that the teaching of two foreign languages in all European education systems must be adopted everywhere.

In the UK, French is by far the foreign language most widely taught. But I know that there has been concern following government decisions which led to a drop in the number of pupils learning a foreign language in secondary schools. On the other hand, the development both of foreign language learning in primary education and of bilingual education are positive signs that give rise to optimism. The need to train French teachers created by these new developments is a challenge to which French Studies departments must respond. But it is clear that only a voluntarist policy can oppose the natural tendency towards monolingualism in a country whose language is a worldwide instrument of communication.

Nonetheless, we must not forget that there is no lack of arguments in favour of the French language. Far after English, French is the foreign language most widely taught in the world: across all five continents, there are more than 85 million learners of all ages and backgrounds. French is also the working language of many international and multi-lateral institutions, and it is the official language and the instrument of international communication in many African countries.

For French Studies departments in British universities, this international dimension of French and of the francophone world must be a trump card in the many and various disciplines of Humanities and Social Sciences: francophone literatures, contemporary history, cultural and linguistic diversity and so on.

I would therefore suggest that this rapid overview suggests that French Studies is in fairly good health in the UK and that its future is promising. In any case, this analysis reflects the importance that we in France give to all that you do to strengthen relationships between our two countries. It also expresses our gratitude for your commitment to the promotion of our language and our culture in your country.

Thank you.

Index

16mm films 173–4

A la recherche du temps perdu (Proust)
　95
A-levels 16, 108
　modern languages 29
　student numbers 242, 288
　syllabuses 275, 281
　teachers 276
A Mission to Civilize (Conklin) 210–11
academic staff *see* staff
access to learning 257–8
ACHAC *see* Association pour la
　Connaissance de l'histoire de
　l'Afrique Contemporaine
Addison, Joseph 80
Adereth, Max 68
AFLS *see* Association for French
　Language Studies
afrancesados 297
Africa 200, 201–3
African literature 209, 212
AHRC *see* Arts & Humanities
　Research Council
Albertine (*A la recherche du temps
　perdu*) 95
Algerian War of Independence 201
Alliance française 63–4
Allison Peers, E. 40
Anglo-Norman Hub 149
Anglo-Norman texts 142–3
Anglo-Saxon intellectual tradition
　149
Anzieu, Didier 99
appendices 291–9
area studies 114, 197–206, 272, 275,
　276, 280
ARTE (television channel) 191–2

Arts & Humanities Research
　Council (AHRC) 33, 34, 126
ASCALF *see* Association for the
　Study of Caribbean and African
　Literature in French
ASMCF *see* Association for
　the Study of Modern and
　Contemporary France
'Aspects of Popular Culture in
　France since 1945' course 191–2
assessment of research 45, 59, 111
Association for French Language
　Studies (AFLS) 20, 63, 150
Association pour la Connaissance
　de l'histoire de l'Afrique
　Contemporaine (ACHAC)
　213–14
Association for the Study of
　Caribbean and African
　Literature in French (ASCALF)
　209, 212
Association for the Study of Modern
　and Contemporary France
　(ASMCF) 20, 62–3, 199,
　272–87
Association of University Professors
　and Heads of French (AUPHF)
　66
associations 62–4, 150
Atelier Doctorants 150
audio-visual resources 289
Audoin-Rouzeau, Stéphane 225
AUPHF *see* Association of
　University Professors and Heads
　of French
Australian Institute for Social
　Research 258
auteurs 173

Barrow Chair of French 38
Barthes, Roland 191
battlefield collections 229
Bayart, Jean-François 214
BBC (British Broadcasting
  Corporation) 61
Beasley-Murray, Jon 43
Beauvoir, Simone de 61
Becker, Annette 225
Beeching Corpus 144
beginners language courses 29
Belles Infidèles 155
Best, Victoria 100
Beugnet, Martine 180
BGP *see* Block Grant Partnership
Biggs, Patricia 143
'black writing' 209
Blanc, Michel 143
blended learning 247, 254–5
Block Grant Partnership (BGP)
  scheme 33, 34
Boccage, Madame du 78
The Body in Pain (Scarry) 221
Bologna Process 10, 256
Bowie, Malcolm 61, 95, 96
Boyle, Claire 100
Branca, Sonia 145
Brassens, Georges 184, 185
Brel, Jacques 184, 185
Bringing the Empire Back Home
  (Lebovics) 211
British Academy 64, 201
British Broadcasting Corporation
  (BBC) 61
Brown, Phillip 263
Browne report (2010) 5–6
Burgwinkle, William 97
Butler, Judith 95–6, 98

Cable, Vince 244
Cahm, Eric 198, 274
Cairns, Lucille 100, 101
Cambridge University Press 44
Cameron, David 244
Campos, Christophe 43
Canning, John 205
career management skills (CMS)
  265–6, 268
  see also graduate employment
Caribbean literature 209, 212
cartes postales 226
CAT *see* computer-assisted
  translation
CBI *see* Confederation of Business
  and Industry

CCWW *see* Centre for the Study
  of Contemporary Women's
  Writing
Centre for European and
  International Studies Research
  (CEISR) 200, 279
Centre National de la Recherche
  Scientifique (CNRS) 119
Centre National du Cinéma 176
Centre for Recording Achievement
  (CRA) 263–4
Centre for the Study of
  Contemporary Women's
  Writing (CCWW) 87, 91–4
Chakrabarty, Dipesh 52
challenges to French Studies
  129–30, 207–19, 262
chanson 185
Chanson de Roland 121, 134, 135
Charlemagne 133, 135
cinema studies 171–83, 290
  research 176–80
  teaching 171–6
  technological changes 173–4
  viewing of films 173–4
citizenship 70–1
Classics Studies 35, 82, 83
Clegg, Nick 243–4
Clifford, James 53
CLIL *see* content and language
  integrated learning
'Club Med' model 244
CMC *see* computer-mediated
  communication
CMS *see* career management skills
CNAA *see* Council for National
  Academic Awards
CNRS *see* Centre National de la
  Recherche Scientifique
Coalition government (2010–) 242
Cohen, Michèle 21
Coleman, Jim 269
collaboration
  language departments/centres 248
  Occupation period 224, 229
  projects 126
Communist Party 68
comparative literary analysis 165
comprehensive schools 4
computer-assisted translation (CAT)
  160
computer-mediated communication
  (CMC) 240, 241
Computers in Teaching Initiative
  (CTI) 65

Confederation of Business and Industry (CBI) 6
conferences 11
  Association for the Study of Modern and Contemporary France 277–8, 284–6
  French in the 90s 16
  Future of French Studies 291–9
  Grenoble conference 213
  Group for War and Culture Studies 227–8
  Institut Français 289
  Women's Writing in France: New Writers, New Literatures? 87
Conklin, Alice 210
Connolly, Kate 243
contact zones, linguistic 54
Contemporary Women's Writing in French (CWWF) 86–94
content and language integrated learning (CLIL) 116
contract academic staff 23, 76
conversation 77–82
Cooper, Sarah 101
corpus linguistics 144–5, 165
Council for National Academic Awards (CNAA) 18
Counter, Andrew 99
course book to case study 191
CRA *see* Centre for Recording Achievement
Crisp, Colin 180
Cronin, Michael 39, 53–4, 55
cross-cultural dialogue 92–3
cross-cultural studies 120–1
cross-dressing 98
cross-language provision 30
Crowley, Martin 100
CTI *see* Computers in Teaching Initiative
cultural studies 107, 108, 120–1, 186, 188
culture
  artefacts 226
  comparative collisions 136, 138
  high/low equivalence 136
  mobility 49–50, 52–4
  projects 128
Culture individuelle et culture de masse (Dollot) 191
Culturetheque 288–90
curriculum issues 6, 17–21, 27, 30–2, 275–6
  defining priorities 129–38
  economies of scale 30

  employability skills 266–7
  literary studies 114
  prioritisation 129–38
  schools 108, 131
  strategies 35
  traditional curriculum 137–8
  universities 17–21, 27, 30–2, 35, 108–10, 203–4
CWWF *see* Contemporary Women's Writing in French

defamiliarisation 35
degree courses
  acquisition of language/content balance 30, 205–6, 238, 264
  attractiveness to students 108–10
  curriculum issues 17–21, 27, 30–2, 35, 203–4
  language-learning component 30, 114, 115, 205–6, 238, 264
  MA/PGDip in French Language and Culture 248–53
  online courses 248–53
  relevance 110–11
  student enrolment 34, 199, 250
  student feedback 250
  undergraduate studies programmes 17–21
Derrida, Jacques 61
desire and sexuality 95–101
Desiring the Dead: Necrophilia and Nineteenth-Century French Literature (Downing) 98
The Digital Divide – Barriers to E-learning (Australian Institute for Social Research) 258
digital resources 239–40, 288–90
  see also online learning
disciplinary identity 37–57
discussion forums 236, 240
distance learning 235–7, 248–53
diversity of French Studies 293, 297
doctoral studies
  employability skills 123, 127
  francophone Africa 203
  French cinema 178, 179–80
  international PhDs 150
  translation studies 165–6
documentary films 289
Dolet, Etienne 155
Dollot, Louis 191
Downing, Lisa 98–9, 101
drama studies 61–2, 122–4
Dubois, Laurent 211
DVDs 174, 175

e-books 289
e-learning 247–61
    benefits 257
    cost 260
    feedback 251–3
    French language and culture
        257–60
    staff feedback 252–3
    student feedback 251–2
    technical support 259
e-moderators 252
e-portfolios 265
ecological movement 69
economies of scale, universities 30
education policy 9–11, 64–7, 242
    see also higher education;
        universities
Educational Rights Agency (ERA)
    174
effeminacy of French language,
    British view 83
email newsletters 90
employability of graduates 27–8,
    262–71
employers
    expectations of graduates 3, 32,
        157, 267
    networking 265
England, conversational arts 79–82
    see also United Kingdom
English character 80, 81–2
English language 80
Enquête Sociolinguistique d'Orleans
    (Blanc and Biggs) 143–4
entente cordiale scholarship scheme
    9–10
environmental movement 69
ERA *see* Educational Rights Agency
esprit 77–8
European Higher Education Area 10
European studies 17–18, 113
European Union (EU) 116, 161
Eustache, Jean 176
Evans, Colin 19, 20
The Evolution of French Syntax
    (Harris) 142
exhibitions 62

Fallaize, Elizabeth 22, 88
feedback
    staff 250, 252–3
    students 250, 251–2, 255, 266
fees, universities 159, 163, 239
feminist intellectuals 69–70
Ferguson, Gary 98

film studies *see* cinema studies
First World War 225, 226, 228
FLLOC (*French Learner Language
    Oral Corpora*) 147
Forbes, Jill 178
foreign correspondents 68
foreign languages *see* modern
    languages
Forsdick, Charles 209
Fox, Seamus 250
France
    African policy 201–2
    colonies 210
    conversation 77–82
    feminist intellectuals 69–70
    government policy 9–11
    higher education promotion 9–10
    national identity 43, 132–7, 207
    national strategy 9–11
    politics 67–8
    postcolonial studies 212–14
    postcolonialism 202
    Quarrels 124–5, 127–8
    Second World War 224, 229
    war and culture studies 220–2
    see also French…
Franco-African studies research
    group 278–9
Franco-British Society 64
francophilia 297
Francophone Africa degree (MA)
    202–3
francophone cinema 179
francophone studies 205, 208–12,
    214–17
    academic status 217
    criticism of 215
    journal articles 215–16
    war and culture studies 220–2
Francosphere 51, 52
Franks 133, 134, 135
Free French texts 67
French: from Dialect to Standard
    (Lodge) 142
French in the 90s conference 16
French in Action modules 267–8
The French Cinema Book (Temple
    and Witt) 180
French Cultural Studies (journal) 12,
    216
French culture, transmission 59–62
French history teaching 211
The French Imperial Nation (Wilder)
    211
French Institute *see* Institut Français

French language
  cultural status 131
  effeminacy characterisation 83
  and gender 75–85
  history 141–3
  importance 299
  in Middle Ages 134–5
  research 141–3
  second language acquisition 146–8
  see also linguistics research
French Learner Language Oral Corpora (FLLOC) 147
French literature *see* literary studies
French for Medics course 249, 254–5, 259
French scholars *see* scholars
French Studies (journal) 20, 60, 215, 216
Frenchness 50–1, 111, 132–7
Freud, Proust and Lacan: Theory as Fiction (Bowie) 95
Frith, Simon 188
Froissart, Jean 149–50
From Latin to Modern French (Pope) 142
Fumaroli, Marc 79
funding of higher education 3, 5–6, 16, 92
future of French Studies 130–1, 257–60, 291–9
Future of French Studies conference (2010) 291–9

Gates, Bill 244–5
'gateway' status, French language studies 34
Gaunt, Simon 98
GCSEs 29, 242, 288
gender
  academic staff 75–6
  eighteenth-century identities 77–82
  French language 75–85
  historical identities 77–83
  language learning/teaching 21–3
  nineteenth century identities 82–3
  universities 22, 23, 75–6
gentlemen 77, 80
girls' education 13
Glasgow University 82–3
globalisation 43, 136
Godard, Jean-Luc 176
Gourdault-Montagne, Maurice 293–5
government policy 9–11, 242
graduate employment 27–8, 262–71

green activism 69
Grémillon, Jean 175
Grenoble conference (2010) 213
Group for War and Culture Studies (GWACS) 220, 222, 226–8
Guillot, Marie-Noëlle 148
Günther, Renate 100, 101
GWACS *see* Group for War and Culture Studies

Hackett, C.A. (Sam) 67
Haiti 211–12
Hammond, Nicholas 98
Harris, Joseph 98
Harris, M.B. 142
Hayward, Susan 178
Heathcote, Owen 101
HEFCE (Higher Education Funding Council for England) xx
heterosexuality 99
higher education
  access to learning 257–8
  challenges 3
  curriculum issues 17–21, 27, 30–2, 35, 203–4, 275–6
  funding 3, 5–6, 16, 92
  gender imbalances 22, 23, 75–6
  modern language student enrolments 33–4, 75
  new models 244–5
  postgraduate enrolments 33–4
  purpose 40
  student enrolments 33–4, 75
Higher Education Funding Council for England (HEFCE) xx
historical studies 44
history of French Studies 4–5
history teaching 211
Hoggart, Richard 185
Holquist, Michael 42
Holy Roman Empire 133, 134
homosexuality 97, 100–1
Hughes, Alex 100
humanity, history of 121
Huss, Marie-Monique 226
Hyde, Ruth 251, 257

identities
  French nation 43, 132–7, 207
  French Studies 7
  gender 22
  linguistic identities 136
  local identities 136–7
  Middle Ages 132–5
  postcolonial period 132

IGRS *see* Institute of Germanic & Romance Studies
impact debate, French scholars in Britain 58–9
In our time (radio programme) 61
independent schools 4
Institut Français 62, 253, 288, 296–7
Institute of Germanic & Romance Studies (IGRS) 87, 88–9
integrated learning, French literature 107–17
intellectual history 121
intellectuals *see* scholars
interactivity 251
interdisciplinarity 51, 92, 93, 277
   Association for the Study of Modern and Contemporary France 279–80
   popular culture studies 185, 186, 189–90
   research 121, 127
   war and culture studies 227
internationalisation of research 40, 47
internet
   Culturetheque 288–90
   translation awareness 160
   see also online...
internships *see* work placements
interpreting studies 158, 163, 164, 165
interviews, sociolinguistics 143–4
iTunes downloads 241–2

James Barrow Chair of French 38
Jefferies, Amanda 251, 257
job opportunities *see* graduate employment
Journal of Area Studies 198
Journal of French Language Studies 150
journal publishing 45, 150, 216
Journal of War and Culture Studies (JWACS) 222, 228–9
journals
   French Cultural Studies 12, 216
   French Studies 20, 60, 215, 216
   Journal of Area Studies 198
   Journal of French Language Studies 150
   Journal of War and Culture Studies 222, 228–9
   Modern and Contemporary France 199, 278, 282–3
   Paragraph 20
   Studies in French Cinema 178

King's College London 247–61
knowledge, nature of 7, 21
Kritzman, Lawrence 43, 207, 215

La Chanson de Roland 121, 134, 135
La Maman et la putain (Eustache, dir.) 176
Labeau, Emmanuelle 148
'lang and lit' degrees 197
language, nature of 21
language acquisition/content balance 30, 205–6, 238, 264
language centres 248
Language and Communication Skills Online Project 255–6
language competence/fluency 18, 19, 37, 50, 120, 130
language degrees *see* degree courses
language departments 242–4, 248, 262
languages *see* modern languages
Languages in Action modules 267–8
Languages, Linguistics and Area Studies (LLAS) 65
Latin 83
league tables, universities 112–13
learned societies 10
Leathes Report (1918) 14, 15
Lebovics, Herman 211
lectureships 22, 76
Leeds School of Modern Languages and Cultures 189
Leeds University 15, 19
Legacies of War: Mourning and Beyond conference (2000) 227
lesbian sexuality 100–1
linguistic contact zones 54
linguistic identities 136
linguistic proficiency 18, 19, 37, 50, 120, 130
linguistics research 141–54
   Anglo-Saxon/European intellectual traditions 149
   associations 150
   empirical tradition 149
   history of theory 143
   international context 150
   outside French departments 148
   phonology 145
   pragmatics 145–6
   second language acquisition 146–8
   sociolinguistics 143–5
   syntax 145
   websites 154
   see also French language

Links into Languages programme 65
literary studies
  A-level syllabuses 157
  attractiveness to students 108–10
  integrated learning 107–17
  publishing 93
  syllabus expansion 114
  theory 121
literary translation 155–6
literature *see* literary studies
Liverpool University 38
LLAs *see* Languages, Linguistics and Area Studies
local identities 136–7
Lodge, R.A. 142
London, University of 5
  see also King's College London
Lumière d'été (Grémillon, dir.) 175

MA Francophone Africa degree 202–3
MA/PGDip in French Language and Culture (online) 248–53
machine translation 165
MacKeogh, Kay 250
Maghrebi-French ('beur') cinema 179
Maison Française d'Oxford (MFO) 119
manifestos 49–50
Marchais, Madame de 79
Marmontel, Jean-François 79
medical students 254–5, 259
medieval literature 120–1
  see also Middle Ages
medieval saints' lives 97
memorial culture 225, 228
MFO *see* Maison Française d'Oxford
Michallat, Wendy 100
Middle Ages
  desire and sexuality 97–8
  identities 132–5
  urban populations 133
Mises au point (L310), Open University course 238–9
The Mismanagement of Talent (Brown and Hesketh) 263
A Mission to Civilize (Conklin) 210–11
MLC *see* Modern Language Centre
mobility, cultural 49–50, 52–4
Modern and Contemporary France (journal) 199, 278, 282–3
Modern Language Centre, King's College London 247–61

modern language departments 242–4, 248, 262
modern languages
  A-levels 16, 29, 108, 275, 281
  academic purpose 37
  benefits of learning xix–xx, 14, 21, 37
  decline in studying 39
  disciplinary identity 37–57
  economic benefits of learning xix
  GCSEs 29, 242, 288
  gender imbalances 21–3, 75–6
  globalisation 43
  graduate employment 115
  mission uncertainty 38
  strategic importance 6
  travelling-in-dwelling concept 53
Modern Studies report (1918) 41
modular learning 237–9, 249–50
Morellet, André 78–9
Moss, Paul 243–4
Mufti, Aamir R. 52
multidisciplinarity 203–4, 298
multilingualism 116, 243, 298
Mythologies (Barthes) 191

nation-state model 43, 55
national identity 43, 132–7, 207
national institutions 64–5
necrophilia 98
Negritude 211
networking
  consolidation 48
  employers 265
  research activities 86–94, 98
  scholars' participation 62–4
'New' French Studies 200–2
New Wave cinema 176
newsletters 90
Notre Dame Convent Grammar 13
Nuffield Report (2000) 67, 242
Nussbaum, Martha 51

OBCE *see* Oxford Besterman Centre for the Enlightenment
'Obscenity in Renaissance France' research group 98
Occupation period, Second World War 229
Online Froissart 149–50
online learning 247–61
  benefits 257
  cost 260
  French language and culture 257–60

staff feedback 252–3
student feedback 251–2
technical support 259
online resources 239–40, 288–90
Open Languages Research Group
241
Open University (OU) 235–46
distance learning principles 235–7
French modules 237–9
modular learning 237–9
research 240–2
residential schools 238
teaching 239–40
tutorials 237
websites 246
oral history 144, 201
Orliac, Marie d' 289
OU *see* Open University
outreach activities 63
overseas students 39
Oxford Besterman Centre for the
Enlightenment (OBCE)119 125
Oxford University 14, 118–28

Paragraph (journal) 20
Parisian French 145
part-time study 235
partnerships 9, 201, 204
PCRN *see* Popular Cultures
Research Network
Pedagogical Grammar course 254
Petrey, Sandy 42, 215
PGCE *see* Postgraduate Certificate
in Education
PhD studies *see* doctoral studies
Philippe Auguste, King 133
philology 14
Phonologie de Français Contemporain
project 145
phonology 145
placements abroad 32, 204–5,
268–71
plays 61–2, 122–4
podcasts 278, 290
poetry 67
political movements 67–70
polytechnics 15–16, 18–19, 66, 276
Pope, Mildred 142
popular culture studies 184–94
'Aspects of Popular Culture in
France since 1945' course 191–2
benefits of studying 192, 193
course description 191
critical perspectives 192
discourses 190, 192

historical view 187
interdisciplinarity 185, 186,
189–90
intersecting approaches 187
not soft option 192
value problem 187–8
websites 194
Popular Cultures Research Network
(PCRN) 189–90
pornography 100
Portsmouth Polytechnic 197–206
postcards 226
postcolonial cinema 179
postcolonial studies 44, 47, 48–9,
207–19
postcolonialism 202
Postgraduate Certificate in
Education (PGCE) 248–9, 254
postgraduate degree courses 248–53
postgraduate enrolments 33–4
pragmatics 145–6
Pratt, Mary Louise 37, 46
pre-modern literature 111, 112
pre-modern studies 107, 110
primary education 298
prizes 265
professional training 10
professorships 22, 23, 76
Proust, Marcel 95
public life, scholars' impact in UK
58–72
public understanding of French
Studies 46, 54
publishing 44–5, 60, 150, 216
purpose of French Studies 137
Pym, Anthony 159–60

Quarrels 124–8
queer theory 95–6, 100–1
'Queer Theory and the Middle Ages'
(Burgwinkle) 97

*RAE 2008 French Sub-panel
Overview Report* 107–8, 186–7
Rambouillet, Marquise de 77
Ramsay, George Gilbert 82, 83
rare books 289–90
Reader, Keith 100
Rebaud, Jean-Paul 296–9
The Red Brick University (Truscott,
pseud. of E. Allison Peers) 40
REF (research excellence frame-
work) 158
relevance of degree courses 110–11
Renoir, Jean 177

research 293
  area studies 197–9
  assessment 45, 59, 111
  cinema studies 176–80
  collaborative activities 6
  cultural projects 128
  embedding 113
  formal/informal networks 86–94
  Franco-African studies 278–9
  internationalisation 40, 47
  linguistics 141–54
  medieval literature 121
  networks 86–94, 98
  'New' French Studies 200–2
  Open University 240–2
  public benefit 59
  quality 113
  Quarrels 124–8
  theatre studies 124
  transatlantic communication 47
  translation studies 165–6
  universities xx, 30–2, 40
research excellence framework
  (REF) 158
residence abroad 32, 204–5, 268–71
residential schools 238
Resistance narratives 224
*Review of Modern Foreign Languages
  Provision in Higher Education in
  England see* Worton Report
Rigby, Brian 12
Robbins Report (1963) 15
role of French Studies 130–1, 137
Rousseau, Jean Jacques 80
Rousso, Henry 224
Routes into Languages programme
  65

Saint-Malo summit (1998) 201
saints' lives 97
Salford University 161
Salmon, Gilly 252
salons 77, 78–9
Sands, Sarah 243
Sartre, Jean-Paul 58
Scarry, Elaine 221
scholarly publishing 44–5
scholars
  associations 62–4
  career management 64
  education policy involvement 64–7
  networks 62–4
  political activism 67–70
  public impact in UK 58–72
  social activism 68–70

scholarship schemes 9–10
School of Languages and
  Area Studies, Portsmouth
  Polytechnic 197–206
schools
  curriculum issues 108, 131
  French studies 28–9
  modern languages provision xix,
    4, 16, 28–9, 294
  outreach activities 63
scientific and academic networks 10
scope of French Studies 293
Scotland, gender identities 82–3
second language acquisition (SLA)
  146–8
Second World War 224, 229
secondary schools *see* schools
*Securing a Sustainable Future for
  Higher Education in England:
  an independent review of higher
  education funding and student
  finance* (Browne report) 5–6
Segal, Naomi 99
selective schools 4
self-identity 22
Senegal 201, 204–5
Sèvres seminar (2009) 27
sexuality 70, 95–103
SFS *see* Society for French Studies
single language studies 92
SLA *see* second language acquisition
SLAS *see* School of Languages and
  Area Studies
SMT *see* statistical machine
  translation
social movements 68–70
social objectives 58–9
Société Internationale de Diachronie
  du Français 150
Society for Francophone
  Postcolonial Studies 209
Society for French Studies (SFS) 62,
  66, 101, 215
Society for the Study of French
  History 63
socio-historical linguistics 142
sociolinguistics 143–5
Sorbonne symposium (2005) 212
Spanish Civil War 228
spoken French 143–5, 147
staff
  contract staff 23, 76
  feedback 250, 252–3
  student–staff ratios 15
  training 257, 259–60

star studies, French cinema 173, 179
statistical machine translation
(SMT) 160
strategically important languages 6
students
feedback 250, 251–2, 255, 266
staff–student ratios 253
surveys 241
studentships 33–4, 158
Studies in French Cinema (journal)
178
study materials 239, 256
sub-Saharan Africa 201
Subject Centre for Languages,
Linguistics and Area Studies
(LLAS) 65
subtitles 175
summer schools 120
supported distance learning 235–7
Sussex University 13, 17–18
syllabuses *see* curriculum issues
syntax 145

taciturnity, English trait 80, 81–2
Tarr, Carrie 179
Tate Gallery 62
teaching
learning materials 236, 239
Open University 239–40
teacher education 254, 298–9
teleconferencing 240
television 191–2
Temple, Michael 180
temporary academic staff 23
textual studies 50
theatre studies 61–2, 122–4
theorists, study of 69
theses *see* doctoral studies
Thompson, Hannah 99
Thompson Klein, Julie 41
threats to French Studies 129–30,
207–19, 262
'three circles' theory 269
Times Higher Education-QS World
University Rankings 2009 112
Times Literary Supplement 60
torture 221
transferable skills 267, 270
translation 155–67
doctoral studies 165–6
economic value 160
internet 160
literary translation 155–6
postgraduate courses 161–2,
163–6

professional entry 159
research 165–6
studentships 158
studies programmes 157–66
studying in UK 161–6
theory 166
thesis topics 165–6
undergraduate courses 161, 162–3
university courses 157–66
websites 167
travelling-in-dwelling concept 53
Truscott, Bruce (pseud. of
E. Allison Peers) 40
tutorials 237

UCML *see* University Council of
Modern Languages
UK-Africa Academic Partnerships
Scheme 201
undergraduate courses *see* degree
courses
United Kingdom (UK)
Anglo-French cooperation 9–11
education policy 64–7
linguistics research 141–54
public impact of French scholars
58–72
translation studies 161–6
war and culture studies 220–31
see also England
United States of America 47, 112
universities
academic staff 15, 22, 23, 75–6,
250, 252–3
attractiveness to students 108–9
Block Grant Partnership scheme
33, 34
challenges 3
curriculum issues 17–21, 27,
30–2, 35, 203–4, 275–6
economies of scale 30
fees 159, 163, 239
funding 3, 5–6, 16, 92
gender imbalances 22, 23, 75–6
language acquisition/content
balance 30, 205–6, 238, 264
languages departments 242–4,
248, 262
league tables 112–13
modern language student enrolments 33–4, 75
partnerships 31, 34
postgraduate enrolments 33–4
purpose 40
rankings 112–13

research xx, 30–2, 40
staff–student ratios 15
strategies 3–4
student enrolments 33–4, 75
studentships 33–4
translation studies 157–66
undergraduate enrolments 34
undergraduate studies pro-
    grammes 17–21
women staff 76
world rankings 112
University Council of Modern
    Languages (UCML) 66–7
University of
    Glasgow 82–3
    Leeds 15, 19
    Liverpool 38
    London 5
    Oxford 14, 118–28
    Salford 161
    Sussex 13, 17–18
    Westminster 265–8, 270
urban populations 133
US Criterion collection (films) 175
USA 47, 112

varia articles, *Journal of War and
    Culture Studies* 229
VHS cassettes 174–5, 176
virtual learning environment (VLE)
    236, 249
vocational education 17, 158–9
Voltaire 78
Voltaire Foundation 119

war and culture studies 220–31
    and the 'cultural turn' 222–5
    diversification 222–5
    francophone studies 220–2
    interdisciplinarity 227
    publications 230
war veterans 201
websites
    Contemporary Women's Writing
        in French 90–1
    EU multilingualism 116
    King's College London 261
    Open University 239, 246
    popular culture studies 194

Westminster University 265–8, 270
White, Nicholas 99
Wilder, Gary 211
Willetts, David 235, 243, 244
Williams, Raymond 186
Williams, Val 222
Witt, Michael 180
Wollstonecraft, Mary 81
Wolverhampton Polytechnic 18
women
    Classics studies 82, 83
    contemporary writing in French
        86–94
    conversation 77–81
    education of 82–3
    film directors 173
    war narratives 225
    writing in French 86–94
    see also gender
Women in French group 22, 69–70
Women Reading Women group 88
women's movement 69
'Women's Writing in France: New
    Writers, New Literatures?'
    conference (2000) 87
work placements 204–5, 269, 270–1
    see also graduate employment
workshops, career skills 265
World War One 225, 226, 228
World War Two 224, 229
Worton Report (2009)
    assumptions of 37
    cultural studies trend 107
    disciplinary identity 45, 47
    employer expectations 32
    language department/centre
        collaboration 248
    modern language community 4,
        38
    relevance of French Studies 108
    university priorities xx
'Writing childhood' seminar (2010)
    92
Wygant, Amy 45–6

year abroad 32, 204–5, 268–71

Zeldin, Theodore 297